AF607878

MBARI
Art and Life among the Owerri Igbo

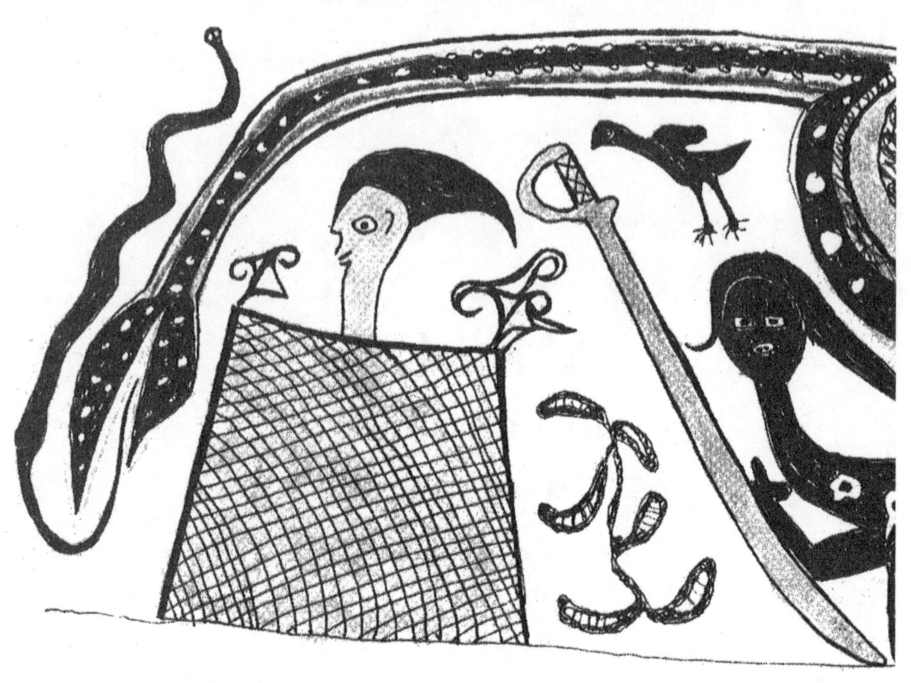

Traditional Arts of Africa

Editors
Paula Ben-Amos
Roy Sieber
Robert Farris Thompson

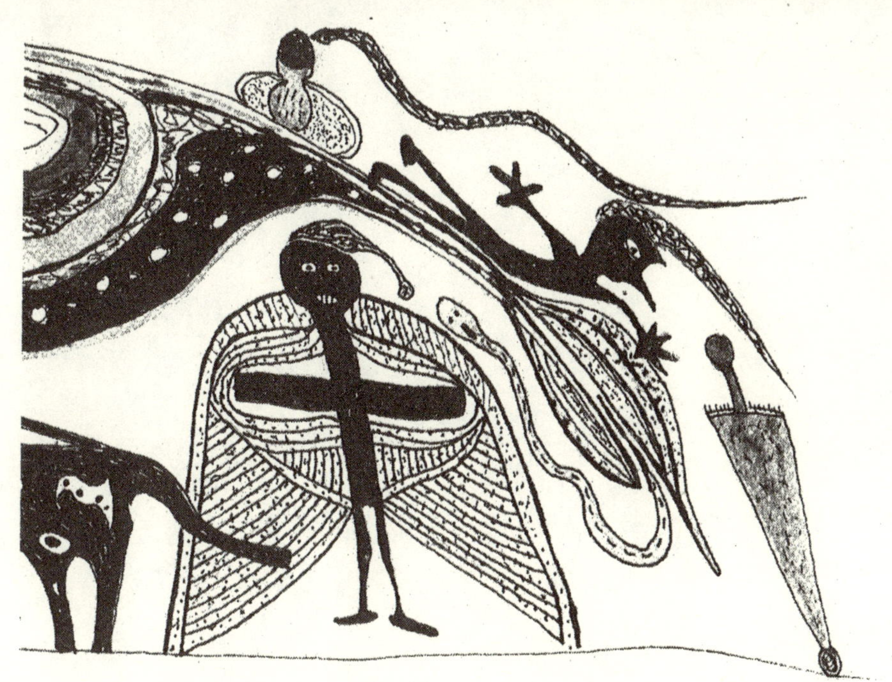

MBARI

ART AND LIFE AMONG THE OWERRI IGBO

Herbert M. Cole

INDIANA UNIVERSITY PRESS
Bloomington

This book was brought to publication with the assistance of a grant from the Andrew W. Mellon Foundation.

Manufactured in the United States of America

Library of Congress Cataloging in Publication Data

Cole, Herbert M.
Mbari, art and life among the Owerri Igbo.

(Traditional arts of Africa)
Bibliography: p. 237
Includes index.
1. Igbo (African people)—Religion. 2. Art, Igbo (African people)—Nigeria—Owerri (Division.) 3. Owerri (Nigeria: Division)—Religious life and customs.
I. Title. II. Series.
BL2480.I2C64 229'.64 80-8094
ISBN 0-253-30397-4 ACCR2
1 2 3 4 5 86 85 84 83 82

FOR Thomas
Peter
Luke

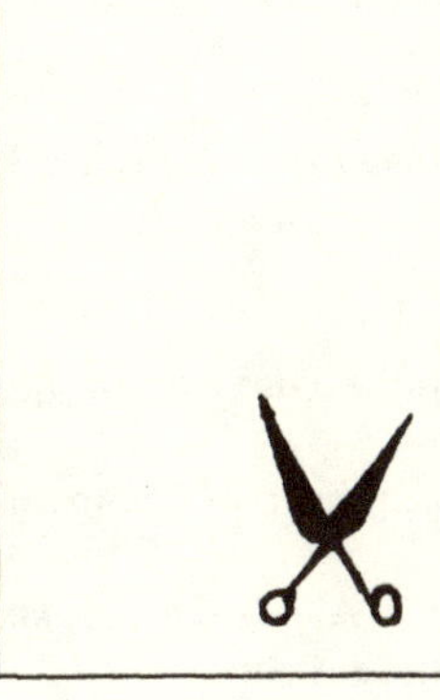

Contents

Color Plates

Unless otherwise noted, all photographs were made by the author during fieldwork in 1966-67.

Plates

Figures

Preface

Mbari—a festival of life, vibrant with color, alive with clay sculptures of gods, men, animals, and monsters set in a richly painted architectural complex. Mud and clay sculpture hardly spring to mind when one thinks of African art, but fine examples of them are found among several African peoples. Mud sculpture, painting, and their architectural settings are of course virtually impossible to transport and thus never reached nineteenth-century curiosity cabinets or modern collections of African art. Nor have many publications dealt with such arts.[1] Rarely, however, do other African clay forms achieve the virtuosity of mbari houses, which are found in a small section of Igboland near the township of Owerri in eastern Nigeria (see fig. 1). Mbari are, effectively, the only forms of visual art made in this region except for some woodcarvings and masks, which are found in peripheral areas.

Igbo art is perhaps best known for masks and figural carvings such as *ikenga* (Vogel 1974, Boston 1977) and village deities or carved doors and stools. Yet the arts of all Igbo-speaking[2] peoples have in fact never been properly surveyed or published.[3] The uneven treatment of these varied arts may be attributed partially to the existence of several separate local traditions, hence a lack of unity which in turn makes generalization unwise and correlations difficult from region to region. Such artistic fragmentation stems directly from the traditional sociopolitical organization of the Igbo people[4]—a fragmentation into small autonomous "subtribes," clans, or village groups which is reflected also in the several dialects of Igbo spoken.

There is no single Igbo art style or object type. A few traits link the various sub-areas, but very few; *ikenga* figures, personal or village shrines addressed for power and success, have become synonymous with Igbo art, but in more than half of Igboland, they are unknown, except in miniature versions in diviners' kits. The art of the Afikpo village group, so well documented by Ottenberg, is different from that of Onitsha, while Abakaliki art bears little relationship to that of the Isu or Ngwa.[5] The performance of masked dances links these areas, but the masks themselves are diverse. Each sub-area has several different types of masquerades, only a few of which may be used by their neighbors. Perhaps the only broadly shared elements are white-faced masks or headdresses and dark-colored grotesque or "ugly" masks; these are seen in Igboland wherever masking is prevalent, although in different styles. Masking may be said to be the preeminent Igbo art, for few regions are without masks. The heartland of mbari houses is one of those rare regions.

Although all areas have had outside economic relationships through a network of markets, with trading contacts and mutual influence on the socio-religious level, regional variation in Igbo culture patterns is the rule. A traditional Onitsha man, for example, will not understand the Owerri word for "god" or "spirit," *agbara,** nor will he know about mbari. All Igbo people, on the other hand, will understand "*mmuọ*," the common word for spirit. Thus some values and attitudes, as well as words, are shared widely, yet regional culture patterns are often quite distinct; mbari themselves prove the point. Two large village groups, Mbiẹre and Mbaise, are situated only about five and ten miles, respectively, from Owerri town, but their peoples appear never to have borrowed the idea of mbari, despite the similarity of their religious beliefs in most essential points to those of mbari builders. In geographic scope the mbari area covers about two percent of Igbo territory east of the Niger River; perhaps four or five percent of Igbo people are involved, for this region is quite densely populated.[6] Clearly, mbari houses cannot be considered typical of Igbo art.

This book will first explore the cultural setting of the mbari area, with emphasis on religion, both because religious values are at the heart of mbari and because numerous gods and spirits are modeled within it. Then in a synthetic account of the building of a "typical" mbari house, ritual and artistic processes will be described in sequence, and the types and roles of various participants will be discussed. This is followed by an analysis of mbari form and style, and then by a discussion of artists' inspiration and individuality, and critical or aesthetic responses to their work. The meanings of both forms and processes are then examined; the conclusion deals with the entire mbari phe-

*Igbo vernacular words like *agbara* and *mmuo* are italicized throughout the text. Orthographic marks and tone marks, both critical to proper Igbo pronunciation, are given in the glossary.

nomenon in a more interpretive manner. As an art historian, I am primarily concerned to document and understand works of art. The ethnographic context is set forth as it contributes to this understanding, but is of course less detailed than it would be if written by an anthropologist.

The study is based on my fieldwork in Igboland in 1966-67, when I saw some one hundred fifty mbari houses of assorted sizes and in varied states of preservation.[7] As far as possible, the statements of men and women involved with mbari houses—as priests, artists, builders—are employed to tell the story. All direct quotations are from informants, and although not always ascribed to individuals in the text, they are taken from transcribed, tape-recorded field interviews. I have relied heavily on the descriptions, stories, and interpretations of mbari people in the hope that this book reflects their attitudes and responses to these fascinating structures, as well as my own. My aim is to describe and interpret mbari houses, not as isolated works of art but as monuments growing out of, and expressive of, the values, beliefs, rituals, and processes of Owerri Igbo culture.

Acknowledgments

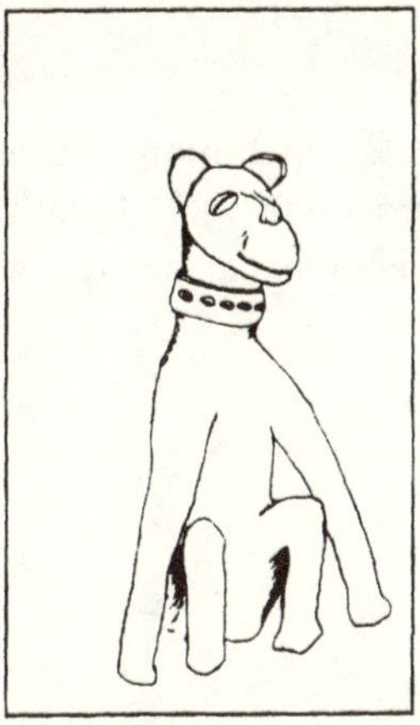

I acknowledge with great pleasure the generous help of many who have contributed toward the publication of this book. For fellowships enabling me to work in the field I thank Columbia University (William Bayard Cutting Travelling Fellowship) and the Joint Committee of the American Council of Learned Societies and the Social Science Research Council (Foreign Area Fellowship). Research grants from the Academic Senate, University of California, Santa Barbara, have facilitated final preparations.

Of primary importance in Nigeria were numerous friends in the Owerri area, priests, patrons, artists, and workers, who unselfishly shared with me the lore of mbari and the life that informs it. Among the many I want especially to thank the following *nnaukwu*: Ugo, Ezem, Nnaji, Eke, Opara, Anyawu, Nicholas Amah, Boniface Nwankwala, Sebastian Onuegbu, and Christopher Onuigbe. Sensitive assistance in the field was rendered by D. C. Okwudili, V. Ugwuadu, T. Uhiara, and especially by Herbert P. K. Opara.

Many other scholars and friends in Nigeria, England, and the United States contributed measurably with suggestions, photographs, criticisms, and other help. Among them are Drs. Mino Badner, John Boston, Tonye V. Erekosima, Robin Horton, Carl Liedholm, Donatus Nwaoga, Labelle Prussin, Arnold Rubin, and Roy Sieber, and Messrs. Ekpo Eyo, William Fagg, John Picton, William Smock, Harrison Shafer, and the late Kenneth Murray. The U.C.S.B. Art Department staff, including Jean Barrick, Linda Callahan, Margaret Dinsenbacher, and Connie Martinez, have helped greatly with the manuscript.

Special thanks are due several people who have carefully read and criticized the manuscript: Douglas Fraser, David Smock, and Paul S. Wingert, in 1968, when an earlier version was submitted to Columbia University as a doctoral dissertation, and more recently G. I. Jones, the late Nora Ottenberg, and Simon Ottenberg.

I would also like to thank Alexandra Cole and our children for their help and support, tangible and intangible, from the inception of this project in 1965 until the completion of the first version in 1968. Finally I am grateful to Patricia Cole for recent and invaluable contributions toward this publication.

MBARI
Art and Life among the Owerri Igbo

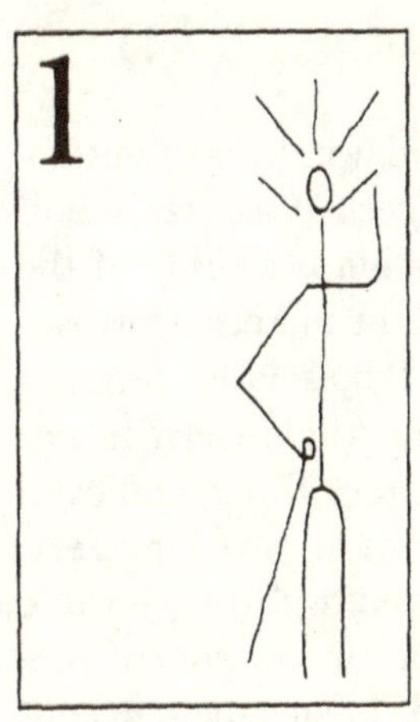

1 Introduction: The Setting

Owerri Today

A few yards from a bustling modern market in the Nigerian township of Owerri, there stood the crumbling, weathered ruins of an mbari house (pl. 1). Worn by rains, winds, and marauding animals, the once colorful monument dimly reflected the glory of a dying institution, mbari. Today that mbari house has disappeared entirely. It is perhaps ironical that mbari houses—more than any other tradition in African art—so graphically illustrate the kinds of change and modernity that have conspired to bring about their demise: a banker at his vault, catechists at prayer, automobiles, radios and telephones, office buildings, uniformed soldiers, maternity clinics, and the white man (color plates 2 and 5, pls. 2 and 3). Similar scenes, vividly modeled in sun-dried clay, still stand in mbari houses erected within the past three decades in villages within a few miles of this West African town, and a few mbari houses are still being made. But Owerri and the progressive contemporary life it fosters have now replaced mbari as a visual and ideological magnet for Nigerians in this part of Igboland. The shift has been fairly rapid, since Owerri became an administrative, educational, trade, and mission center in the first years of this century. By 1963 Owerri town had 26,017 inhabitants,[1] more than five times its population in 1935; before 1900 the "town" was no more than a loose collection of semi-autonomous villages whose inhabitants, like villagers throughout the mbari region, were striving to stay alive on the fruit of the land.[2]

In earlier times the area had been a crossroads between Onitsha and Aba, between fishermen to the south and yam-growers to the north. It has long been a collecting point in palm-produce trade,[3] and a famous and powerful oracle was consulted nearby.[4] Today Owerri is an outpost of the wider world—Lagos, London, New York. Children of the area return from abroad as doctors, teachers, scientists, economists, and lawyers. Other Owerri people work today in Kano, Onitsha, Enugu, Benin, and Lagos, as well as outside Nigeria. Cars, taxis, and trucks ply even on the back roads, so real isolation is a thing of the past. Indeed, the mbari themselves have charted the increasing worldliness of Owerri people for several generations. Igbo soldiers brought back tales of the 1914 Cameroons campaign of the Anglo-German war (pl. 2); and policemen, court messengers, western clothing, and even colonial administrators have long been stock items of mbari imagery. Today men sit at telephones in mbari "office buildings" (pl. 3), while nearby operators—somewhat incongruously clad in traditional patterns of body paint—relay silent messages of Igbo involvement in contemporary life (pl. 76). Scenes of women giving birth, once portrayed in a traditional native pose (pl. 4), now take place in the kinds of maternity clinics that dot the countryside, where uniformed nurses are in attendance (color plate 5). Even if many of these modern realities appear in mbari tableaux, Igbo interest in the institution is on the decline, along with the socio-spiritual and artistic values that lie behind it.

Mbari History

The origins of the mbari institution are obscure. In 1904 Whitehouse photographed an mbari and asked questions about it, but attempts to reconstruct the history of mbari before 1900 have been frustrated. Elsewhere (Cole 1975) I have tried to speculate on the growth of the tradition and its relationship with other artistic phenomena both inside Igboland and beyond, but nothing of its pre-1900 history is certain. We may suppose mbari evolved gradually from small structures with a few mud figures—known widely in Igboland and elsewhere in Nigeria, especially among related Igbo and Edo peoples west of the Niger—into the elaborate complexes photographed by Murray and Jones in the 1920s and 1930s (pl. 5). Since the 1904 "Whitehouse mbari" (pl. 6) is fully evolved, with most of the artistic features, including a fairly large architectural core, still seen in the late 1960s, we may suppose that mbari houses containing several figures, even a dozen or two, existed before 1900. As still earlier sacred figural sculptures became more numerous and were integrated with their architectural settings, it is probable that building processes were also elaborated, that a fenced enclosure was eventually built to insure surprise when the structure was unveiled, that the rituals attending various construction stages became embroidered and increasingly complex. Three essential and underlying aspects of mbari surely existed in Igboland and beyond well before 1900: sacrificial rites aimed at human and agricultural productivity and renewal, cult sculptures (and/or masks) representing deities and their families, as well as assorted local character types and genre activities; and formal, elaborated structures linking these figural representations in space and time. Multi-figured and colossal *ijele* masks from northern Igboland, and the formalized setting of several large wooden sculptures in Ohaffia village shrines, *obu,* reflect similar impulses inside Igboland. The large, carefully structured complexes of representational mud sculptures devoted to Olokun, the Edo god of waters and creation, are the closest non-Igbo comparisons. Mbari seem to have evolved earlier than these Edo shrines, but this hypothesis is far from certain.

Even though the ritual underpinnings of mbari as well as aspects of its form and building ritual probably existed outside Igboland during the years of its elaboration, there is still no evidence that mbari was anything other than a local, Owerri-area development. The Uratta clan or village group is considered the originator, both by themselves and by neighboring peoples who learned the mbari tradition from them. But oral traditions are shallow in this part of Igboland and no one recalls the first mbari house. This suggests that mbari were being made much as we know them at least as early as 1850, well within the memories of my informants' grandfathers. My informants were, however, clearly in agreement that the 1920s and 30s were the halcyon decades, the time of the largest and most spectacular mbari houses, which contained upwards of 100 modeled figures.[5] Kenneth Murray documented one in 1946, quite possibly the grandest and most complex mbari of all time, which included about 230 clay figures in several related structures (see appendix D).

As the influence of European education and European missionaries grew in the 1940s and 1950s, the institution began to change and to decline. Changes in both form and ritual processes have certainly been evident in the history of mbari during this century, and doubtless change was also apparent in earlier times. Sculptural and painted themes reflect, through time, a continuing impulse to contemporize, to incorporate the world around at the time of building and even to anticipate the future. Changes in building rituals are less easily documented, although informants made it quite clear that the leaders of any given mbari project had a good deal of freedom to invent new procedures and festivities. The houses built after about 1950 rarely contain more than 30 or 40 figures; those of the 1960s, rarely more than 25. The decline in size and grandeur has been paralleled by shorter, less elaborate building rituals and more concessions to the social and economic lives of the builders outside mbari. I estimate that in the late 1960s perhaps 90 percent of Owerri people below the age of 35 were at least nominally Christian; thus the pool of available traditional worshippers was small then and is shrinking every year. Most of the ceremonial elaborations and many of the restrictions reported for the 1930s were no longer to be observed in 1966-67. Many essential rituals remained, on the other hand, and I witnessed several. The overall decline of the mbari tradition, however, is symbolized by two events: the construction, about 1965, of a cement and concrete mbari house, and the Nigeria-Biafra civil conflict of 1967-69. In the first instance it seems that the builder sought to freeze mbari and render it permanent—in direct contradiction to the tradition itself. The second event, a devastating civil war, raged with particular intensity in the Owerri area, and it is doubtful that mbari, except perhaps in a revivalist form, can have withstood its devastating influence.

During the time of my fieldwork, however, the traditional character of mbari remained alive in the memories of older informants, in their stories, and to some extent in ritual practices still observed. The mbari houses illustrated and discussed in this book were almost all made after 1930. The hypothetical reconstruction of mbari practices in the next chapter is rooted in observable fact and in the memories of my intelligent informants. It is a composite account but, I believe, an accurate one. The stage can best be set by recounting fragments of creation mythology, then by assaying the environmental, economic, and political situation that prevailed for most of this century, the only time we have hard evidence for the mbari insitution.

The Land and the People

Chineke wanted to create the world. He wanted to create the days. Chineke created man, the gods, animals, trees, everything. . . .

Chineke created four people. He created all the gods and kept them, making spirits more numerous than men. He gave us cloth, the basket, the knife, yams, and everything we eat, and put them in the house he built. He put everything inside it and put those four people inside it in four rooms. He put them into the house: Eke, Orie, Afo, Nkwo. These are men, and he also put women in a separate room. He fixed the house well and gave them everything to eat in plenty. Then Chineke called in all the gods and fixed a time for creating the days.

Chineke asked, "Which of you knows the days?" Agwushi, god of divination, said he knew. "This is Eke, the next is Orie, then Afo, then Nkwo. These are the four days of the world."*

Then Eke suggested it would be a good idea for Ala (land) to exist. The land just came out. The land and the sky are the same. The nature of how both of them came out is not known. No one gave birth to them.

There has always been land. The land existed before we met it. The land was all a big forest when man came. The palm tree and all the trees were here before we came to meet them. Chineke first kept them. He made the skies too and kept them in the same way. And all the grass that grows on earth came down from the skies, and the soil we have also came from the skies. Then man worked on it. When you point to people with land, they did not get it themselves but from the strength of their ancestors who first cut paths and cleared in those old days.[6]

The land of the Owerri region was once densely forested, but by 1900 it had been largely cleared. It is a gradually inclined peneplane 30 to 50 miles north of the Niger River delta and 200 to 300 feet above sea level.

This land is bordered on the east by a major river, the Imo, and is cut through by three smaller river valleys (map, fig. 1). Under the pressure of slash-and-burn agriculture, less than a sixth of the region retains heavy growth—most of it protected forests sacred to local deities. Soils are acidic mixtures of sand and clay (called Benin sands) that are only moderately fertile; so despite heavy rainfall (80-90 inches per year), people struggle to take decent harvests. And lush speedy growth threatens continuously to engulf farm and village alike with thick brush. Villages are nearly hidden from one another although many are only 200 to 400 yards apart. Sweltering heat in the dry season and torrential rain with constant and oppressive thunder in the wet season are deterrents to concentrated work.

The Uratta[7] people, acknowledged originators of mbari, share this distinctive artistic world with five or six other groups, several of which are known as Ngor peoples. All together the mbari-building groups number somewhere between 250,000 and 300,000 people, spread

*Eke, Orie, Afo, and Nkwo are the four days of the common Igbo week. Some areas observe eight-day weeks, in which case the same day names are used but are preceded by "great" or "small" if the specific day is not clear in the context of the conversation.

among roughly 90 village clusters.[8] Before colonial times, most of these village groups were politically independent from one another, without any common meeting place, ancestors, or deities. Beyond occupation of contiguous tracts of land and some sense of commonality against neighbors, unity was perceptible only in a near-identity of customs and beliefs. Mbari is without question the most visibly striking of these.

Neither the Uratta nor neighboring groups have traditions of origin,[9] just as none of them remember when the first mbari was made. Apart from local displacements resulting from warfare and the sporadic short-distance shifting of village sites, the people seem to have occupied their homeland for a very long time.

Villages or village segments were moved infrequently, perhaps every twenty-five to forty or fifty years in the old days, to sites usually less than a mile away. The shift was made when things went wrong, when "the land got hot" causing "people to die in numbers": "People steal or commit other crimes, and some are debtors of the gods. All these things are bad, and when the gods start killing them they will blame it on the land—while it is really they who have defiled the land. People cause good land to become bad." Various ritual steps involved in the shifting process underline its significance to the people;[10] these will be discussed below.

Economy

Agriculture is the main occupation; by 1935 bare subsistence harvests were supplemented only by petty trade and the sale of palm produce as a cash crop. Despite a broader economy today, agriculture is still of prime importance. Crops and weeds struggle upwards for sunlight during the heaviest rains of April, May, and June, after yam and cassava farms are planted. People weed the farms, and the crops win the battle of growth. This damp season of cold and of want brings luxuriant growth but little food. Not until August are the first New Yams ready to be eaten ceremonially.[11] The main harvest of December and January brings bounteous months when yam barns are full, when it is dry and hot, when men can afford to avoid the heat of the sun for days on end. But then the yearly cycle must be repeated, the bush cleared and the debris burned. People re-enact the ceremonies marking the beginning of this new agricultural year and once again bend to the land.

With such a dependence on agriculture for subsistence it follows that most people, even in the 1970s, are farmers. Both men and women go to farm in this area, though tasks are differentiated. Even men with other specialized jobs, native doctors, palm-wine tappers, diviners, and priests, are also farmers part if not most of the time. Almost all women, in addition to tending gardens near their homes and larger farms farther away, are petty traders. The collection and processing of palm fruit may be either communal, for village self-help projects, or by household.

The crisscrossing paths and roads that break up the terrain lead almost inevitably to markets, the nerve centers of Owerri life. Markets have been an important adjunct to subsistence agriculture since long before European trade goods were introduced. Here women converge to trade excess garden foods in small quantities and to socialize. Other traders, both men and women, travel between larger bush markets dealing in heavier crops such as yam and cassava, and trade goods, today ranging from tinned foods or cloth to jewelry, kitchen utensils, and radios, bought in modern cities like Aba or Onitsha.[12] The people themselves consume most of the food they grow, with only small quantities left over for sale to the more overcrowded Mbaise. The only real cash crop still is palm produce, much of which is exported southward eventually to leave Nigeria altogether.

Wealth in this society was not traditionally calculated, however, on money income or the rapidity of capital turnover. In a polygynous social system with a land-based economy it was the size of the family that really mattered. A man with many wives was a man with many children. These in turn led to well-stocked yam barns, to the acquisition of goats and cows, pawns and slaves, and titles—the public validation of status achieved. Such prestige, added to free birth and the wisdom gained with experience, helped project ambitious men to positions of power and leadership.

The striving for status and power has for some time been a major preoccupation of most Igbo people who, as Uchendu points out, conceive of their world as a marketplace in which people compete and bargain not only among themselves but with their gods as well.[13] As a proverb seen frequently today on the trucks of aggressive Igbo traders has it, "No condition is permanent"—neither poverty nor wealth. Any man can improve his own lot, if he is alert and ambitious, while conversely he may find himself surpassed by others if he relaxes his vigilance and loses initiative. Status and power seekers manipulate not only other men but the very rules of competition in an environment that stresses both change and equal opportunity.[14] The Igbo man is largely responsible for his own destiny, *uwa* (the same word as "world"), and thus embraces the new perhaps more readily than most African people. Nor is this desire for change and improved status simply a product of the dynamic economy and technical progress introduced in this century by white men, for scholars have demonstrated an "Igbo receptivity to change" that predates the large-scale infusion of European culture and values during the last sixty to seventy years.[15] The contemporary Igbo, progressive, educated, and aggressive, simply embraces modern means to work out his traditional need for competition and status-seeking.

Social and Political Organization

The fundamental Igbo belief in equality also precluded the development of any centralized authority in the Owerri area before colonialism. "The Igbo have no kings," runs the proverb.[16] Distrust meets any one man with great power, and every freeborn male has the opportunity to achieve wealth and stature; even without them he may speak at the village meeting which, in pre-colonial times, constituted the local government.[17] Since the building of mbari houses appears to have no relation to the administrative chiefs and territories instituted by the British and maintained after independence, this description excludes these later offices and structures.

Traditional social and political organization was fragmented and segmentary, based on patrilineal family structures which began to operate at the level of the compound, or household unit. Compounds are still territorial, architectural units usually bounded by a continuous wall enclosing a number of small undecorated buildings. Smaller compounds contain two or three related married men with wives and children, while larger ones may house fifty to sixty people in ten or more separate structures. Each compound is an effective household under a recognized leader who holds *ofo,* a secular and spiritual symbol of headship in the form of a short staff deriving its power from lineage ancestors. An *ofo* brings to its guardian numerous ritual and social rites and obligations.[18]

The *umunna* ("children of father"), however, is more important than the compound as the basic social unit. *Umunna* are patrilineages that vary greatly in size. A single compound *can* be called *umunna,* but more usually the designation is applied to several related compounds and is used for the successively larger lineages that arise when descent from one man is traced for several generations. Large *umunna* can be hamlets or villages.[19] *Umunna,* or patrilineages, must therefore be defined by context because they constantly overlap and are often confusing.[20] Thus villages are usually made up of a number of small sublineages, more or less balanced and distinct, but related in claiming descent from the same founding father. Slave or stranger elements are often partially assimilated, so that not all the members of an *umunna* are necessarily actual descendants of the founder. The system is in fact more complicated than is indicated here, partly because of the instability of the units.[21] Bisection seems to have been the most usual kind of segmenting, though, since dual organization is very common.[22] Lineages, like most villages which they make up, are exogamous, and their headmen hold *ofo* as symbols of their position and authority.

Although the largest effective political unit was a group of villages (or town), the most important unit was the village itself. That most government functions—administrative, legislative, economic, judicial—were focused in villages and their meetings indicates the independence and autonomy of these units. Villages within a town often competed fiercely with one another, and before the Pax Britannica, warfare was as frequent between "related" villages as against a common enemy.[23] As G. I. Jones has indicated, many villages in this area "are not really sure whether they want to be independent local units or part of a larger group. In some social situations and in some periods of their history they act as independent units, in others, as part of a larger one. One of the ways of defining their position is by combining to build an mbari house if it wants to unite, or by building its own (mbari) house if it does not."[24] The minimal unity felt in the village group stems from a sense of remote common ancestry, from the contiguity of their farmlands and dwelling areas, and from a few common cults, particularly that of the land itself. The infrequent meetings on this level are convened to deal with common external enemies, markets or roads, or important shared deities and their propitiation in either annual festivals or in exceptional situations, such as the building of an mbari. These meetings are attended by older freeborn men, *ndioha,* "people of peace," who hold *ofo* for the major component lineages in each village.

The same *ndioha* have an important place in village meetings, which are open to all freeborn adult men, *amala,* "owners of the land."

Women take no part in such meetings and ordinarily have little to say, directly, in village affairs. On some ceremonial occasions, however, women who have married and moved away, *mgboto,* are called back to their fathers' villages where they wield a power usually denied their sex. Leadership, then, stems from male consensus as determined in village meetings, which lineage *ofo*-holders, elders, and other powerful men (i.e., cult priests and the wealthy, persuasive speakers) dominate. Nominal chiefs are appointed or elected, but few wield widespread political authority and none dared to be autocratic.

The democratic and communal character of village social life and political organization both supplements and complements the individual Igbo's preoccupation with status. Prestige is achieved only with the cooperation and support, material and moral, of a man's lineage. For his superior status to be validated; he must in turn share its benefits. This pattern permeated the whole social fabric. Ozo and other title systems, for example, institutionalize the sharing of fees in some mbari areas.[25] Similarly a village or town recognizes and respects an individual for the benefits he can confer upon the group. A persuasive man may forge consent among his townsmen—a reward for the powerful—but he generally faces competition and opposition. Each new proposal or dispute is hammered out in democratic meetings that nevertheless swing according to the persuasions of forceful speakers. The essence of these meetings is dispute through oratory; their inevitable conclusion is compromise.

The laws or conclusions of all meetings, whether town, village, or lineage, must be ratified by oaths sworn upon *ofo,* the socio-religious symbols held by "first sons", *okpara,* lineage heads at various levels. They invoke *ofo* to bind all villagers to a decision and to kill all transgressors. The *ofo* itself dramatizes the spiritual basis of even the most secular matters even today, for its power represents the authority of the high god, Chineke, channeled through lineage ancestors, *ndichie,* without whose support and concurrence men dare not act. Thus the ultimate sanction for human activity—law making, war, buying and selling, changing village sites, planting or harvesting, making and using "art"—comes not from living men but from supernatural beings. In the socio-religious sphere of mbari activity, neither colonialism nor the modern governmental infractruce has very much affected the beliefs and practices of Owerri peoples.

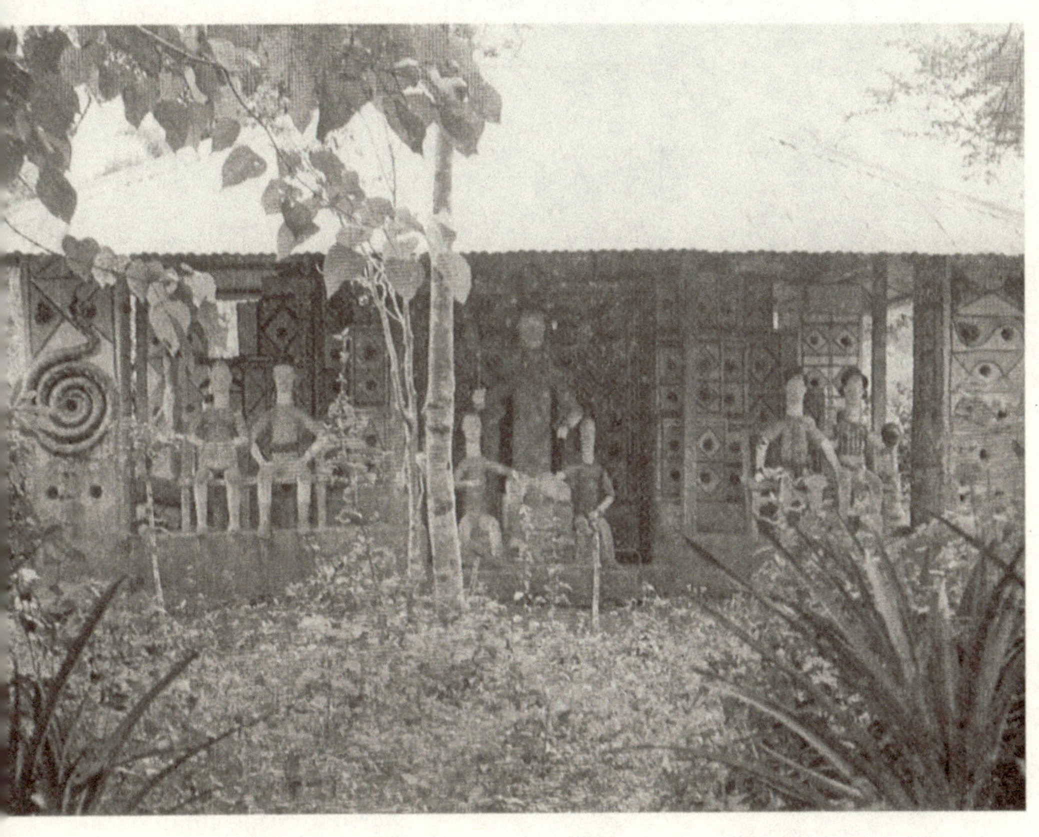

1.
This fine and quite typical mbari was opened about seven years before the picture was taken.

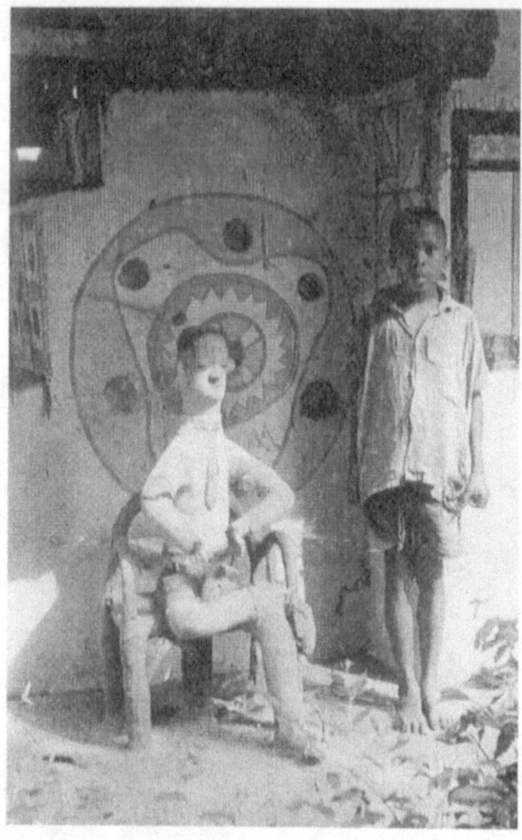

2.

The faces of white people are often painted the same colors as those of Igbo people but are often distinguished by special poses and accoutrements, in this case the nontraditional crossed-legs pose.

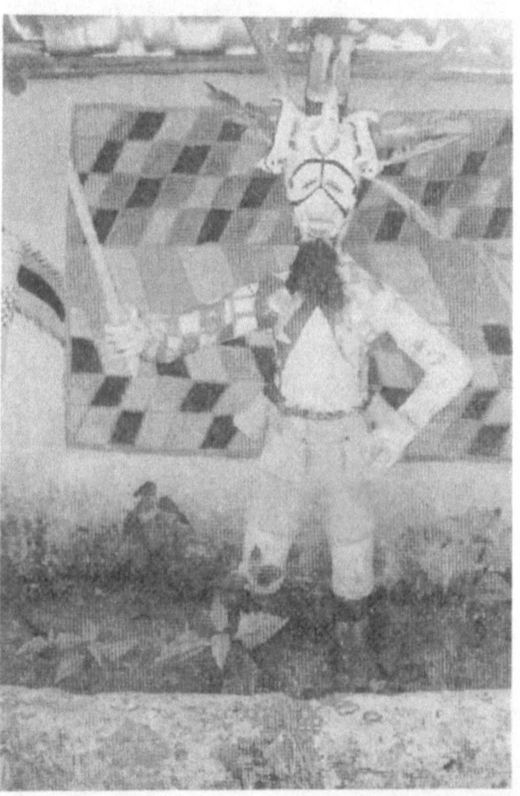

3.

Agwa, a village group of the Western Uratta, is one of the few mbari-making places where masquerades are danced.

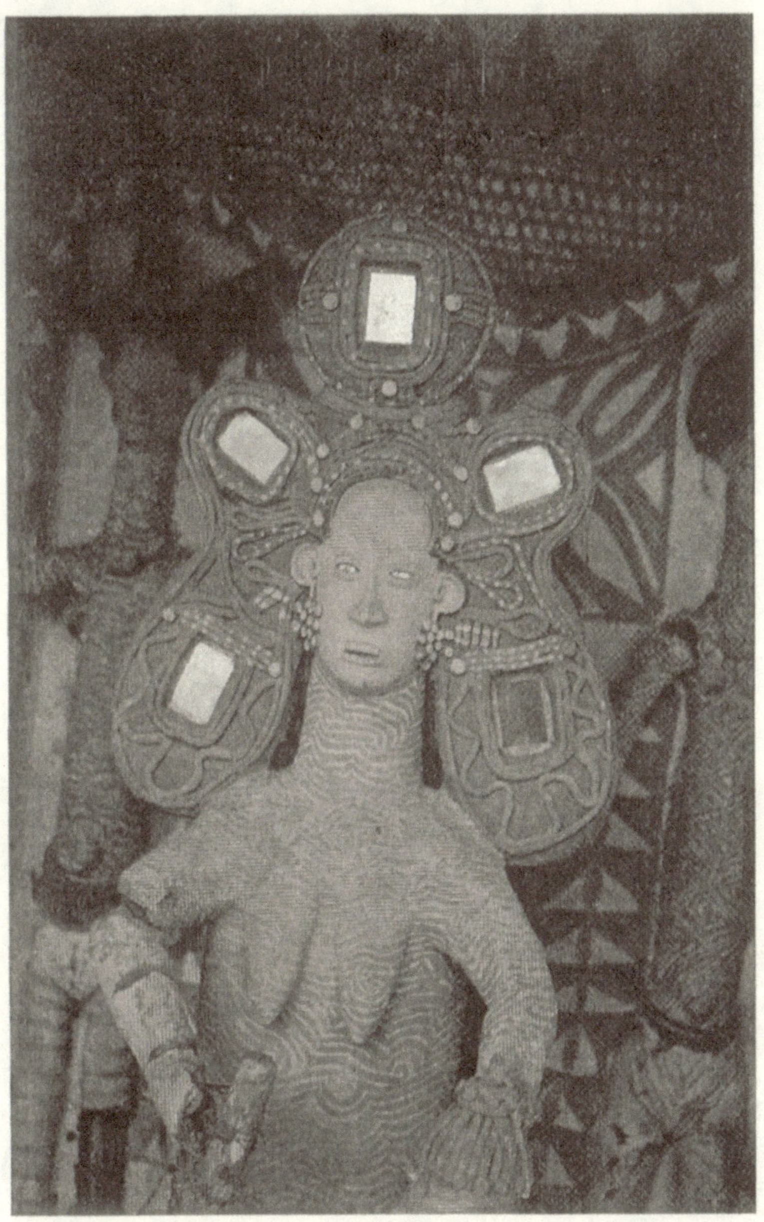

4.
The dignified formalism of an mbari's owner, rendered well over life-size, often contrasts with other mbari figures and groups.

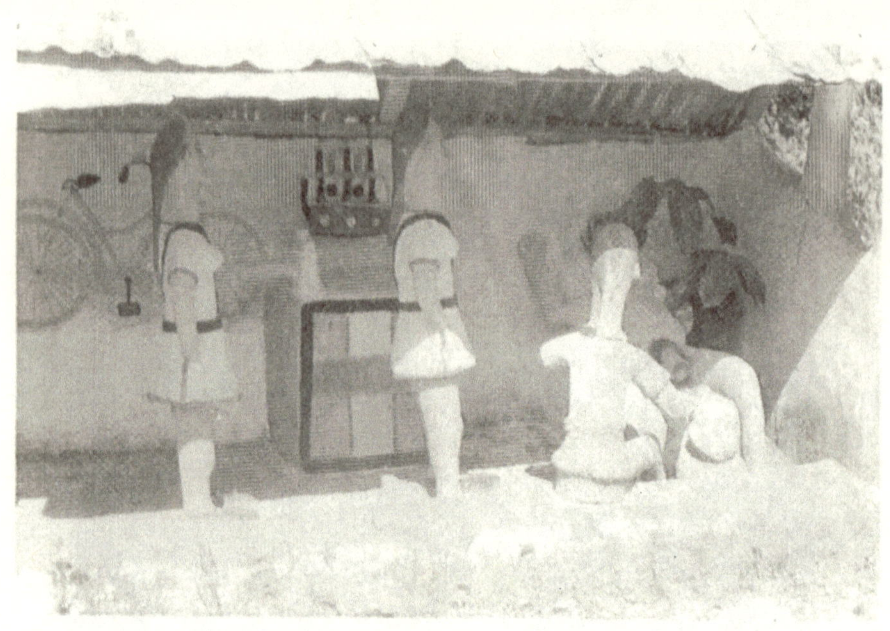

5.

This contemporary scene of a woman giving birth is typical of both the graphic quality of much mbari imagery and the quasi-journalistic, reportorial impulses often observed.

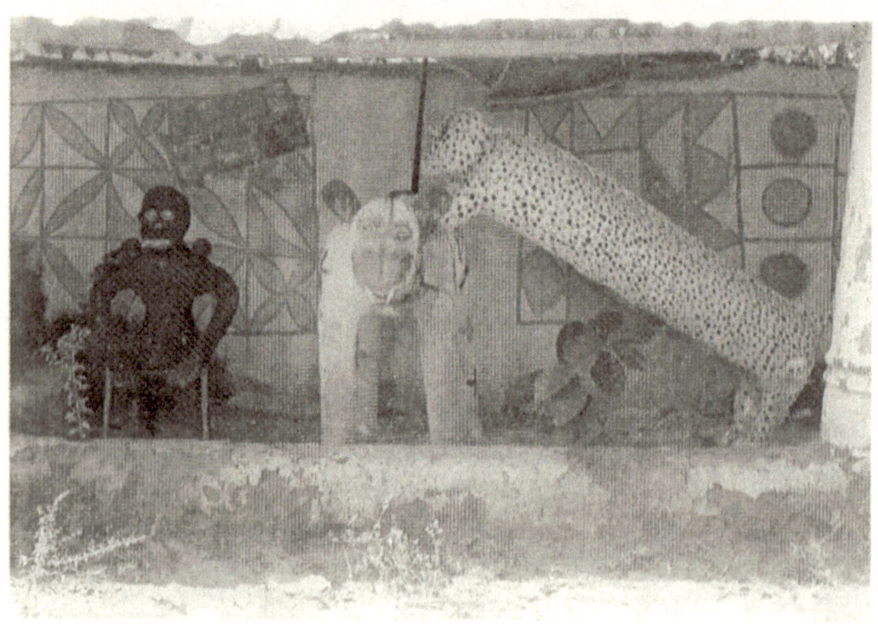

6.

Animals are favored mbari subjects even today when few villagers have seen them. In the twenties and thirties the animal poses tended to be more active.

7.

Ala's sword has fallen here, but her painted body patterns, more detailed and precise than in life, have been protected well by the overhanging metal roof.

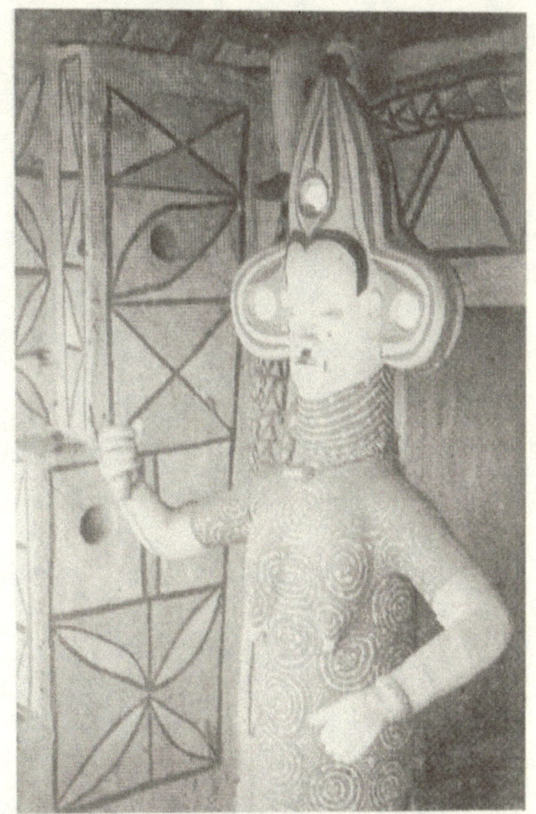

8.

Akakporo's helper, Godwin, has had twenty years of mbari experience. He is primarily a farmer and domestic house-builder but would prefer full-time mbari work. His style is very similar to, and often indistinguishable from, Akakporo's.

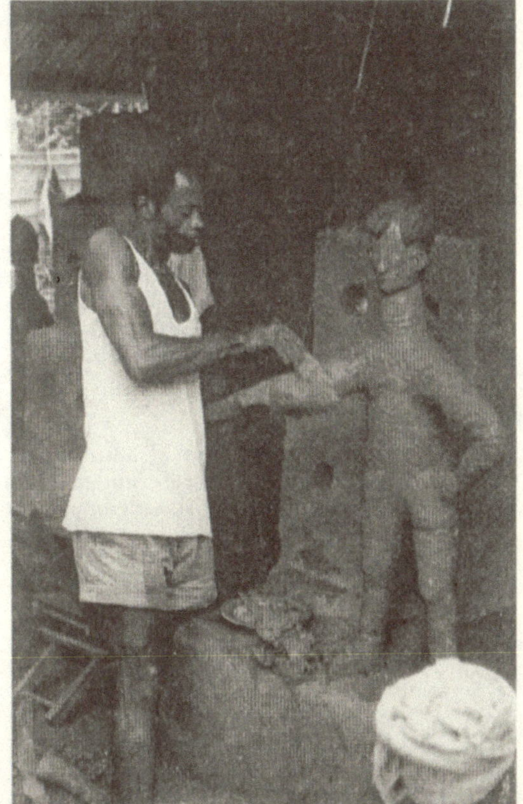

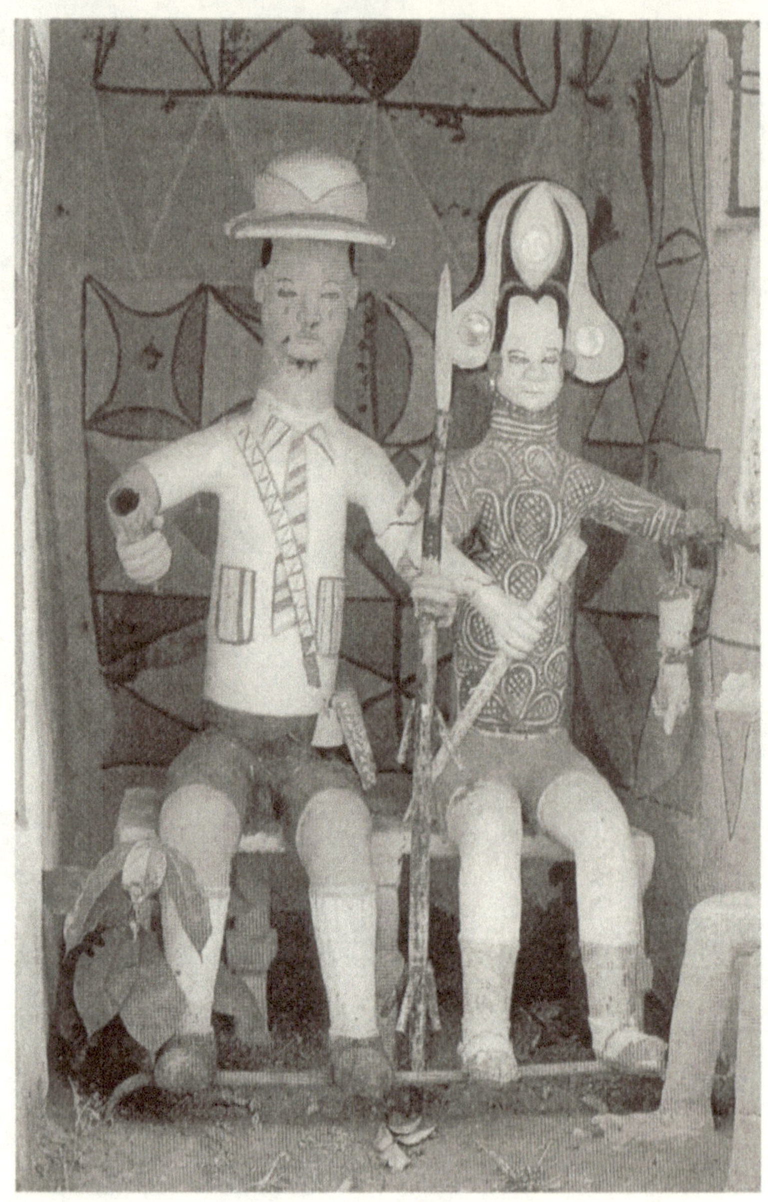

9.

The traditional god of thunder in modern dress. The greater conservatism in rendering females may stem from the pleasure the artists take in painting the decorative body patterns, which they find challenging as well as aesthetically pleasing.

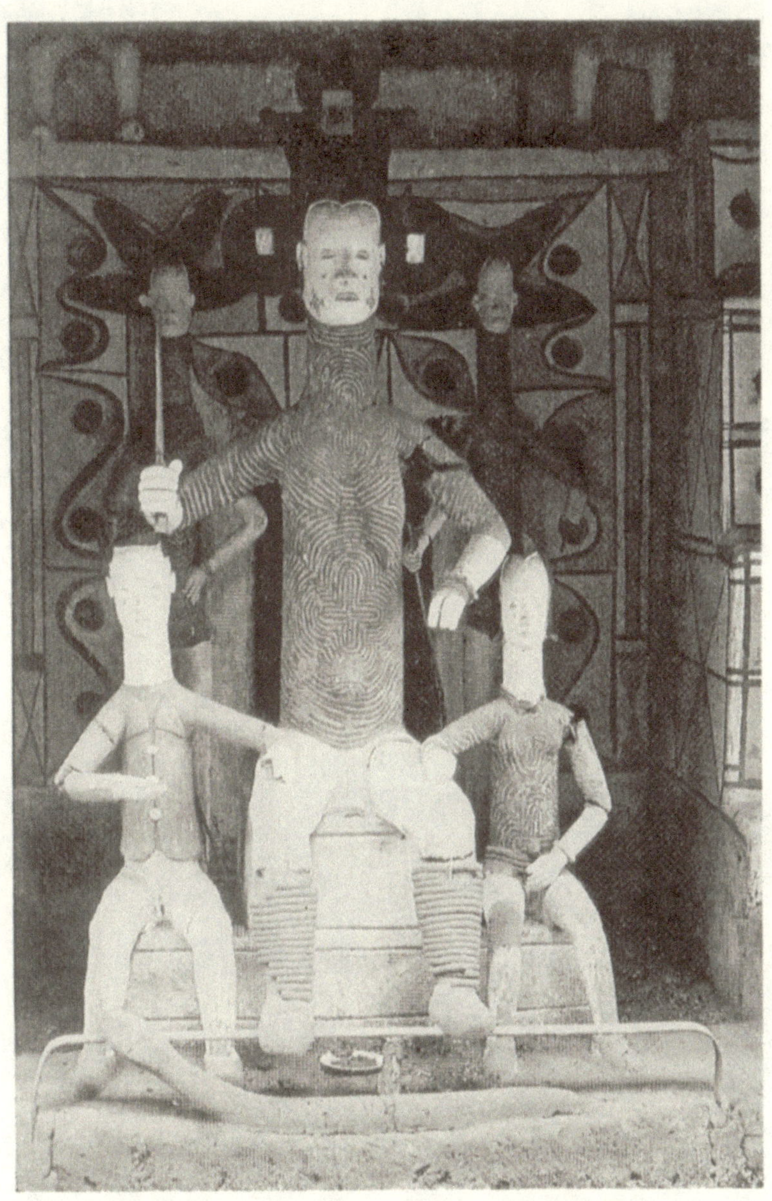

10.
The artist Ugo of Ihitte has a personal style marked by his frequent use of small units and curvilinear ropes of modeling clay.

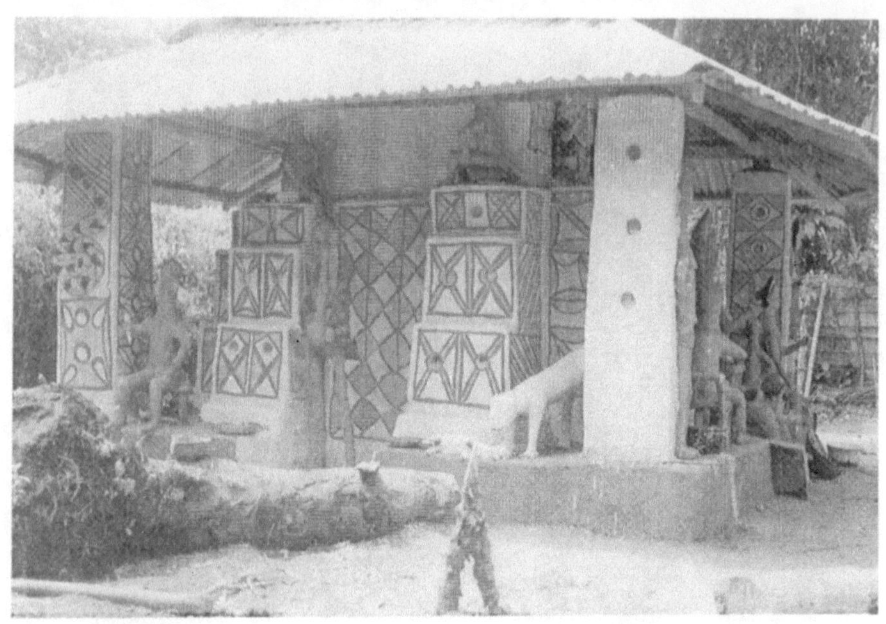

11.

The Nnorie mbari moves on toward completion. Next the front side, right, will be painted. In the foreground stands the incomplete first figure, which will be destroyed on opening night.

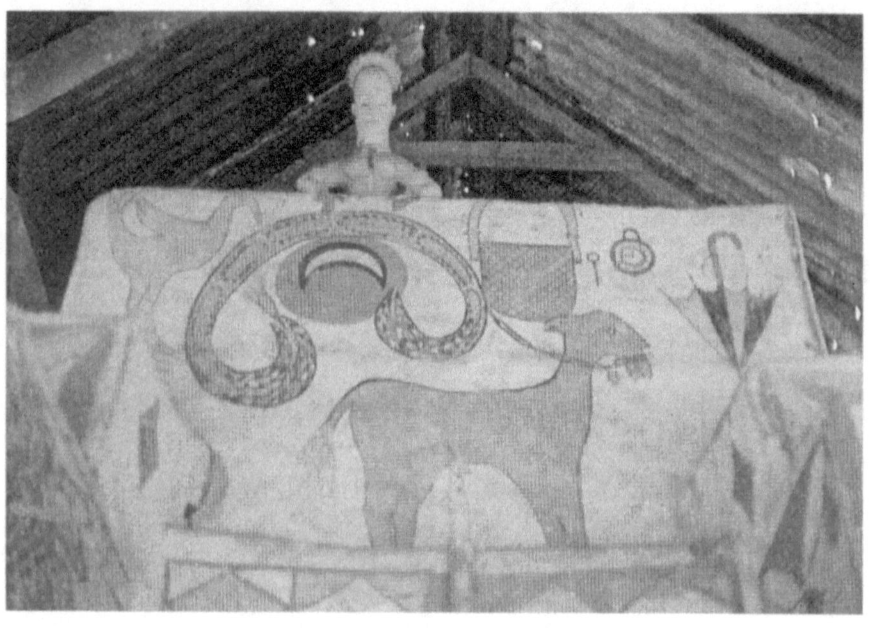

12.

The "free" paintings on upper walls often increase the subject range of mbari imagery, and the depictions here may or may not relate integrally with mbari activity.

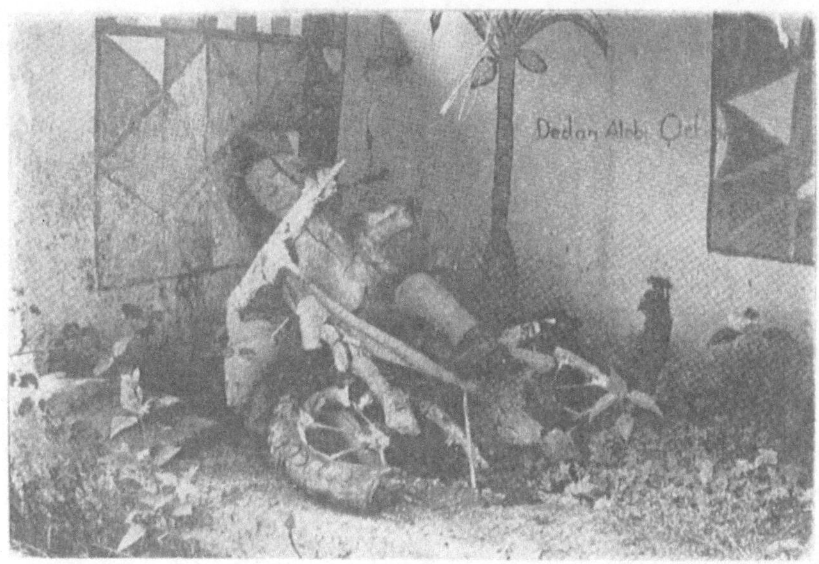

Plate 1. Mbari built with mat roofs may last only a short time; this gallery was finished only two years before the picture was taken.

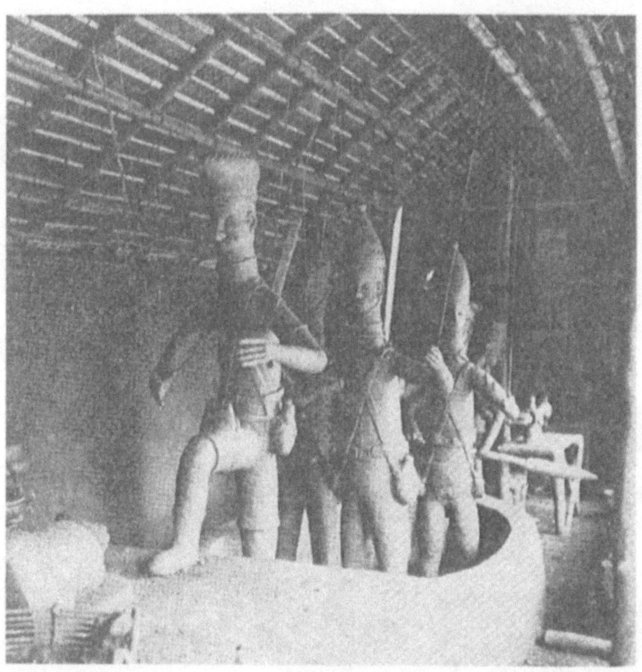

Plate 2. Superior modeling and complex grouping characterized the work of the thirties, perhaps the golden era of mbari. Note the carefully constructed mat roof.

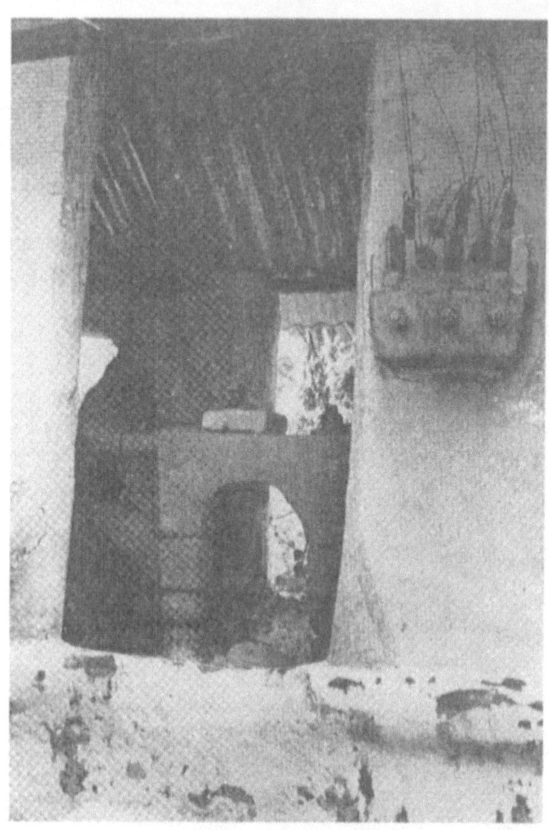

Plate 3. A business man, with telephone, sits at his desk in an office building. Telephone unit, right, is made with discarded flashlight batteries.

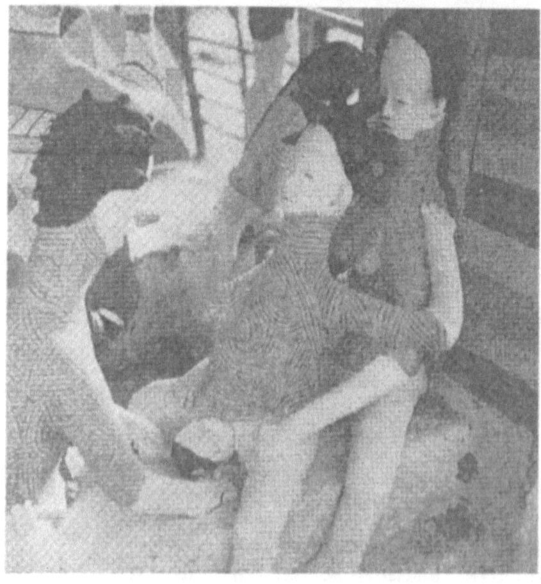

Plate 4. The dramatic moment of childbirth is recorded in a great many houses, as if to emphasize the fructifying aspect of the mbari phenomenon.

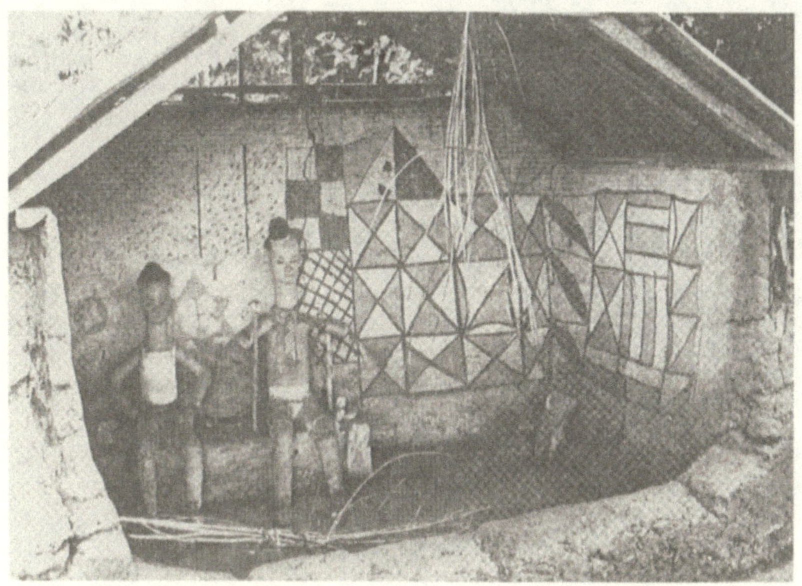

Plate 5. Countless small mbari, like this one, are found in the area, but they do not, of course, receive the attention accorded large ones.

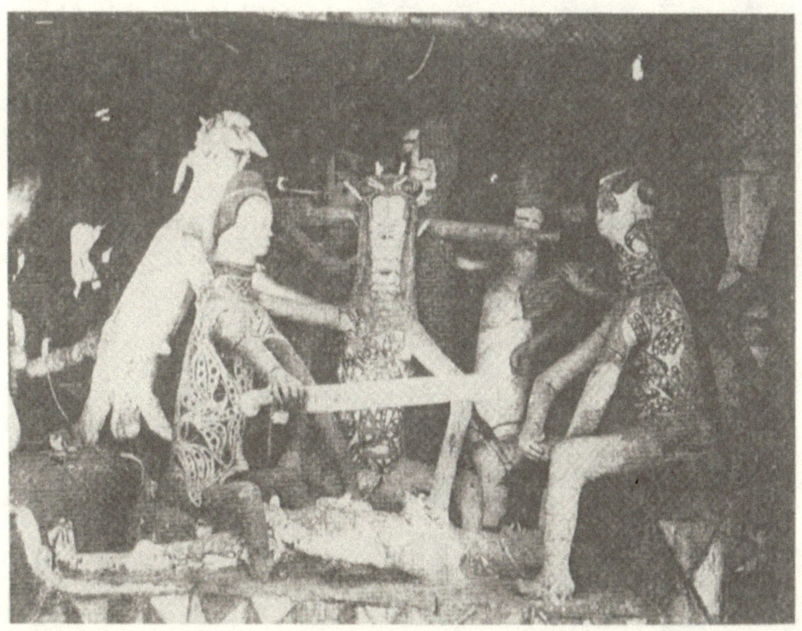

Plate 6. Elaborate body painting was the principal "clothing" of mbari figures, and their makers, before the turn of the century. This appears to be an execution scene.

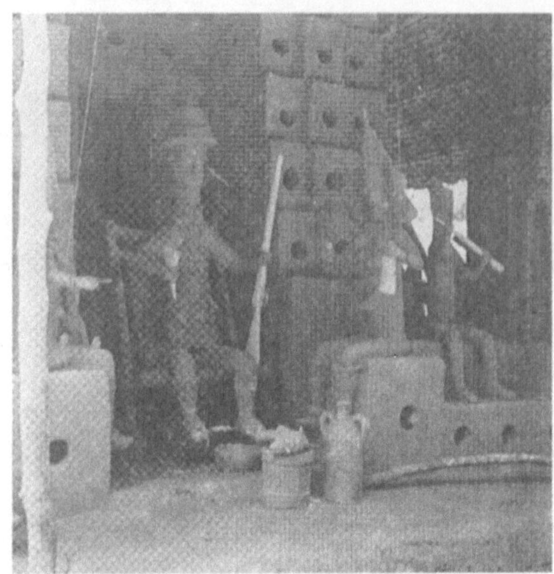

Plate 7. A large mbari to Amadioha, shown here with a gun, will soon be painted. Note the precise detailing.

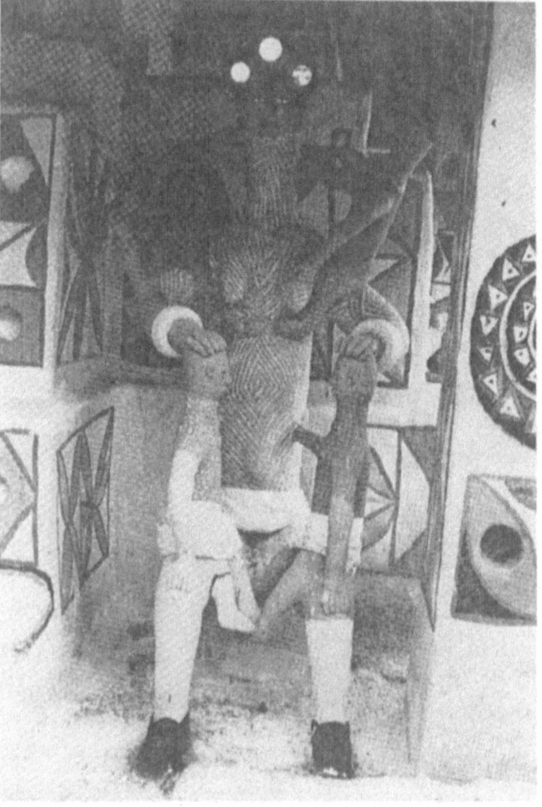

Plate 8. This frequently seen image, a goddess with many children posed precariously about her, is often identified as Ekwunoche, a river deity.

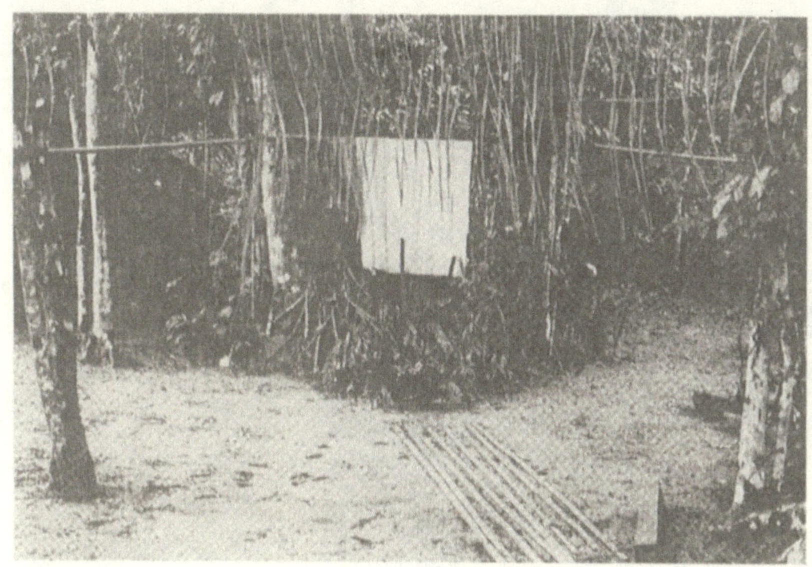

Plate 9. Typical shrine and altar for an important deity. The white cloth provides visual focus, but the god's symbol is the cluster of trees behind.

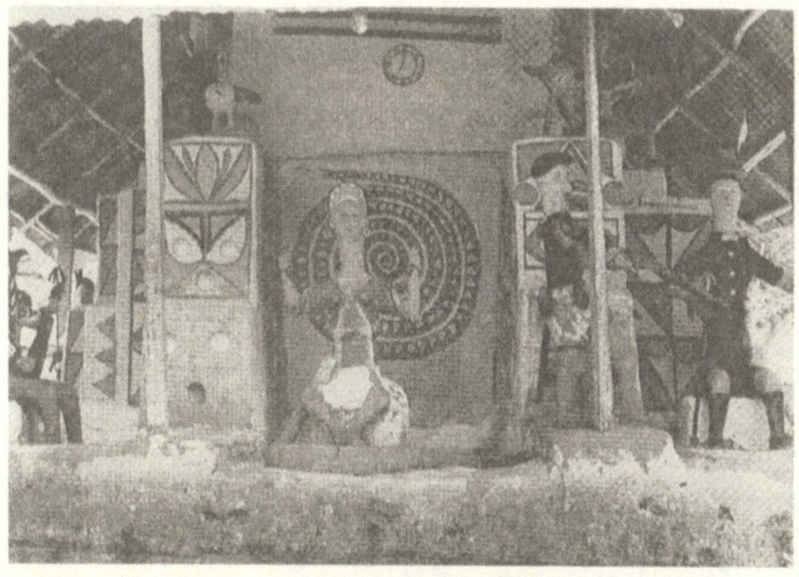

Plate 10. This fairly recent mbari still contains traditional images, like Mamy Wata, the python, and a hunter, while the guitarist (left) and the chief (right) reflect modernity in a more obvious way.

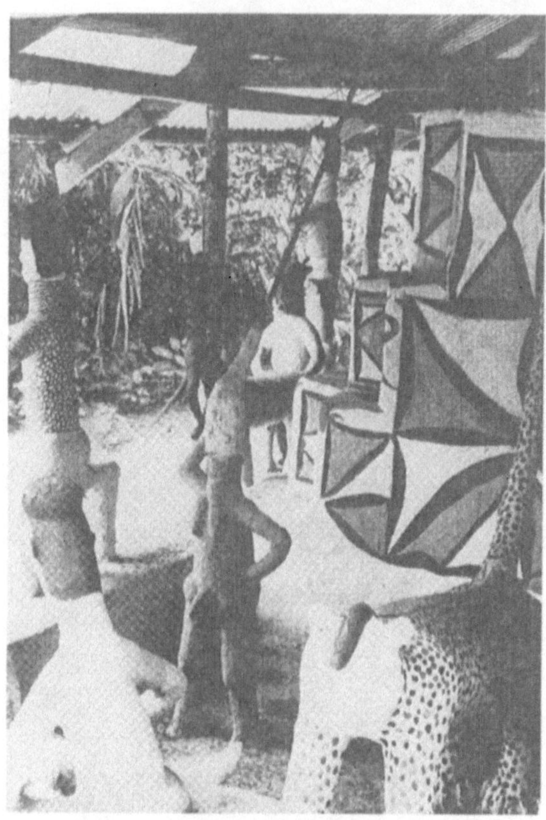

Plate 11. View across the corner of one mbari shows how figure placement encourages visitors to move around the house. In the center is a monsterized *mmuo* image.

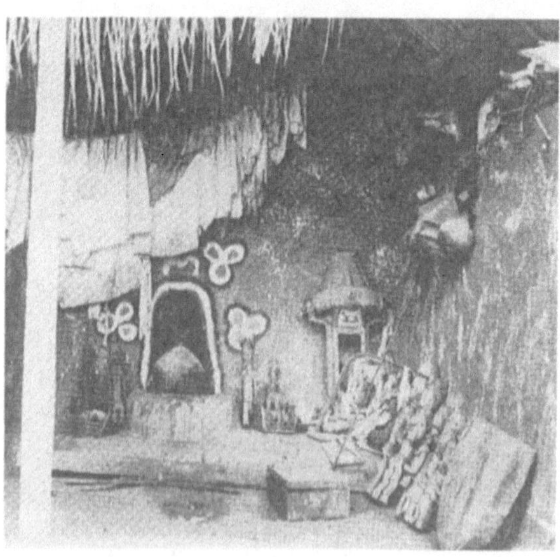

Plate 12. The inside of the "public" part of a goddess's house with wooden figures representing her messengers, iron objects and skulls given in sacrifice, and cloths, which are gifts to the deity.

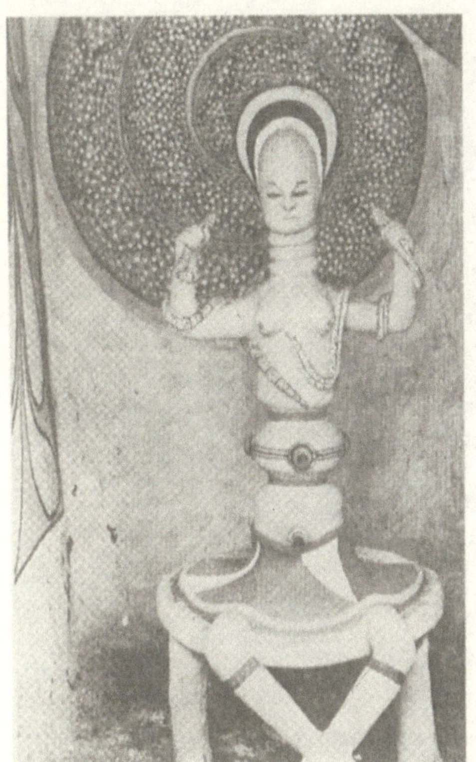

Plate 13. This highly conventionalized rendering of the goddess Mamy Wata was photographed by the late Kenneth Murray in 1936.

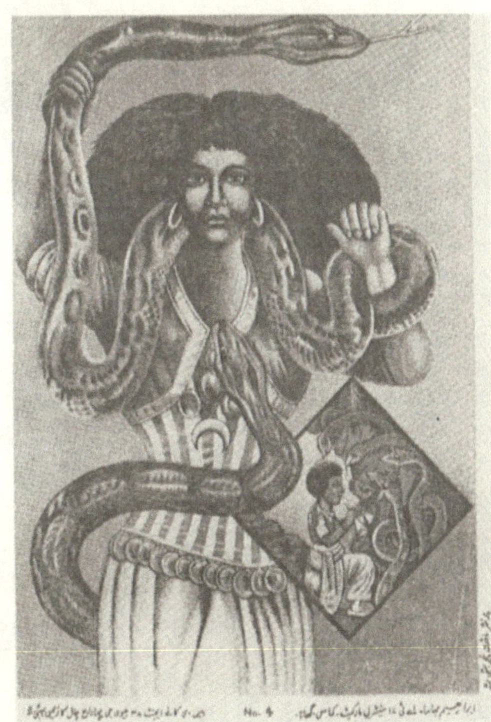

Plate 14. Other versions of imported prints of Mamy Wata exist, but this is the one most frequently seen in the Owerri area. See plates 56 and 57.

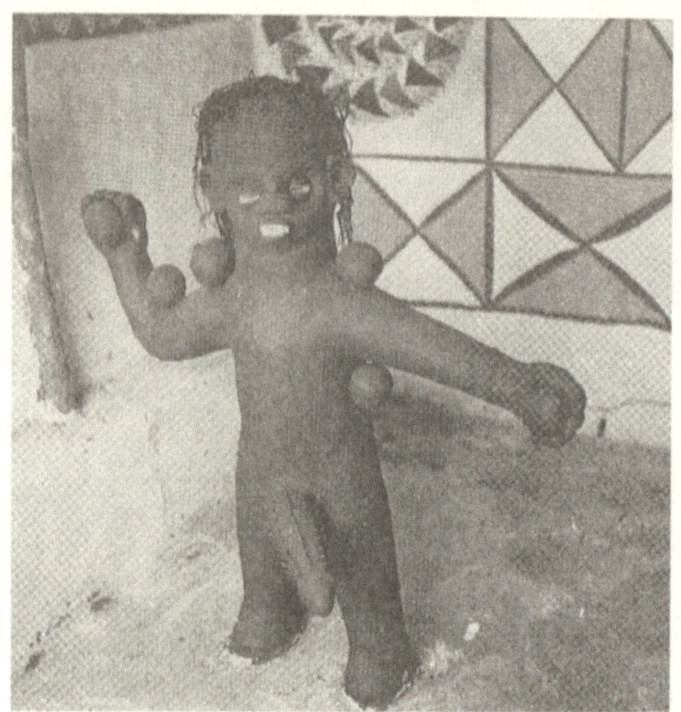

Plate 15. Okpangu, a dreaded but popular creature, is the villain of many Owerri folktales.

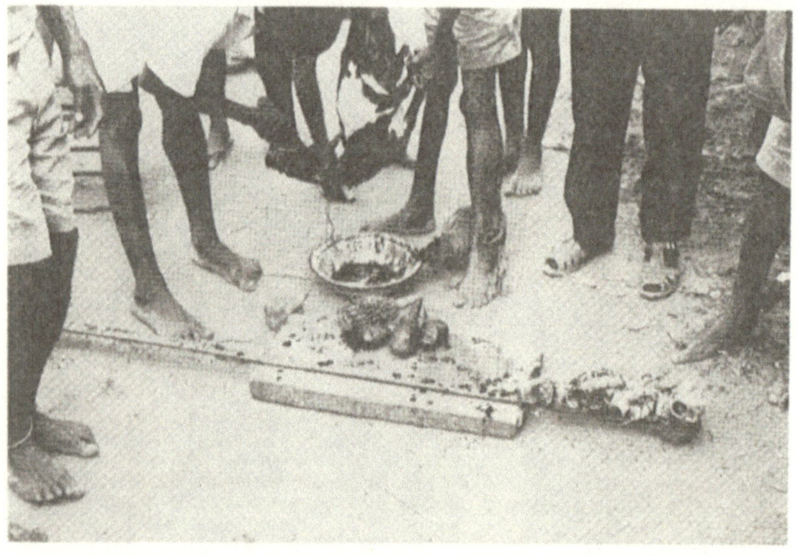

Plate 16. The "tied iron" and the ọfọ symbols of the god and his priest are here being empowered with the blood of a goat.

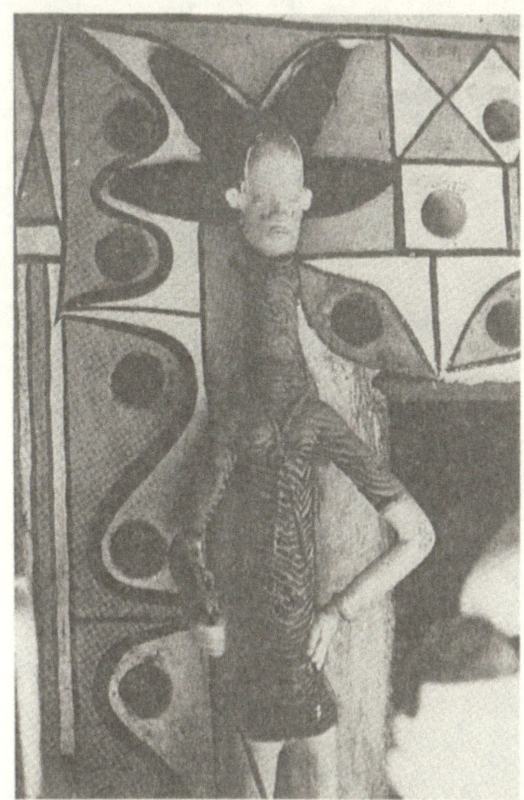

Plate 17. Nnaji's version of an *ijeremgbe,* who represents an mbari worker and who guards the door to the inner chamber.

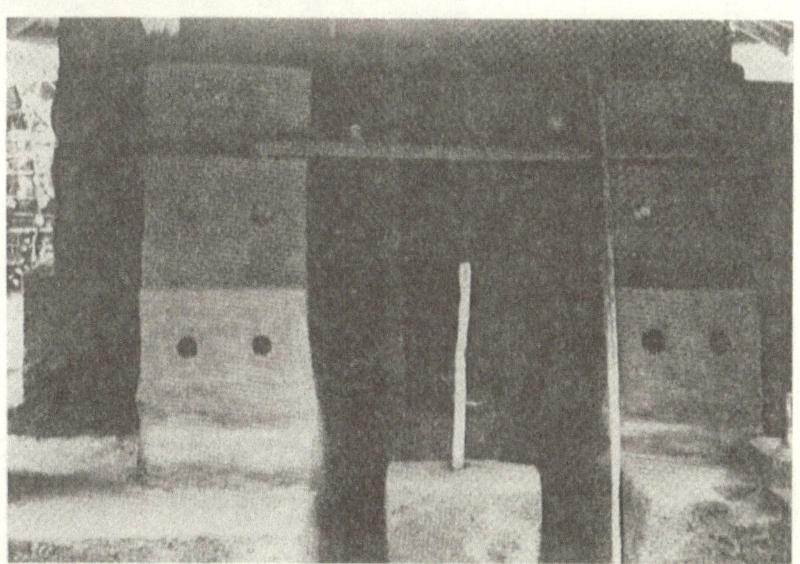

Plate 18. The architectural core of an mbari in 1966. The "owner of the house" will be modeled on the large pedestal (see plate 22).

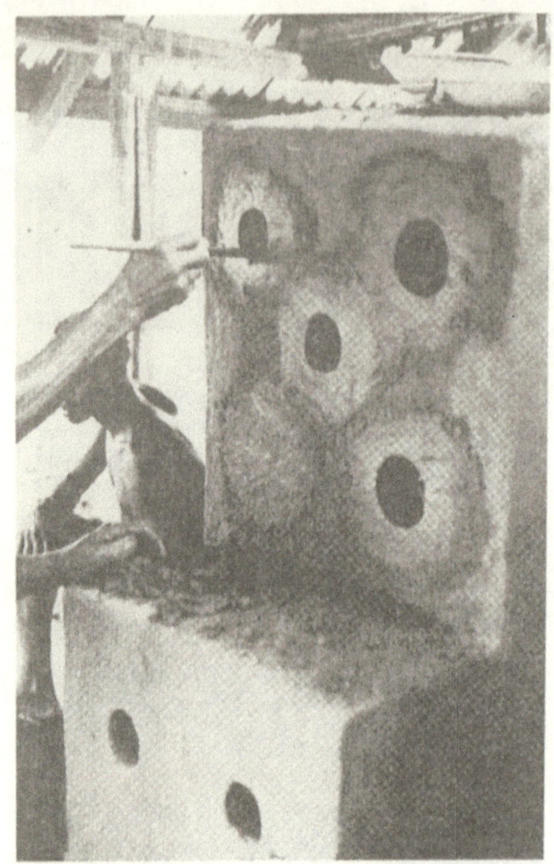

Plate 19. Ugwuanya shown imbedding plates or saucers into a buttress. First a hole the size of the dish is excavated.

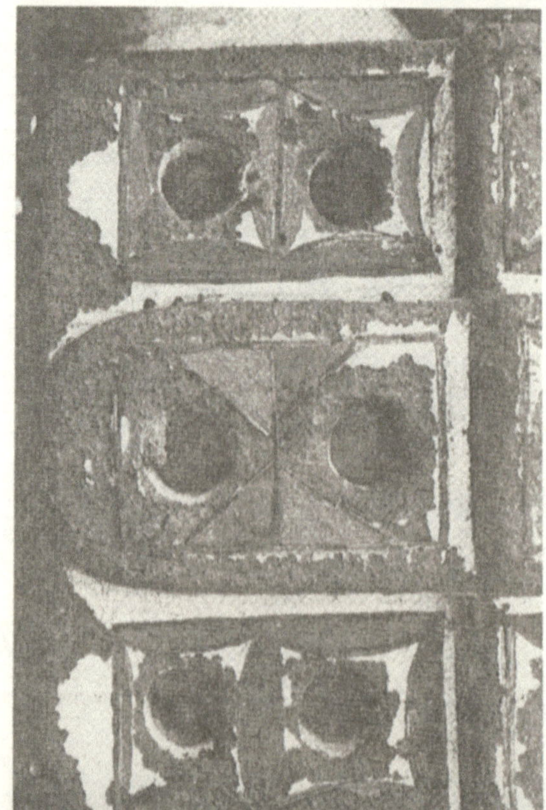

Plate 20. Slivers of bamboo, used as painting guides for geometric patterns, may once have been common.

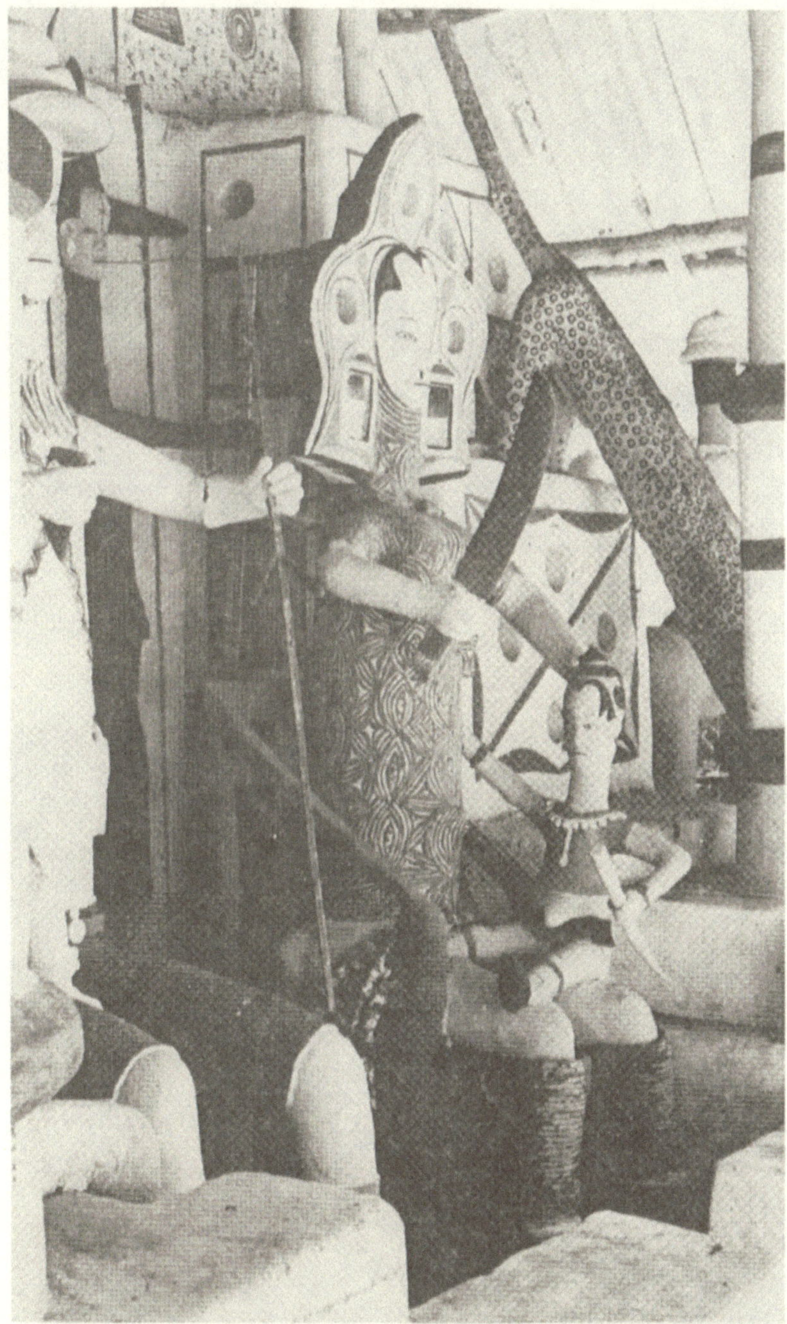

Plate 21. Iron bars, if the deity owns many, are used in several ways: imbedded in walls, placed in the hands of *ijeremgbe,* and set as footrests for important figures.

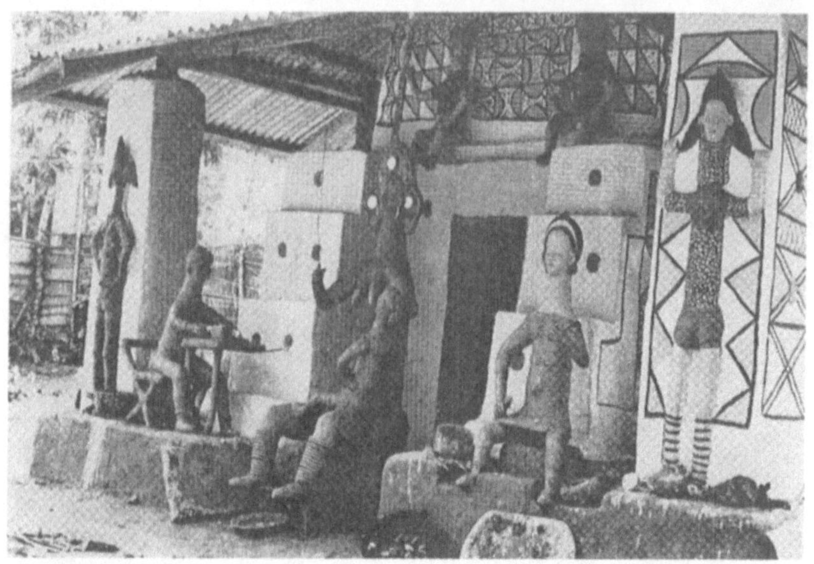

Plate 22. Most plane surfaces on mbari are whitewashed before colored pigments are applied. Painting implements line the lower wall.

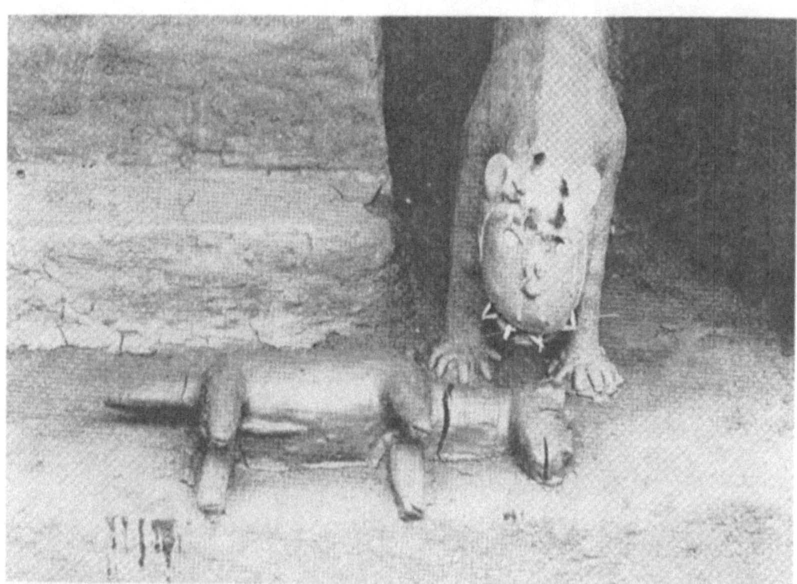

Plate 23. Cracks develop as "yam" dries. Note that sacrifices have been made on the leopard's head; feathers are stuck to the wet blood.

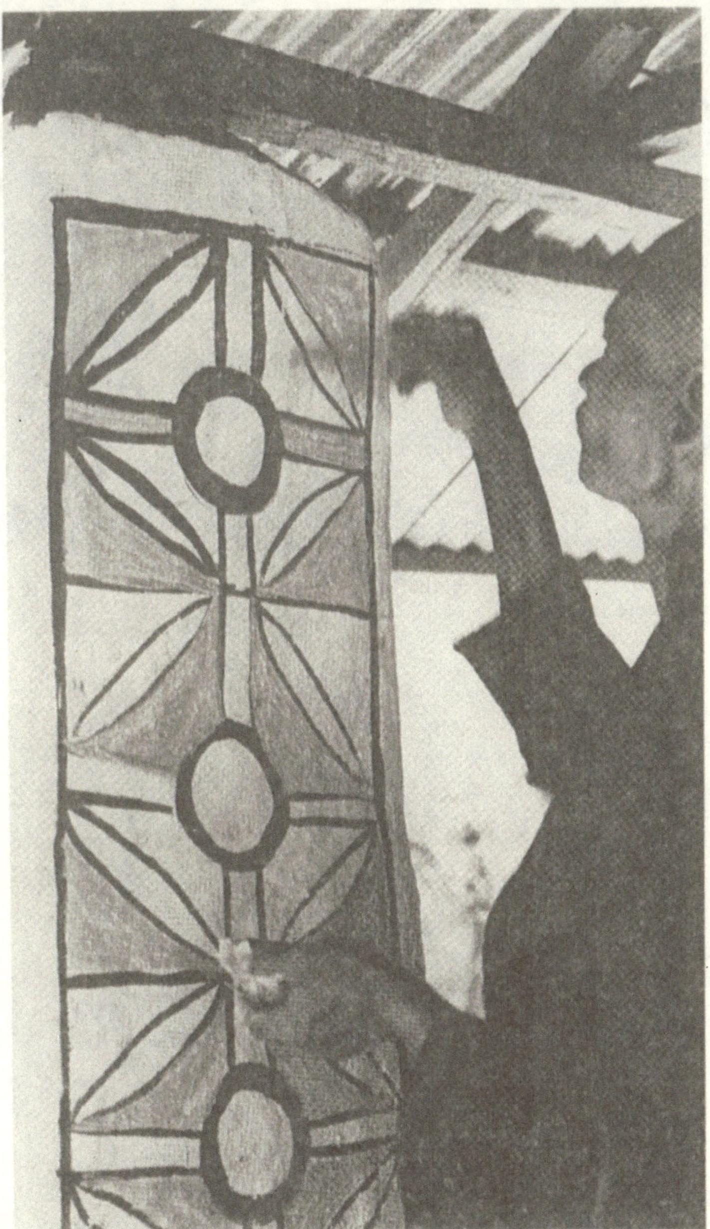

Plate 24. Geometric patterns often end up being quite different from their early versions, and they are sometimes overpainted six or eight times before they are considered properly finished.

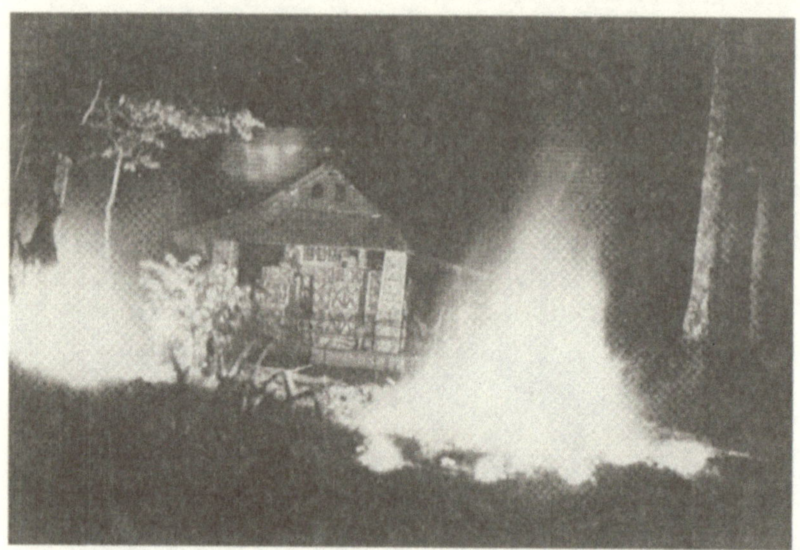

Plate 25. The Nnorie mbari lit by bonfires on the first night it is revealed to the world.

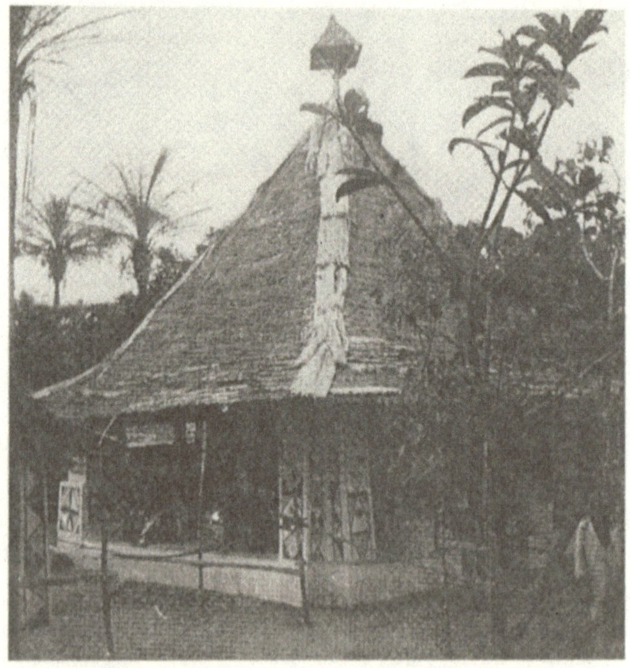

Plate 26. Many mbari houses of the 1930s, like this one photographed by G. I. Jones, had mat roofs, although metal ones were occasionally seen. Some informants said this plan, with the house built around a central pole, was the most common one in the old days.

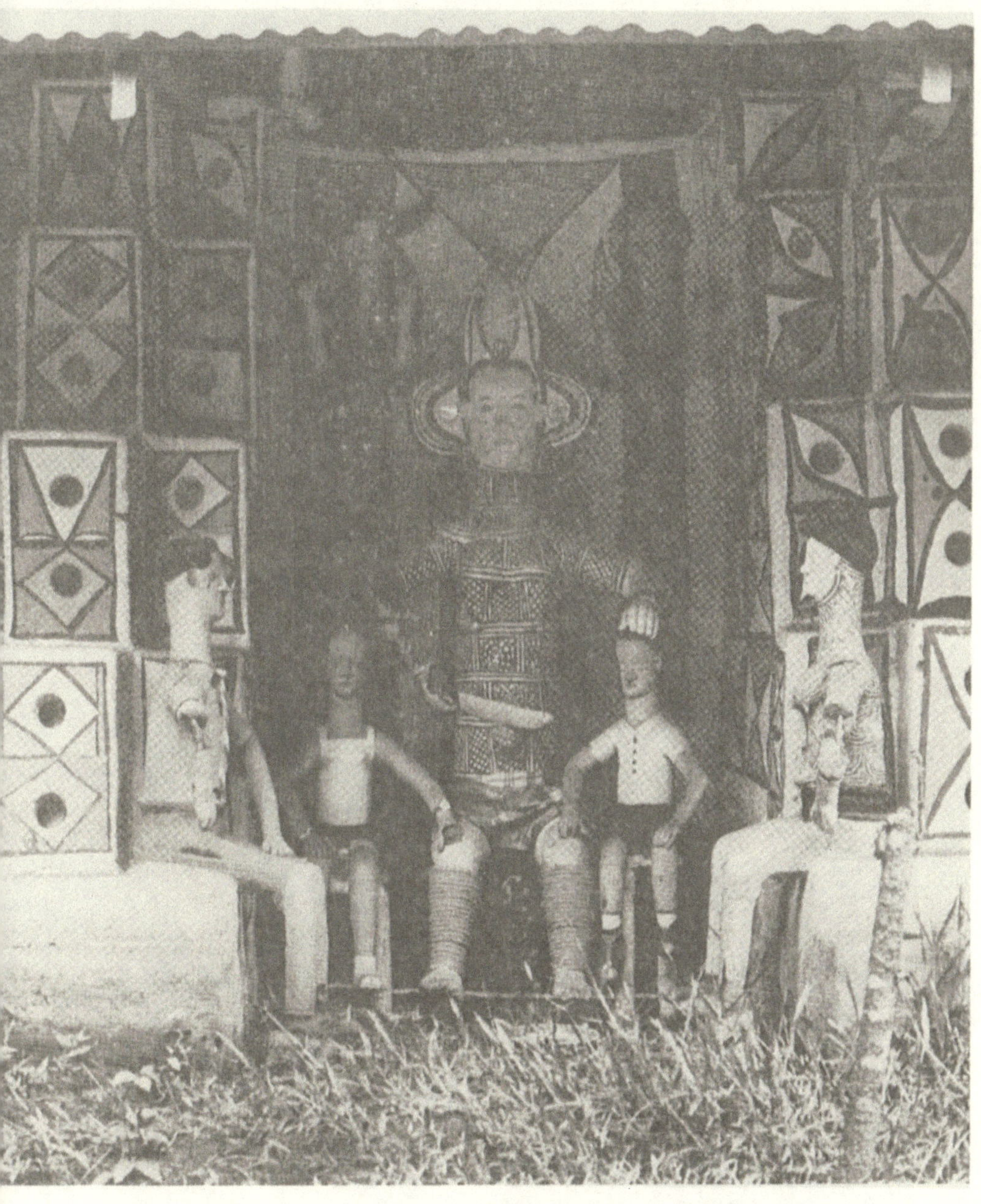

Plate 27. The front side is often the most formal and complex, for here the deity is surrounded by her entourage—her children and supporters.

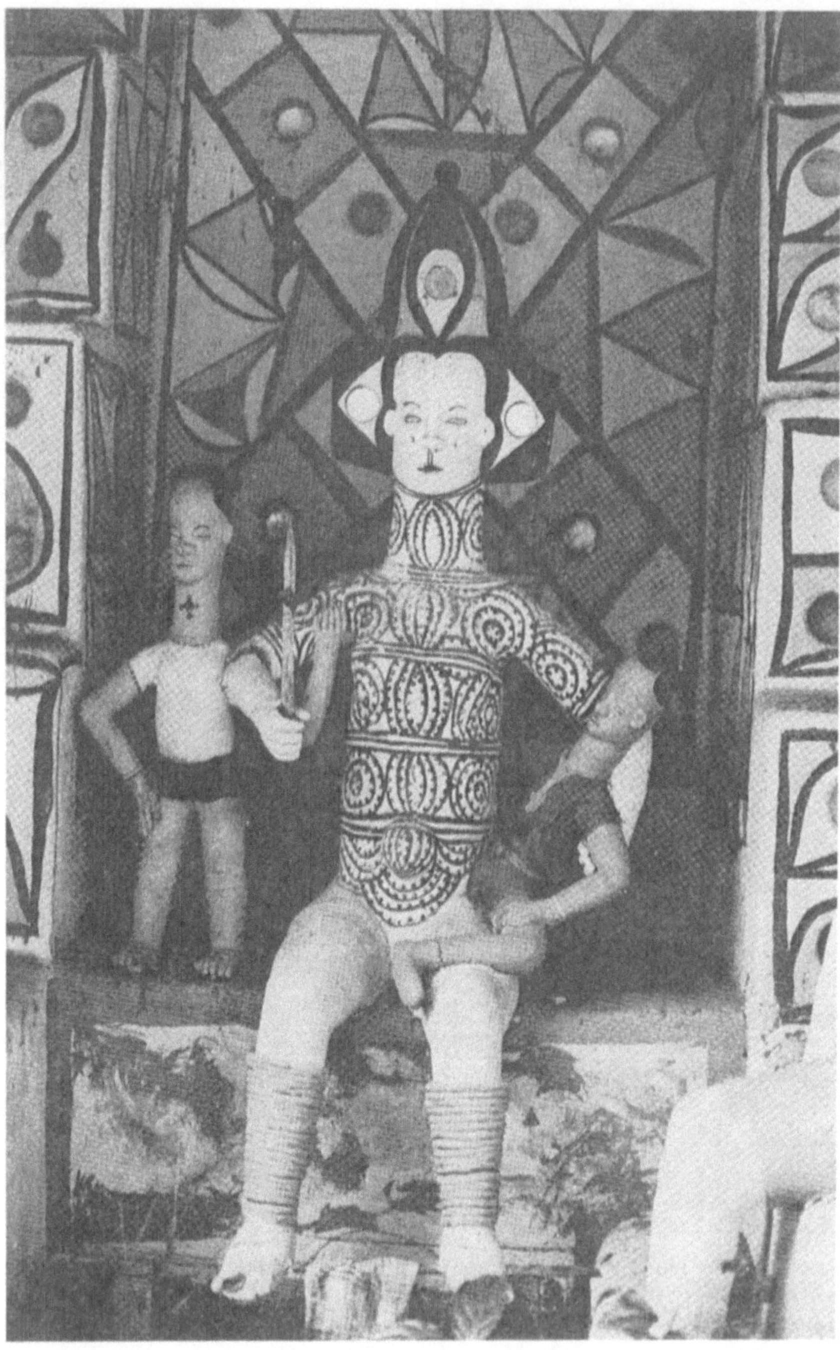

Plate 28. In a large house a subsidiary deity may receive prominent placement but she may not outshine its owner. The owner of this mbari is shown in plate 27.

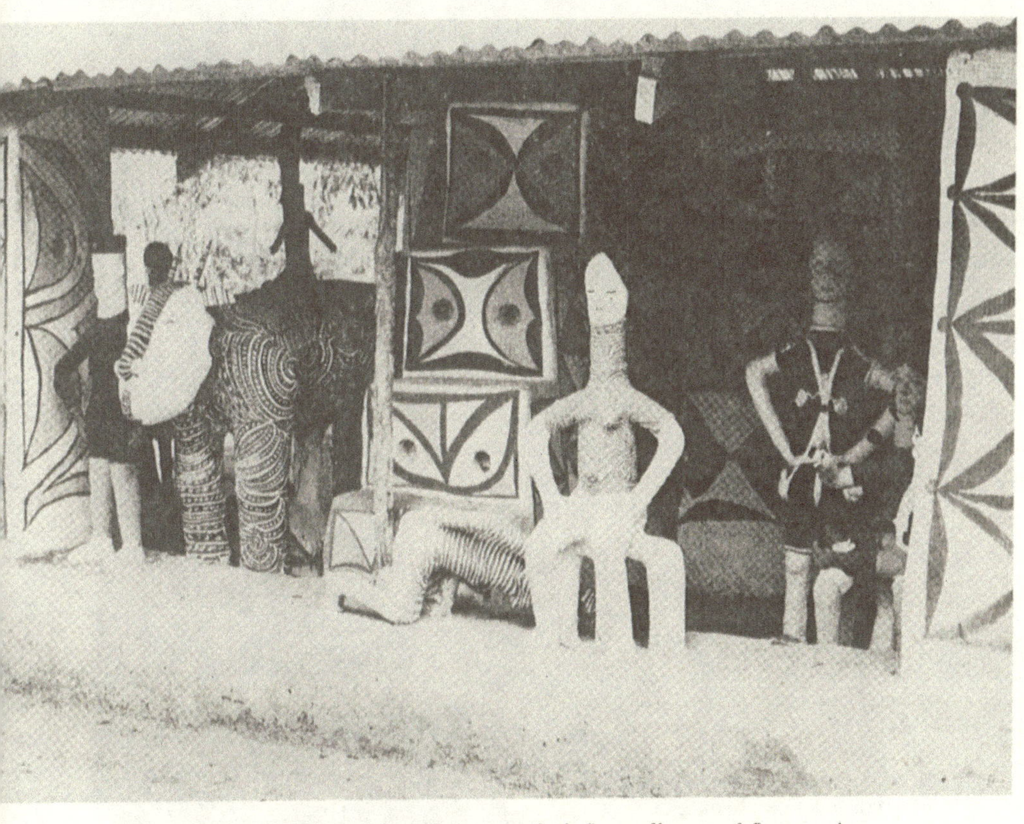

Plate 29. Subsidiary sides often contain informally posed figures, in this case, a shameless woman displaying herself to passersby.

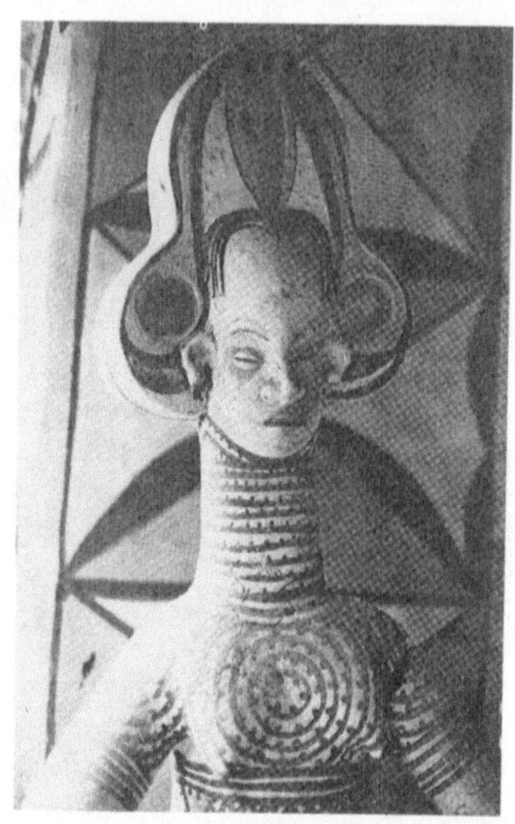

Plate 30. A finely rendered female figure by the artist Ezem.

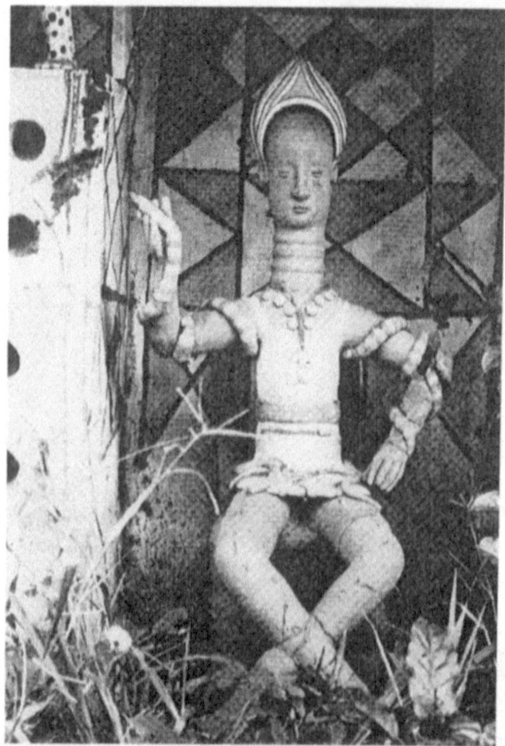

Plate 31. Mamy Wata with the typical cross-legged pose and ringed neck. She wears a cross, and her left arm has been broken.

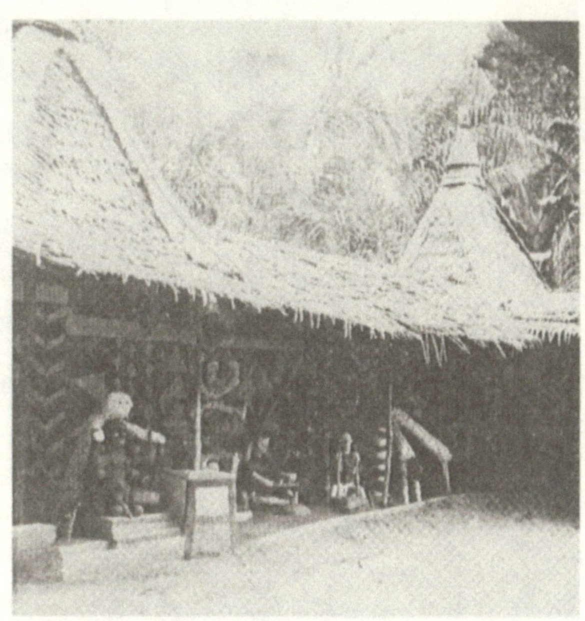

Plate 32. View of the gallery of a large mbari; it houses a number of relatively informal figures and groups.

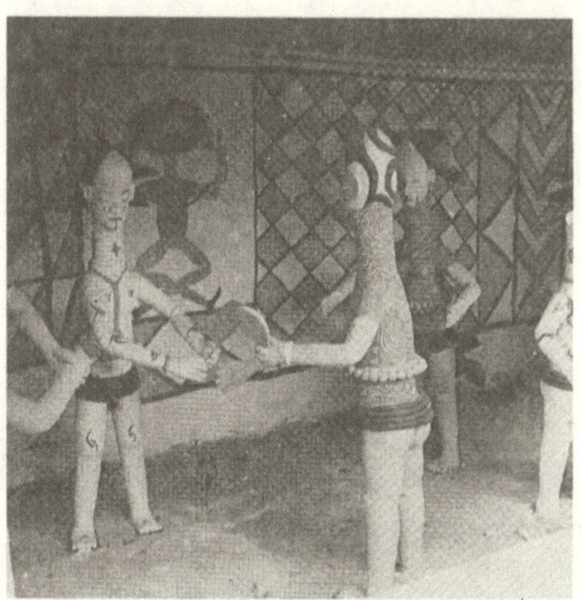

Plate 33. Dancers in the gallery of a recently opened mbari, with a painting of Mamy Wata on the wall behind.

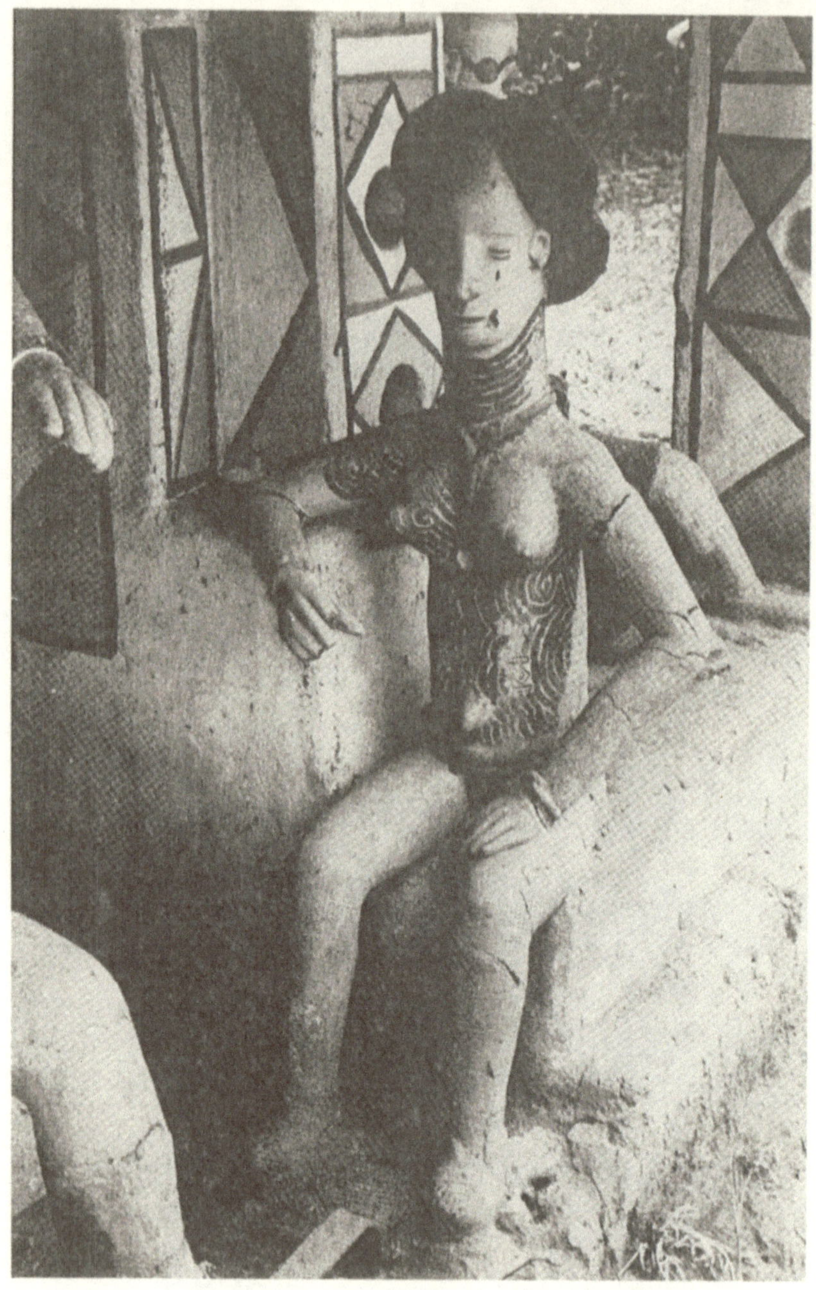

Plate 34. A well-modeled female figure which is informally posed.

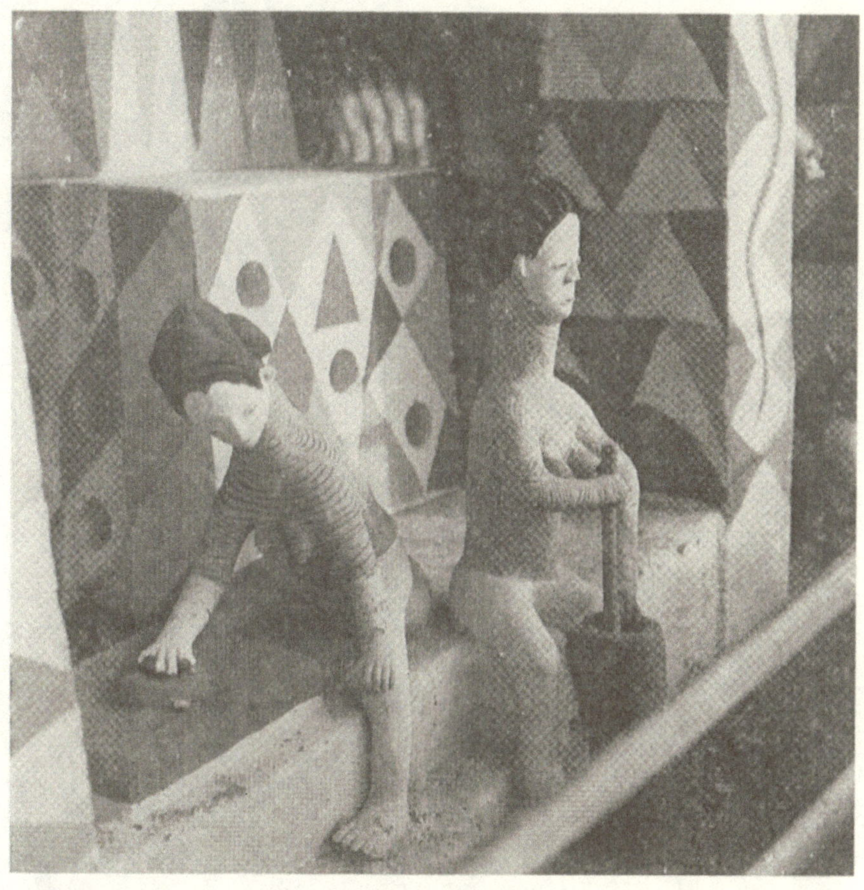

Plate 35. Scenes like these of women grinding camwood and pounding yam explore the domestic life of the community.

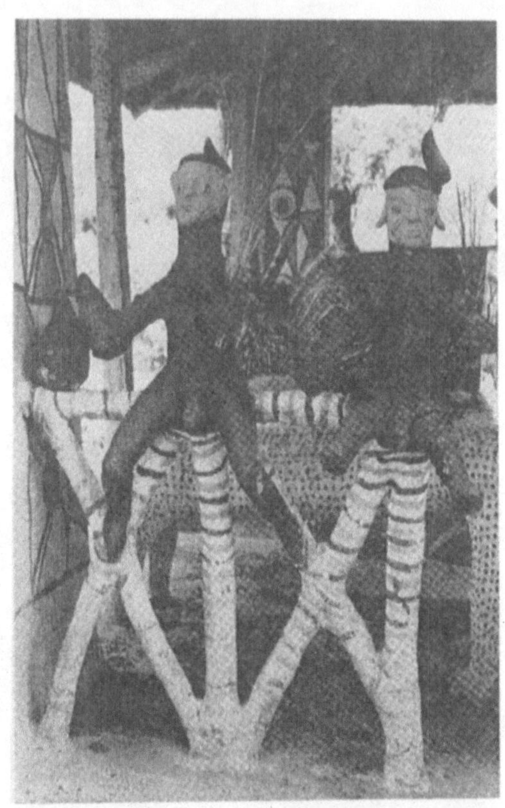

Plate 36. The airy pose of these rainmakers reveals scenes from other parts of the house.

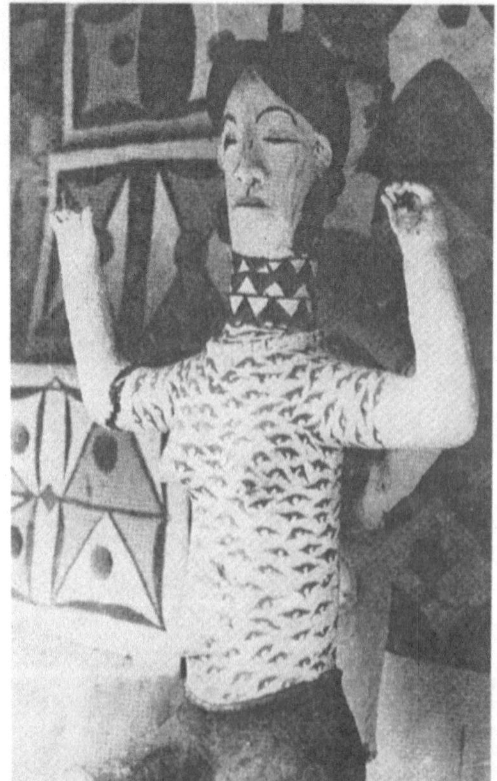

Plate 37. The idealized, hands-raised position of women often encountered. Compare the insecure modeling of this figure with plates 31 and 34.

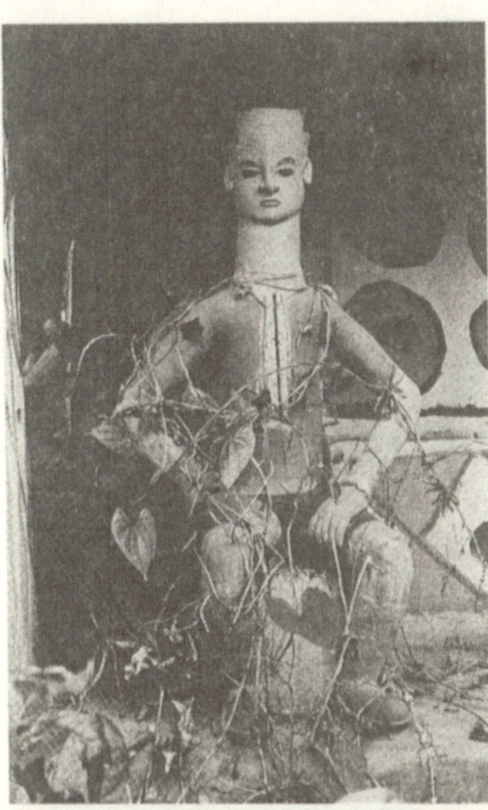

Plate 38. A dignified, carefully-rendered male figure by Ezem. Compare this pose with plate 29.

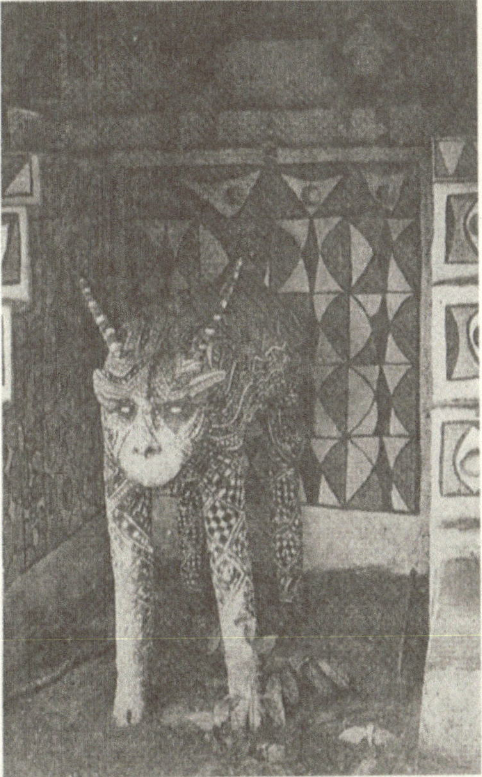

Plate 39. Elephants like this one suggest that sculptural conventions are often more prominent in the creative process than is descriptive modeling from nature.

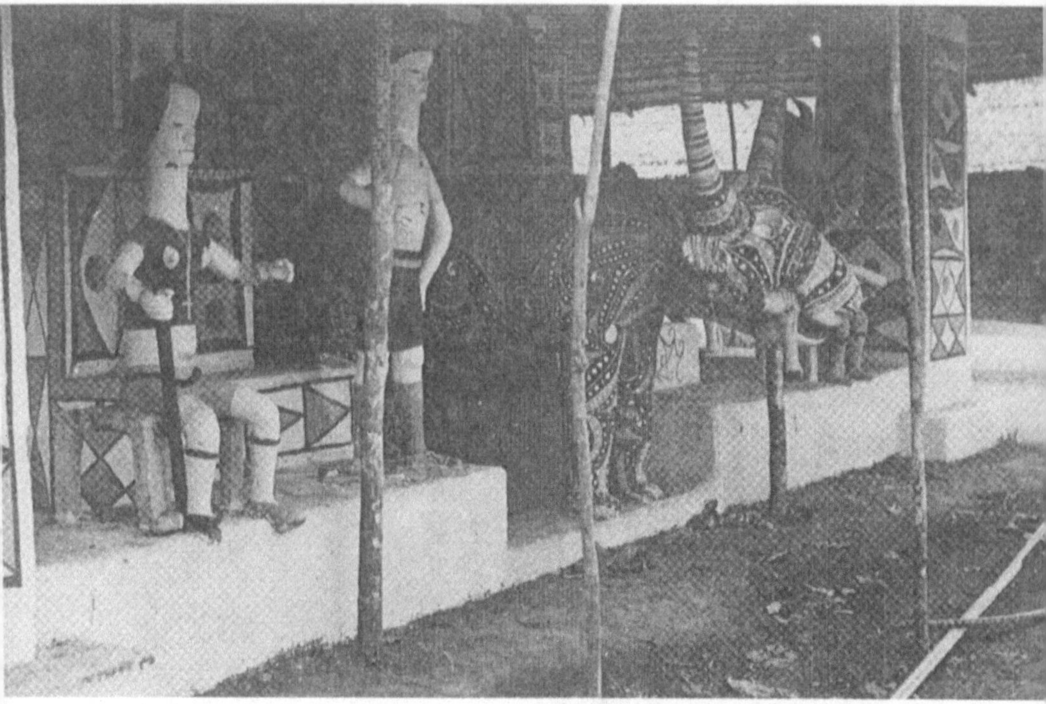

Plate 40. A fancifully sculptured and painted hippopotamus grasping a child in its jaws.

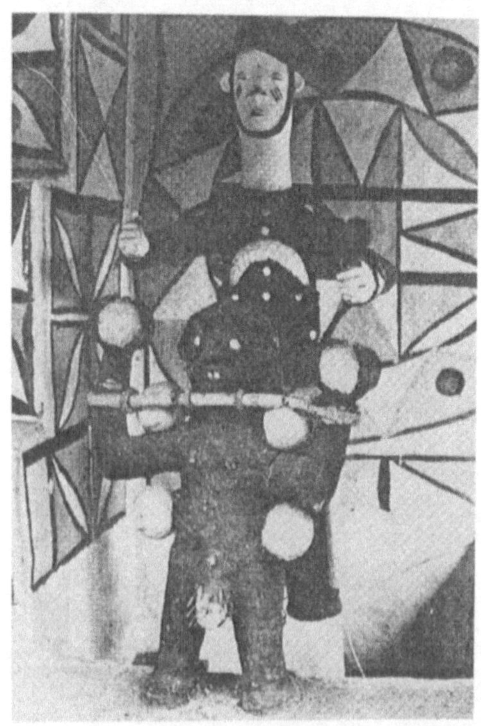

Plate 41. Ogidi, the giant policeman, holds the mythical ape-man Ọkpangụ ensnared with chains.

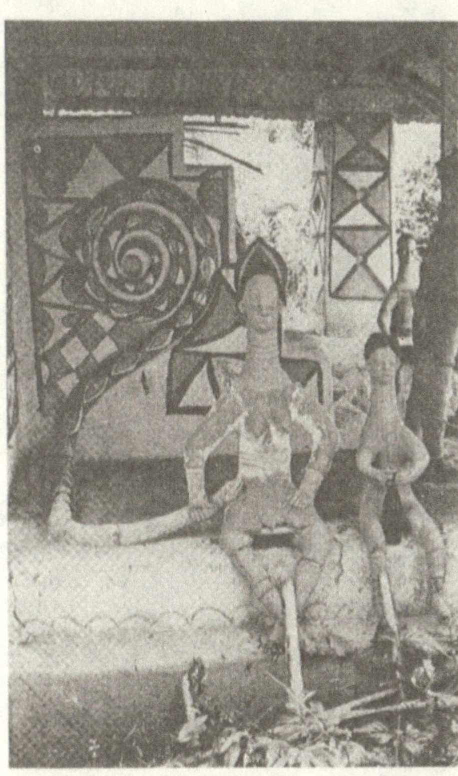

Plate 42. This variant on the common subject of Mamy Wata suggests that many artists are not satisfied by merely copying traditional imagery.

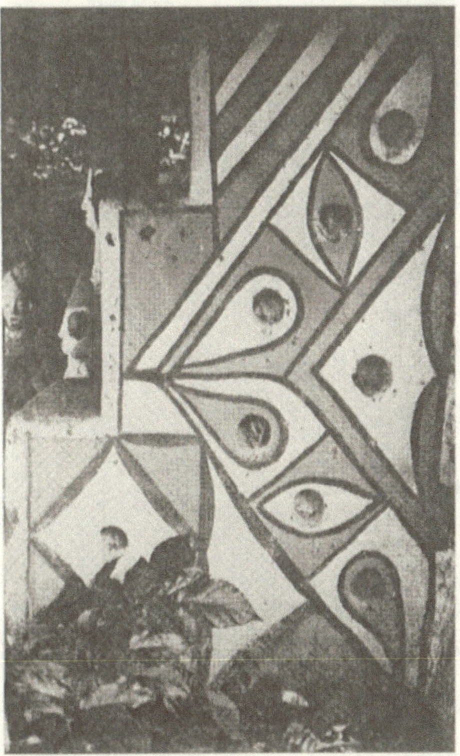

Plate 43. Outline, contrast, and subdivision are primary concepts in painting buttresses and lower walls.

Plate 44. Visible here are slight variations and color changes that add visual interest to geometric background patterns.

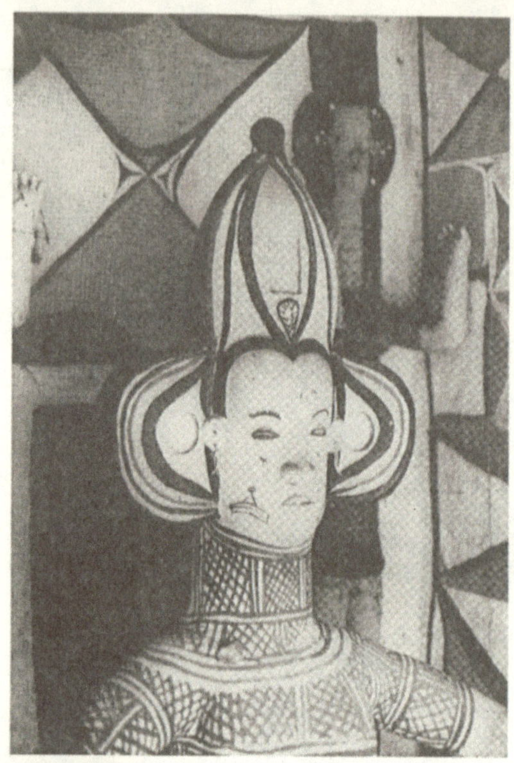

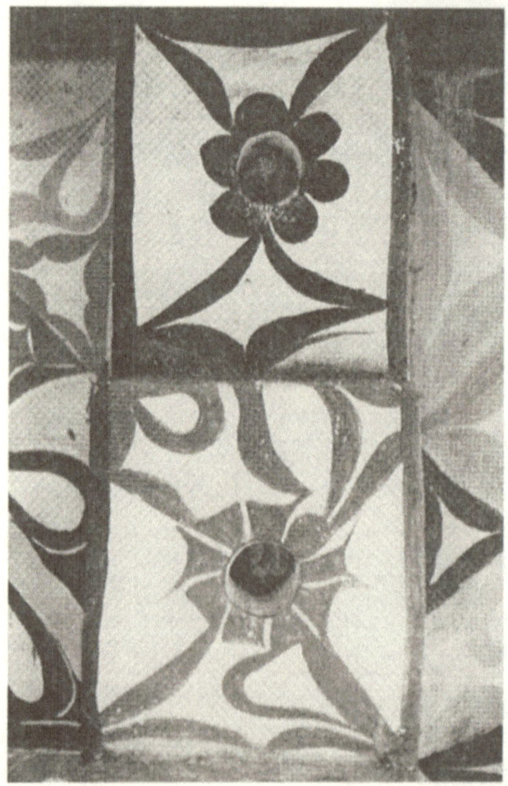

Plate 45. Artistically drawn curvilinear designs draw attention to the plate openings.

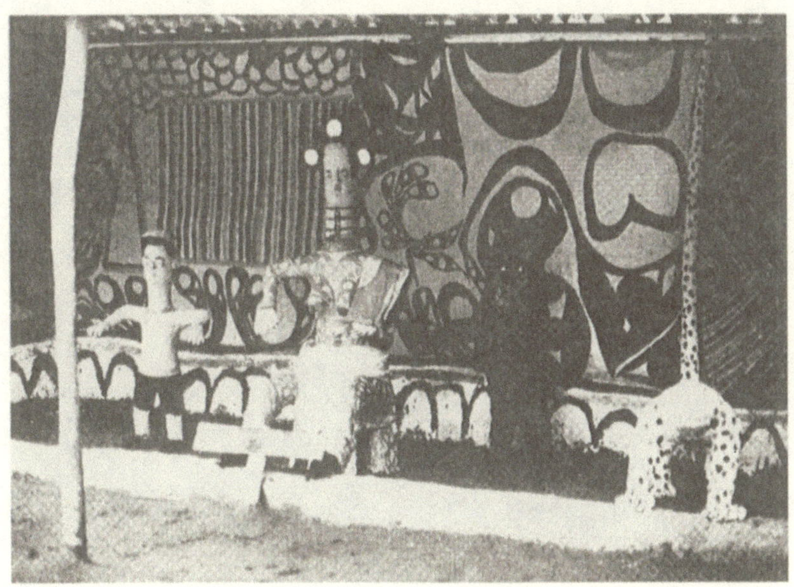

Plate 46. Rather dark, flamboyant, and arbitrarily applied wall paintings that some critics found unacceptable.

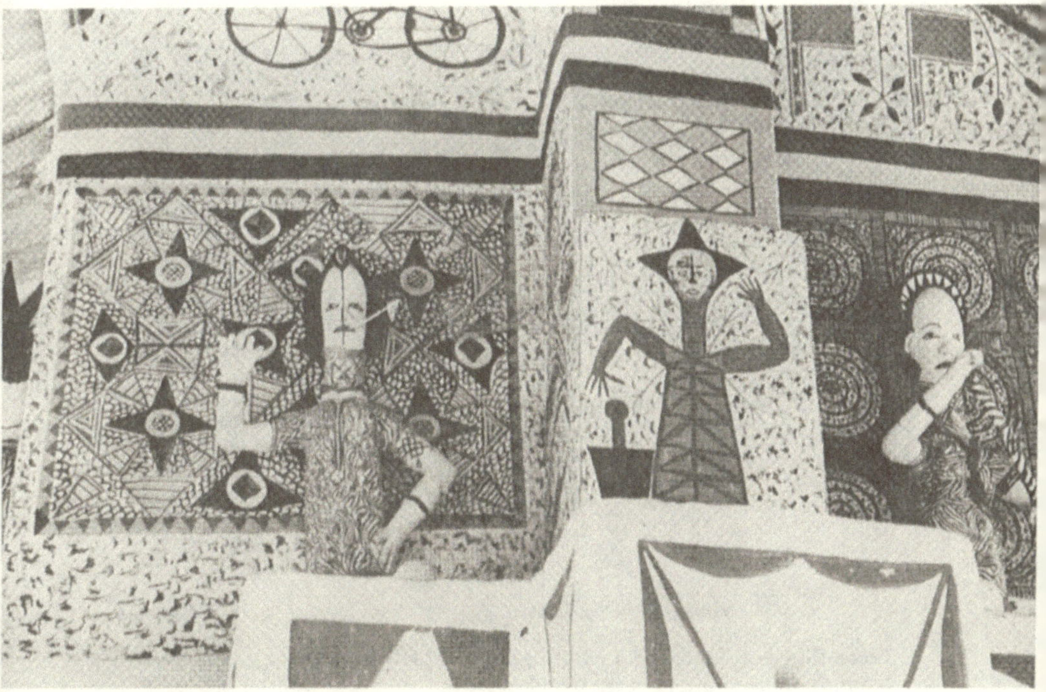

Plate 47. Upper wall paintings of great detail and precision; behind the sculptured women appear renditions of cloths.

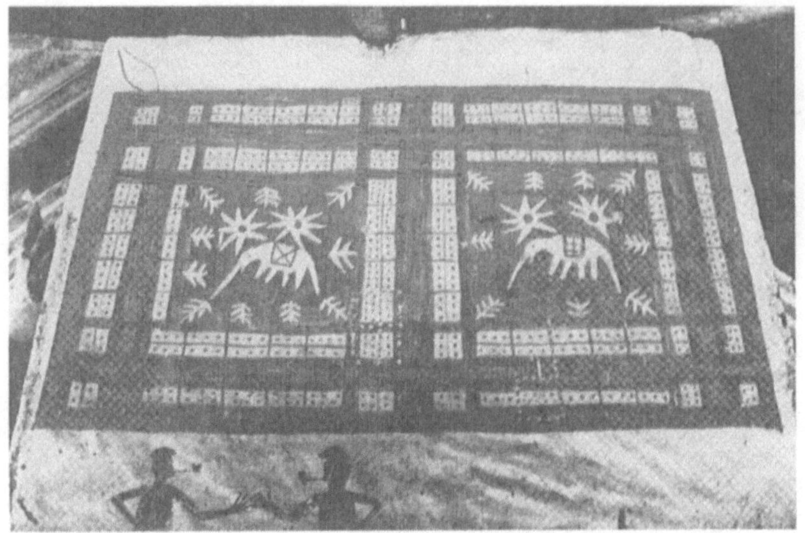

Plate 48. A simplified version of imported "George" cloth above a simple figural scene.

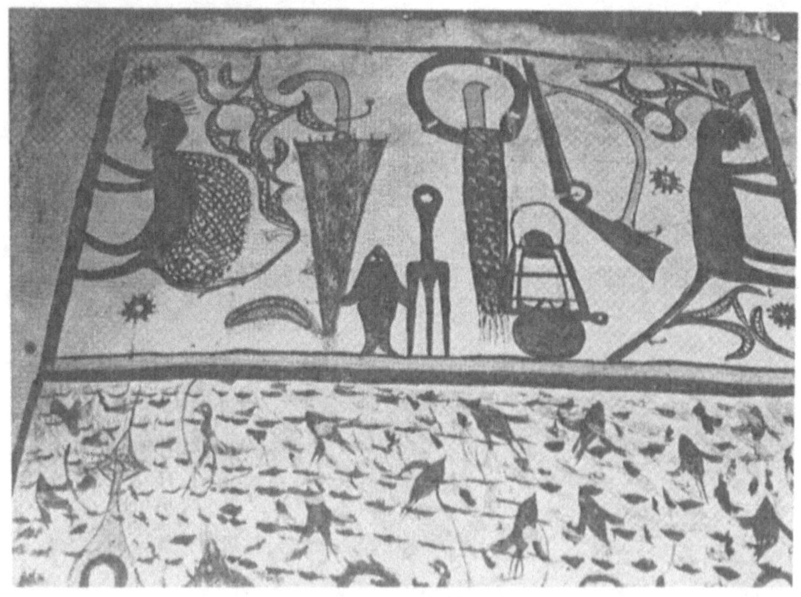

Plate 49. Few upper wall paintings are framed, and we may suppose framing to be a fairly recent development.

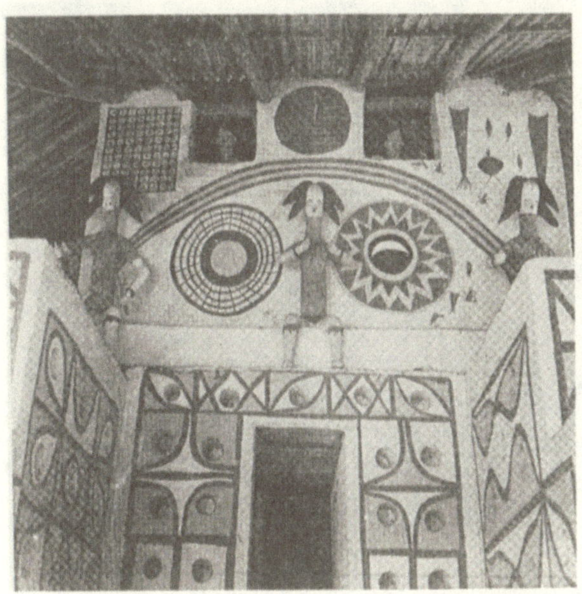

Plate 50. A symmetrical end-wall painting with celestial symbols dominant. Note the two white men peering from the "second story" windows.

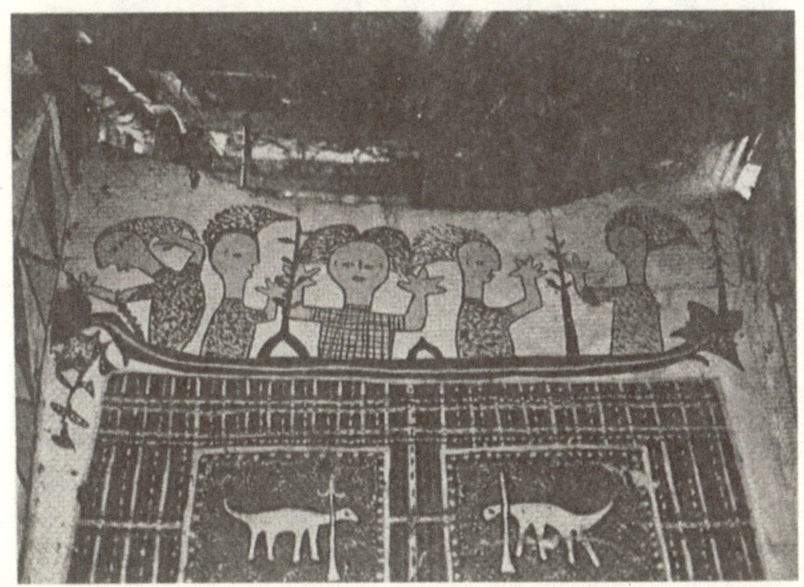

Plate 51. An imaginative wall painting of women and trees in a boat, above a more traditional theme, cloth.

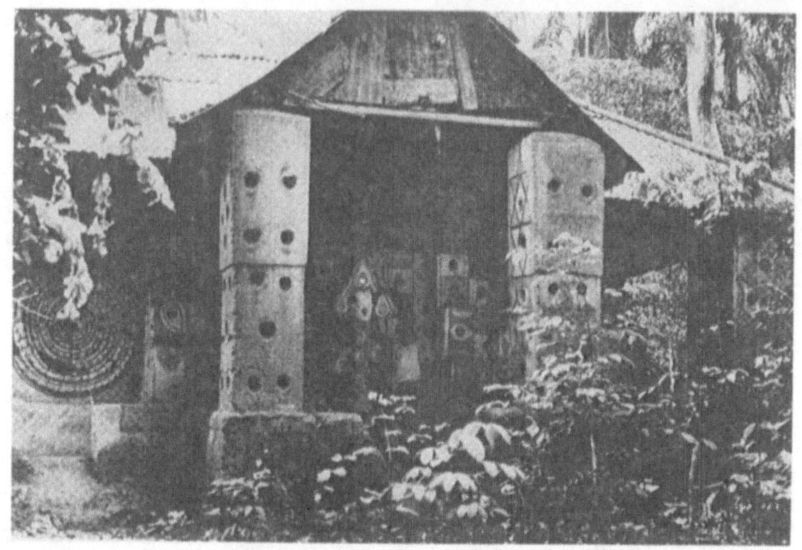

Plate 52. The largest single mbari structure still standing in 1966–67, and perhaps one of the largest ever built. Note the size of the priest who is standing beside the seated deity.

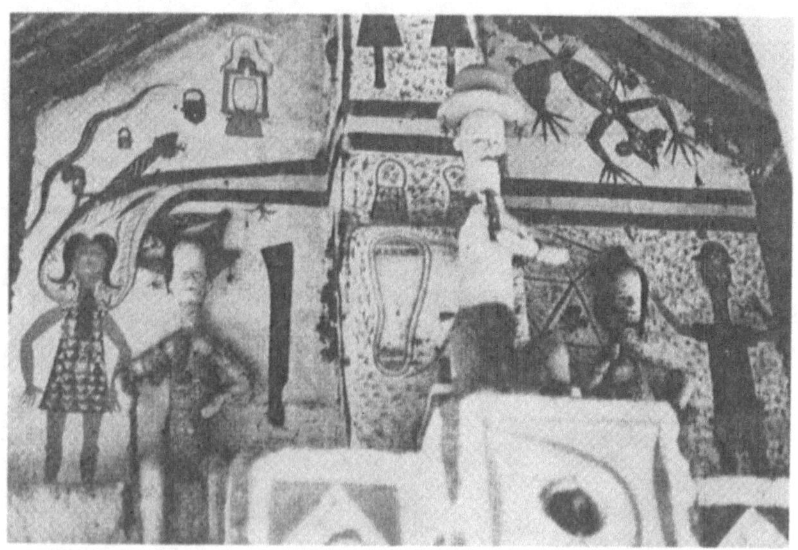

Plate 53. Lively and varied upper wall painting, with the schematized rainbow python biting a girl.

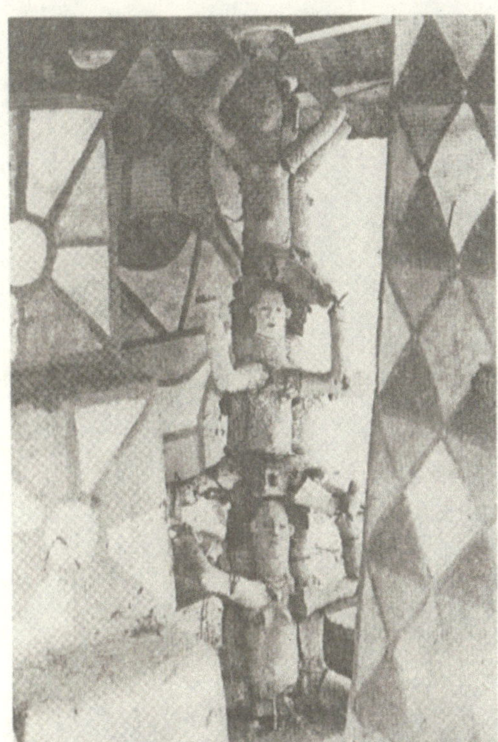

Plate 54. One of the more complex figural groups, which includes nine women holding up a keg of palm wine. It is derived from a proverb.

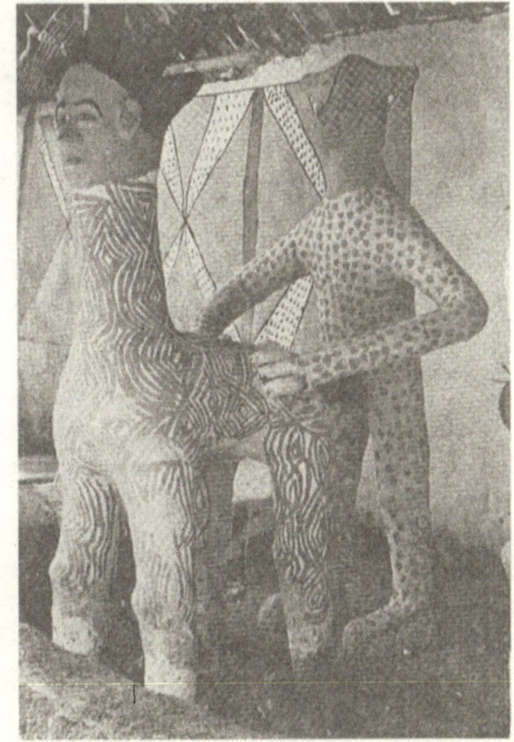

Plate 55. This group—a goat-headed man copulating with a woman-headed goat—is often used; it refers to a proverb.

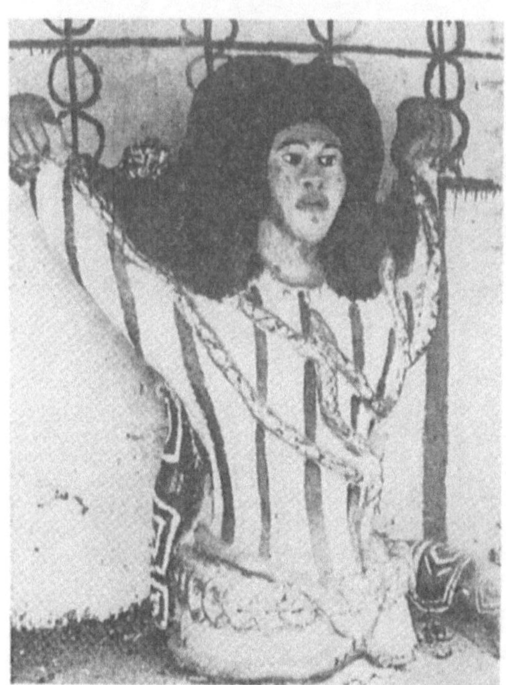

Plate 56. A modern sculpture of Mamy Wata inspired directly by the imported image in plate 14.

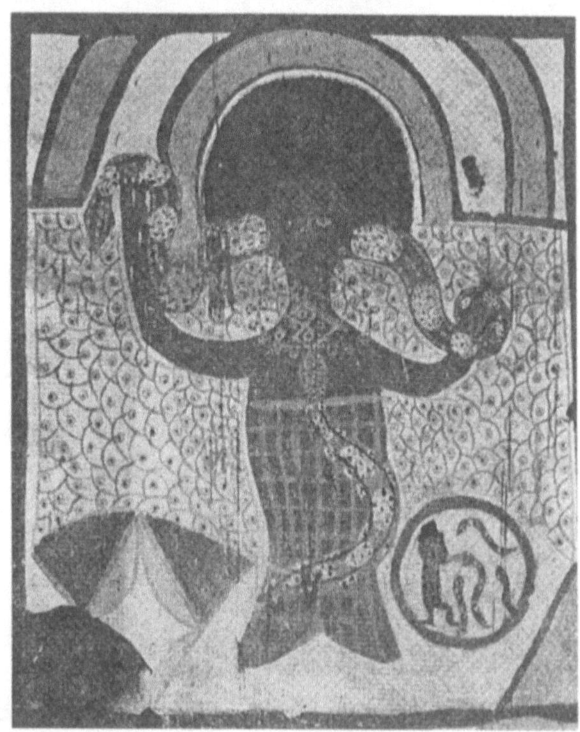

Plate 57. Wall painting of Mamy Wata derived directly from the imported lithograph.

Plate 58. An adaptation of the Crucifixion. Notably, Christ is shown with the navel rupture once common in the Owerri area. The actual cross has been omitted.

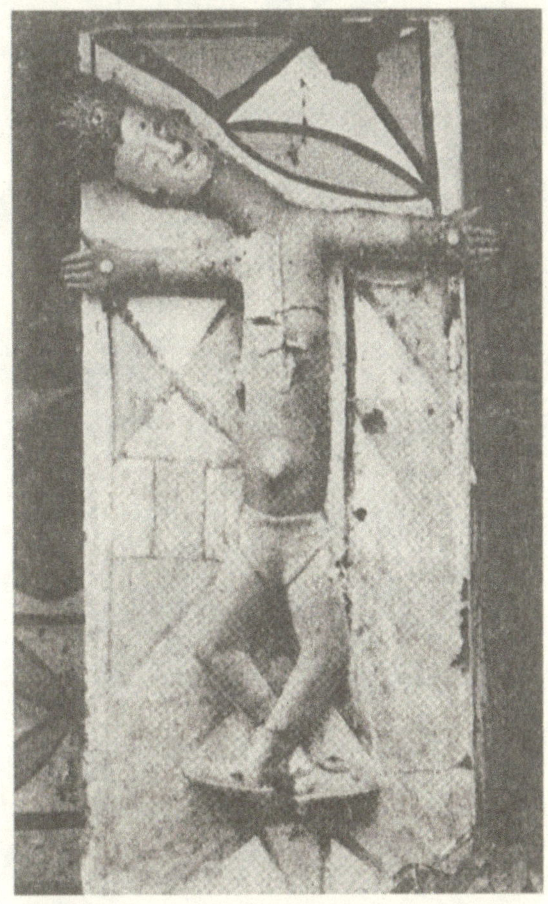

Plate 59. A realistically detailed, but still unpainted, mbari image taken from life in the community.

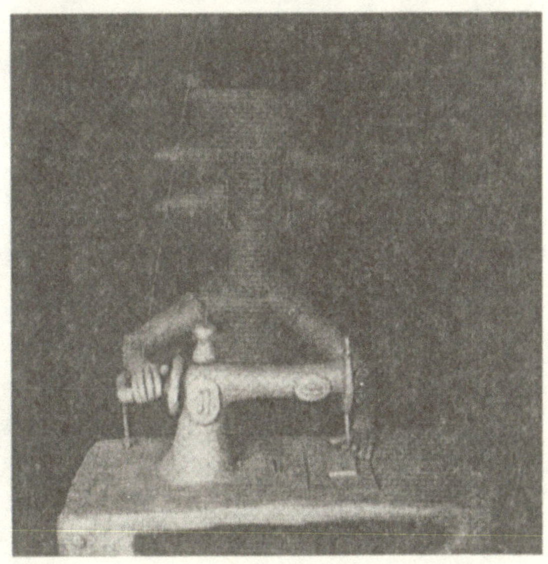

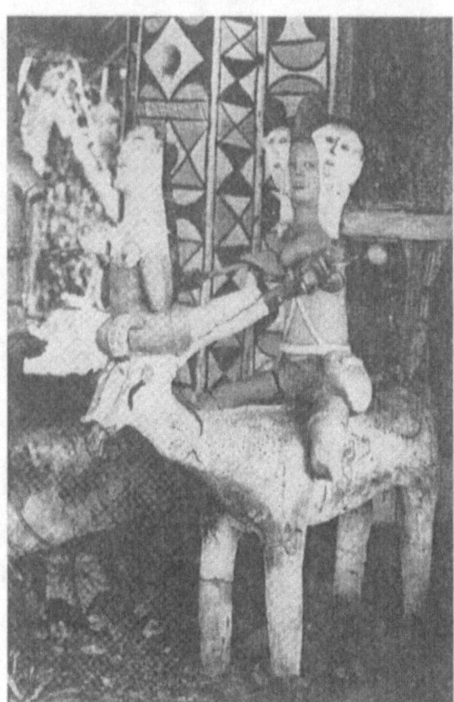

Plate 60. Figures like this seem to be without historical precedent, but after they are made they are often called *mmuo*.

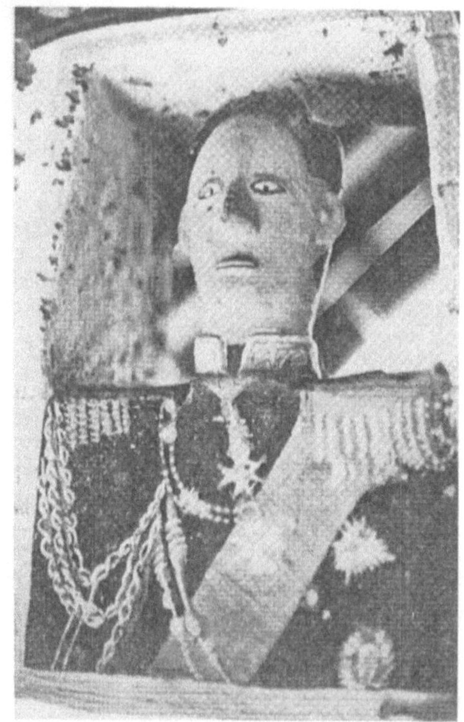

Plate 61. A cleverly rendered general, perhaps inspired by a magazine illustration.

Plate 62. A seated male, the body of a schematized beast, with Nwa Alakandu, the dwarf, sitting beneath.

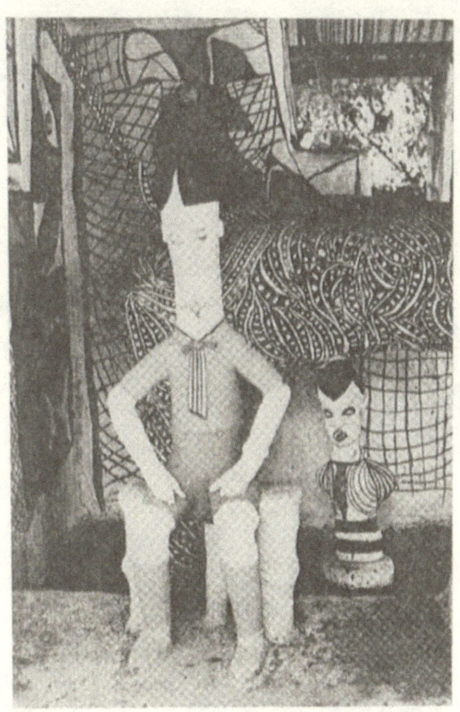

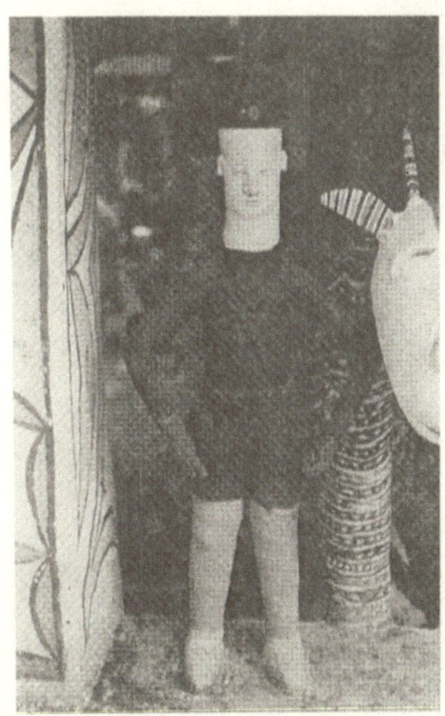

Plate 63. Ezem's soldier, which critics preferred to Akalazu's, plate 64.

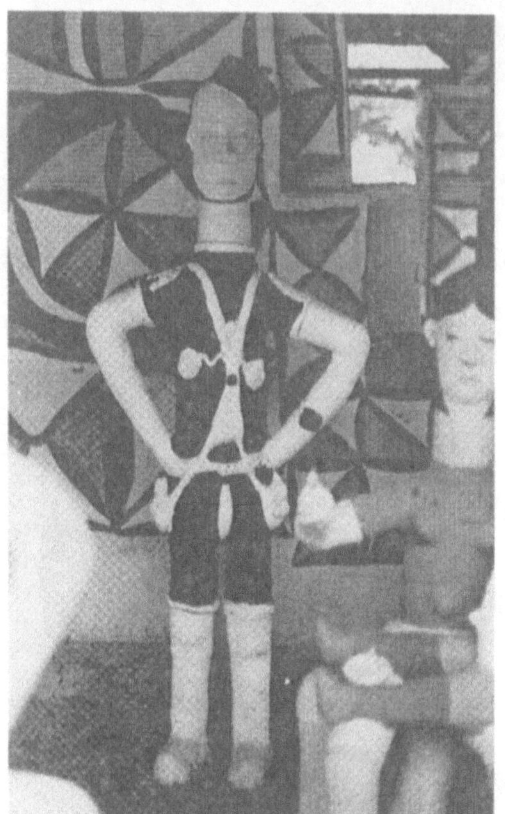

Plate 64. Akalazu's soldier, in the same mbari with Ezem's.

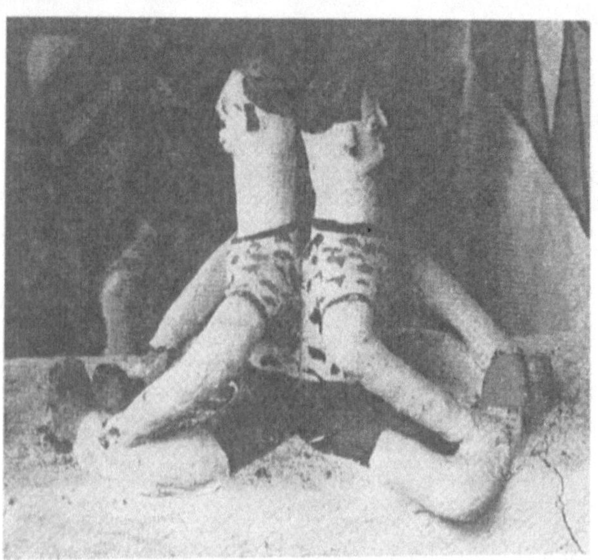

Plate 65. Twins, until recently, were considered an abomination in Igbo country.

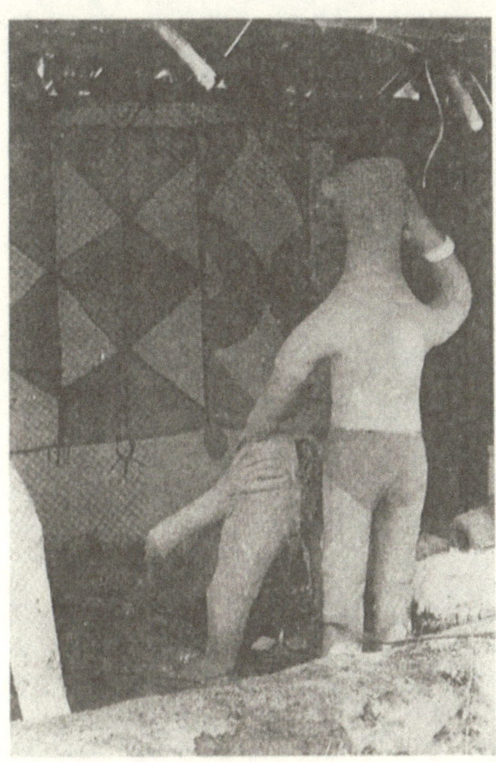

Plate 66. Graphic sexual scenes are found in most mbari of medium or large size.

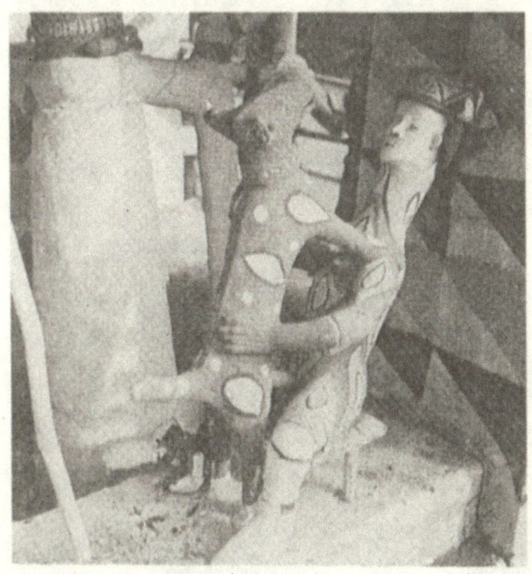

Plate 67. Scenes like this are always favorites of the mbari-viewing public.

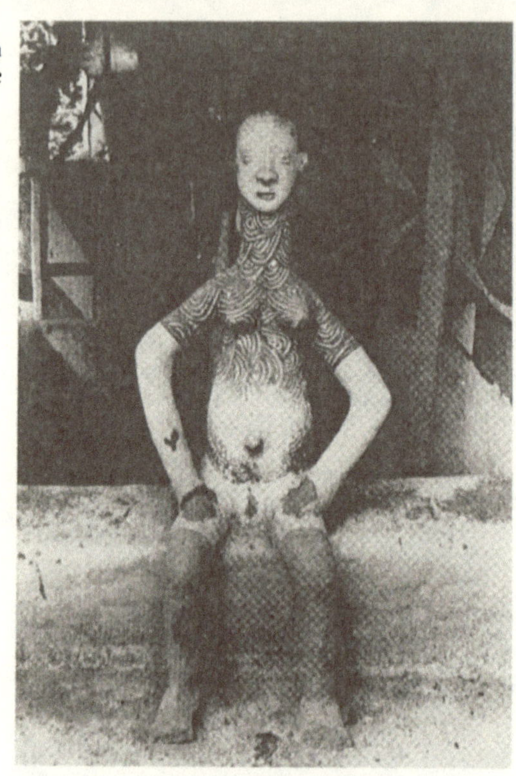

Plate 68. A pregnant woman whose belly is dramatized by the washing-away of surface paint.

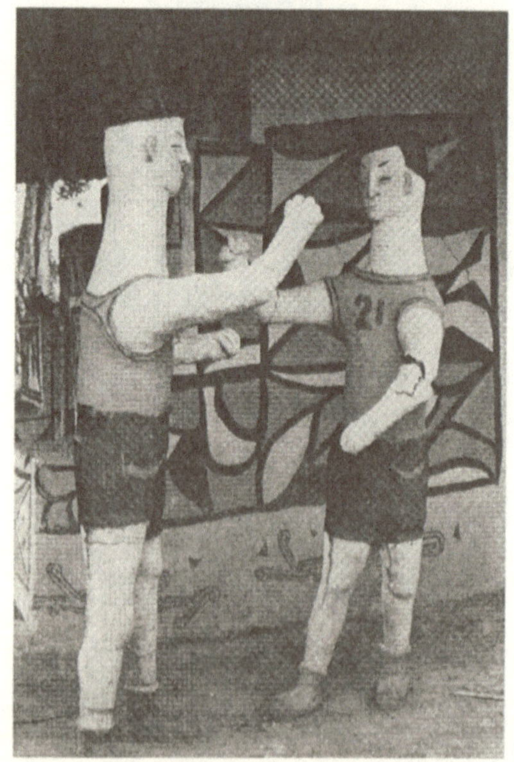

Plate 69. Boxers or other sportsmen are fairly common subjects in large mbari.

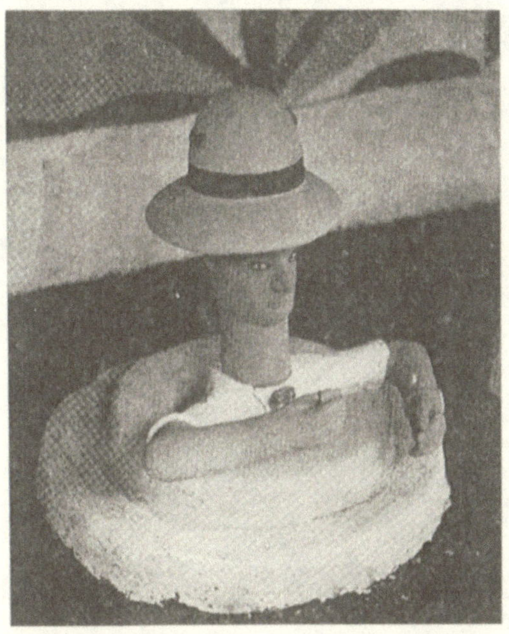

Plate 70. Myths of the origin of the white man have him emerging from a hole in the ground.

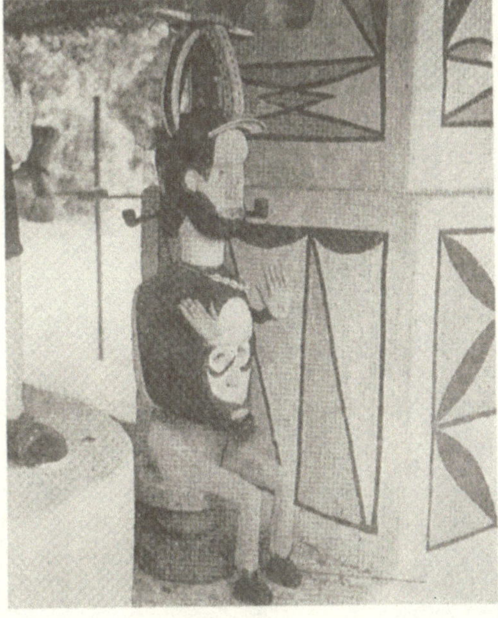

Plate 71. This figure is unusual in having been constructed primarily of wood—for unknown reasons.

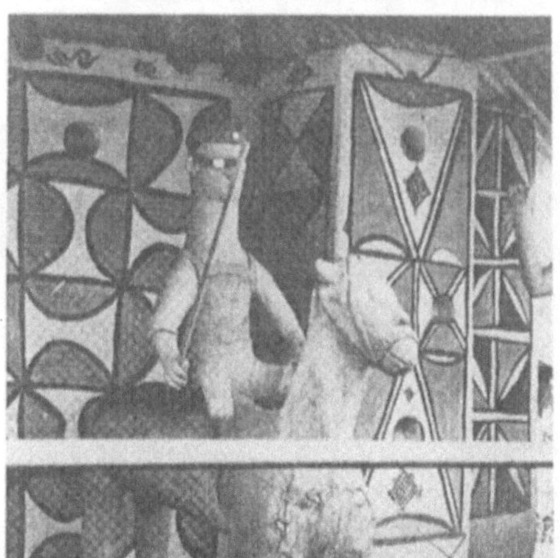

Plate 72. Equestrian scenes are at least as old as 1904, when one was photographed by Whitehouse. This one is quite recent.

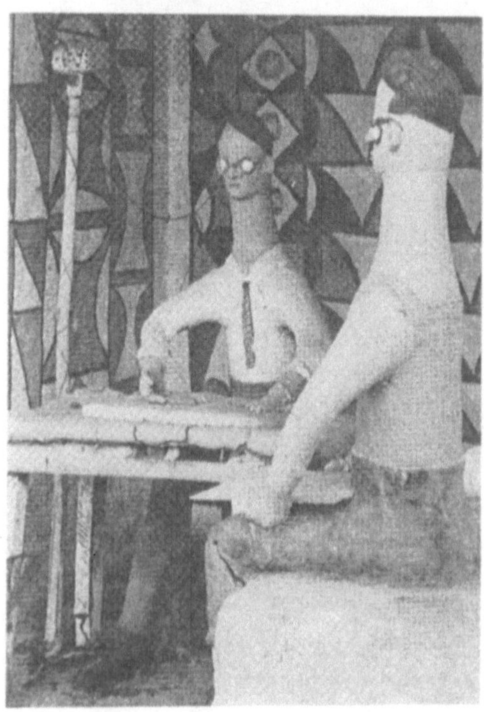

Plate 73. This scene from a radio studio indicates that subjects are taken from outside as well as from within the local community.

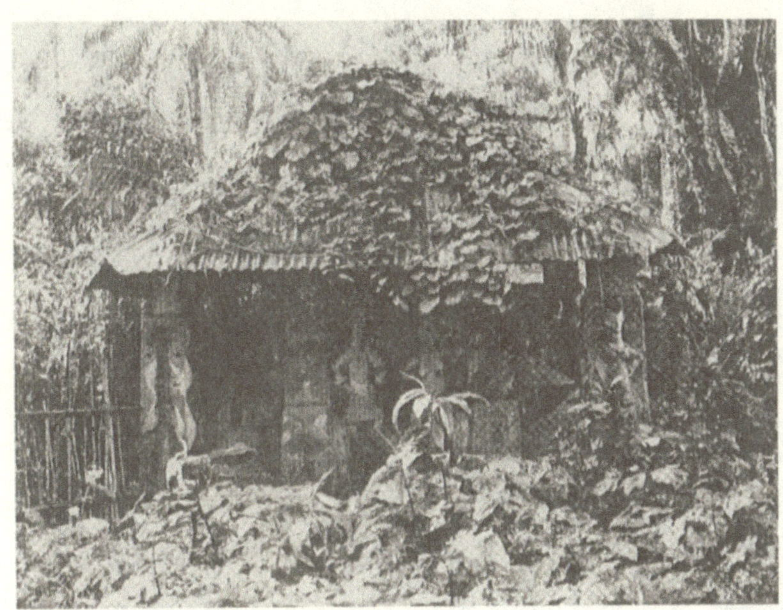

Plate 74. Metal roofs delay the disintegration of an mbari, but nature ultimately wins.

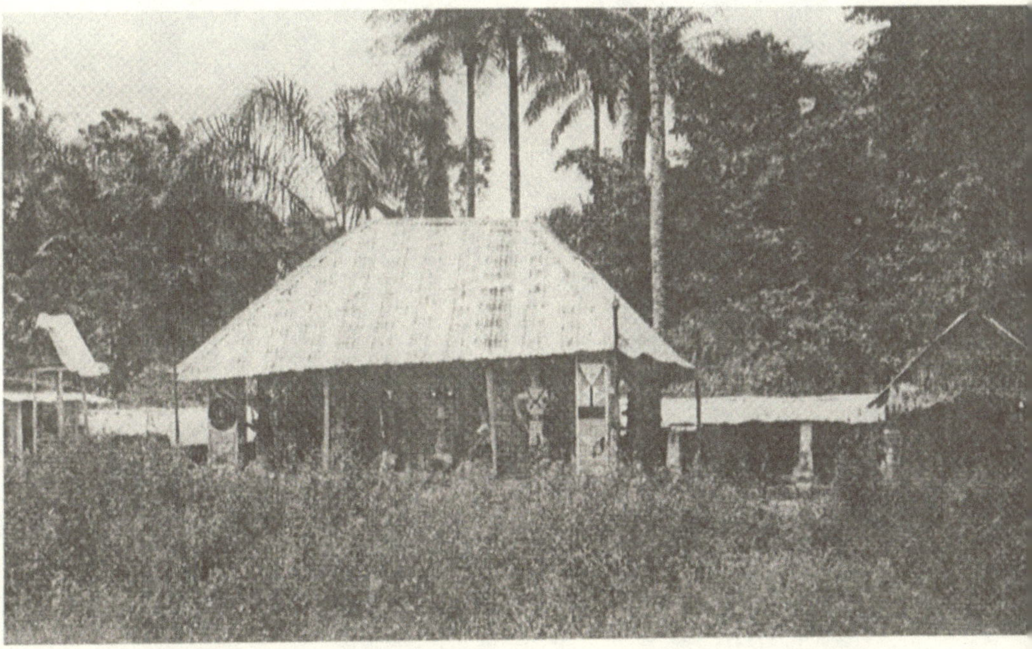

Plate 75. View of the largest complete mbari extant in 1966–67. Note the telephone poles at the corner of the main house and the small airplane under its own tin canopy, to the right.

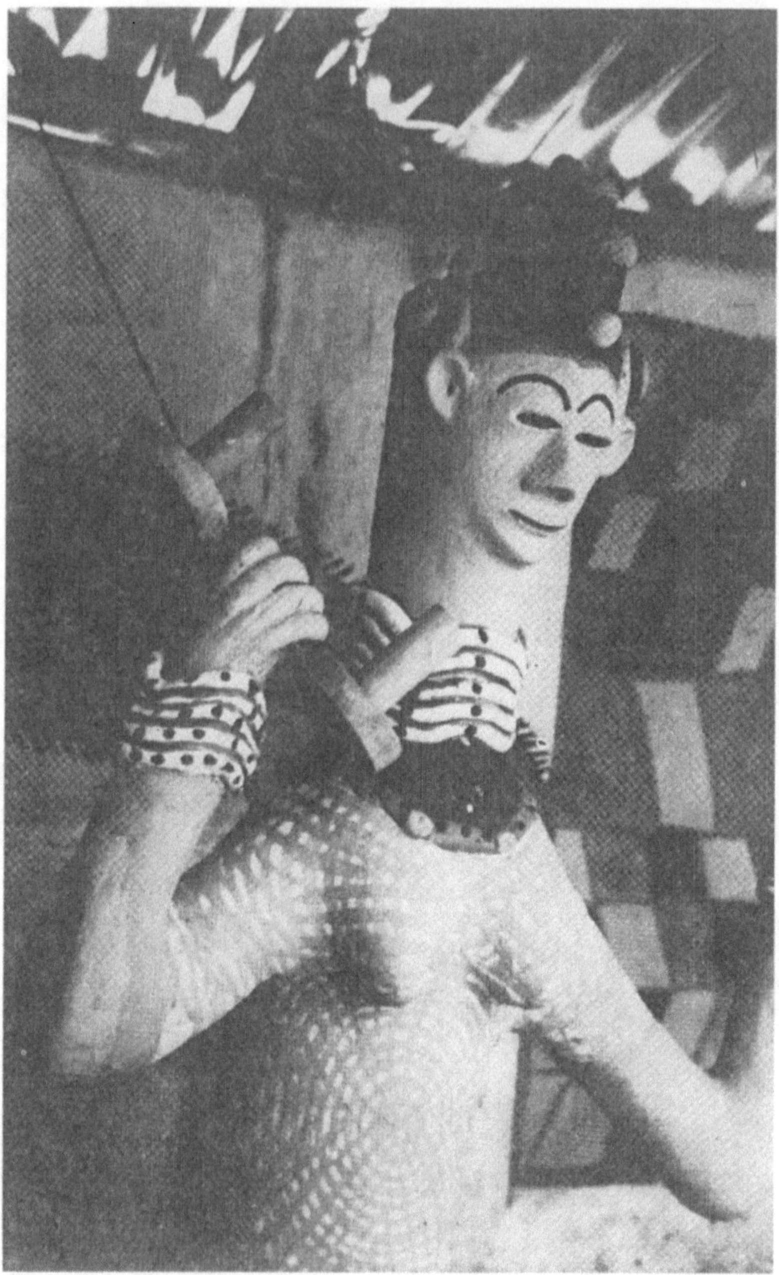

Plate 76. Telephone operator in the gallery of the mbari shown in plate 75. Two telephone terminals are also present, and the telephone wire is string.

2 The Gods and the People

Owerri Igbo ideas about man, spirits, the world, and their interrelationships tend to be neither analyzed nor highly systematized by the people themselves. The following is an outsider's attempt to classify spiritual beings and ideas, an effort to understand how the Owerri man visualizes and acts upon his own fate, the success or failure of his crops, the wealth of his lineage or village, and so forth.

In the Igbo view the Owerri world would appear to have four quite distinct but closely interrelated levels. The first of these is the land of human beings and the physical, observable world of nature—farms, rivers, buildings, and so forth. The second is quite different—the "land of spirits," *ala mmuo,* in which things are intangible and insubstantial. Living men may inhabit this world when asleep or possessed by a spirit, but normally it is the realm of supernatural beings of three major types: the ancestors, *ndichie;* tutelary deities, *agbara,* who are the objects of cults; and other spirits related to the cult system but outside of it, which I shall call *mmuo.* Beyond this second level of reality, the "land of spirits," inhabited principally by ancestors, cult deities, and other spirits, is a third, more abstract level, that of *chi* and *eke,* which may be thought of as the animating forces of each human being and which combine to form his personal "world" or destiny. The fourth level, more impersonal yet, is of *chi* and *eke* combined and unified in a single word/concept, "Chineke," which stands for the creator god, the original *anima mundi.*

In this chapter[1] we will first examine the Owerri concept of the high god, Chineke, and the principles he comprises, and then the three categories of active supernaturals. We will turn then to brief discussions of sacrifice and magic and conclude by discussing the place of religion in an Owerri person's life and why a community undertakes the building of an mbari house.

The High God: Chineke

> Chineke molded the world; then Eke divided the world. Eke came out of the hands of Chi, so they became the same. They are of the same mother. It is like the creation of the world: the world is one. That is the way Eke came out of the hands of Chineke. But they are the same.
>
> If it were only for the hands of Chineke no one would die a violent death. It is Eke who divided the world and after that people died in power. Eke is the tricky one who portioned out these things. Chineke is straight and long, and he made the lives of the people upright and good. Eke played this trick we are now inside.[2]

Chineke (or Chukwu[3]) is the creator, the high god. Though distant and not the object of images or direct sacrifices in Owerri, he is often addressed by name in prayer and does receive offerings indirectly. He knows what people are doing but does not himself intervene or punish. The etymology of his name suggests that he is both a deity and a concept, for "Chineke" is a contraction of *chi, na* ("and"), *eke: chi* apparently meaning "god" or "soul," with *eke* approximating "creation" or "division."[4] *Chi* and *eke* are also personifications, as suggested by the quotations above and the words of another informant: "Chi and Eke represent male and female. Chineke—I don't know if he is a man or a woman.[5] He is up, up, up, and we don't see him." As male and female principles Chi and Eke have a dualistic role in creation, a role that is both complementary and contradictory, a duality that may also be seen as an explanation for the differentiation of the sexes. Chi, as the male idea, being first, was responsible for forming the untarnished world as it existed, apparently, in that split second before Eke, the female, came to divide and therefore spoil it: "Eke played this trick we are now inside." But *chi* and *eke,* as Chineke, are the same, the fecund unity of male and female, harmony and completion. This cosmic dualism reverberates on many levels in Owerri Igbo life, not least in the symbolism of mbari.

The notion that Chineke represents completeness is also supported by the custom of a man's establishing *chi* and *eke* symbols in a small personal shrine after he has fathered male and female children. All Igbo people have a *chi,* a personal spiritual guardian or soul, which they acquire at conception and which helps to determine their destiny (or world), *uwa,* their success or failure in dealing with other people and various supernatural beings.[6] The Igbo people believe in reincarnation, at which time, in Uchendu's view,[7] a man's *chi* bargains with the creator for his role in the next life. This role seems to be a man's personal world or destiny, *uwa.*[8] The person who fails to achieve the goal he has set for himself can take solace in the fact that "no condition is permanent"; he may improve his lot in the world of ancestors or be born again with a more kindly *chi* and more prosperous *uwa.*

While on earth, however, man deals not with the remote creator but with other people, ancestors, nearer gods and spirits (*mmuo*),[9] to whom Chineke entrusted the conduct of the world after creation. These spheres of activity concern people most of the time, for one cannot change his or her *chi,* short of death, and cannot reach the high god directly.

The Ancestors: *Ndichie*

The ancestors are the spirits of certain people who have died. They are thought to live in the land of spirits, *ala mmuo,* and to pursue much the same activities as people on earth. Ancestors are the concern of families and lineages, who erect shrines for them at which are offered, periodically, food, drink, and prayer. Ancestors affect the morality, prosperity, and general well-being of the family or lineage.[10] Each lineage maintains at least one shrine to *ndichie,* a notched timber, stuck vertically into the ground or into a low mud platform, where offerings are made.

On this family level ancestors wield considerable power, protective and beneficent when they are well-treated, angry and unmerciful when wronged or neglected. "Ancestors (*ndichie*) own the land near us. Anything that will destroy the harmony of the compound, *ndichie* will not like. So that [referring to the ancestor symbol] is where we settle disputes."

Family ancestors are the most personal of spiritual beings, but even so they are not often named and their tangible symbols are never anthropomorphized. In speaking of an older man who was present during an interview, one informant said, "The real *ndichie* are our dead fathers, but this man here holds the *ofo ndichie* and we sometimes consider him an ancestor." This statement crystallizes the idea of an unbroken continuity of supernatural beings running from the remote Chineke to living men. Even the unborn are included, for human spirits are waiting in anthills to be reincarnated. Reincarnation renews and maintains family lines, as Shelton has noted,[11] and links the current members of a family to both the past and the future.

The Nearer Gods: *Agbara*

"Chineke created *agbara* and gave them power."

"*Agbara* are very close to us and fast-working."

Of the many deities in the Owerri pantheon, *agbara* are the most commanding, the most insistent, the most feared. But unlike Chineke, these gods are local and neither omnipresent nor omniscient. They correspond to parts of the immediate world of nature, time, and space that affect men and that men wish to affect: land, thunder, rivers, war, and markets or days. They are, however, clearly more than personifications or deifications of these things. Asked if Amadioha as thunder and as *agbara* were the same, for example, a man said:

> What tells us that Amadioha really exists and has power is the thunder. Thunder is the gun of Amadioha (pl. 7), one of his powers, what he shows the world to demonstrate his existence. Amadioha is *agbara*. He is thunder. They are the same and they are different.[12]

Also, although the god Otamiri in the town of Egbu takes his name from the stream he brought to the people and in which he lives with his wife and children, his "work" includes punishing local criminals, giving work, children, or other aid to people who need it, and killing those who catch or eat fish from his stream. His anthropomorphic role as provider, protector, and prosecutor belies his existence as a particular body of water. It is as if a prominent part of the local world is named an *agbara*, while the character of the god combines the general features of all such deities, cast as they are in a human mold (color plates 4 and 9), with more specific responsibilities associated with, or deriving from, an influential part of the world, in this case a river. Each *agbara*, moreover, is a public cult under the leadership of a priest. Cult priesthood may be inherited within a specific lineage, but it is in the nature of many such cults to cut across lineage lines, to integrate varied family groups and therefore to help define villages and their segments.

What are the broad traits ascribed to all *agbara*? They may be either good or bad, beneficent or malevolent. All can settle disputes, be sworn upon, and hurt or kill false swearers or trouble those who neglect them; their behavior is often capricious. Once informed of breaches, they punish common criminals, such as thieves or cheats, and deal with the transgressors of taboos concerning the aspect of the world associated with their "homes." *Agbara* are called fathers or mothers of their people. Each is particularly responsible for the fertility of his or her people and for general nourishment and help. In spite of the potential goodness of all *agbara,* though, people like to stay away from them, for he or she who gets too close to a god will die, viz., "any man who sees an *agbara* is a dead man." *Agbara* are essentially unknown. People who feel they are "near" *agbara* act cautiously, carrying protective charms and medicines (*ogwu*). These tutelary deities, then, fulfill multiple roles, many of which they share with each other, in a jurisdiction that goes beyond lineages to villages and even village groups.

Ala and Amadioha: Earth and Thunder

> The first *agbara* to come out were Ala and Amadioha. . . . Ala is a female, this Earth we walk on, and that is where she gets her power. . . . Everywhere Ala has great strength and is very wicked. Ala kills instantly if someone steals or swears falsely in a dispute. Ala comes instantly. Amadioha is more gentle—he does not kill at once. Ala is evil, she is dark. She kills people, then eats them (when we bury them). But Amadioha is fair and good. His heart is clean. He is peaceful and a merciful man. Ala kills, Bwimm!! and eats, always swallowing people.[13]

Ala (color plates 4 and 7) and Amadioha (color plate 9, pl. 7) are certainly the most eminent and commanding gods in the Owerri pantheon. Together they oversee all essential aspects of village life. The cult of the land, however, is preeminent; in some instances it is the only institution that integrates the component villages in a village group. Like other gods, Ala is provider and protector, the owner and mother of her people. She is a god of peace, but when offended, she reacts violently. Her special province is of course the land, "from which she derives her strength." Apart from controlling its fertility and productivity, as the ultimate source of yams and other crops, she is the judge in disputes over boundaries or land tenure. She decides the time for planting, for harvesting, for moving to a new village site. To defile the land—whether by incest, adultery, stealing, giving birth to abnormal children, fighting, kidnapping, or murder—is to incur her wrath, which means violent punishment if not death. As Meek aptly says, "Ala is the fount of human morality, and is, in consequence, a principal of legal sanction."[14] Many laws are made and sworn to in her name; if they are broken she punishes the transgressors. Few activities escape her control; few people can neglect her. With such responsibilities, it is not surprising that Ala is the most feared and respected of *agbara.*

Nor is it puzzling that beside Ala, Amadioha emerges as a gentleman, a god of cool temperament and peace, despite the fact that he sends lightning and that his priest may sieze property struck by it.[15] Just as Ala is called queen of the earth and underworld, so Amadioha is king of the skies, though a less frequent, less insistent meddler than she in the affairs of men. He has ultimate responsibility for rainfall and sunshine, and is considered by many to be the custodian of the rainbow, itself a portentous celestial symbol.[16] In contrast to "dark Ala," Amadioha is considered fair-skinned (color plate 9), an attribute that puts him in charge of all light-skinned Igbo people. White or other light colors are symbols of the thunder god and are given to his cult as presents and worn by his priests. As a man of highest title Amadioha is the patron not only of males generally but of those of exalted rank in particular. Like Ala, who is often considered his mother or wife, Amadioha is often worshipped and petitioned for his powers in promoting human fertility. Amadioha has many mbari built for him, and he invariably appears in the houses built for other gods.

Other *Agbara*

Despite the preeminence of Ala and Amadioha in Owerri religion, their cults are equalled or occasionally surpassed by those of other deities who may also be known over wide areas for their special powers. Such is the case, for example, with Otamiri in Egbu, with Afo at Umuahiagu and Ekwunoche at Umuekwune. Umuahiagu holds a very large market on Afo day, and both the day and the market are overseen and regulated by the goddess Afo. Ala Umuahiagu seems to have neither the wealth nor the influence of Afo. The same holds true at Umuekwune, served principally by the river goddess Ekwunoche, whose reputation as a "mother of many children" is known for miles around. Her special success with human fertility—the production of large families rather than merely one or two children (pl. 8)—has caused the local eclipse of Ala, who is normally charged with that responsibility. Ekwunoche's powerful reputation brought her great wealth and one of the largest mbąri houses remembered in the entire region. In much of the area Oparogu is the god of war who, though more powerful before the *Pax Britannica*, still commands respect as a general tutelary deity.

Simply to list the many *agbara* of the Owerri area would not serve the present purpose.[17] Suffice it to say that every town[18] and village, besides worshipping Ala and Amadioha, has several other public cults that belong to major lineage divisions within the community and may have mbari erected in their honor. The priesthood is hereditary within a given lineage, although worshippers come from outside as well as inside that unit. Like lineages and communities themselves, however, cults may be unstable. They split, languish, or flourish in seemingly arbitrary ways, though their composition and strength apparently depend largely on the relative ambition and sagacity of the priests.

The Priest: *Onyeisi Agbara*

The wealth of an *agbara,* or its status among other deities, cannot, and perhaps should not, be distinguished from the position of its custodian "husband," the priest (*onyeisi agbara,* literally, "person at the head of a god"). Competition is highly developed in both human and supernatural spheres of the Owerri world, where the emphasis on prestige appears as status-consciousness and jealousy. A deity who fears herself slipping in relative position troubles her priest, asking for more attention, more wealth, more servants, a new house (mbari), all in an effort to regain her proud place in the conference of gods. "So that our *agbara* can hold her head up among the others" is a frequent response to the question of why an mbari house was built. These matters of a god's prestige, revealed in divination, are of course parallel to the preoccupations of men, always anxious to improve their own lot, in earlier times by marrying more wives or taking titles and today by building two-storied concrete houses with corrugated zinc roofs. The prestige of one village or village group, in competition with others, can often be directly measured by the wealth and stature of its principal deities and priests. And mbari houses, which are conspicuous symbols of status, often figure prominently in such competition.

A number of other factors, aside from the wealth of an *agbara* gained through sacrifice, contribute to establishing and maintaining her status and that of her priest. Influential gods get considerable service from the community, for apart from their cult slaves, *osu,* they have five or six freeborn males helping them with cult activities. Moreover, a priest may demand three days of farm work per year from his entire male constituency in the name of his god: a day each for clearing, planting, and harvesting. Despite his expenses in feeding the workers, the priest can complete much of his farm work with this labor, a sure economic gain.

Informants stress "paying" a deity when petitions are answered. "You ask the *agbara* to make your house cool, to make your wife pregnant, and to keep harm away, and if the god does these things, you will pay her. . . . You have to thank her." But people bargain with their gods, procrastinate, and sometimes refuse payment until they are forced into it by injury or catastrophe. Despite the *agbara*'s basic kindness she is often remembered by her power to harm, and her strength is so measured. When offended or provoked, a god "comes to fight," to demand her due. Many occasions for honoring gods are irregular and unpredictable, yet all gods are also propitiated regularly every four days, and during one or more major festivals each year.

Thus a wealthy priest—or *agbara*—is often a substantial force in the socio-political arena. While an individual man can seldom rule in any accepted political sense in this area, strong priests, more than powerful men of other professions without spiritual backing, can frequently swing a meeting to their own advantage, and may become *de facto* leaders of great influence.[19] As leaders of cross-lineage institutions, too, they have opportunities for exercising social control in the many cases—dispute, sickness, law-breaking, and other crises of varied sorts—in which their *agbara* are invoked.

In summing up these major deities as the most notable and conspicuous of Owerri spirit beings, it is well to stress their ascribed human characteristics, "They like to live as people, beside humans, so they can do the work that pleases humans." *Agbara* are in and of this world, though they are said to live also in the underworld, especially in anthills. Like people they are ill-tempered or kindly disposed, ambitious and competitive, jealous and proud. Some few *agbara,* notably Ala and Amadioha, moreover, have great power, for their cults cross lineage and sometimes village lines and thus become forceful integrators of disparate and even competitive community elements. The "family" character of *agbara* is stressed over and over again on several levels in ritual, language, and art. Gods are considered related both to humans and to one another, to have wives or husbands or children among other deities and among living people.[20]

An extension of this "family" character of these tutelary deities may be seen in the three classes of beings considered "children of the gods," *umuagbara.* These are the modeled clay figures in mbari houses, discussed below, the subordinate tree altars within an *agbara*'s ritual area, and the various animals held sacred in Owerri communities. None of these may be considered true gods, but rather they are different manifestations of the work, methods, or jurisdiction of *agbara.* They are the signs that deities exist, that they maintain certain controls over humans and stand ready to help or harm them in a variety of ways.

Small tree shrines, called the children of their deities, are found on the sites where mbari are built, and it is worthwhile to discuss these sacred areas briefly here. A village's ritual area(s) is called "The face of the god," *ihu agbara*[21] (pl. 9, fig. 2). An *ihu agbara,* as opposed to domestic compounds, which are usually enclosed by continuous mud walls, is a relatively open space, distinguished by small, usually undecorated mud buildings and especially by trees planted in patterns, with the most prominent tree or cluster of trees symbolizing the god itself (fig. 2). Other features include small zinc "roofs," iron rods, cloths, numerous pots or bottles sunk in the ground, and ropes of palm leaves strung together, *omu* (pl. 9). The small pieces of roofing tin are erected to accompany a goat sacrifice made by a man when he is building a new house with a prestigious tin or zinc roof. They are symbolic shelters for an *agbara* whose protection and blessing is asked when the sacrifice is made. Libations are made at the pots and bottles, which themselves have been offered in sacrifice. The strings of young palm leaves symbolize the presence and influence of an *agbara.* They mark off boundaries, ritual areas, and individual shrines. The iron rods and cloths will be discussed later.

The lines or clusters of tree shrines contribute strongly to the visually distinctive nature of these sites. Each tree has a specific name and each in fact represents a principle active in everyday life. Appendix A elucidates these shrines in some detail.

Another class of beings called the "children" of *agbara* is the extensive but varying list of animals considered sacred throughout the area. Some animals are forbidden by a god and are taboo rather than sacred, for reasons given in myths, while others are protected as the messengers of the gods, frequently because they live in the "homes" of deities, such as streams and forests. The python (pl. 10), revered throughout much of the mbari region, is in this protected category, as are monkeys in some areas. Though pythons are dangerous, many Owerri Igbos claim safety in their presence. Should one be found in the village, however, it is carefully and quickly removed on sticks to a nearby forest or stream. Still other animals, especially monkeys and leopards (color plate 6, pl. 11) are protected because killing them is considered tantamount to killing an old man, about to die anyway, whose spirit has temporarily entered the animal.

The list of sacred animals includes most large and small animals both harmful and docile found in the area today and many, such as the elephant and leopard, which are either extinct or not very common.[22] The major practical effect of an animal's sacredness is the ban on harming, killing, or eating it, all considered offenses against the god who "owns" it. These restrictions in turn tend to integrate and identify the groups adhering to the taboo.

A few animals are also notable by virtue of their association with prominent deities: he-goats for Ala, white rams for Amadioha, dogs (fig. 3) for Agwushi. As representatives of their gods, these three common animals also constitute rich sacrifices to them, while in turn the animals, as symbols of the power of their gods, may stimulate peculiar reactions, particularly fear, in people who encounter them under unusual circumstances.

Other Spirits

A third category of supernatural beings, distinct from the cults of ancestors and *agbara*, comprises the various free spirits for which, generally, there are neither cults nor priests and which, therefore, lie outside the public cult system.[23] Men are individually concerned with these spirits, as opposed to the cults discussed above, which operate also on a village level. This class of supernatural beings, then, is a means for individuals or social units to adjust their spiritual, social, and economic environment. Thus it includes the god of divination, Agwushi, as well as other oracular deities like Mamy Wata. It also includes Mkpataku and Anyawu, the "coming in of wealth" and "sun," respectively, and Ajiokuji, the yam deity. There are also several malevolent spirits of destruction and disease whose influence men seek to avoid; they cause men to be divisive and disorderly, to suffer misfortune in the marketplace, or even death.

Agwushi, the god of divination, is clearly the most important of these free spirits. After a discussion of divination, other spirits in this group will be discussed in turn.

Divination and Oracles

Agwu or Agwushi,[24] the divination deity, is the foremost messenger of *agbara*. The role of Agwushi's priest, a diviner, *dibia*, is to uncover and illuminate the desires of the gods. "Agwushi will tell you what the gods have done and what they want. Diviners interpret the mind and will of *agbara* through Agwushi."[25] His essential work is thus to elicit the meanings of things and actions that are not otherwise clear, to see the past, the present, and the future.

Agwushi is also the patron of the abnormal or insane, for whom he offers guidance, cures, and protection. This link with insanity may also relate to the state of emotional and psychic frenzy, or possession, entered by many diviners during the divination process. In any case, Agwushi is mysterious and very much feared by ordinary men who nevertheless depend on him to uncover hidden things, to clarify the obscure.

Agwushi's primordial act of discovery or clarification is set forth in mythology:

> Chineke asked, "Which of you knows the days?" Agwushi said he knew. "This is Eke, the next is Orie, then Afo, then Nkwo. These are the four days of the world." Chineke took Agwushi and gave him to all because he had said this. "As you have said this, Agwushi, you should take Ala." Then he took Eke and gave him Agwu and asked them to go to a foreign land to live, saying that they should take this *agbara* (Ala) and go, and that Agwushi should produce for Ala what she will eat. Chineke then called Orie and said "You go to this land and live," and he gave them Agwushi and Ala and Amadioha to live with them. Agwushi was to feed them. . . .
>
> Then Chineke told Agwushi to go to man and leave part of himself with them, and also to leave part of himself with every god—Amadioha, Ala, and all the others. "When you get there, give the people a part of you that will look after them."[26]

This quotation reveals Agwushi's ambivalent position in "gathering things for the gods" as well as looking after man. All diviners as well as cult priests keep wooden figures called Agwushi Ala, Agwushi Amadioha, etc., which seem to represent the part of Agwushi sent along with the gods, the part that shares in the transactions between men and *agbara* (pl. 12). If a god wants to hurt or kill someone, Agwushi must approve, and he will take a portion of any sacrifice offered—though he receives few sacrifices directly, except those of the diviner, who is both priest and devotee of this divination spirit. Agwushi both serves the *agbara* and is served by them. He helps men but also aids in controlling them.

The part of Agwushi given to man would seem to be the Agwushi addressed by the diviner and represented by several small wooden figures in his kit called Agwu—Agwu himself, Ikenga Agwu, Agwu's wife, his son, his dog, and so forth. So Agwu is one and many at the same time, just as he is in many places at once. Diviners say they keep only the "small Agwushi," that the big one is "out on the road." Thus, Agwushi's precise position in relation to other supernaturals might be interpreted as a calculated mystery, for it seems likely that Agwushi, as the main clarifier of the obscure, must himself be a cryptic, ambiguous fellow. He is well known to be tricky.[27]

A deity closely related to Agwushi is Mamy Wata (pls. 10 and 13), whose intrusive, oracular cult is held by diviners and priests.[28] Mamy Wata, a charismatic water and snake goddess, has in recent times come to supplement, and in some cases even eclipse, Agwushi as god of divination and principal local oracle. Like Agwushi, she is associated with insanity, but unlike him she is particularly famous these days as a dispenser of riches. She is known to have been brought by white men, whom people consider to have endless supplies of paper money and coins. This connection with money, as distinct from traditional wealth measured in yams, family, and social position, has undoubtedly helped project Mamy Wata to center stage, where she now performs many tricks of legerdemain under the clever tutelage of adroit diviners.

An analysis of the intrusive Mamy Wata cult shows much about religion and belief in the Owerri area. How the cult became established is unknown, though its major stimulus may have been one or more color lithographs imported from India or Germany. One print, found today as a kind of icon in many parts of Nigeria and beyond (pl. 14), shows the head and upper body of a woman with luxuriant dark hair, on whose upraised arms snakes are entwined. The ready acceptance of the cult and the extent of its local power today suggests that while *believing* may be deep-rooted in the Igbo culture, the *focus of belief* can shift rather quickly. Surely the Mamy Wata cult has had neither the central authority nor the organized proselytizers of the Umunoha and Arochukwu oracles, or of Christianity. Its spread and current importance stem in some measure from the charisma of its captivating "imported" icon, the image of an exotic woman controlling pythons or other snakes, creatures already sacred throughout most of the area.

Mamy Wata is a mysterious and appealing character, appealing perhaps *because* she is mysterious. She is openly linked with money and innovation, both of which play strong roles in contemporary life, and which, more than anything, contribute to the success of the cult. Although much about Mamy Wata is new, she is consulted and manipulated in an age-old manner. Unlike Agwushi, though, she is not represented at the shrines of *agbara* by wood figures, although she is represented in mbari houses whereas Agwushi is not. She has many devotees but still does not replace Agwushi, who would not easily relinquish his role as chief mediator between gods and men.

Unlike the other spirits in this third class of Owerri supernatural beings, the oracular cults of Agwushi and Mamy Wata are held by priests, who, by their initiation and often considerable learning, can communicate directly with their deities on behalf of clients. The traditional Owerri man consults a diviner often, and sometimes the divination ceremony is rather awe-inspiring and cryptic—the diviner may become possessed by his god, in which state his voice and actions are unusual. At the same time he will chant, sing, say prayers, hit gongs, or shake rattles, so that the ritual is often quite an impressive performance. Still, the diviner's role is to reassure his clients and, ultimately, to reorder and rebalance a personality or a community. His paradox is one of clarifying some of life's mysteries in rites which are themselves mysterious.

Most spirits in this third category have few if any redeeming features; they are opposed to orderly conduct or unity in anything. Most of these are unnamed, unlocalized spirits who have neither priests nor shrines. They are seldom offered animal sacrifices, are not sworn upon, and have no mbari erected in their names, although images of them are found in mbari. For purposes of convenience I will call the supernaturals *mmuo. Mmuo* do not help or protect or provide; they are known principally as forces of evil.

Mysterious and devious, *mmuo* are creatures of the black night, thick bush, or unknown lands far from home (color plate 6, pl. 15, fig. 4). Some of them, at least, seem to be spirits of the unhappy dead, spirits of men who were cheated at their final burials and therefore roam dark places to plague the living. These evil-working spirits are also called *ekwensu.* The victims of *mmuo* (or *ekwensu*) are people lacking confidence or those especially foolish in contravening well-known (but often not terribly serious) rules. Others disturbed by these spirits are the conscience-ridden, the insecure, the fearful: "Any place you go and feel very afraid—this is the land of spirits (*ala mmuo*)," an underworld largely defined by its spirit inhabitants. Like them, it is a fearful, not quite human place, one to be avoided at all costs. Like *agbara, mmuo* live in impressive tall constructions built by white ants (termites); anthills are said to have four (or sometimes eight) "eyes" or "doors" through which spirits pass. Mbari images of these evil spirits always violate human anatomy with sometimes bizarre distortions and deformities (pl. 11, fig. 4); images of Mamy Wata are exceptions, and indeed, they are often considered by Igbos to be among the most beautiful of mbari figures. Mamy Wata, like the modeled image of an *agbara,* is rendered in idealized human form.

Mmuo might be considered "junior" deities, for they plague people, and are provoked to anger in much the same way as are *agbara.* On the other hand, the consequences of crossing their paths in the wrong direction are likely to be lighter than in the case of the more powerful gods. These spirits are often considered "messengers" of gods, sent out to do their dirty work or at least to warn. They harass, wound, and maim, but normally do not kill.

One of the few spirits with any real personality is the antic Okpangu (pl. 15, fig. 5), a mythical youth who was partially transformed into an ape by other *mmuo* as punishment for his refusal to work. Okpangu is a favored character in folk stories, all of which have their moral lessons, especially for silly or lazy people. Okpangu is at once foolish and shrewd, humorous and dreadful. His character is a capsule of those qualities associated with all *mmuo:* mysterious and deceitful, unexpected, tricky and rather brutal, but often still comic. People cannot really see, feel, or hear Okpangu, but they know he is there and they must believe in him.

Mkpataku, Ajiokuji, and Anyawu are other spirits that can be either beneficial or harmful to an individual or family, or even an *agbara.* Small shrines to these spirits are therefore found on all levels, from a domestic family compound to the sacred ground of a village group's integrating Ala. Wealth, and the status and prestige it brings, are such preoccupations for Igbo men that nearly everyone designates part of his threshold as *Mkpataku,* "the coming in of wealth," and the "faces of gods" have similar thresholds. Libations or other small offerings to this spirit are meant to insure that wealth will pass over the threshold into this world. Similarly, people honor the yam goddess, Ajiokuji, so as to harvest large and healthy crops. Anyawu, the sun, can contribute to individual or family prosperity by providing either children or wealth. Libations are made at the small Anyawu shrine, a tree planted either in a domestic compound or as part of the landscaping on a sacred site, whenever people need to petition for success or prosperity in an undertaking.

Sacrifice and Medicine

Offerings are brought to appease a god, to remove an offender from the oppressive hot breath of an *agbara,* to lighten the burden of guilt, and, sometimes, to give thanks. A god's strength is said to bring wealth; a successful and powerful god is a wealthy one.

All presents or offerings, regardless of their motivation, are sacrifices,[29] the major source of a deity's wealth. The rich fabric of Owerri religious and ceremonial life stems in large measure from the elaborate weaving of many strands of sacrifice. Individuals, lineages, villages, and village groups all seek to reach, to influence, or at least to respond to their gods by sacrifice. Some offerings are expected and recurrent, while others are irregular and more occasional.[30] Owerri sacrifices include all major types outlined by Hubert and Mauss (1964), and a recent book by Francis A. Arinze (1970), an Igbo, discusses the varied forms of Igbo sacrifice in some detail. They may be small and quickly executed or elaborate and time-consuming; they may be given grudgingly or joyfully; and they may range from a piece of kola nut or a splash of wine, to a cow or a human being.

In most cultures a human being is the largest offering one can make to a god, and this is not less true of Owerri where a human is given as a living sacrifice. Such persons become slaves, *osu,*[31] to the *agbara,* and are never put to death. *Osu* are given to cults by offenders or their families as penance for very grievous offenses or, very occasionally, in thanks. They are dedicated to serve an *agbara* and by extension his priest, a service that binds both the *osu* and his descendants to perpetual cult slavery.[32] An active major god, with *osu* sacrifices from time to time and a steady flow of smaller ones, may have quite a considerable stream of wealth coming in, from which he or she may build up an impressive estate: a yam farm, innumerable chickens and goats, and a hamlet of faithful servants, *osu.*[33]

Men deal with their gods by magic or medicine as well as by sacrifice. *Ogwu,* best translated as "medicine," is the name for magical material, each dose being composed by a medicine man or diviner, *dibia,* from a variety of carefully prepared substances. When an *ogwu* is used with appropriate incantations, it is expected to exert a power or influence on the recipient, whether man or supernatural. If the power of *ogwu* is rather undefined,[34] it is nevertheless meant to be directly activating, needing no intermediary to do its work. Sacrifices and *ogwu* often seem to merge, because both involve ritual formulae—the careful manipulation of prescribed substances, with incantations, to influence supernaturals—but the two are quite distinct. Sacrifice seems to be more powerful but less versatile than *ogwu*, which has combined positive and negative uses, in formal or informal situations, directed at or against men, animals, or various supernaturals. Once it is prepared by a specialist, *ogwu* can be used anywhere, carried, rubbed on something, scattered, taken hunting, or to war. Sacrifices, on the other hand, are carried out under more formal circumstances, usually at prescribed shrines, and as directed by priests. Both medicines and sacrifice are used extensively in mbari building processes.

Summary: Life and Religion

Spiritual symbols and rituals, though perhaps taken for granted by many Owerri people, are pervasive in time and space, in the life of both a single man and an entire community. Notably, each of the four major days of the Igbo week is given over to one of the four most important cults, Orie to the ancestors, Nkwo and Afo respectively to Ala and Amadioha, who together encompass the world, and Eke to the great mediator, Agwushi. Every other deity is worshipped on one of these days as well. Spatial coordinates are also governed by the gods, who oversee the markets near a man's home. These ramifications suggest how well religion is integrated into the practical social and economic life of the community on its various levels.

Ancestors are revered by families and lineages, that is, within a distinctly local and kinship-based social unit. Thus the exalted collective dead of a lineage oversee and enforce kinship rules and morality on that level only. These ancestors watch out for the general well-being of a lineage in return for periodic food and drink, prayers of thanks, and gestures of obeisance. These dead people come back into a family through reincarnation and thereby assure both its historical roots and its continuity.

Agbara cults, on the other hand, apply to corporate social units that transcend, in size and geographic scope, the individual family or lineage. These deities account for the world as men find it, particularly the local environment and its major division. Such gods and their priests have jurisdiction over community lands, streams, markets, and roads. As tutelary gods, they control the physical and moral well-being of village segments, of villages especially, and in the case of the integrating earth cult, Ala, of entire village groups. Deities are thought to reward people who uphold community laws and those of the named entity (land, war, streams, etc.), but to punish or kill those who weaken the community by disrupting the market, polluting the earth, offending the sky god, and so forth. Thus *agbara* control the well-being of the village and village group in return for generous, continuous offerings of food, care, shelter, and propitiatory rites, and extraordinary sacrifices on demand.

Those supernatural beings I have designated as "Other Spirits" (for lack of an Igbo name covering them), constitute a far more heterogeneous group than either ancestors or deities. These spirits, moreover, are not always easily distinguished from *agbara*, and some, in fact, appear to have been elevated to deity status. This category comprises the spiritual beings or, in some cases, the principles (*Mkpataku* = "coming in of wealth"; Ekwensu = evil-working spirit) that help individuals, families, and even gods adjust to the social and economic environment. In an explanatory sense these varied spirits also account for those aspects of human behavior that are above and/or below accepted social and economic norms, as well as a person's upward or downward mobility in the socio-economic sphere. People either very rich or very poor or constantly in debt, excessively bright, shrewd, or stupid—all these are affected by such spirits. If the marketplace itself and the rules governing it are overseen by an *agbara*, then one or several "other spirits" watch over a man's actual transactions and account for his profit or loss. These spirits, along with a man's *chi* (and presumably his *eke*), provide for his particular "world," *uwa*, or destiny. Thus these spirits are not identified so much with kinship or territorial groups as they are with man's activities, his successes, confusions, and catastrophes. And since these are not gods who are fixed or isolated either temporally or geographically, they tend not to be honored regularly, as the ancestors and *agbara* are; instead they are acknowledged when they are needed, more especially when they have caused trouble. They may be petitioned before a journey or a transaction, and thanked if it goes well; or, if things go wrong, they must be placated or persuaded to retreat. Shrines associated with many of these spirits are located on all community levels, from the private domestic compound to the "face of Ala," the precinct of a communal earth cult. Individual people and gods hold" these cults, and in a sense become their "priests." But the cults tend to be private and noncorporate, by and large addressing those aspects of life, nature, or the world that are not governed by lineage ancestors or the public cults of major tutelary deities.

There are varied, complementary concepts of anthropomorphism with regard to these three supernatural categories.[35] Ancestors, who were living humans, are of course conceived of in entirely human terms. Yet they are never represented by human images in the Owerri area. *Agbara,* in contrast, are represented by humanoid, even relatively naturalistic images in mbari houses (color plates 4 and 7) as well as by nonfigural symbols such as trees. These gods are thought of as anthropomorphic only in a limited sense; they may have children and consorts, but often do not have parents. They do not live in real houses (except mbari), but in forests, streams, the sky, or the earth itself. An Igbo might speak of the "will" of an *agbara,* but not of its thought processes; of its need or desire for wealth, but not of its labor to accumulate such wealth; of its "heart" or "mouth," but not of its legs or genitals. The "Other Spirits," as we have seen, tend to take nonhuman or distorted human shape (pls. 11 and 15). The naturalistic rendering of Mamy Wata (pl. 10) may be attributed to both her newness and the fact that realistic visual prototypes exist for artists to draw upon. Diviners hold images considered Agwu and his family, but these are usually very simplified, highly stylized renderings. Most other spirits—generalized *mmuo,* Ekwensu, Okpangu, etc.—are strong departures from human realism and naturalism. This concept of relatively abstract, or at least non-naturalistic, depiction quite closely parallels the very limited list of human traits associated with these supernaturals. Because most of them operate in the "land of the spirits" (*ala mmuo*), it would not be appropriate for them to take human form. Yet as the most heterogeneous of the supernatural categories in terms of concept and purview, it seems appropriate for images of them to vary widely from the nonfigure symbol for Mkpataku to the attractive, long-necked Mamy Wata as she appears in mbari houses.

On the everyday practical level, of course, religion in the Owerri area is quite different from the preceding classification. Although Igbo people *understand* their religion, and in it find the rationale for life itself, they neither analyze nor systematize their beliefs. A person sees gods, cults, prayers, and sacrifices as practical, more or less efficient means of explaining, and then dealing with, the world. Since no alternative system existed until the advent of Christianity in this century, Owerri people played by the spiritual rules passed down to them.

If a person is troubled, he or she consults a diviner. One reacts to a verdict either by doing the required ritual or by putting it off because it involves more than he wants to do, or because something else intervenes. In any case, he believes, and in real crises he musters the resources needed for sacrifice. In neglecting or procrastinating over a stipulated action, he is not really bargaining; rather, he is simply continuing his life as easily and painlessly as possible.

A major catastrophe or a series of crises will, however, plunge a person into a state of overriding anxiety or fear, so that he calls upon all the resources of those known to deal with such things, the diviners and priests. With things going well, people are able to hold the unknown—capricious nature and the various supernatural beings—at some fixed distance away. But this delicate balance is thrown out of equilibrium in times of crisis; either the gods and nature become too close because someone has broken the law, or people have neglected the gods and they take offense. In both cases the gods are "hot" and dangerous.

Similar observations obtain for a family, a larger lineage, and up the hierarchy of segments to include the village group or town. When marking the agricultural or yearly cycles, for example, lineage representatives will convene to carry out prescribed rituals. Because a large group of people is involved, these rites may not be taken for granted, nevertheless, they seem habitual. Nor is the entire catalogue of a town's deities any more relevant on this level than it is for the individual, for most *agbara* are worshipped *within* and not *across* a town's component villages. Only a few strong *agbara* cults, usually including those of Ala and, less often, Amadioha, are addressed by all segments across village boundaries. People naturally turn to these when the equilibrium of the entire community is threatened. Such occasions are of course rare, taking place only "when the land gets hot," after multiple deaths from plague or war or pollution or serious drought or famine. In such major, pervasive crises when nature and the gods have tipped the scales against a community, no ordinary sacrifice can redress the balance, not even a pair of human beings, *osu*. An *agbara* is calling for the greatest offering it can demand: mbari.

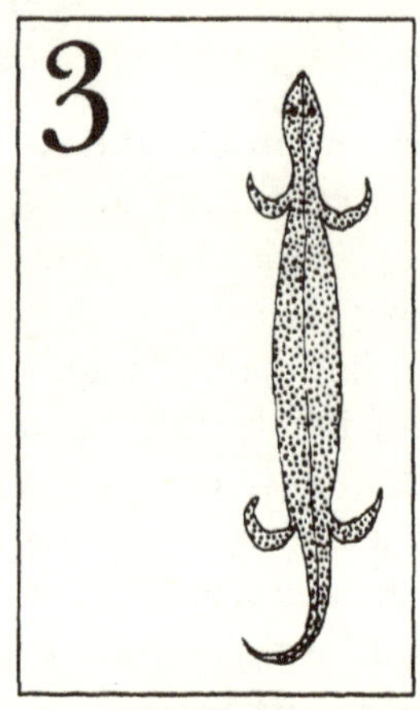

3 The People and Processes of Mbari

"I will tell you about how mbari came to our place. Our Ala is the head Ala of the town, and when she wants an mbari she shows certain signs: things like bees, a leopard, snakes, and other animals. After seeing these things I took money and went to a diviner to inquire what they meant. He told me . . . that Ala did that work . . . that Ala needed an mbari.

"I called [representatives of] the whole town. I gave them drinks and food and money according to our tradition, and they distributed the goat I killed for them. After that I got one iron bar and plunged it into the ground; I knew it was time for the yam festival. So I asked the diviner to call the *agbara*. After invoking Ala he selected some people who first of all worked with iron. We called them *ndishigwi*. They were given cocks and goats before they started their work. After staying a week at my house the *ndishigwi* went around the town. . . . The thirteen villages killed thirteen goats when they reached there. When they returned, they stayed four days in my house. I kept them in, and they were called out only for two shillings each when their husbands or brothers needed them. That money is to say: "May the *agbara* not kill me." When those women went, I took money to buy zinc, and I called the carpenter. Then I went to the artist and said: "This is money for calling you," and I swore that nothing would happen to him, that I would not kill him.

"Then I called the diviner so that I would avoid any troubles and to persuade the *agbara* not to kill anyone, and he invoked the god to show us how she wanted the mbari to be. Then a fence was built. Before the mbari workers entered, we got some medicine to rub on their bodies, and we did the same for the people who brought the mud. After it was finished, we called the owners of the land to see whether it was good or not. . . . Then we invited our friends, our daughters married abroad, our in-laws, to enjoy the mbari festival. When they were called, the fence was removed so that everyone could see mbari. After that I bought a cow to take around the god's market. Then the cow was killed and distributed to the whole town. This is mbari. We are giving the *agbara* a thing of pride."

This is an account of the mbari house built in Umuedi Nnorie in 1965-67 and was given by the officiating priest of Ala. Four or five other informants gave similar reports, varying in details, of mbari erected in their communities since about 1930. No two mbari are alike, either in the forms and subjects of the clay figures or in the ritualized building processes. Accounts of larger mbari houses of the 1930s and 40s mention ceremonies and ritual elaborations no longer observed in the late 1960s. On the other hand, when small mbari were built, even in the 30s, their building processes were neither lengthy nor complex. At some undetermined time in the past, however, a number of symbolic rituals came to be accepted as necessary for large mbari of the type discussed in the synthesis that follows. This hypothetical ritual and technical process is typical for the 1930s and 40s even though each building campaign is in fact unique. Rituals and building steps that I have witnessed will be clearly identified; others were reported from earlier times, and almost always corroborated by different informants. The account is a composite, yet the village, its people, and the mbari process are based in reality.

The Demand for Mbari

We shall assume that a village, the oldest in a hypothetical village group or town, has been in its present location for about a decade. The people moved from their old village site following a catastrophe, such as an unusually high number of infant deaths.[1] Ala's last mbari opened some fifteen years ago in the old village. Things have gone well for the people until recently, when a severe drought has worried many elders and given them bad dreams. The rains have been scanty, forecasting a poor harvest. Some young adults have died without apparent cause; one old man has seen a python in his yam barn. To the *amala* (freeborn Igbo landowners) and their senior spokesmen, *ndioha,* these are signs that a powerful god is restless; more than that they dare not guess. So they decide that the gods must be consulted through Agwushi, their messenger. The matter appears to be serious, for Ala's priest has recently found another supernatural sign, a goat dead for no apparent reason. A delegation of prominent elders and the priest visit one of the town's respected diviners.

The verdict is that the earth goddess of the village, the senior and most powerful Ala in the village group, needs a thing of pride: mbari.

Divination reveals that Ala feels neglected and is thus offended. Shortly thereafter the priest calls a meeting of all the lineage representatives, including the priests of lesser Alas, to inform them and seek their support. They are not enthusiastic about another mbari because they spent so much money only fifteen years before. They realize they must consent, however, to avoid angering Ala, "their owner," to avoid more deaths in the town. Reluctantly they set a date for the building of an mbari, making it three years hence, to give them time to grow yams for the *agbara* and collect money for the building fund. By sacrifice the people seal this early agreement to build mbari. They sprinkle the blood of a he-goat, the first of many for Ala, both at her own tree, central in the *ihu agbara,* and at the shrine tree called "I have agreed," *ekwelem.*

During the next few years, however, rainfall and thus harvests are plentiful, and few mysterious signs or untimely deaths are reported. Ala's priest holds a few "contribution meetings" for the building fund, but the response is poor; with things going well, people have other ways to spend their money. Two or three villages threaten to break away by withholding contributions and by claiming that they intend to build an mbari by and for themselves. The original three-year deadline comes and goes. The people have almost forgotten about mbari, and even the priest has spent the little money he had collected, on himself! Suddenly one of his wives dies in childbirth. Through divination he is reminded that the mbari deadline has passed. In remorse he promises again, realizing that the *agbara* is punishing him for his procrastination. Yet, as one informant relates:

> They still will not build mbari at the time promised. The *agbara* has come with another fight. If the time is exceeded by three or four years, she will come again with a fight, and only then will people really agree. They will not be ready, but they will make motions. Then they will start getting ready. They will plant and collect yams, remembering that "the thing that eats yams" is coming. But the *amala* might still prolong it for another two years. We just do not do these things suddenly. The *amala* will say to the priest: "You have been eating the things brought to the *agbara* without bringing us in. All our shares—have you ever given them to us?" They will do this just before "tying the head" and when the time comes they will still try to think of how the priest has offended them. But eventually they will come to decide firmly. They start tying the head on the iron and then they are united.[2]

Thus a new date is established for the ritual launching of the mbari; this may be several years after the deity first requested a new house.

The Agreement: Eating the Yam of Mbari

Before the day set for sealing the ritual contract to build mbari, a diviner goes through the whole town to identify all the women past child-bearing age. From this group he can then select, through divination, the *ndishigwe,* "leaders of iron" or "people at the head of iron." A day or two after they are chosen[3] comes the ceremony of "tying the head on iron," or "establishing the leader of iron," *ikeishigwe.* This involves the town's most prominent priests and diviners—no less than twenty and as many as fifty men—called by the priest. It focuses on an iron bar, *igwe,* which was given to Ala previously as part of an *osu* sacrifice. After arguing over their fee, the diviners collaborate in tying several sacrificed goats' skulls to the iron and in preparing a complex medicine to be rubbed on the bar and on the strings prepared simultaneously for the chests of the bearers of the iron (pl. 16). The *ogwu* requires the blood of two fowls, whose feathers are tied to the strings.[4]

The importance of rod iron, used variously in mbari, should be noted: it is a symbol of strength, wealth, and supernatural power, having been used as a form of trade currency from the slaving era onwards, and it is encountered frequently in Igbo shrines and rituals.

The men then formalize the commitment to build mbari by sacrificing a goat and two more fowls over the tied iron and on their own *ofo.* The host priest makes a speech establishing stringent laws for the building period: No one will fight or steal, no one will cut another with a knife, no one will poison or murder; all must obey Ala. The goat killed during the rite represents the penalty for any offender in the town. "They ate a goat when the laws were being made, so anyone breaking them will have to pay for the goat. . . ."

The tied iron, *igwe,* is a symbol that mbari is to be built; it is itself considered so powerful that these female "iron leaders," *ndishigwe,* are reluctant to carry it. In the old days the task fell to a female ritual slave (*osu*) who, being owned by and therefore part of the deity, was more immune to its power than the others. Both the bar and the women are thought to be invested with the strength of the god. They begin and end their tour with four days at the priest's compound, where the first of many fowls and goats are killed for them. Then the old women walk through the whole town, to each village, carrying the long iron bar with its strong medicines, announcing mbari and its laws. "You know the *ndishigwe* have run into the hands of *agbara.* If they come to your house and put that iron on the ground, you can never succeed in pleasing them enough." They are thus feasted and entertained lavishly.

In contrast with the serious mission of these old women is the light-hearted celebration, called "eating the yams of mbari" (the "thing that eats yams"), which occurs a day or so after the women leave each village. One informant expressed the relationship between the "tied iron" and the yam festival by saying: "This iron we have tied is the leader of those who are going to eat yams." The festival is often a period of sexual license for all except *ndishigwe,* who were strictly forbidden any sexual contact. Extramarital liaisons are apparently frequent, even between members of the same exogamous group. This behavior is explained, on one level, by the statement that "any yam eaten without great sexual freedom will not be strong enough," as if the success of mbari depends on the intensity of the celebration launching it. All *mgboto,* women married into other towns (or villages, if a village rather than a village group is erecting the house), return home for the feast, bringing much food for their families and for the men who are expected.

The festival seems to proceed as follows: First the *ndishigwe* come to a village and are feasted; a day or so later a large group of *mgboto* convene there to cook for and entertain the many men who arrive a few days afterward; the men and women enjoy their own feast while the *ndishigwe* move on to the next village. After a few days the men and women also converge at the next village.[5] So the festival of "eating yam" continues until all the villages have been visited, each for four days. Then the *ndishigwe* return to the priest's house from which they must be ransomed away by their own families, "to pay for all the food they have eaten."

So ends the first peak on the graph of mbari activity. The people are now wholly committed to the task and work hard to insure its success. The priest has consolidated community sentiment and collected some money for the expenses to come, and has probably been provided with a new wife by his constituency, who also pay off his personal debts.[6] It is important that the priest be a prosperous representative of his god.

Mbari People

Before the actual construction of mbari begins, several individuals and groups are selected and prepared for their jobs. Three essential men are the priest whose *agbara* demands the mbari, one or more diviner(s),[7] and one or more mbari artist(s). In theory the three should be in concert on the overall project, yet because each has his own prerogatives and spheres of influence, conflicts arise. The priest considers himself in charge and is in fact responsible for seeing the program through to completion. His basic work, in addition to the continuing duties of his priesthood outside mbari, is to feed the mbari workers periodically and to carry out the many sacrifices required during construction. But he cannot really do very much independently, as nearly all decisions or undertakings start with divination, which is controlled, of course, by diviners. Yet because a priest may call in other diviners and can release the first from service, he has some control over a diviner's behavior. By the same token, since a diviner's own economic and other less tangible gains are likely to be considerable before the mbari is finished, it is worth his while to avoid offending the priest. The diviner need not always be present, but he must come whenever problems requiring consultation with the *agbara* arise or whenever new medicines are needed. He generally attends and helps with major rituals, and in the old days, he seems to have virtually lived at the mbari site, as the artist(s) did.

Artists

Of the three, the artist(s) or craftsman (pl. *ndioka*, "people of skill"; sing., *onyeoka*) is in many ways the most crucial. No medium-sized or large mbari can be constructed without this man, who is architect, sculptor, painter, building supervisor, and priest. His position and influence are analogous to those of the European medieval master builder, for even though he may delegate much of the work to others, the completed structure bears his unmistakable stamp. Usually he works a great deal himself, especially on figure-modeling and finishing, because he knows his professional skill will improve the mbari; this is a matter of pride and importance to him, for if the standard is not high, he may not be commissioned again. Little mystical aura appears to surround the artist; he is appreciated simply as one who does well the job he knows. Both his attitude toward himself and that of others toward him suggest that "craftsman" may be a more appropriate description of his function than "artist."

The craftsman for a given mbari is selected from a widespread group of known professionals by divination. If particularly skilled, and hence in some demand, he will be offered presents and promises by the priest in order to secure his services. He and his patrons, the priest and *amala*, then establish his fee through bargaining. If the mbari takes more time or ends up larger than anticipated, it is agreed that he will be paid more. The artist and his patrons realize of course that the contractual agreement is only part of the benefit. Artists and diviners are notorious for devising methods of extracting money and goods from the community throughout the construction period. Many of these occasions are ritualized, and in them the diviner and artist share the role of priest. Because such schemes are announced as the will of the deity, they are officially sanctioned and therefore must be accepted by the workers and the cult priest as part of mbari.[8]

Most master builders came to the craft either as local builders, chosen by a god to work for their lineage, or as assistants to professional artists, relatives perhaps, who took them under their wing. In either case, once an artist chooses this profession, he serves a more or less formal apprenticeship of six to ten years. During this time he may work on fifteen to thirty mbari. In some cases apprentices paid their masters to learn the work, in others they did not. In recent years lesser artists have accepted commissions after working on only one or two mbari, perhaps as hired helpers and in one case as a priest, but they are exceptions; their mbari houses are usually small and artistically mediocre.

Although it is difficult, if not impossible, to establish the number of active artists in any given historical period, some figures will help. In 1966-67, I identified twelve living men who were or had been professionals, of whom seven were still active. The work of another eight to twelve individuals (dead in 1966) can be discerned from my photographs and those of G. I. Jones, and in some cases their names can be correlated with their sculpture.

Clearly, not every village group had an artist, and it was not uncommon for a man to accept a commission twenty or twenty-five miles from his own home. I was told on several occasions that "artists come from Ulakwo (Obube) or Egbu," but this does not accord with the facts in 1966-67, for none of the twelve living artists hailed from those places. Such statements probably reaffirm these village groups as early mbari regions or originators. The residence distribution pattern of the twenty to twenty-four artists does not in fact appear to be significant, although some clustering can be noted. That two or three artists live quite close together can be attributed to master-apprentice relationships—a master has more opportunity for attracting helpers and apprentices from among his own people. I am not aware of any father and son artists.

Young artists do not break away from their teachers at any fixed time, rather, when the master feels the time is right; usually this occurs when the older man passes along a commission he is too busy to accept. Even then the separation is not final; the older man traditionally recalls the younger to help on unusually large commissions. Although an artist emulates his master's work, the thought does not occur to him to compete with his elder, for, as one artist said, "A servant's work cannot exceed his master's." Yet competition among artists of the same generation is fierce: no man admits to a superior; few acknowledge equals: "the thing that spurs me on is my willingness to make my own work more beautiful than that of any other artist."

All mbari artists are proud, and many are gifted, yet most of the eight men interviewed placed financial gain higher on their scales of motivation than the "urge to create." Ironically, some cited to me their lack of western education, and hence their "inability to do anything else," as the reason they entered this profession. They seem just slightly more prosperous than the average farmer; none I met appeared to be genuinely wealthy. They combine their mbari work with other jobs, such as farming and wine tapping, done during that part of the dry season when mbari work may be suspended because the ground is too hard. In any case, artists seem to enjoy their work and bring to it great imagination, patience, and perseverance.[9]

Although the patrons (*amala*) do not model or paint an mbari, they certainly contribute to its progress and success. Asked how important the *amala* were in the building process, one informant turned the question back on me, "Will an *agbara* build himself an mbari?"—indicating that as owners of the land, senior *amala* are the only real patrons. They must agree to build an mbari and share the economic burdens on a half-and-half basis with the priest. *Amala* (or in the old days their slaves) also build the high fence within which the mbari is constructed and make the large building that houses the mbari workers. Selected *amala* must also approve the completed house before it can be unveiled, and naturally they are on hand to take part in the festivities and rituals of the opening. Some are also chosen by the *agbara* to do her work.

The Workers

Ndimgbe, "people of *mgbe,*"[10] (sing. *onyemgbe*) are those plucked out of society and isolated for service to their god. They are in many ways the most fascinating people involved in mbari, for they do much of its work, carry out many of its ceremonies, and are central to its symbolism. The prevailing method of *ndimgbe* selection, in spite of temporal and regional variations,[11] is clear. The *agbara* chooses them one evening through divination at the *ihu agbara.* Immediately after they are named, probably not individually but by family or lineage, the diviner and priest proceed through the town making a chalk mark on each compound from which a worker is required. It is quite probable that in the old days all major lineages were required to send at least one mbari worker. Then the compound leader chooses the person to represent his household or lineage, again by divination. A son and daughter of the priest are chosen first and automatically become leaders of the group. For the others there are apparently no selection criteria, so they vary widely in age, occupation, temperament, and sex. Since compliance and unanimity are essential, strong sanctions were undoubtedly available in former times to those in charge.[12] In recent years, however, a person chosen for mbari has been allowed to find a substitute or buy his "freedom" at a substantial price.

By the 1950s and 60s the population available for mbari work had shrunk; Christians or those working away from home were not chosen, and even some believers found ways to avoid service. But out of fear most of those named will enter mbari. In the old days the same fear gripped the entire community, and while people may have been reluctant then, they nevertheless went readily without questioning the diviner. There was first the belief that he who refuses must face the *agbara*—and death. Beyond such a negative reason was a more affirmative promise of life; the presumed benefits to participants were long-range: more children, the general health of both one's immediate family and the whole lineage, larger harvests. A former *ndimgbe* would tell the people selected that the work is easy, a vacation from normal cares, but this contradicts the more frequent comments that the life of *ndimgbe* is hardship, suffering, and loss. Both these statements are true. Actual mbari work is certainly less taxing physically than farming, and workers always eat and drink well inside the mbari fence. Yet they suffer indignities and harassment and are constantly fearful of the deities' proximity and power. They must endure being away from home and family for a year or two, having to trust their relatives to tend farms and cut palm fruit, having to pay relatives or others to mend their roofs and plant their yams. Then, too, the family or lineage has to support the absent worker, sending him food, cloth, and money while helping to care for his or her spouse and children. "Being an mbari worker spoils the wealth of the family and wastes time. If you think of what you could have produced while there, you will not want to do it." This attitude is more typical of the 1960s than of the 1930s, when there were fewer alternatives.[13]

Shortly after selection a potential *onyemgbe* undergoes a rite called "locking the armpit" while he or she is still at home; a protective and strengthening charm (*ogwu*) is tied to his body, and a fowl is sacrificed. The next stage may be as much as several months later. On a prescribed evening[14] diviners go out to the compounds of all selected workers, pack their baskets, then escort them with three relatives as attendants to the meetinghouse, *obiama,* of the priest. This is called "bringing in *ndimgbe,*" and is done individually for each member of the group, no matter how many there are. The basket contains a few things necessary for mbari rites and its sequestered life.[15] From that day as much as two years may pass before the worker will sleep again at his own compound. All that night the *ndimgbe,* each guarded by his or her three attendants, keep a vigil: "The three people who own them will sing until morning. Then they will chew pepper and put it in the eyes of the workers so they cannot go to sleep," for the next day an important initiation ceremony is to be held.

Walking the Iron

"Walking the iron," *izo igwe,* is the crucial ceremony held the morning after the vigil. Mbari workers prepare themselves for this by beautifying their bodies with camwood and rubbing their legs with a freshly concocted medicine to "cool and strengthen them" for the arduous task ahead. Then long narrow iron bars are laid down end to end, stretching, if there are enough of them, from the priest's meeting house to the mbari fence (fig. 6). Beginning with the leaders,[16] the son and daughter of the priest, each worker in turn must "walk the iron"

> which is . . . a difficult thing. Pieces of iron are put on antelope skins. One after another each *onyemgbe* has to walk on the iron—on tiptoes—from beginning to end. Three helpers are there to make sure his feet do not touch the ground. All successful walkers will be cheered but anyone who fails cannot be *onyemgbe.*[17]

The irons are placed in a path that passes through a part of the *ihu agbara* called the "coming in of wealth," *mkpataku.* When the walkers reach this point, near the most sacred part of the shrine, onlookers yell to them, "Go and come back safely" ("*ejialo*"). The last to walk the iron is an *osu,* or if the *agbara* has none, the priest's son. This last position is dreaded because it is considered closest to the *agbara*'s strong and potentially evil influence. At the end of his walk, each person turns around to enter the enclosure backwards, as if to signal the symbolic importance of the event. Artists and diviners, rather than "walking the iron" themselves, supervise and direct the activity, but they, too, are protected with medicines.

Once inside the fence, *ndimgbe* cannot act normally until after the mbari opens. No one sees them for three eight-day weeks; they are secluded in the priest's compound, where they will live for the duration.[18] Once "inside," moreover, they undergo other rites before real work begins. They receive more charms as well as the mbari "uniform" and they are cut twice with knives. The first time a broad "X" is lightly scratched across their chests, and *ohihe,* or bandolier-like strings with *ogwu* rubbed on them, are then tied on over this in the same "X" pattern. Next they are laid on banana leaves and touched or lightly cut with a knife red hot from the fire. On the same fire boils a medicine which they drink "to make the body strong." They are supposed to wear the uniform of *ohihe* throughout the building period, on bodies dyed red or orange with camwood or, for very special occasions, painted with elaborate patterns (*edeala*). As one former worker observed, they "looked like carved and painted figures." No sewn garments are allowed; men wear loincloths and women wear special raffia skirts, with beads at their waists, a uniform reproduced in some mbari (pl. 17).

On the day they "walk the iron," the *ndimgbe* move to their special living quarters, *eke nwaori,* either through a narrow communicating fence built expressly for them from the mbari enclosure, or in open procession accompanied by a special gong (*ogene* or *igbugbo*), rung to warn people away from the area. *Eke nwaori,* not far from the mbari site (fig. 6), was apparently a single, large, long room in which all *ndimgbe* sleep, men and women on opposite sides. Both sexes also used the same bathing area[19] and toilet. Such communal living arrangements are highly unusual in a society where the sexes are separated.

After the *ndimgbe* have entered the *eke nwaori,* the diviner may prepare still another medicine for them, called "tying the head," *ike ishi.* This *ogwu,* made with the head of a sacrificed chicken, means "may neither this *agbara* nor anything else harm us or kill us until we are out of this place." Since the head represents life, the rite symbolically secures each *onyemgbe* for the *agbara* for the duration of mbari building.

During the three weeks of seclusion *ndimgbe* are expected to rest, eat well, decorate their bodies with camwood, and learn songs and dances. They do not work; it is as if they had entered a "fattening house" in which nubile girls are prepared for marriage. Within the first few days they all select new names, another clear signal that they have changed status and are no longer part of the real world outside. The priest's son and daughter, as the two leaders, are always called "goat killer" and "meat eater" respectively, though other *ndimgbe* can choose any name that appeals to them, or be given one by a fellow worker, out of the common pool of mbari names from the past, such as "camwood rubber," "child atop drum," "knife sharpener," "plate," and so forth. (See list of names and their meanings in Appendix B.)

At about the same time the men and women pair off as mbari husbands and wives, in relationships that are usually platonic but in some mbari apparently sexual. In most towns for *ndimgbe* to have sex even with members of other exogamous groups was a serious offense against the god, who killed both offenders. The great majority of informants said that sex was entirely illegal, although some admitted that it was inevitable; nevertheless people chose what could be called "joking spouses," *dinwanna* (literally, "husband who is a brother").[20] In a few towns, however, sex between *ndimgbe* seems to have been common.[21] Where sexual relations were allowed, even if illegal, the partners were strictly enjoined from working on the mbari the next day because intercourse defiled them and would in turn pollute the mbari materials and jeopardize the entire project.

Before *ndimgbe* emerge from their seclusion in *eke nwaori*, they acquire their iron staffs, *ofo igwe* for men, and *agalegbe* for women. *Ofo igwe* is a six-to-eight-inch piece of iron that, like all the iron used on mbari, has symbolic properties and has been previously sacrificed to the *agbara*. It is shaped at one end with molded mud enclosing *ogwu*, and it somewhat resembles the ancestral *ofo*.[22] Yet these *ofo igwe* were given even to the youngest male *ndimgbe*, some of them boys of twelve or fourteen who under normal circumstances would rarely if ever hold an *ofo*. *Agalegbe*, a thin iron staff with decorated top (pl. 17), which looks like the ramrod of a Dane gun, from which it takes its name, is a similarly powerful instrument. Each worker theoretically kept his symbol with him at all times, for it simultaneously protected him and served to identify him closely with the god.

The next ceremony, marking the end of the twenty-four-day seclusion period, is "end," *mmaru,* when *ndimgbe* are said to be "killed out" of *eke nwaori.*

> They came out in full regalia with *ohihe,* and the women with elaborate hairdresses. A crowd will come to see them, and the diviner will cut some *ogwu* into their bodies and chant some prayers. Everyone eats well and we know that the *ndimgbe* have come out. Anyone who sees them from now on is not bound by the law.

The "law" referred to here is that any "civilian" who sees a spirit-worker, *onyemgbe,* will be fined a goat. This ban is now lifted, except for certain sanctified working periods announced by loud gongs. Shortly after the *ndimgbe* are "killed out," they are ceremonially fed by the diviner. After that comes another rite called "greeting the mbari workers," *ekele ndimgbe.* In some areas they are saluted first by the town's oldest man, who brings them a goat. In all towns, their relatives and other townspeople greet them with small gifts of food, kola nuts, or money. Then, as in most other ceremonies, the *ndimgbe* enjoy a considerable banquet, with only the finest foods served. Notably, *ndimgbe* are not allowed to eat cassava, the starchy staple, but are served only yam with the richest of soups made with meat or fish.[23] Later on in the day of the "greeting," the *ndimgbe* are allowed to go to their family homes for a few hours before returning to *eke nwaori* for the night. They are again feted by their families, who treat them with extreme deference, as if they were dignitaries. From this time onward they can return home occasionally, but must always spend the night in *eke nwaori.*[24]

"Walking the iron" and subsequent ceremonies clearly involve the symbolic death and rebirth of the workers; this and other symbolism will be interpreted in detail in chapter 6.

Tying and Building the House

Before turning to actual construction, we must go back briefly to the preparations made by the *amala* weeks before the workers walked the iron and entered their special compound. First the *amala* select, by divination, a piece of land large enough for the mbari enclosure, usually on the margin of the existing sacred site. They clear the area of debris for the stout fence, seven or eight feet high, that will hide mbari activity from strangers and villagers alike. After they erect the framework for the fence and lash thick mats of palm leaves to it,[25] they make a doorway in one corner, with a small vestibule on the outside of the fence (fig. 6). At the same time they proceed with *eke nwaori,* which they build in a style similar to that of ordinary houses although many times larger to accommodate all the workers under a single roof. All these preparations, made openly by the *amala,* provide secrecy for both the workers and the mbari during the construction period.

Once mbari workers have emerged from their twenty-four-day seclusion in *eke nwaori,* three or more ceremonies precede the erection of the first mbari supports: "clearing the site," "blessing the artist," and "covering the ground." The first of these, clearing the stumps and debris, *ikwa achichi,* has the same name as the rite performed annually at the beginning of the farming cycle after the land has been burned. Here it is intended to smooth the site, now partially overgrown since the first clearing, in ritual and actual preparation for the new building. Later in the day the artist is formally honored for the first time by the priest and *amala,* who give him a cock and a hen and promise to insure his well-being for as long as he works. Then, before the first posts are erected, he and the priest sanctify the ground. A cock and a goat are killed, and their blood is sprinkled over much of the enclosed area. The ceremony, called "covering the ground," *ikpushi ala,* is performed "so there will be peace." Then the first vertical supports can be sunk at the spots marked by the artist, and the first lintels lashed to them. This activity, marked with still another sacrifice, is called "tying the house" since, in the days before carpenters and nails, the entire framework was lashed together with strong liana or raffia ropes. The whole understructure is built in the ensuing days, and is then roofed over with hundreds of palm-leaf mats either woven by *ndimgbe* and their helpers, "the four-day-workers," or provided by various lineages. Since about 1950, a carpenter has usually been hired to erect the wooden framework and the roof. Even before that, beginning about 1935, mbari were sometimes roofed over with imported tin sheeting.

Building an mbari would be quite impossible without a group of laborers called "four-day-workers," *ndionuabaliano.* They are men (never women) selected by divination from the same units, either compounds or larger *umunna,* as the *ndimgbe.* Although they did not undergo the same elaborate preparation and initiation and are ritually less important than *ndimgbe,* they are indispensable to the actual work. Some, and perhaps in the old days occasionally all, of these workers are cult slaves, *osu.* They have an anomalous place in the hierarchy of mbari personnel. They are called four-day-workers because they come to the mbari only once every four days, when they do many of the heavy and unpleasant jobs. They help to cut timbers for the basic wooden framework, to erect this structure, and to make mats for the roof. Then, after they have been prepared with a protective medicine (*ogwu*) and the ground has been "softened" with the blood of a sacrificed goat, they begin to dig the laterite mud used for the mbari walls and columns. Each man has his separate mud pit, with a competition determining the best laborer. The *ndimgbe* are strictly forbidden to enter these pits; should one fall in by mistake, he must pay for the offense with a goat. The relationship between four-day-workers and *ndimgbe* is a curious one, for while the latter consider themselves far superior, they nevertheless defer to the four-day-workers a good deal of the time at the site. For if the four-day-workers should take offense and walk off their jobs as mud diggers, mbari would have to stop:

> *Ndimgbe* have to beg these people, and they act as if they are greater than *ndimgbe*, yet *ndimgbe* are the beautiful ones chosen by the god, and they don't have to soil their bodies. . . . The four-day-workers do the tough jobs for the *agbara*, in fact they are the ones who suffer. *Ndimgbe* come to kill wealth [eat sacrificial animals], while four-day-workers come to work.[26]

The clay these laborers dig up and then "puddle" into balls of workable consistency is then carried the few feet to the mbari itself by the *ndimgbe*, who are not forbidden to handle the mud after it has been worked. The master builder has by then measured the ground and planned the walls and columns. He supervises while the heavy work is carried out by his apprentices, mbari workers and laborers. Progress on this part of the building is often slow and apparently uninspired, requiring perhaps several months. The work is heavy and hard, for more mud is used in a single large mbari than would be needed for ten, even twenty, ordinary dwellings. In the first place an mbari may cover as much as ten times the ground plan area of a regular house, and furthermore, the higher walls are enormously heavy, in some cases four to five feet thick. Each corner post alone may be enveloped in eight or ten cubic yards of mud. Gradually, however, workers cover most of the timber framework. If the mbari is to have a gallery or cloister around it, the workers will also build its walls and columns will be built and a roof affixed. Toward the end of the building activity the buttress walls of the main house are cut precisely into their characteristic stepped profiles. Then the entire red-brown house is polished with a slip of finer clay unti it is smooth and glistening (pl. 18).

During this whole period there has been no mention whatever of mbari, either inside or outside of the fence. The building is considered just "an ordinary house with an ordinary roof. . . . From the time a deity says she wants an mbari until they come out of the *eke nwaori,* we never refer to this as mbari. Rather, we say '*ndimgbe* are doing their ceremonial things.' " Asked if this was regarded as preparation for mbari one informant said: "No. We say 'They have gone to *mgbe.*' "[27] There is a clear difference in people's minds between erecting the basic mbari building and the work that follows, despite the thin veil of secrecy that surrounds the entire project.

Mbari Arrives

> First the talk is: "We are going to work, we are going to work. We have prepared the mud and are beginning the walls. When we finish the walls then we cut them. . . . " People say: "*ndimgbe* and *mgboto* are buying plates (*efere*)." The next thing is to push in mbari. From that day on which the plates and saucers are gathered the whole thing takes on a new name: mbari, mbari, mbari, mbari. On the day these plates are brought and inserted *mgbe* adopts a new name.[28]

Now an abrupt change of tone, a heightened drama, enters the proceedings. No longer are the *ndimgbe* building an "ordinary mud house"—they are "dancing mbari." From a laborious task, this effort is transformed into a joyful dance. Why? Apparently because of ordinary European soup and dinner plates or saucers. Also called "mbari," these plates are collected in great numbers; for larger mbari as many as five hundred may be brought to the site by representatives of all compounds, by native women married into other towns, and by the *ndimgbe* themselves. The day of their insertion into the mud walls is one of great ceremonial activity at the mbari site; indeed, it is a festival itself.

> When the plates are put in, they kill a goat and sprinkle its blood on plates. . . . The priest's wife assigns a number of bowls of the best kind of food to the leader of each lineage, and these old men have food prepared and bring it, too. . . . Much food is cooked that day and much wine is drunk.[29]

It may take two or three months to lodge all the plates in the walls and columns of a large mbari. For each plate a hole the width of the plate and four to five inches deep must be dug in the now solid wall; then the plate is inserted and wet clay is repacked around and over it so that only the center shows—an area only a few inches in diameter (pl. 19). Walls are then repolished and the plates cleaned deep within their sockets so they will shine out brilliantly in contrast with the brown mud. The cleaning "reveals the eye sockets of mbari"; in the metaphoric language used, the columns are called *anyanama,* "eyes on the road."

A parallel activity, called "hitting the iron," *iku igwe,* involves embedding "slivers of iron", *mkpeshi igwe,* or wooden substitutes into wall and column surfaces to serve as guidelines for the geometric patterns to be painted later (pl. 20). Although this is no longer done and may never have been done extensively, several informants considered it an essential part of mbari building in the old days.[30]

In earlier days of mbari construction (1920s and 1930s), at least in some areas, iron rods, *igwe,* were used symbolically in several parts of the structure. Depending on the wealth of the god, which can be partially measured by the number of *osu* sacrifices offered since the last mbari, several full-length irons of the type used for "walking the iron" were embedded in the walls and columns. If the *agbara* had only a few bars, the artist would put them on either side of the small door leading to the mbari's interior chamber, or occasionally, in the hands of relief figures modeled in the same locations (pl. 21).

Harvesting "Yam"

Once the plates and slivers of iron are inserted, the *ndimgbe* prepare to "go to farm to collect the yam of mbari," a symbolic activity that is in actuality no more than collecting the clay from which mbari figures and animals are modeled. As in all mbari activities, however, there are ritual preparations, sacrifices, medicines, songs, and prayers. On the appointed night *ndimgbe* are led out of the mbari enclosure by the priest's son, *ogbokiri* (or an *osu*), in the order established when they "walked the iron" some months before. Gongs are sounded whenever this procession is abroad, to warn people away, as it is dangerous for anyone to get too near *ndimgbe,* particularly on the way back from the "farm," for a stranger would "defile the yam" if he saw it or got too close. If the *ndimgbe* see any villager while abroad for this work, they are entitled to fine him a goat—on the assumption that he also saw them. It is a cult slave's job to seize the goat from the man's compound; he need offer no explanation.

On the first night of this work *ndimgbe* are accompanied by a diviner whose job is to prepare the "farm" by sacrifice and special medicines (*ogwu*). At an especially impressive anthill chosen previously, the diviner blows from his hand a black *ogwu* designed to chase away any malevolent spirits lurking in the area. A goat is then sacrificed to "soften the yam mound," that is, to make it easier for workers to dig the anthill clay—"yam." Workers rub another medicine on their bodies to protect them in this dangerous work; they are dealing with the "heart and vestibule of *agbara*," *obiama agbara;* and as a gathering place for both deities and other spirits, as well as the spirits of men waiting to be reincarnated, an anthill must be approached and conditioned with the utmost ritual care. This task of digging down into anthills is taxing, for the clay is extremely hard, and it is hazardous—physically hazardous, because the disturbed ants bite fiercely, and psychologically hazardous, because of the proximity of the spirits. Any *onyemgbe* who says he has been bitten by an ant is fined a cock; instead he must say he has been "pricked by the thorn of the yam vine." As if to make the work still more difficult, only the clay deep within the anthill, that called the "mother of yam," is considered fine enough for mbari figures. While some workers dig the clay, others carry ants away on sticks. After enough "yam" to fill each worker's basket has been dug, the chunks of clay are carried back to the mbari in procession, again to the accompaniment of warning gongs. A brief rite to "cool the yam," *ibujuji*, to neutralize it, is performed before it is brought inside the fence.

The next morning the *ndimgbe* busy themselves soaking the clay to soften it; they then pound it in wooden mortars (of the kind normally used for pounding yam or cassava) until it is the sticky consistency of *fufu*, pounded yam. Throughout the ensuing months this pounded clay is called only *fufu*, which is the name for the preferred way of preparing yam for the best meals. Repeated trips to the "yam farm" are required, and the preparation and pounding of this clay seems a never ending task.

Modeling Figures

The first figure to be constructed of this material is called "bad" or "ugly person," *onyeojo*, or "child of the bad mortar," *nwaokwaojo*. It is neither a complete figure nor is it placed inside the waiting mbari structure (color plate 11). Intended to draw off any "evil that might disintegrate the mbari" building process, it is either thrown away directly after the ritual, erected in the *agbara*'s forest, or placed to the side of the mbari within the fence, as in the illustration. Even in the latter instance the "bad person" is later thrown away. Deliberately incomplete, it represents any "big or little evil" that might plague the mbari or its people during construction. The blood of a cock or a goat is dripped on it. People say that without the construction of the "ugly one" none of the figures subsequently modeled in mbari would stand up.

The final activity in this round of preparatory rituals is "planting the skill/art," *iruoka*. What is actually planted is the stick (or iron bar) on which the torso of the principal deity, the owner of the house, will be modeled (pl. 24). The stick has in fact been in the pedestal seat for some time, since it was sunk there to make the hole in the drying mud. But at this ceremony the blood of a goat sanctifies the stick and the entire pedestal, as if it were an altar, thereby preparing for the whole modeling phase of mbari. Some blood may also be dripped on the armature of the first clay figure actually modeled that day, one which, aside from being first, is in no way more important than many others.

Mbari has now properly begun, and the mood of exhilaration that accompanied the insertion of the plates is revived. Indeed, the first day of modeling may also be transformed into a minor festival. Although the work of pounding anthill clay is not easy, singing and dancing spring up spontaneously. Hardly a day goes by without such entertainment, supported by generous amounts of palm wine. Each day, too, the spirit workers decorate their bodies by rubbing them with camwood. The first figures modeled are those on the left of the mbari's front side. Work progresses from left to right and thence counterclockwise around the house, bypassing the owner of the house and sometimes the relief figures behind her. The house begins to fill up with lively mud-colored inhabitants, called *ewuwu*:[31] animals, children, adults, monsters, and gods. Soon red-brown figures are seen everywhere in all subjects, shapes, and sizes: in relief on the walls, high up under the roof, sitting on a step, peering around a column, climbing up a post or stalking down the steps of a buttress (color plate 11).

All figures first need an armature of some kind to anchor them in place and to support such projections as free-standing arms. Most armatures are sticks sunk into the clay wall or into a specially built pedestal. Because it is difficult to sink such sticks in hard, dried mud, however, the artist must plan the better part of the mbari in advance, choosing where he wants to place his figures so holes can be made for the sticks while the clay of the understructure is still soft. He also decides which are to have earthen seats so these supports can be made. In this way all will be properly positioned when he is ready to model figures on the brick-hard foundation.

Though the artist need not determine the exact nature of each figure, such as the precise activity or sex or body position, he must have in mind generally what he wants and its location, before much figure modeling is done.[32] As one craftsman said, "The whole mbari must be laid out as an imagination photograph." The entire conceptual projection of a completed mbari house, especially if a large one, required imaginative, careful advanced planning on the part of the artist/master builder, who works without either models or sketches.

Armatures are essential for modeling and tend to be as complicated as the main outlines of the intended figure or group; for while anthill clay does have quite remarkable plastic qualities, it has little tensile strength. It cannot support itself in thin projections, especially horizontal ones. Thus complex figures or groups, like the rainmakers in plate 36, have an equally complex understructure of thin green branches lashed together in the pattern which is now visible. The actual procedure for making an armature for a simple figure was explained by the artist Ezem:

> You get sticks and you tie them the way you want them with cord and you break the bones which will be the arms and legs of the figure. Then you place the feet. . . . The sticks . . . are the bones of the figure and the yam is the flesh and muscle.

Strong cords from raffia palms are used to lash sticks half an inch or more in diameter in place. The entire armature is completed for each figure before any mud is applied, and the artist stabilizes cantilevered arms or other projections with strings running from them to a roof beam (pl. 22). He usually removes these strings after the clay has dried.

A relief figure is anchored somewhat differently. First the outline of the figure is drawn, then incised, on the wall, followed by excavation to a depth of two or three inches within that outline. Short slivers of wood are then pounded in within the outline to hold the shaped clay in place. Excavation is a clever if difficult structural solution, for if a half figure were modeled entirely on the surface rather than partially within the wall, it would fall off or deteriorate much faster than is actually the case.

On completing the armature, the artist calls for *fufu* (the word used for pounded yam = clay), brought to him by an *onyemgbe,* which he applies to the lower and heavier parts of the figure (color plate 8). Next the sticky but easily modeled clay is plastered roughly over the whole figure, except for the arms and other delicate projections. Then the artist shapes the entire torso, smoothing over with wet hands the mud he has just added, pushing and kneading the pliable clay to the exact shape desired. He may add some more mud or scrape away any excess with a spatulate wooden tool. The legs and head are shaped roughly and smoothed in the same way. Though no clay is yet on the arms, the artist begins to add and model the facial features by pinching and depressing the basic shape with his fingers and then building it up with small shaped lumps. He uses small wood or bone tools for fine detailing, of an elaborate hairdress or costume for example, and in finishing the facial features. Properly pounded clay can be modeled into remarkably fine ropes and filigrees.[33] The head, hair, and most of the costume of a figure are usually completed before the projecting parts are begun. From time to time the artist is likely to step back and to the sides "to see if the figure is complete"; "completeness" is his way of expressing aptness, correct proportions, and general "rightness." A fairly simple seated female figure with a delicate but not overelaborate hairdress might occupy him for forty-five minutes or an hour. Artists never like to leave a figure unfinished at the end of a day's work, for next morning the clay is partially dry and difficult to handle.

Mud settles and develops surface cracks overnight in drying through contraction, even though it does not become firm throughout for a week or two. As soon as the inevitable cracks (pl. 23) appear *ndimgbe,* rather than the sculptor, patch them and smooth them over with wet hands. The cracking, patching, cracking, patching sequence may continue for two weeks or more for each figure depending upon its size and complexity.

Only rarely, it seems, does an *onyemgbe* try his hand at modeling figures. Besides the professional artist(s), the only sculptors who make complete forms are the artist's apprentices and possibly one or two of the four-day-workers. Some larger mbari houses of the past, on the other hand, employed as many as five well-known professional *ndioka,* but only rarely did so many artists work together, as when a community had to finish its mbari especially fast because of alleged pressure from the deity. In recent years mbari seldom reveal the handiwork of more than two men. In instances where several artists participate, the first one called oversees the whole operation.

Life Inside the Fence

The various participants in mbari activities get along together remarkably well. In the mbari construction I observed, almost no bickering or friction marred a period of six months.[34] In addition to being generally friendly and calm, *ndimgbe* are very democratic about the division of labor; men and women are considered equal, with no visible gap in social position. Asked about this unusual situation, one informant insisted that "all duties are equally shared among *ndimgbe* . . . men and women do the same work." Both men and women pounded "yam" for example, a job usually done by females. Yet a natural and expected division of labor did occur when someone particularly good at a specific job spent most of his time on it. Conversely, where another was unequal to a task he was usually assigned elsewhere. For example, one woman who did a sloppy job of painting left that work, at the artist's suggestion, after about a half hour on the job. Someone else, with a steadier hand, was assigned to repaint her mistakes. Also, men frequently performed the heavier or more acrobatic jobs such as those high up under the roof. It is nevertheless important that most of the work, food, and living conditions were shared between the sexes on a relatively undifferentiated and equal basis.

The period of modeling figures was not an unbroken drudgery of endless workdays. Diversions were created when animals, such as fowl or goats, wandered or were lured into the mbari enclosure, where they were at once seized, sacrificed, and eaten.[35] Furthermore, special ceremonies accompanied the modeling of as many as ten to twelve figures considered so important that they "cannot be done for nothing"; the blood of a fowl was dripped on such figures as the python and leopard, deities other than the owner of the house, and the relief figures. Often, when two sides of an mbari are full, a goat is killed to "get them [the workers] onto the other side," as if to spur on the activity. If the mbari includes a cloister, its figures will be modeled at the same time as those of sides three and four, with special sacrifices for some of them. In the old days each occasion of sacrifice became a small feast, or festival; and the workers, in costume with decorated bodies, drummed, danced, sang, joked, ate, and drank palm wine.

As the fourth side nears completion a new surge of ceremonial activity heralds the construction of the *agbara,* the owner of the house herself. This activity may begin with the modeling of two female figures in relief, called *ijeremgbe,* "You went to *mgbe.*"[36] These two elongated figures stand behind the owner of the house on either side of the door leading to the inner chamber, or, occasionally in smaller mbari, on the two front corner columns (pls. 21 and 22). As important figures, each *ijeremgbe* has a fowl sacrificed to it, as if in preparation for the he-goat that will be killed shortly thereafter for Ala, owner of the house.[37]

Artists consider the owner of the house very difficult to model, because this very large figure must be completed in one day. Artists claimed the difficulty is technical; they may also find constructing the image of their most feared god psychologically taxing. In any case, the modeling procedure is the same as for other figures except that the priest reserves one iron bar for Ala's footrest, and in some places, another is used and placed beside the wooden armature for her backbone, ". . . so when ants and goats attack the stick, they cannot attack the iron. The figure is stronger." This is true, yet since the brick-hard mud accounts for most of the figure's durability, this artist seems also to be referring to the symbolic strength conferred by iron, obviously of utmost importance to an influential god.

Painting

To inaugurate the painting of the mbari the artist or an *onyemgbe* chosen by divination runs around the whole mbari quickly splashing white paint on every wall and column surface; sometimes a praise song is chanted at the same time. This rite is done just after a goat's blood is dripped at the *agbara*'s pedestal and on the painting equipment—lumps of unground colors, grinding stones, and mixing bowls. In some areas this ceremony preceded the whitewashing of all plane surfaces with a chalky solution (pl. 22). I heard one unconfirmed report that the figures themselves were then blackened with charcoal. If this was indeed the case, and it seems to accord with the elaboration of symbolism and ceremonial, an mbari must have presented a very striking appearance at this point. That day the *ndimgbe* begin to prepare the colors, starting with white, which is needed in great quantities. White, like many of the colors, is a coarse earth pigment requiring considerable grinding before it can be mixed with water for a smooth application.[38] The common pigments used (before the introduction of Western oil paints, which are occasionally used now) are listed below:

White, *nzu*: an earth pigment also widely used in rituals. It can be purchased in markets.

Black, *inyiri*, *oji*, or *uri*: from charcoal prepared at the mbari site.

Red-Brown, *ajanchara*: from anthill clay.

Yellow, *ovuvu* or *ajaumukabia*: from a clay specially procured at some difficulty and expense in the old days by *ndimgbe* men, from a sacred site near the town of Umukabia on the banks of the Imo River. The same color as *udo*, a pigment prepared from a yellowish wood and used in many sacrificial rites.

Green, *akwukwo ndu*: clay from the Imo River. Procured, however, with less difficulty than *ovuvu*.

Blue, *baluu* (Igbo-English): from European washing blue.

Red, *ocha obara* (literally, "the color of blood"): from camwood, though it seems to have been used as a bright red only infrequently, and was proscribed in some places.

Pink, *uforo*: an earth color, also from the banks of the Imo, was used more often than a true red.

To obtain intermediate colors these pigments are mixed. The range is quite wide, for there are sometimes as many as ten or twelve distinct colors, all natural or native-made except for blue. Artists make small paintbrushes from fowl feathers saved after sacrifices and tied in small bunches up under the mbari roof. They make larger brushes of coconut ruff for the broad white areas, while inner coconut shells serve as paint containers.

All the *ndimgbe* apply pigments under the close supervision of the artist, who usually decides where a color is to be used. For patterns on columns and stepped walls the artist or a trusted assistant marks out the basic designs, either scratching the pattern using a stick rule, or by drawing the lines freehand with brown or black paint (pl. 24). If satisfied with the pattern he may go over his preliminary sketch with thicker lines, or he may simply indicate the colors to be used by putting a small dab of the proper color paint in each space. It is not uncommon for these patterns to be painted, repainted, emended, or touched up four to six times. Generally only three or four colors—white, red-brown, yellow, and black—are used for plane surfaces, with brown or less frequently black, as the guide or outline color. In most mbari houses, only the columns, steps, niche backdrops, and smaller wall surfaces have these patterns. The larger paintings on upper wall surfaces are the province of the artists who often take special pride in them, particularly in "weaving the cloth" which appears on the high wall behind the "owner of the house" (pl. 22).

The sculptured figures are usually painted in the same order in which they were modeled. Thus, the last figure to be painted is the "owner of the house." By this time the mbari is bright and colorful, and the workers are buoyant with spirit. Utmost care is taken in painting Ala; her body designs, *edeala,* must be elegant and precise, close parallel curvilinear lines; her head and hairdress detailed, strong, and dignified (color plates 4 and 7). She must dominate the front of the house. As Ala is being completed, finishing touches are applied elsewhere; lines are straightened, dull colors are repainted, and imprecise patterns are reworked. The priest sets a day in the near future for the visit of the *amala;* mbari has yet to pass the test of its patrons.

Criticism

When the artists and the *ndimgbe* consider their work finished, a group of senior *amala* come to examine it. They buy their way into the mbari enclosure with a goat or two and some jugs of palm wine.[39] Apparently it is customary for the *amala* to be very critical. They will countenance neither indistinct sculptural rendering nor sloppy painting. Any mistakes they find or anything they feel should be changed must be rectified quickly. If any cracks in figures are detected, for example, they must be filled in and repainted, or if splashes of paint are observed on a section intended to be white, they must be painted out. An artist may be asked to remodel a foot or head, perhaps occasionally an entire figure, if the *amala* judge it to be misshapen. Depending on the amount of further work required, a date is then set for the opening. Apparently even inferior mbari strongly criticized by *amala* have still been opened, but in such cases the artist is discredited and the priest's prestige declines. On the other hand, regardless of an mbari's artistic quality, the *agbara* still appreciates the effort, and all the people involved with it look forward to opening day with anticipation.

It may happen that a figure seems to resemble—quite by accident—a particular real human being known to people in the community. This is deemed inauspicious, for it is believed that if the figure is still there when the mbari opens, the person portrayed may die at the hands of an irate *agbara*.[40] If the *ndimgbe* notice such a resemblance, a delegation is appointed to apprise that person or his family of what has happened. The usual procedure then is for someone in the family to come to see the figure; if it is a sufficient likeness or portrait, the man will pay with a goat to have the figure destroyed so that another one, not his likeness, can be built in its place. No figure in an mbari may resemble a living person. As one artist expressed it: "Mbari figures do not look like people. They are more beautiful than human beings. . . . "

The Unveiling—The Sacrifice Completed

The people have been thinking about and working on the mbari many years. This long process draws to a swift and dramatic close when it is revealed to the world. The complete unveiling takes a night and a day: a night for the private and spiritual part, and a day for the more secular and public aspects of the celebration.

Evening Rites: After dark on the appointed evening the priest, the diviners, and the *ndimgbe* assemble inside the enclosure. First they "close the path" to the "farm." They have previously covered the excavated anthills with leaves and other debris; now they do the same to the path leading from the mbari enclosure to the "farm." This done, they seal off the usual door into the enclosure, the one made originally by the *amala,* with a sacrificial goat or fowl. If *onyeojo,* the incomplete first figure built, remains inside the mbari site, they now remove it.[41] Heaped by it on the ground are paintbrushes, stirrers, and containers. All the *ndimgbe* cluster around this pile while the artist kills a cock and drips its blood, then sprinkles a yellow powder, *udo,* on the feet of the *ndimgbe* and then on *onyeojo* and the other things. The group then tears the *onyeojo* and gathers the painting implements from the ground and, as one knot of bodies, takes them over to a pit and flings them in, shouting: "We have thrown away the bad child; look at him!" Thus the site is cleared of all bad things, and the *agbara* can now be formally invited into her new house.

The symbolic presence of the *agbara* is announced by the ritual establishment of her spirit or soul, *chi,* or by the transfer of a symbolic stone,[42] to the inner chamber of the mbari. After that the diviner prepares a purifying medicine for the workers. The priest brings two bowls, one for the *chi* and one for the medicine. He and the diviner make the *chi*, dripping the blood of a hen first on it and then on the feet of all the more important mbari figures,[43] beginning and ending with Ala. After the priest places the *chi* a few feet behind Ala inside the inner room, the artist seals the entrance, usually with a wooden door without hinges.[44] The priest meanwhile intones a lengthy prayer reminding Ala that he has made a "porridge of yam for her, the yam of mbari." He also asks blessings for the community, for the workers, and especially for himself, with a special plea for relief from his debts—presumably those incurred in erecting mbari.

Next all the workers—*ndimgbe*, four-day-workers, and artists—are purified. Their heads are bathed with unripe coconut milk "to wash away all pains and fevers, to let the god restore them to normal health." The *ndimgbe* each contribute other preparations, including an egg, a yam leaf, a snail, and two pennies to the artist and the diviner, who pocket the money and prepare the rest as a purifying *ogwu* in the second bowl. The artist then touches each *onyemgbe* in turn with this substance on several parts of his or her body saying:

> Please, Ala, our owner, let evil leave our bodies. Anyone who does well, let good follow him. We have done the thing [mbari] for which you are known; have mercy on us. Give us children. We did the work of the spirits so let us go now and rest.

Each worker takes a lump of this purifying medicine away with him for use after each bath for the next several weeks. In accepting this ball of *ogwu* the workers say something like this: "Anything I have done, let not the consequences of it eat my head [kill me]. Please, we did good work here. . . . Let no trouble come near us."

While some are still completing this purification, those who have finished raise a loud curse on the mbari and themselves:

> Whoever did this, you are dead and lost; Chineke burnt you. The uncivilized people who did this should die. The hands of them that made these things are deformed. Whoever made it did a terrible thing; whoever made it is dead.

In the meantime the artist has cut a door-shape in the mbari fence directly in front of the honored god, leaving the "door" in place but ready to fall. After the *ndimgbe* and the artist have cursed themselves and one another for a few minutes, their leader rushes at the fence, breaks down the new exit, and runs out, followed by the others one after another, to the jubilant sound of horns and gongs sounded by diviners and others who have collected at the site. As the female *ndimgbe* reach the outside world,[45] they fling off their raffia skirts and accept new cloths from members of their families who have gathered to await and participate in the opening.[46] The women quickly wrap the new cloth and continue on their way; with the male *ndimgbe,* who have also donned new clothes, they set out for a neighboring town, where the priest of another deity welcomes them back into the community and feasts them. As the workers are running away from the mbari, a spectacle unfolds.[47] When the first gongs sound, more villagers converge on the mbari site, for they too have been anticipating this moment for years. After a number of important elders have appeared, a diviner gives the signal for them to smash down the mbari fence. Seconds later, the new mbari emerges—dimly reflecting the light of the moon. But half a minute later the scene is again transformed—the fences are heaped up or thrown into the mud pits near the mbari and are set on fire. The drama of the next half hour surpasses anything the town has known for years. With huge bonfires lighting the monument, the noise of horns, gongs, and guns fills the night air, while young people seize fence supports, create torches of them, and dance, chanting praises, in procession around and around the new mbari (pl. 25). A gathering crowd joins this spectacle to celebrate the god's acceptance of her mbari, her "thing of pride." The pride of the people, in turn, knows no bounds. So ends the first drama of an mbari opening.

Public Announcement: The next morning the *ndimgbe* go to the compound of the priest to be formally returned to their families. The mbari priest says: "Take back your son (daughter). He was alive when he came and you get him back alive." A few days later the *ndimgbe* and the diviners form a procession, which always includes a cow, and go to the largest nearby market to announce Ala's new mbari to the people from surrounding communities who convene there. On the morning of the ceremony all the workers reconvene at the priest's compound wearing their best "civilian" clothes.[48] As if to match their splendor, the cow, like the men, is decked out with feathers and a small white cloth sprinkled with yellow powder, *udo,* on its head. The cow and the people are adorned with symbols of praise, coolness, beauty, and pride for all to see when the procession tours the market. The procession, following the established order for the *ndimgbe,* weaves through the thronged market to great cheers, the blowing of horns, and the firing of guns, with the workers receiving small gifts along the way.

As they walk back to the priest's compound, they avert their eyes when passing mbari, for the *ndimgbe* are always careful, once released from service, to avoid the mbari and if possible to refrain from talking about it. A former *onyemgbe* fears that he might slip up and say, " 'Look, I did this figure.' If he does that he has killed himself. The god that owns that work will kill him." Later, workers may even express surprise at the very existence of the mbari.[49] They pretend to have had nothing whatever to do with it even though many people in the community know they served as *ndimgbe.* Of course, those who made it are "dead and lost. . . . "

In contrast to the attitudes of mbari workers, villagers and people from nearby areas flock to the mbari for days after it is formally opened. People of all ages come to admire it, crowding and jostling one another to see the "owner" and other popular figures, sometimes making small offerings of kola nuts or coins. Everyone chats and comments, seeking out especially those figures they expect or new ones they have been told about. The mbari is entertaining and amusing; people often laugh and cheer. Indeed the general mood is of elation and festivity, and special pride if one is a member of the village or town that built the mbari. People from outside that group, on the other hand, may mix their own admiration with silent feelings of jealousy and resentment, for their own god has not got such a splendid house.

For the priest and his family these days after the opening are splendid but hectic. The revelation of a new mbari is an important time for visiting, gift-giving, and feasting. This priest entertains many from surrounding areas who come bringing presents from their own gods—cloths, palm wine, yams, fowl, perhaps a goat or a sheep. Since he must entertain such visitors well, his wives are busy cooking most of the time. The men sit around eating and drinking. The *ndimgbe* themselves are well entertained and feasted, first in the priest's compound and again by their own families. They receive many gifts from their relatives, for a released worker is a hero; he or she has saved his lineage from destruction by the god. And for a time, at least, Ala must keep her distance from all her people; she can be comfortable and content in her new house. The mbari festival is a time of joy, good health, and peace.

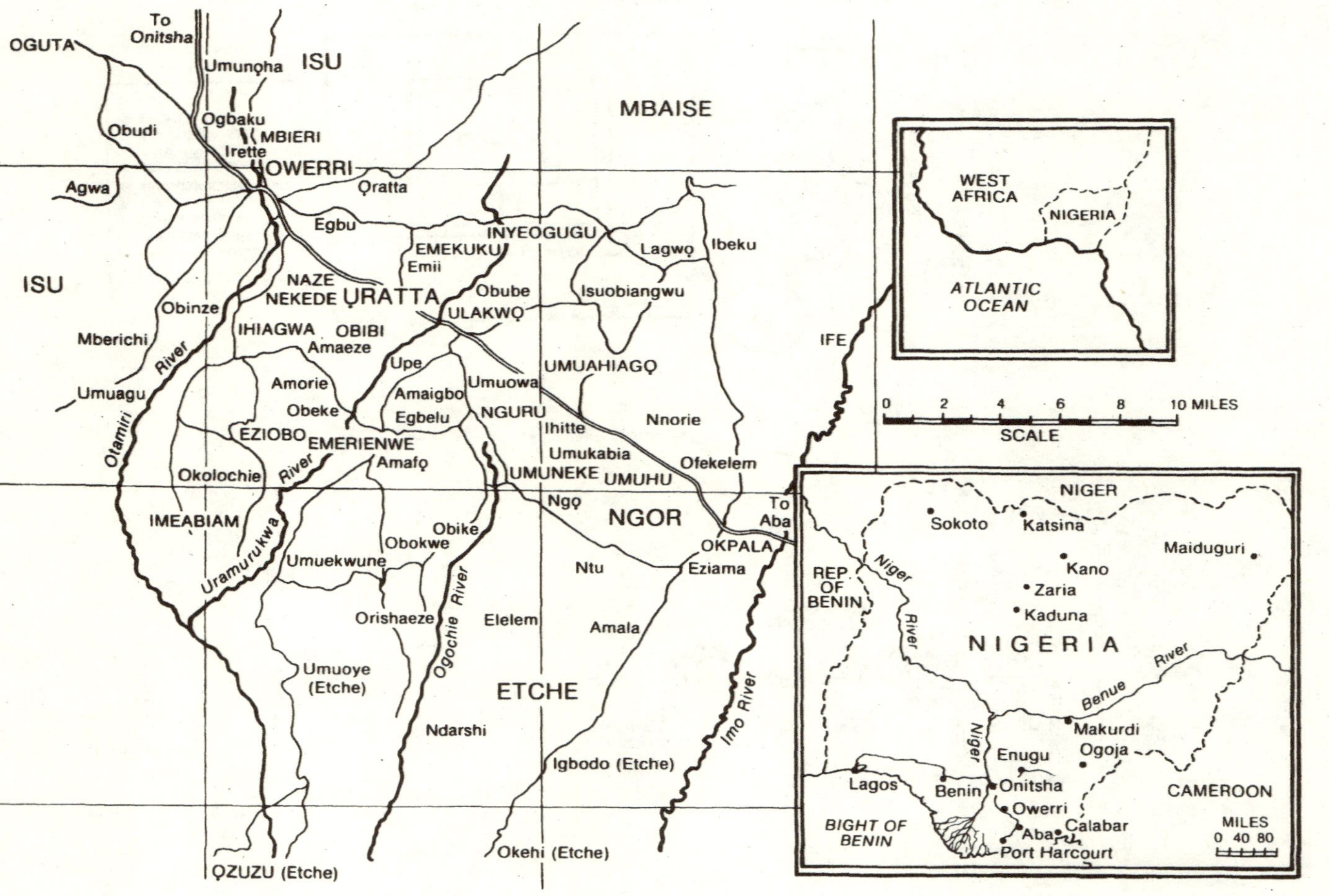

Figure 1. Map of Owerri area.

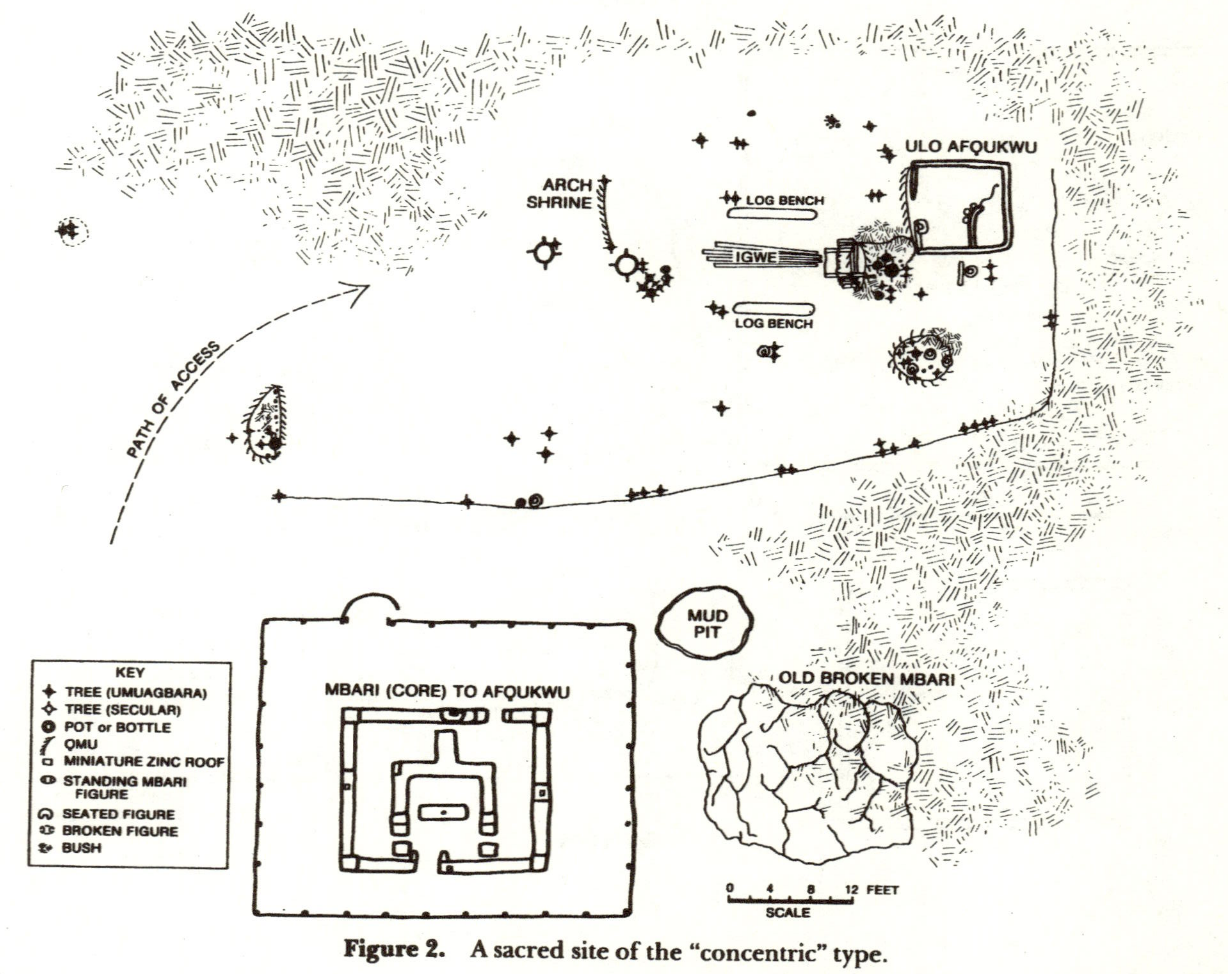

Figure 2. A sacred site of the "concentric" type.

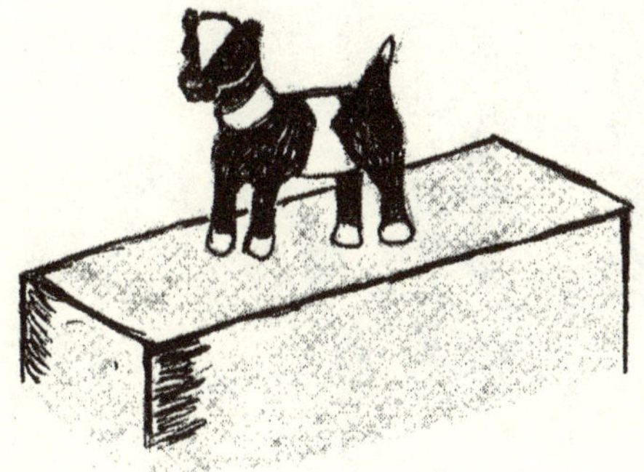

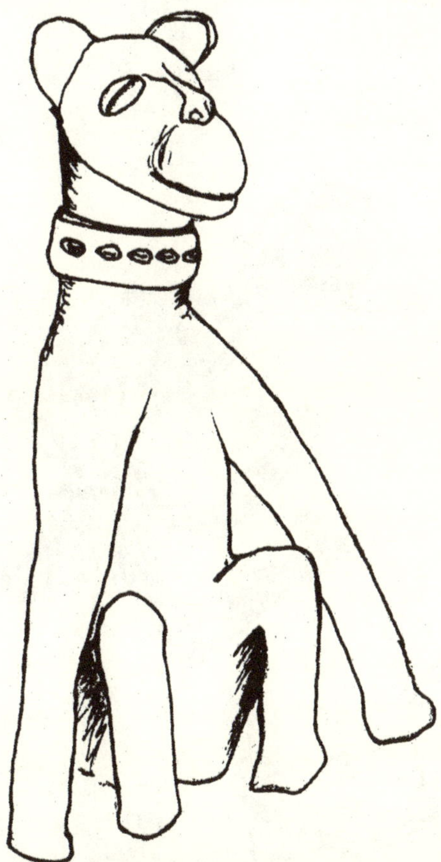

Figure 3. Two different versions of dogs.

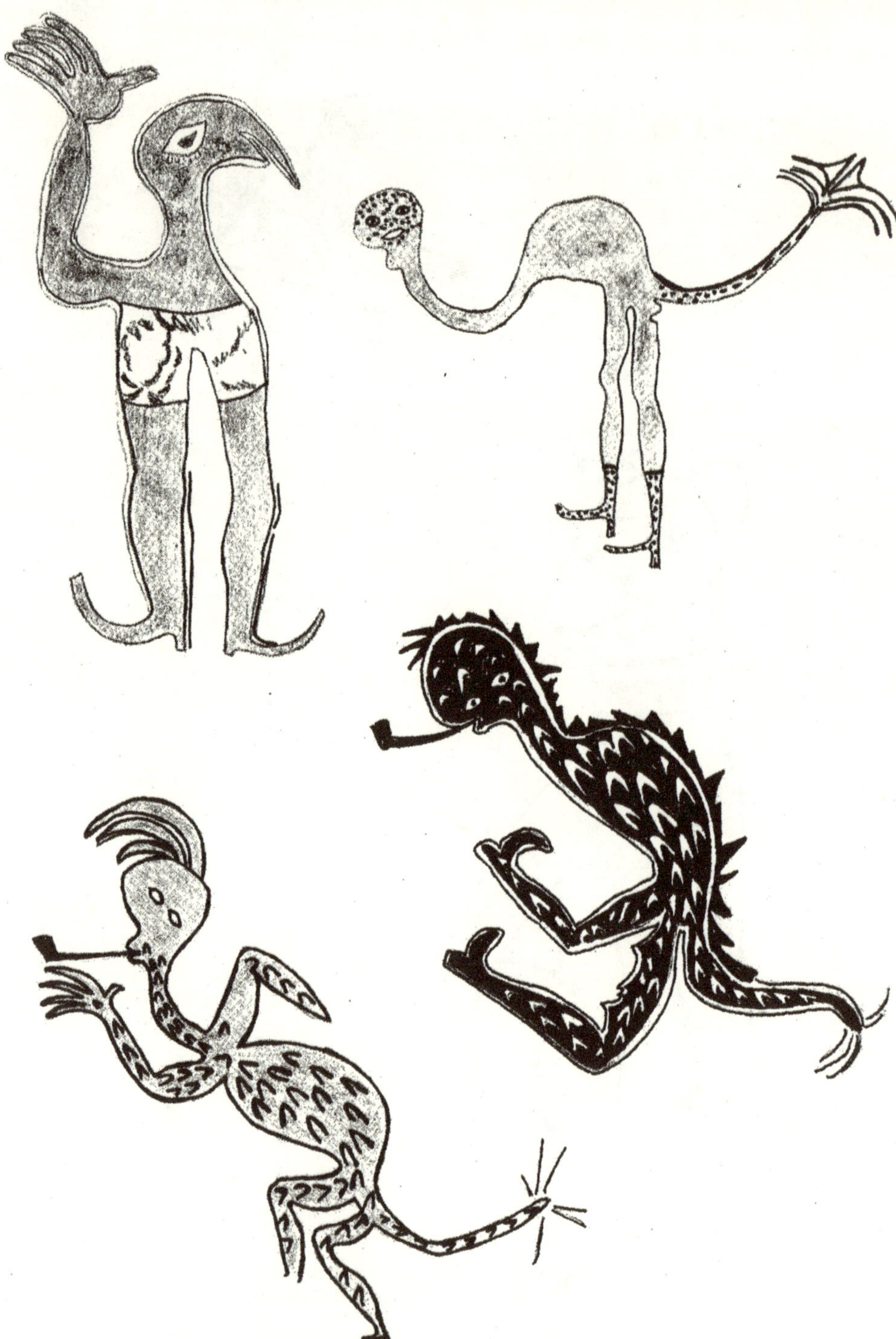

Figure 4. Paintings of the evil Ekwensu probably derive from the Christian concept of "Devil."

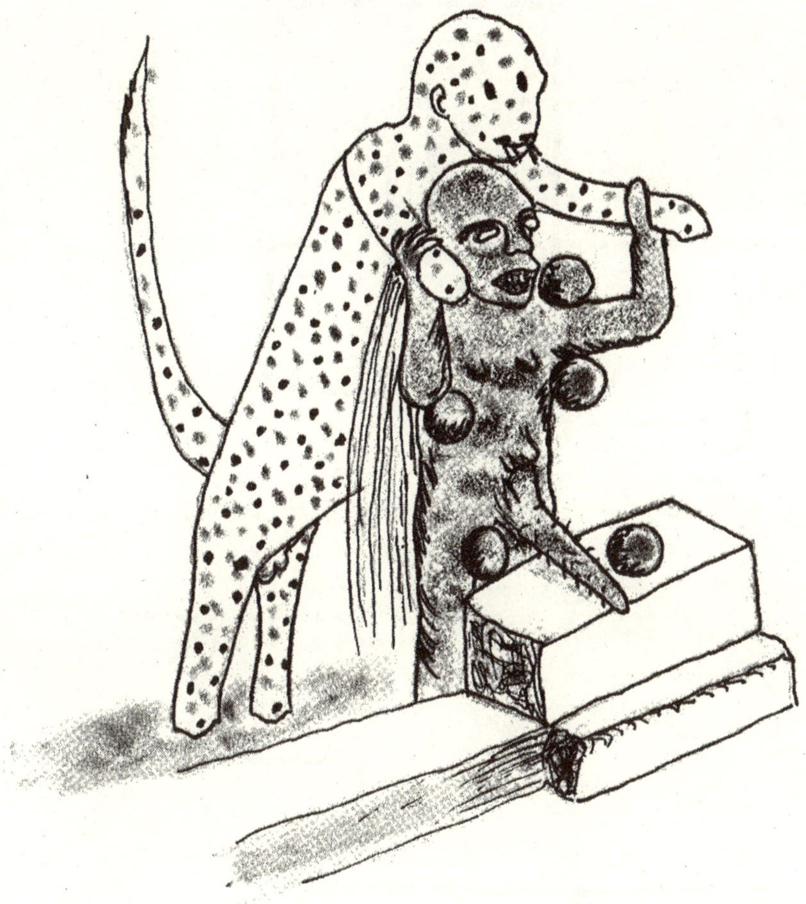

Figure 5. These two favorite mbari beasts are shown in a wide variety of poses.

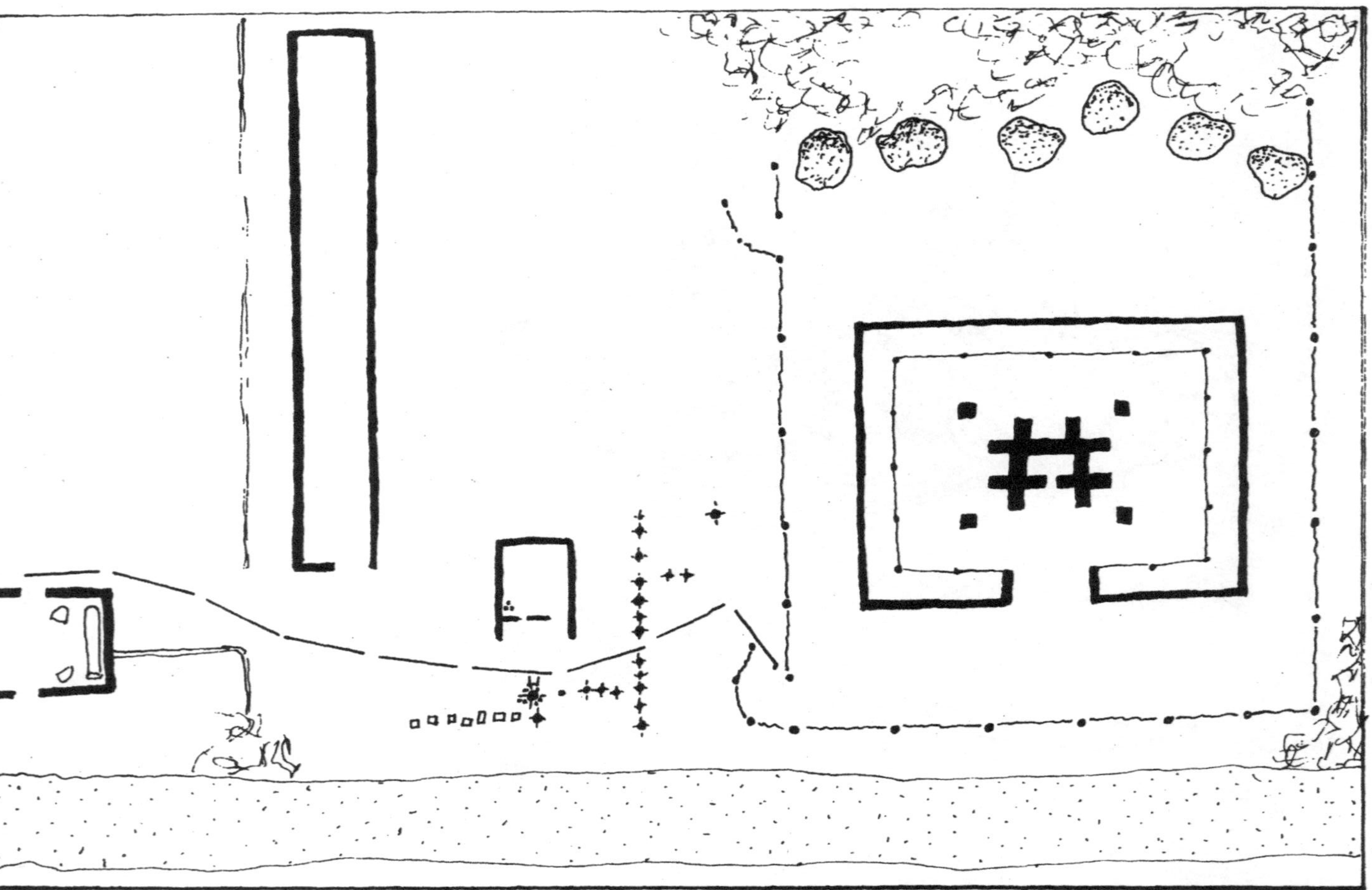

Figure 6. Sketch plan of hypothetical site showing route of *izo igwe*.

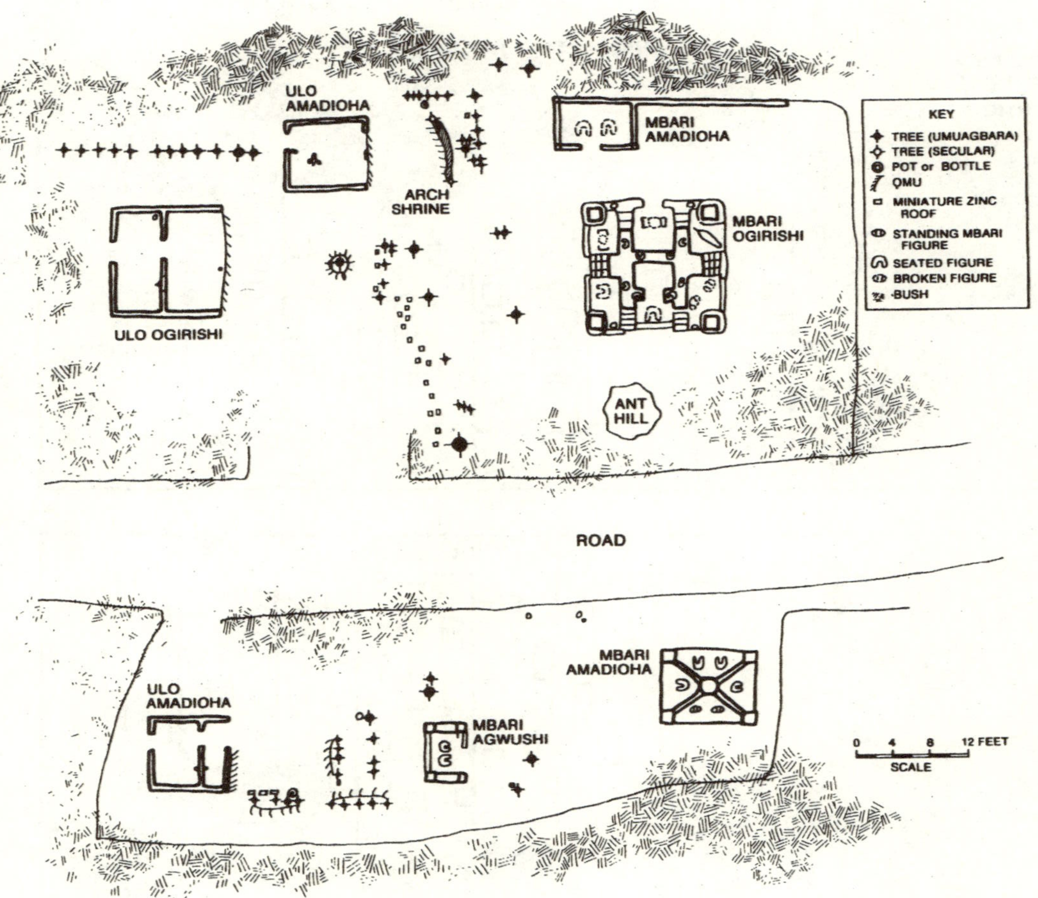

Figure 7. Plan of a group of sacred sites of the "rectilinear" type.

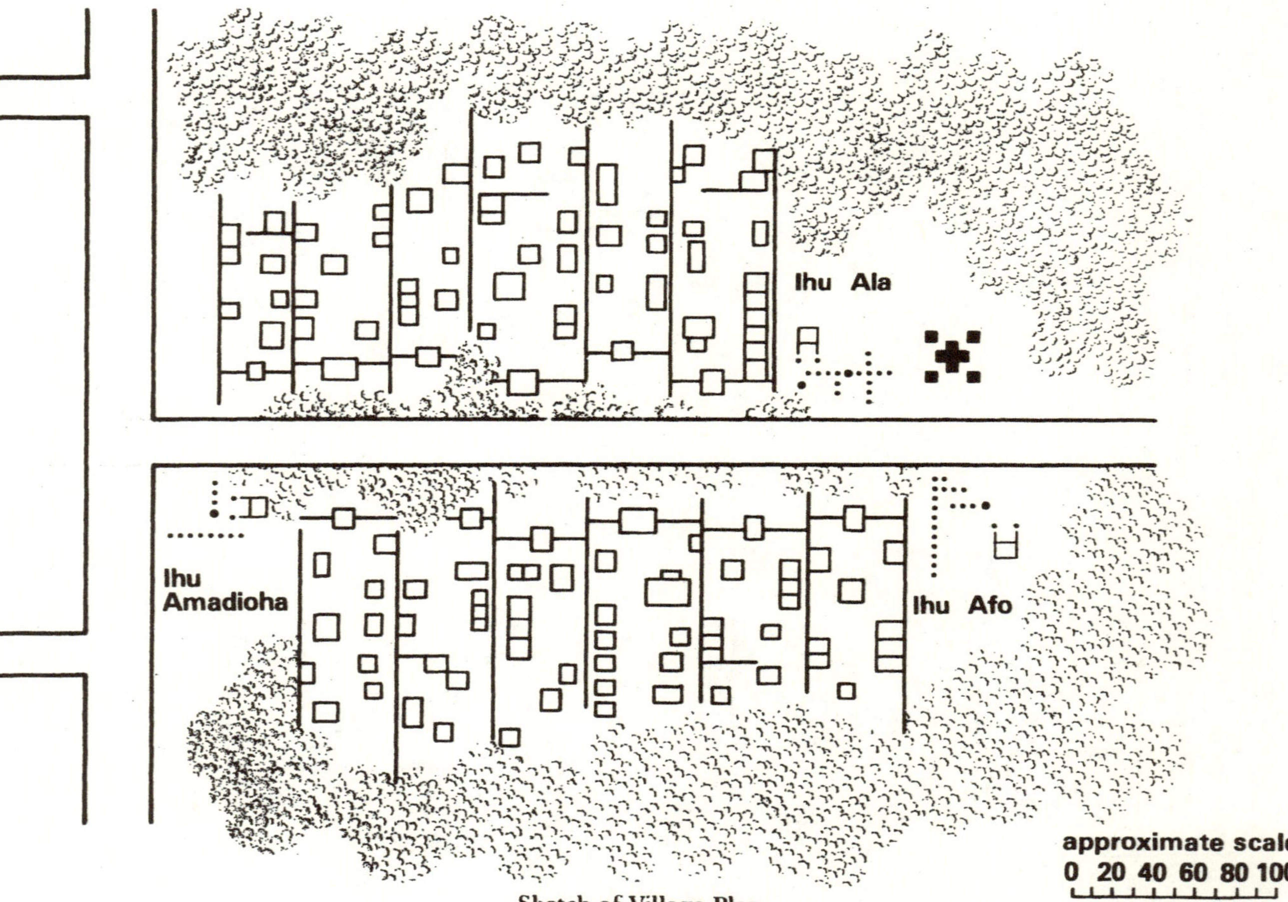

Figure 8. Sketch plan of a "rectilinear" village.

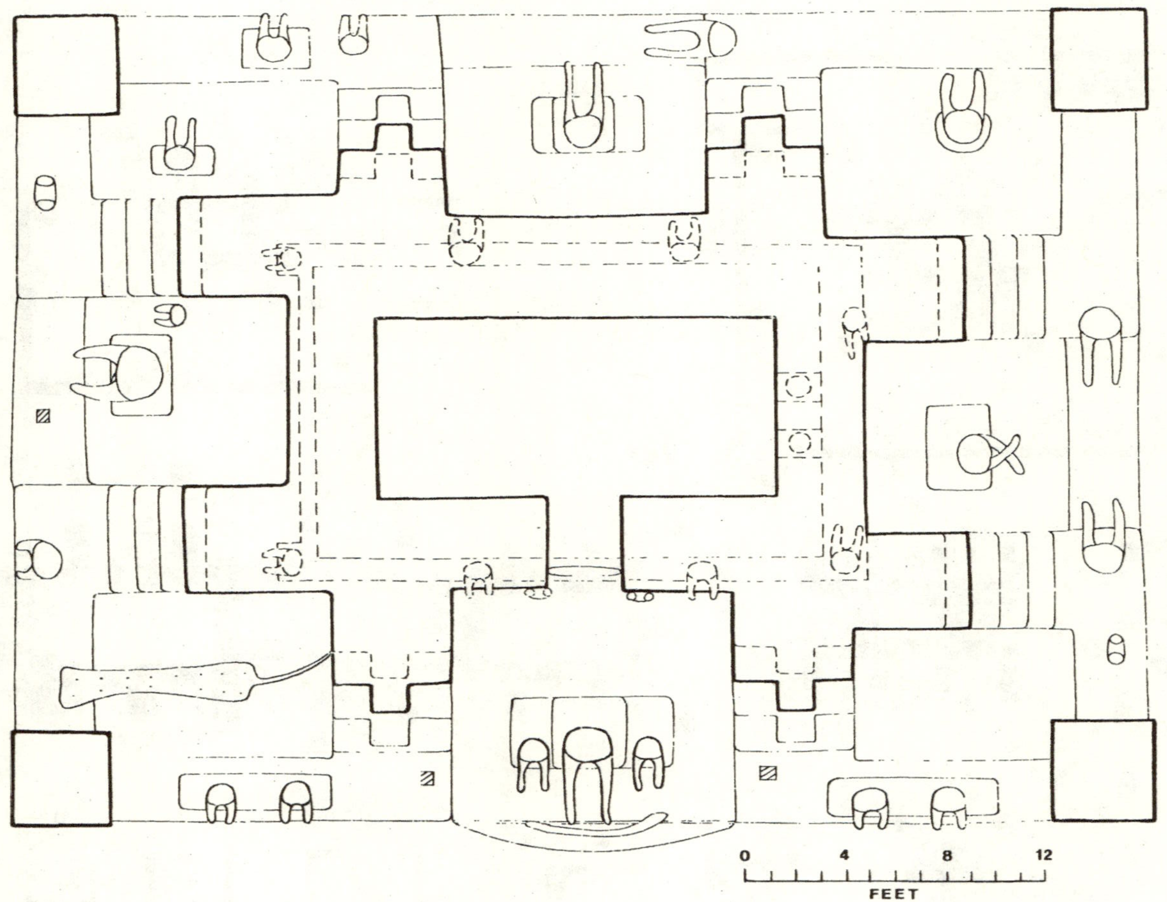

Figure 9. Plan of the mbari at Ndiama Obube. See color plate 1.

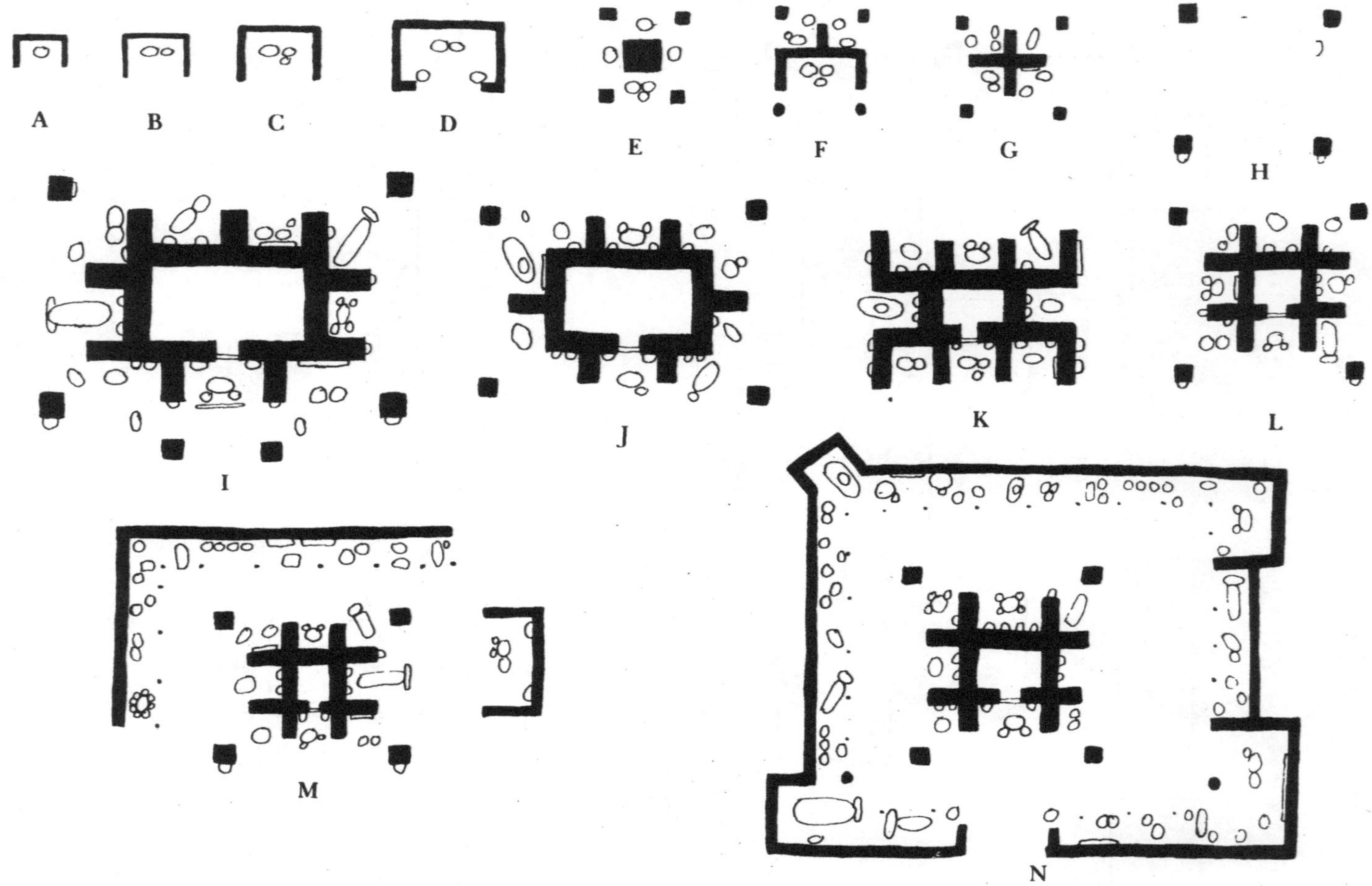

A B C D E F G H

I J K L

M N

Figure 10. Mbari are built in many shapes and sizes.

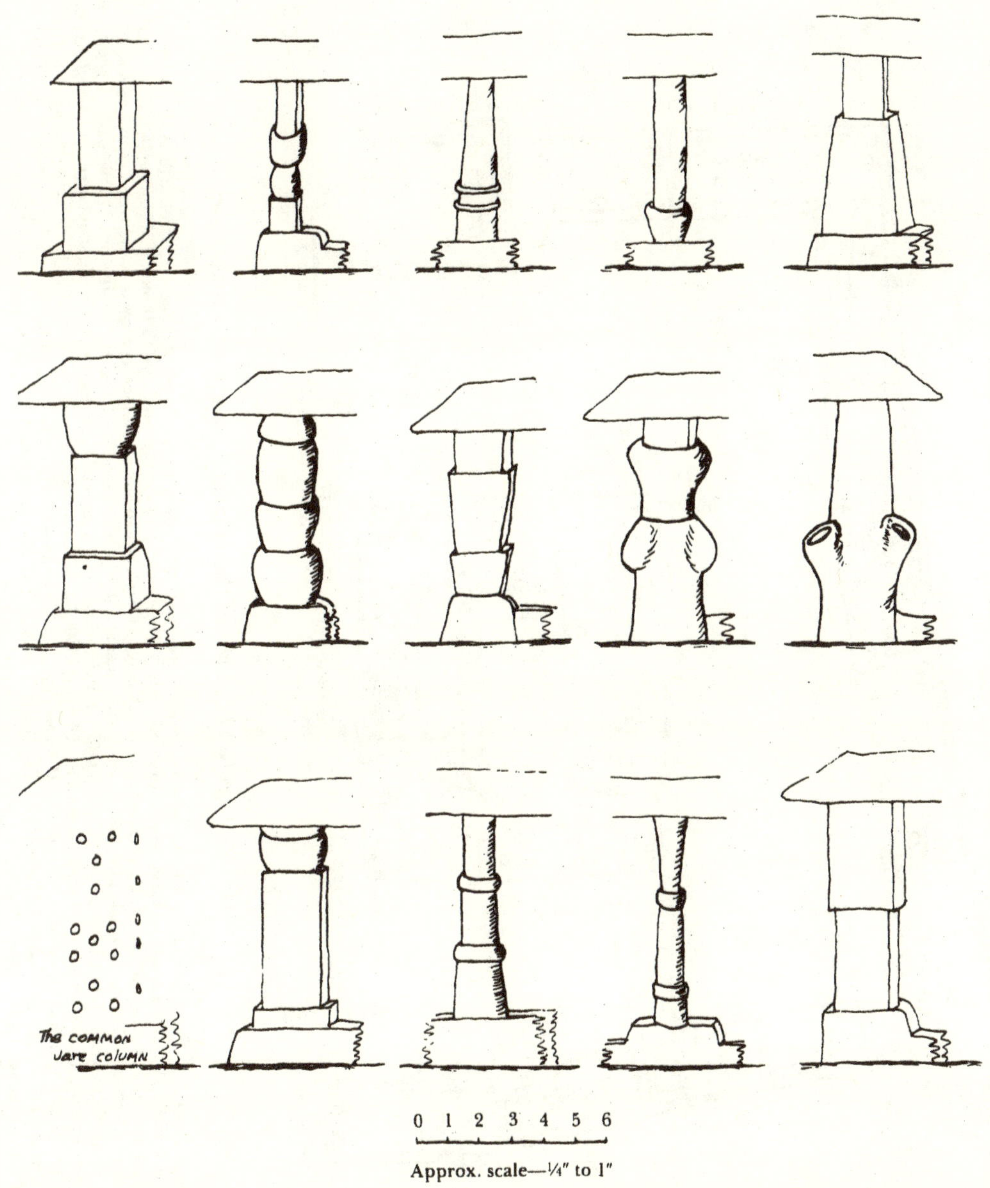

Figure 11. Variations in column shape. The standard column is shown as if painted.

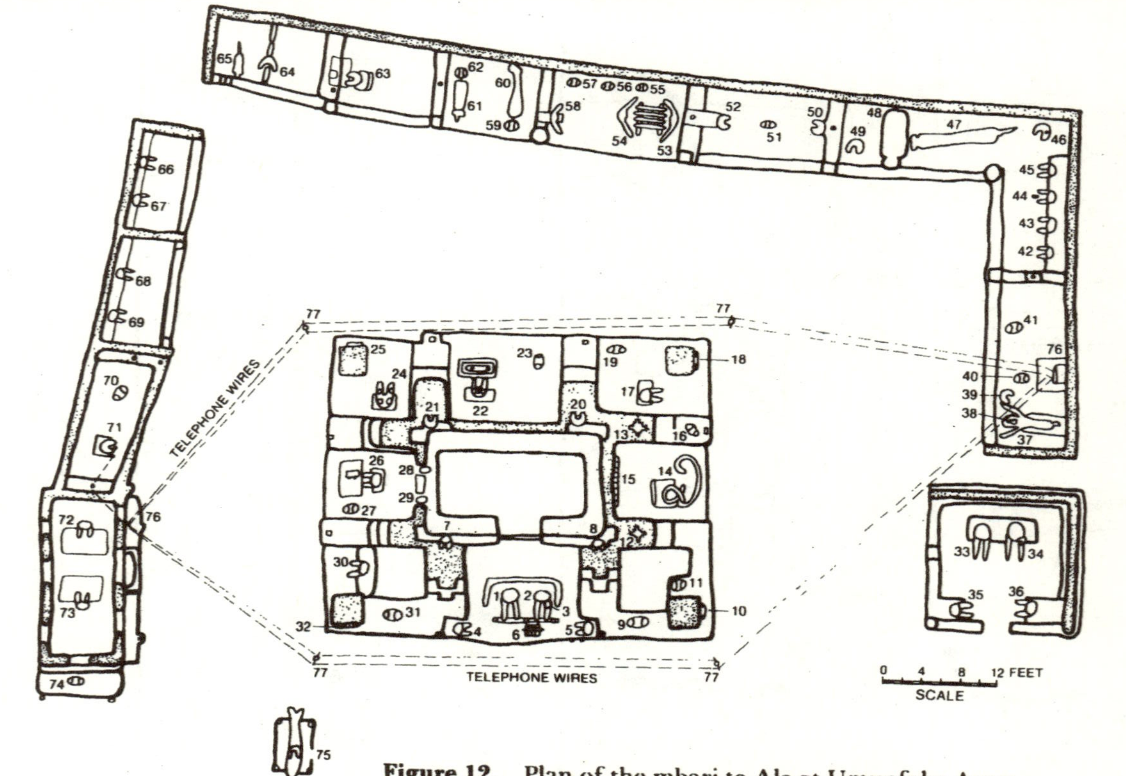

Figure 12. Plan of the mbari to Ala at Umuofeke Agwa.

1-Ala's husband; 2-Ala; 3-Her child; 4-Her first son; 5-Ada, her first daughter; 6-Tortoise; 7-Ala's daughter; 8-Another daughter; 9-Police (bodyguard); 10-*Ijeremgbe*; 11-Guitar player; 12-Guinea fowl; 13-Guinea fowl; 14-Mamy Wata; 15-Python; 16-Hunter; 17-Chief Emederonwa (Ala's brother); 18-*Ijeremgbe*; 19-Football player; 20-Female *onyemgbe* with mirror; 21-A lady (*onye missus*); 22-Female tailor; 23-A lady; 24-Ala's queen among women (Ezenwanyeala) with four children; 25-Viper; 26-A father (*nnaukwu*); 27-His son; 28-A whiteman at window (*nwa beke*); 29-A whiteman at window (*nwa beke*); 30-Oriefi Ala (an *agbara*); 31-Police for Ala; 32-A snake (*eru*); 33, 34, 35, 36-Amadioha Ala, his wife, his son, his daughter; 37, 38, 39, 40, 41-Delivering mother, her child (emerging), midwife, standing nurse, standing nurse; 42, 43, 44, 45-Four *ndimgbe*; 46-Orphan; 47, 48, 49-Leopard (*agu*), lion (*dom*), Okpangu; 50, 51, 52-Drummer, dancer, dancer; 53, 54, 55-Egwu musicians; 56, 57, 58-Egwu dancers; 59-Hunchback copulating with 60-*mgbeknwaokpere*; 61, 62-*Madu bu ewu*; 63-Man writing book at desk; 64, 65-Motorcyclist (*onyeigwe*), dog; 66, 67-Obube Ala's wife, Obube Ala (an *agbara*); 68, 69-Diviner's wife, diviner (*dibia*); 70-Okorosia masker (Agiriga Okorosia Ala); 71-Pretty woman (Ochonma Ala); 72, 73-Telephone officer, businessman; 74-Court messenger (*kotima*); 75-Airplane pilot.

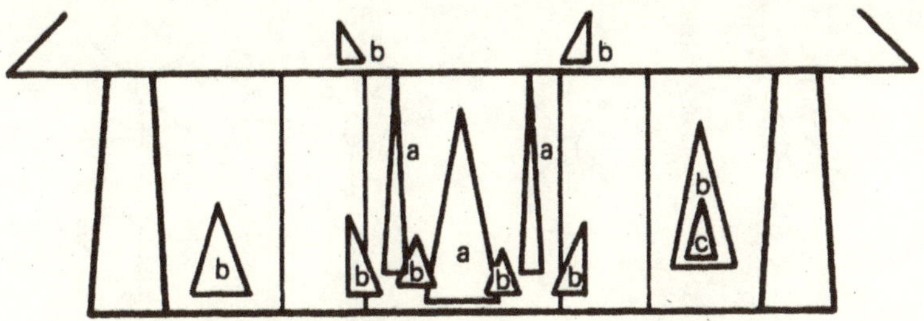

Side One: 12 figures (a = 3, b = 8, c = 1, d = 0)

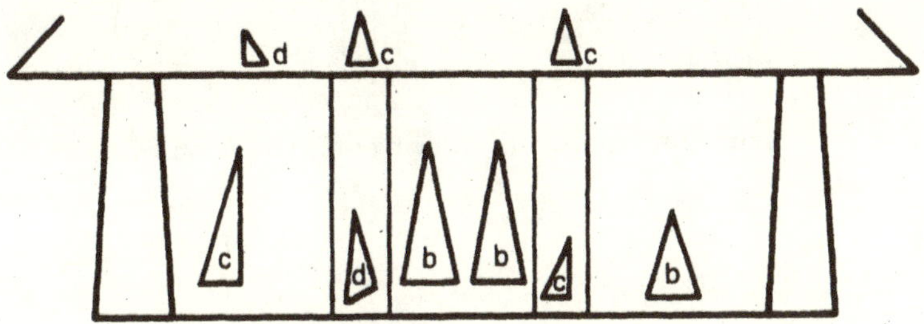

Side Two: 9 figures (a = 0, b = 3, c = 4, d = 2)

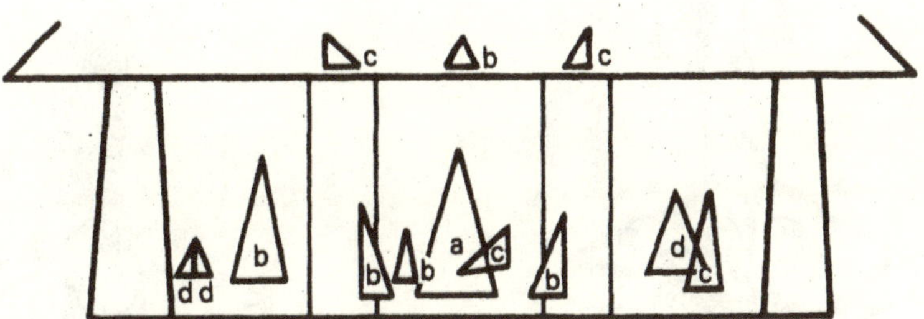

Side Three: 12 figures (a = 1, b = 5, c = 3, d = 3)

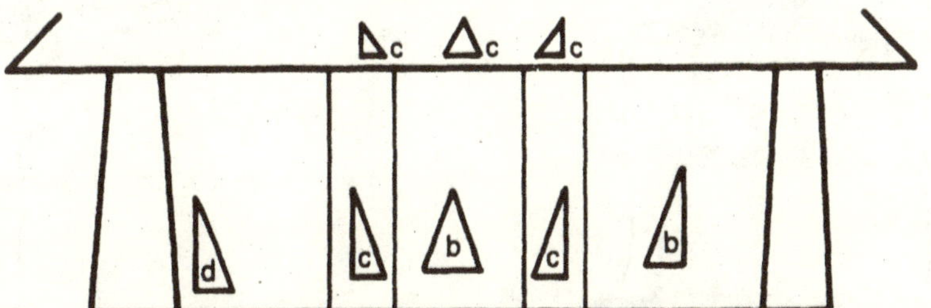

Side Four: 8 figures (a = 0, b = 2, c = 5, d = 1)

Sketch elevations, Mbari to Ala, Umugote Orishaeze, showing figure distributions on the hieratic continuum. Scale of formality: a = most formal, d = least.

Figure 13. Diagram showing the relative formality of sides and the placement of figures.

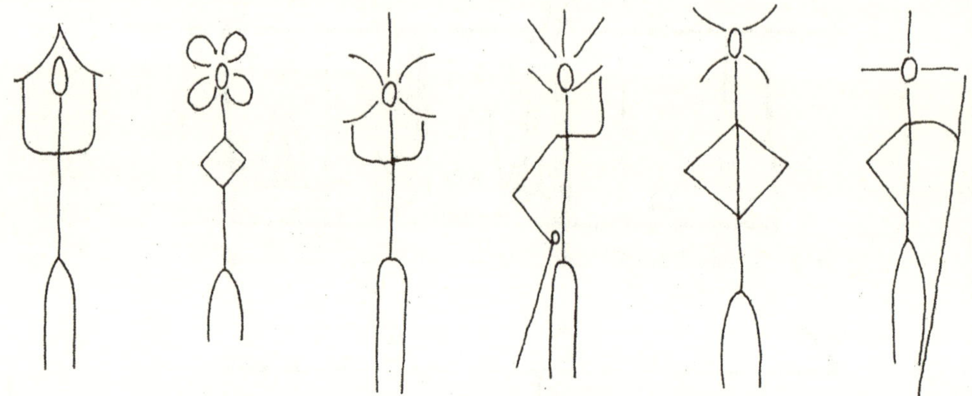

Figure 14. Schematic drawing of *ijeremgbe* poses.

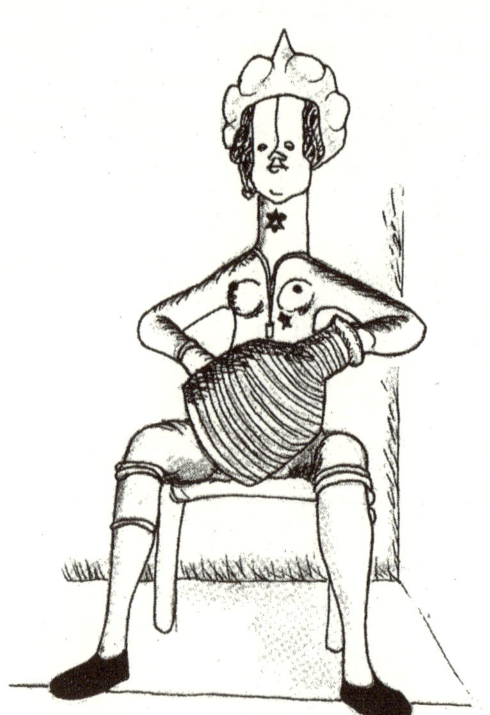

Figure 15. Woman with a demijohn.

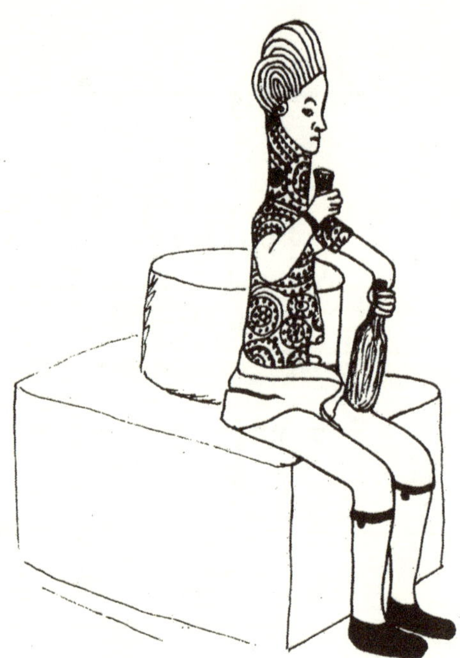

Figure 16. Woman with a bottle.

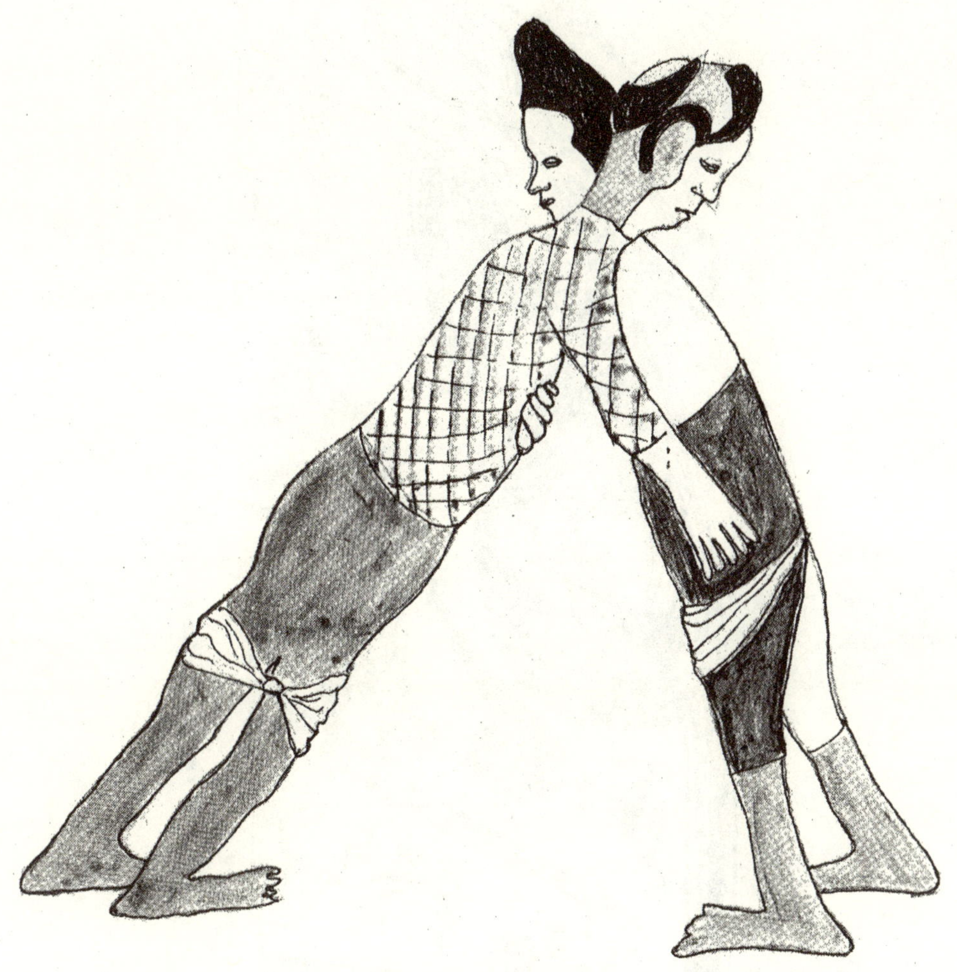

Figure 17. Wrestlers.

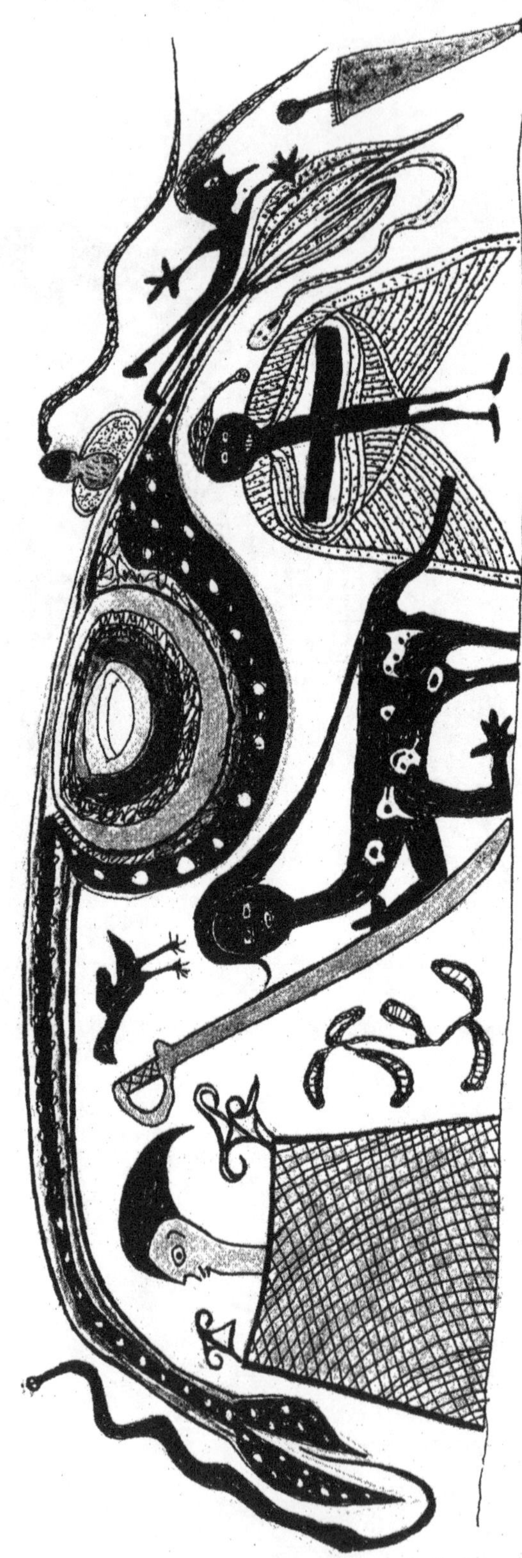

Figure 18. An upper wall painting by Ugo.

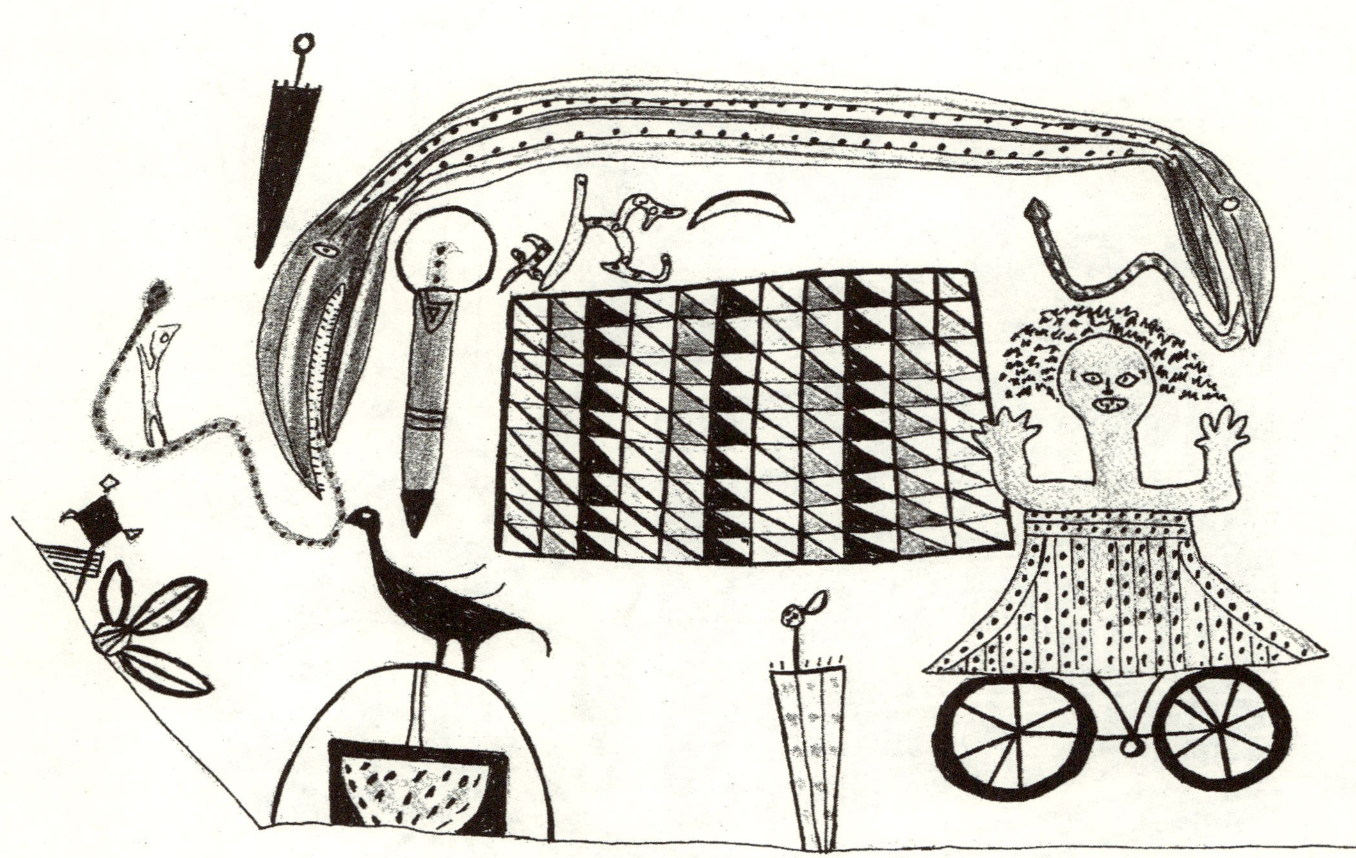

Figure 19. Upper wall painting by Ugo. The cloth and the rainbow are standard subjects.

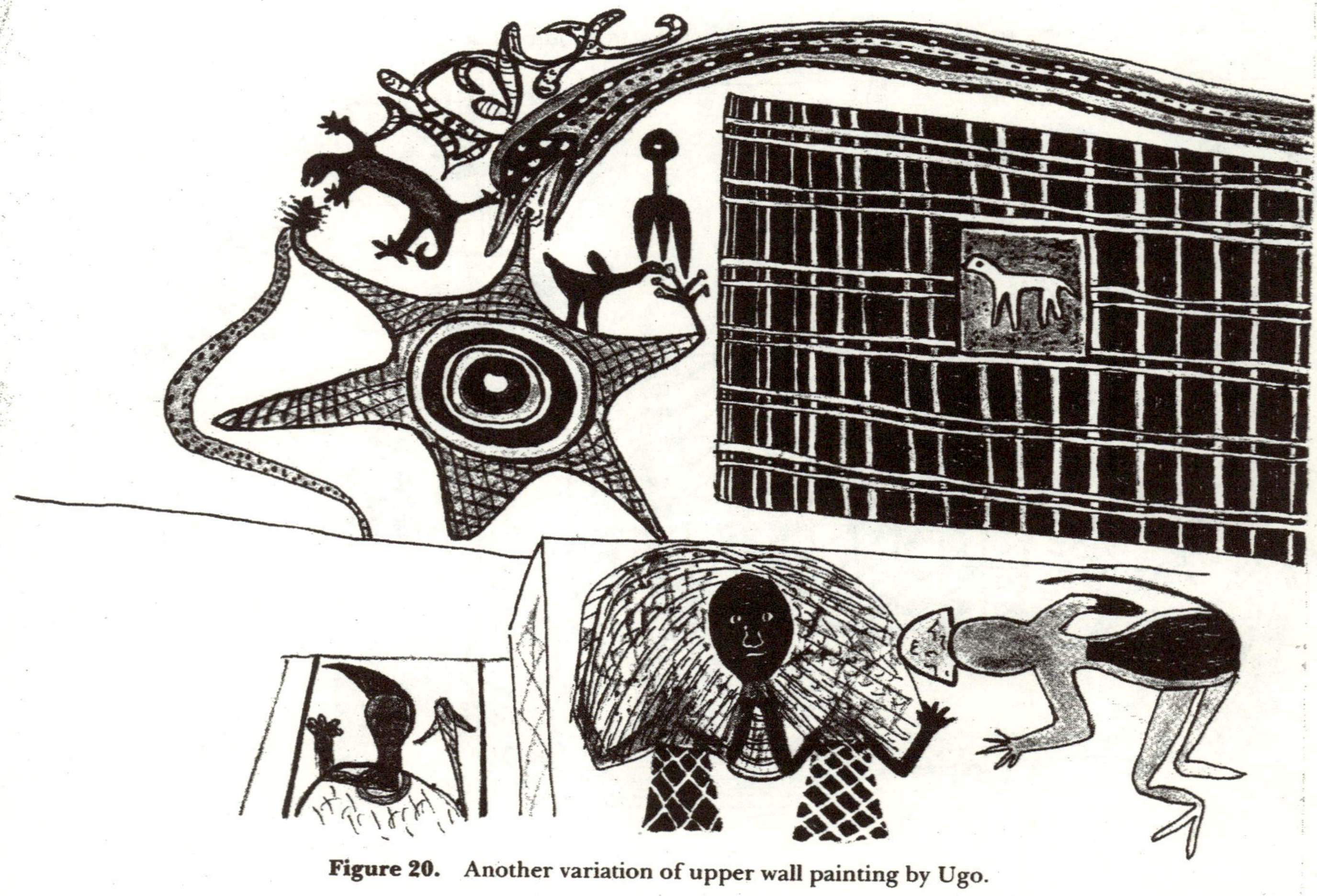

Figure 20. Another variation of upper wall painting by Ugo.

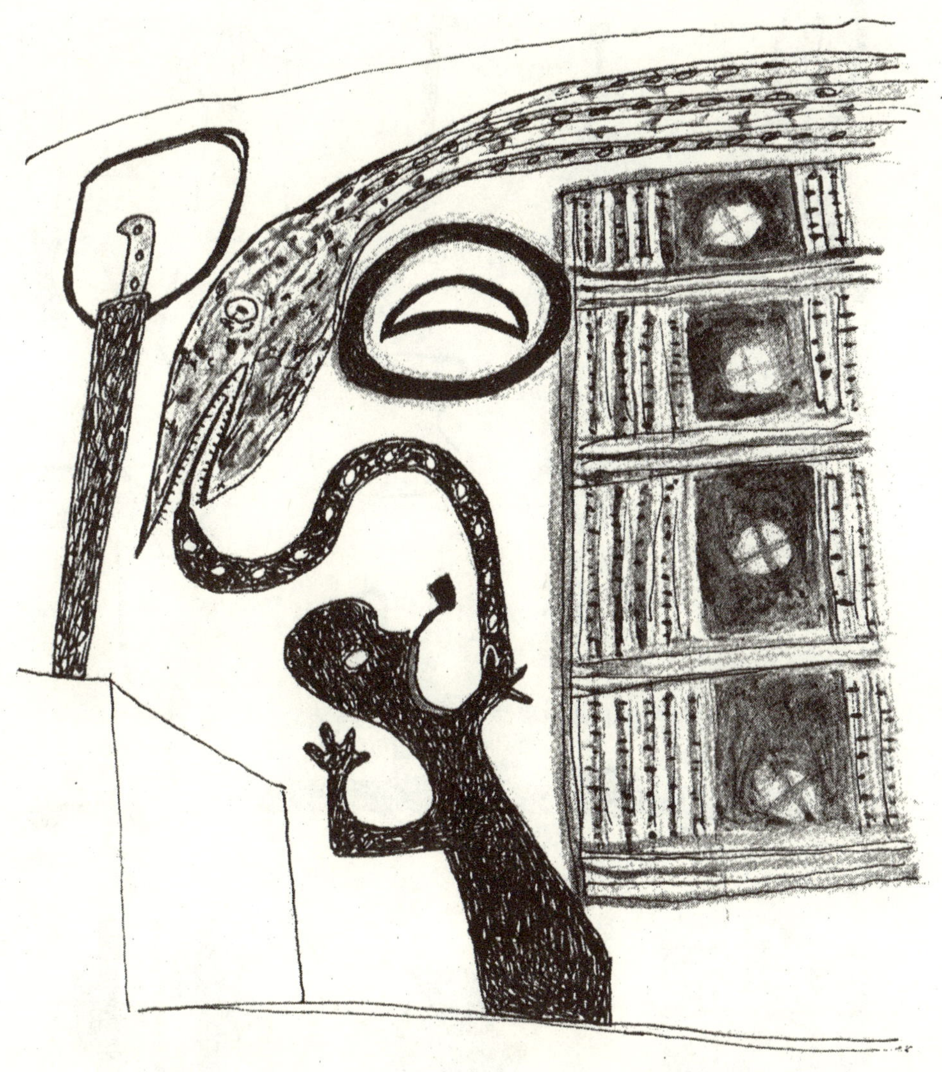

Figure 21. Recurrent and new elements characterize Ugo's paintings on upper walls.

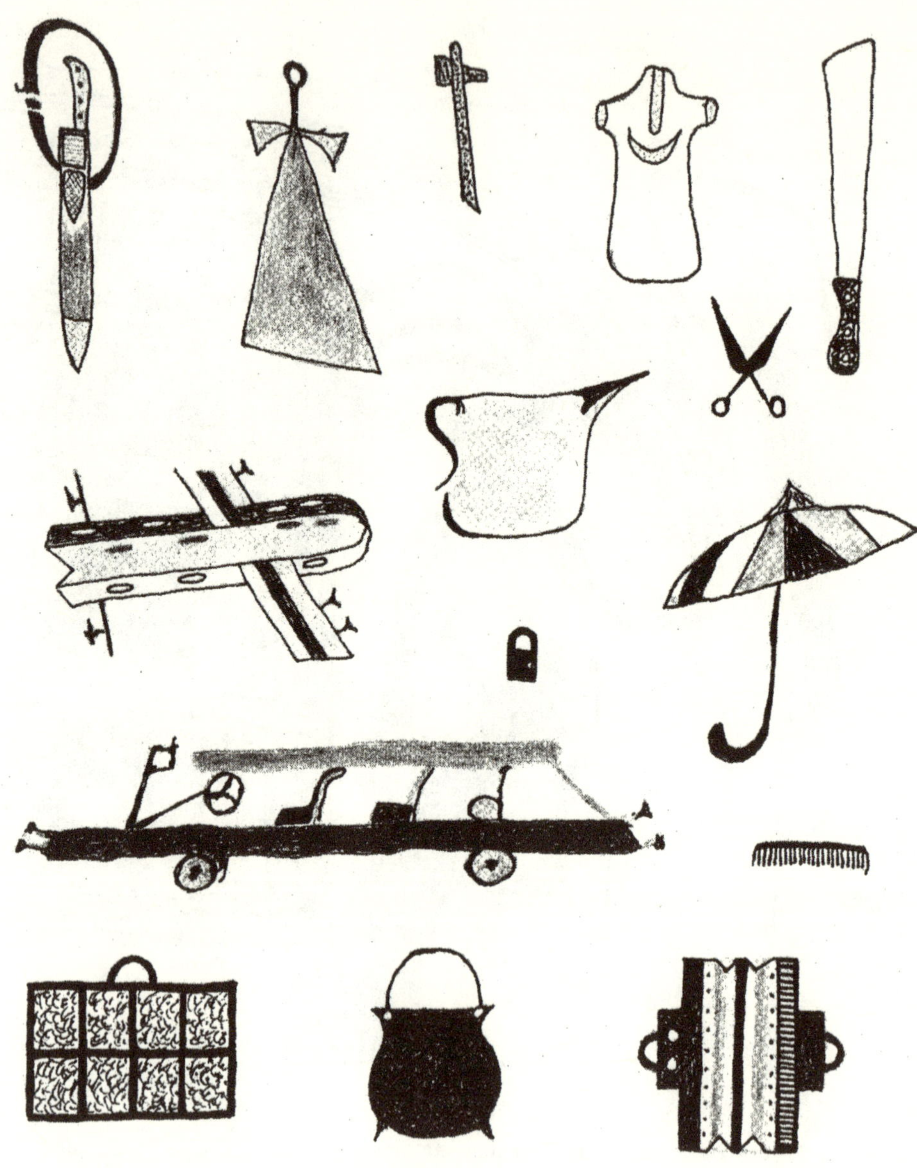

Figure 22. A selection of actual objects depicted on upper walls.

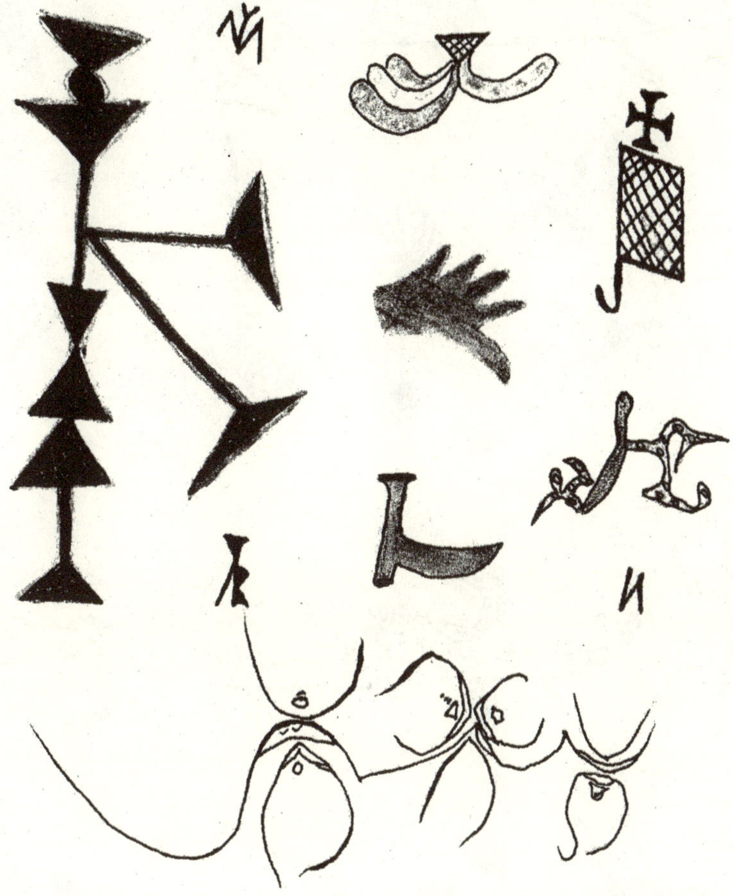

Figure 23. Abstract or nonrepresentational shapes seen on upper walls.

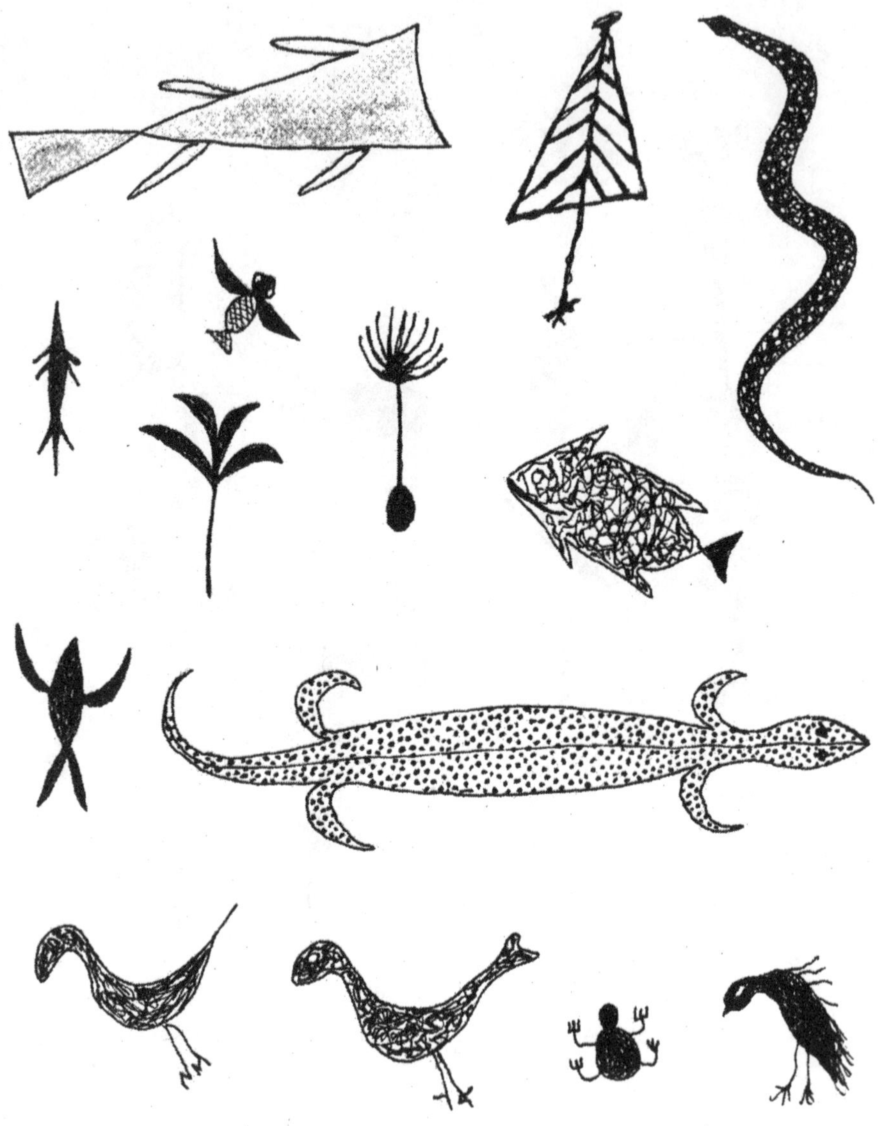

Figure 24. Plant and animal images depicted on upper walls.

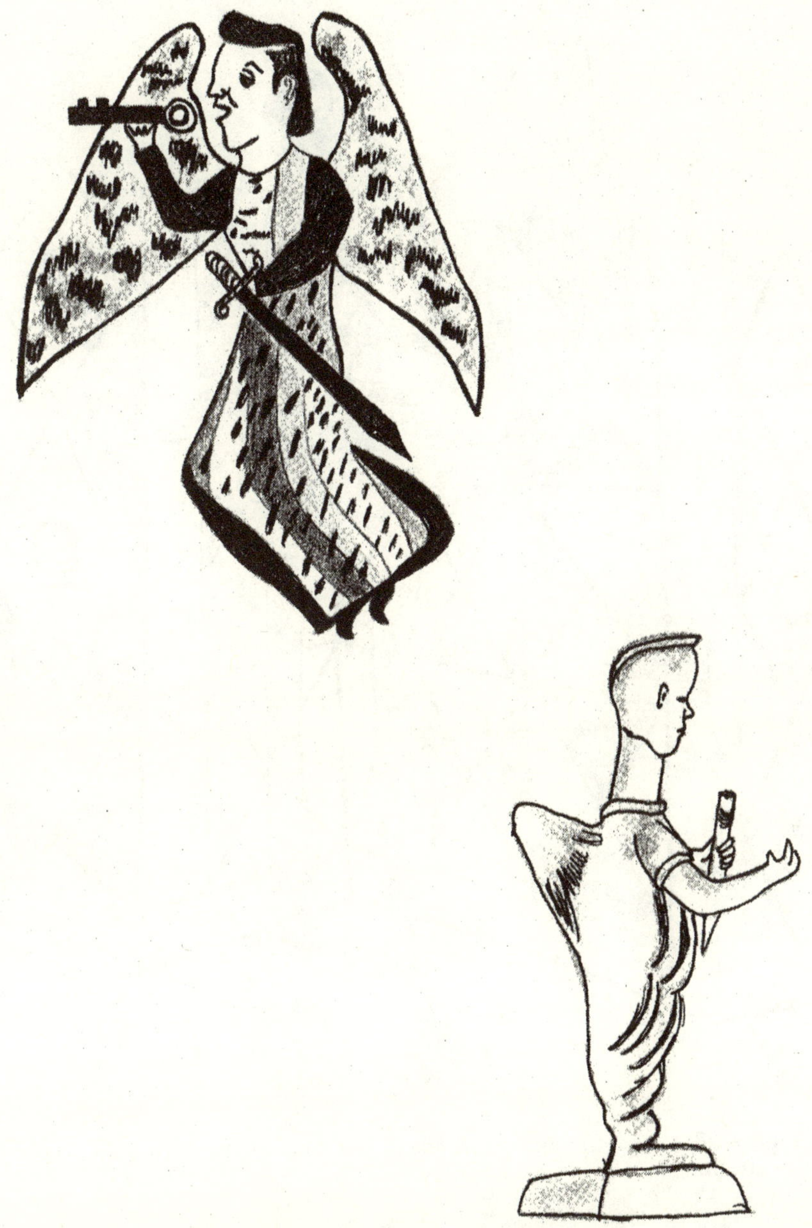

Figure 25. A painting (*a*) and a sculpture (*b*) representing angels.

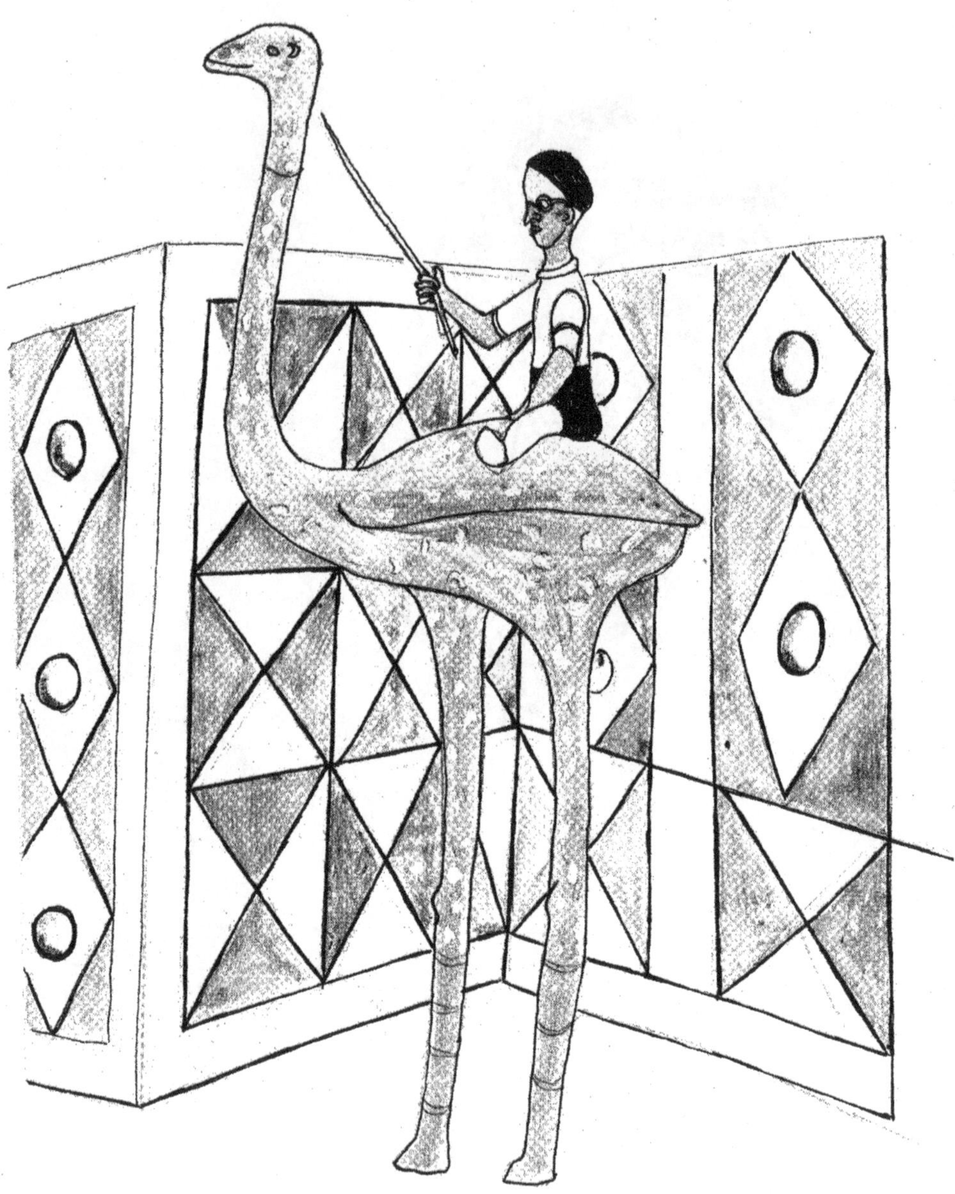

Figure 26. A group common since at least the 1930s: a boy riding an ostrich.

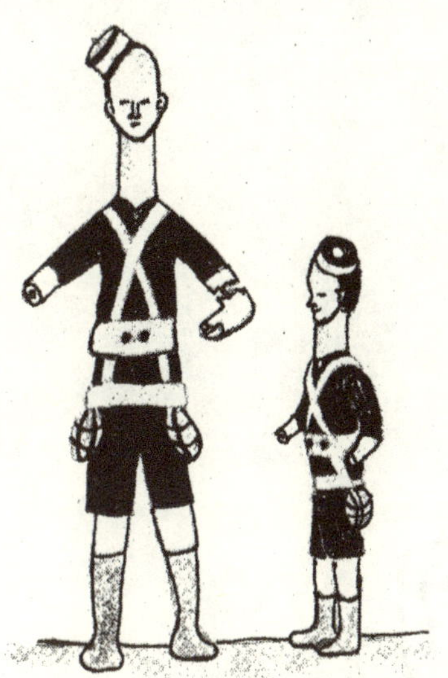

Figure 27. Ogidi, the giant policeman, shown in relation to a figure of normal size.

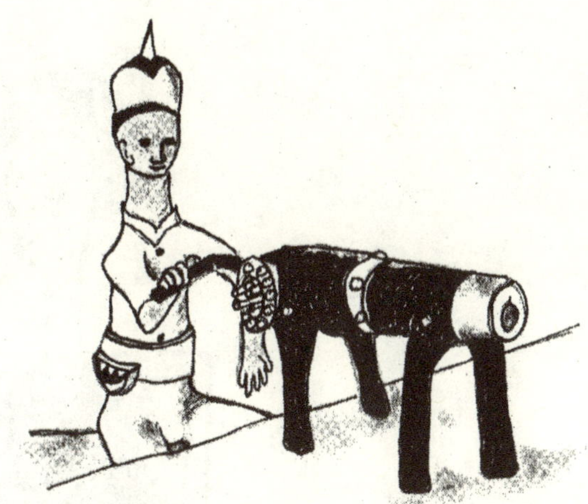

Figure 28. Soldier and Gatling gun.

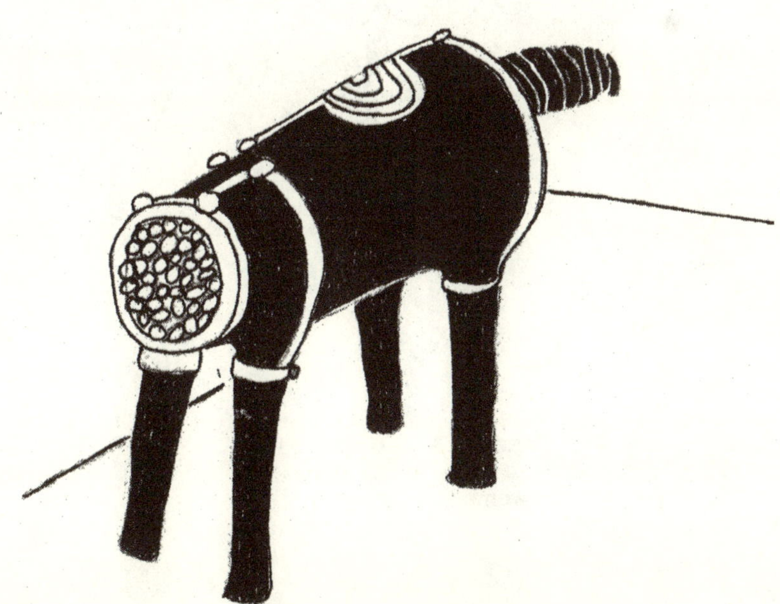

Figure 29. Gatling gun.

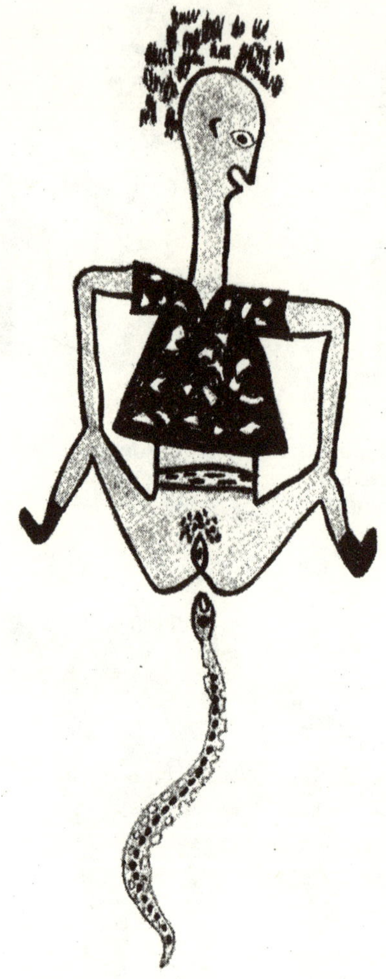

Figure 30. Upper wall painting of a shameless woman.

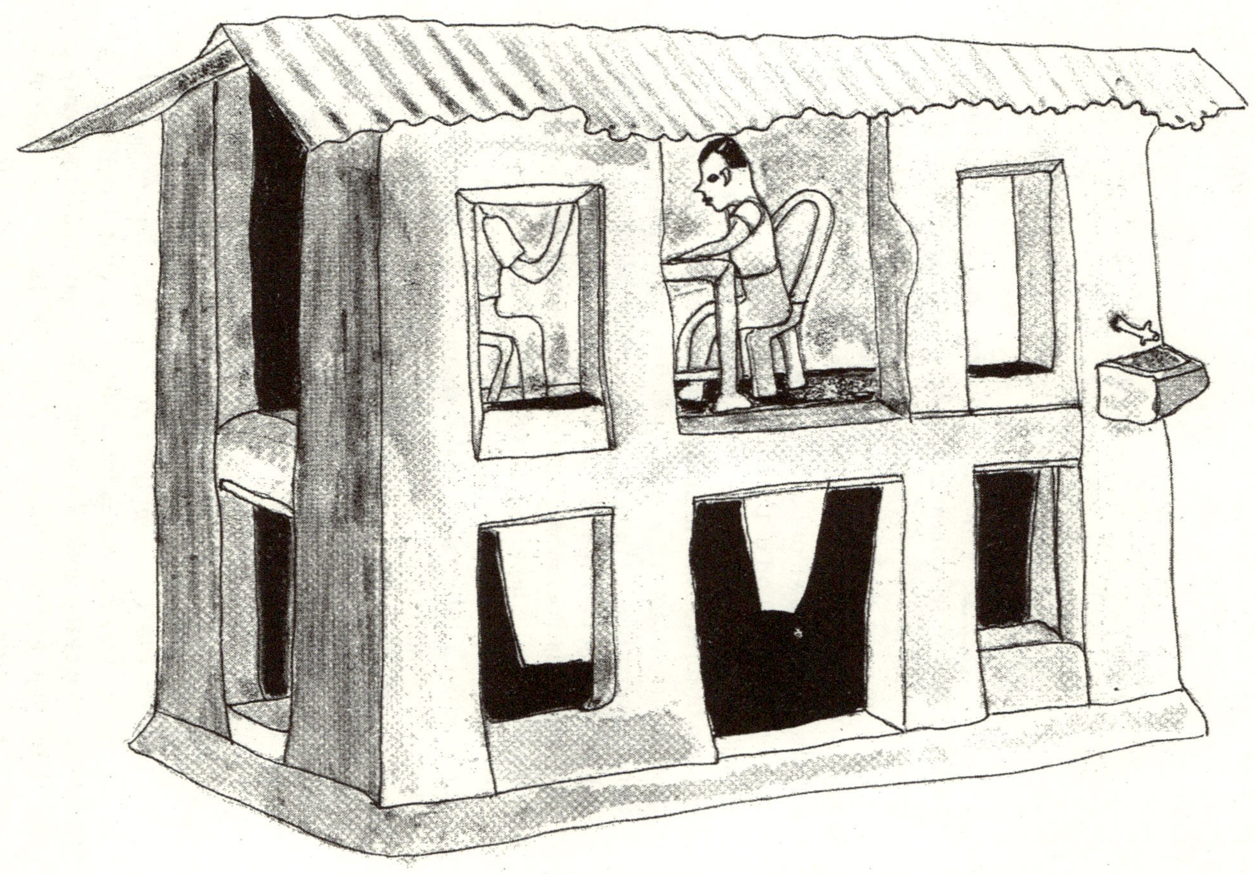

Figure 31. A miniature "storied building" called "Zik's house."

4 Form

Whether an Owerri Igbo person or an analytic Westerner, the mbari visitor knows he is in the presence of a consciously planned and carefully executed work of art. The Owerri person when questioned about this might reply that if mbari were not beautiful, there would be no sense whatever in building it. People will say, "Mbari is the crown of our god,"[1] as if to emphasize the colorful, decorative orchestration of the god's "fancy" house. The fact that this is an artistic display, and not a god's real house, is well known. This discussion of form and an analysis of mbari houses as illusions, works of interrelated sculpture and architecture, are consistent therefore with the Owerri Igbo's vision of his own world. We are not isolating a "work of art" that perhaps only we would label as such.

Component parts of mbari will first be described and analyzed: the site, architecture, sculpture, figural styles, and wall painting, each treated separately. Then these sections will be integrated in a discussion of mbari as an artistic unity. In this chapter I shall refer to various parts of many mbari houses rather than confining analysis to a single example. This is necessary to cover the significant variations in form. When generalities are expressed the reader may assume we are discussing a hypothetical but typical mbari of the larger sort, probably one made before 1960.

The Mbari Site

An mbari house is not simply erected in any convenient place. It is usually built upon, and comes to dominate, a precisely located sacred area, the "face of the god," *ihu agbara,* which has been in existence as both a religious and an artistic entity long before the mbari is built—twenty years or more in some cases. When a village changes its site the *ihu Ala* is one of the first plots of ground located, by divination; it is cleared, "landscaped," and consecrated; unlike domestic compounds it must be completed before the new site may be occupied. Men must care for and house their gods. The sacred sites of the Owerri area are of two main types, differentiated by the principles on which they are ordered, which may be either "concentric" or "rectilinear."[2]

The concentrically organized "face of the god," exemplified by that for the goddess Afo at Umuoye Etche (fig. 2), gives strong emphasis to the large tree chosen to represent the deity. Such a focus is achieved by clustering vegetation around the tree so as to expand its image, and by directing vision and circulation thence by the judicious location of other plants and objects (fig. 2, pl. 9). The main access path to this ritual area, located next to the priest's compound, leads directly to a secondary clump of shrine trees that soon catches the visitor's attention. From there he is pulled toward the sanctuary by the funnelling effect of the trimmed secondary growth on either side of the wide, carefully swept path. As he enters the sanctuary, he passes under an arched shrine, while his gaze is involuntarily drawn to the focal clump of trees and ritual objects. Thus the plan, aided by the log benches and a "carpet" of sacrificed iron rods, *igwe,* leads him to the "heart of the god," *obi agbara.* The small "house of god," *ulo agbara,* containing such things as the wooden Agwushi figures attached to each deity, the "kitchen" and other ritual props, is just behind this area, nearly obscured by the plantings that bulk out the "heart." The entire site may seem to be random but is actually carefully planned.

In contrast, rectilinear sacred sites (fig. 7) depend less on clustering and more on the linear disposition of shrine trees. The striking patterns presented impress one as landscape architecture, for the screen-like lines of trees, like the planting of a formal garden, order the whole site. Small pieces of roofing zinc and bottles or pots sunk into the ground for libations reinforce the geometry. Although the space is open, leaving all parts of the site visible, formal arrangements do establish circulation patterns within the area. In sites without mbari houses, attention is focused on the sacred tree of the deity or her house, or both.

Owerri village planning tends not to stress long vistas that terminate at visually or culturally prominent buildings or sites. Apart from market approaches, roads and paths lead to other roads or end at nonfocal locations. Hence the visitor seldom notices sacred areas until he is near them, and to see them fully he must often turn to face them. The sketch plan (fig. 8) of a small village of the more formal linear Owerri type shows three sacred sites, *ihu agbara,* in their usual positions at the ends of the residential areas beside the compounds of their respective priests. This sort of planning usually determines the locations of mbari, since they are most often built on part of the sacred site. Thus mbari are generally found at the sides of roads rather than at their ends.

Although divination determines the general location of an mbari, the artist himself pegs out the perimeter on the ground, squaring off the new building in relation to the tree lines or small buildings already on the site (fig. 7). Mbari siting is invariably appropriate because the house itself is so dominant visually that focus and circulation are reorganized by its location and orientation. Previous focal points dwindle in comparison. When an mbari is built, it is as if a formal garden had been much altered, but somehow perfected and completed, by the addition of an elaborate fountain.

Architecture

For a short time in the mbari construction process before any figures or colors have been added, the emerging building can be seen as pure architecture, solids and spaces, columns and rooms, stairs and walls. If we isolate and examine the underlying mbari structure, we can better understand some of the formal and spatial complexities of the completed monument, although the building is obviously not meant to be seen publicly at this stage. The plan of the mbari for Obiala at Ndiama Obube may be considered typical (fig. 9); variations from this norm will be discussed below. The basic structural elements of mbari are a proportionately small enclosed box supporting a steep roof that extends well out from this central mass, over four corner pillars. The interior block, occupying about one-third of the ground plan, is supported in turn by eight buttresses, two springing perpendicularly from each wall. Each buttress is cut into four or five steps ascending toward the central core, and sometimes the steps have three-part lateral divisions as well. This plan—four columns enclosing an externally buttressed box—is fundamental to mbari except where its small size precludes an elaborate interior structure. Except for the core, which is seldom used, no space is *interior* space; the house is open, with spatial demarcations more implicit than explicit.

In most mbari houses therefore each side has a mass-space-mass rhythm of ABA, or ABABABA for the entire wall, with the central space being the largest (color plate 1, fig. 9). In mbari with central cores there are few variations on this plan. A low wall around the whole structure, broken only at the central niche on each side, often links the four corner columns and marks off the sets of deep niches, each of which is open on three sides.

The horizontal axis formed by the base and roof lines is modified by vertical steps climbing each buttress. Lateral buttress steps reduce the severity of buttress masses while easing the visual transition to the spaces on either side. Although the corner pillars rise to seven or eight feet, the interior walls are double that height; and because the steps end at buttress height the four upper walls present vast plain surfaces of mud. They are not visible from a distance, however, because of the rather low overhanging roof. Sometimes window holes relieve the severity of two of the four flat surfaces, those on the gable ends (pl. 50). The tops of the walls intersect with the roof, which pitches steeply down over the viewer as if to shelter him as well as the mbari under its broad expanse. Four heavy columns and the base wall anchor the open house in place, while the buttresses carry the eye diagonally up and forward to the interior mass, a closed block. The less massive buttresses and columns complement this central block and modify its heaviness. The geometry of an mbari plan, therefore, resolves not only in a simple ABA rhythm of mass and space, but also in hieratic ranking in which the central niches dominate because they are larger and have solid backdrops that contrast with the more open lateral niches. Nothing in domestic building nor in any architecture from surrounding Igbo or non-Igbo areas competes with the visual complexity and sophistication of these structural features, for virtually all domestic architecture deals only with enclosed space of simple rectangular plan rather than the implied demarcated spaces in rhythms and hierarchies that characterize mbari.

In contrast with the impression of measured space, there is a marked freedom in the execution of edges, angles, surfaces, and measurements which suggests such paradoxes as "unruled straight lines," "rounded right angles," or "unmeasured modules." Much of the work is freehand, measured only by sensitive eyes. For this reason there is a superficial unevenness, an imprecise geometry that in no way destroys the illusion of straightness, flatness, angularity. On the contrary, an impression of marked precision and control is presented, especially at a distance. Textured, irregular surfaces offer variety in the close view. The stepped buttresses, notably, are wider and heavier than is structurally necessary, and neither they, the clay walls, nor the columns actually support the roof, which is completed on its wooden frame before the work with mud is begun.[3] These factors illuminate the artistic character of mbari architecture, since the shapes and subdivisions of "structural" members serve primarily as a visual or programmatic function and not a structural one.

Despite the prevalence of the Obube mbari plan just described,[4] there were in fact many variations in the sizes and plans of houses observed in 1966-67 (fig. 10). The rule is clear: the smaller the mbari, the simpler the plan, and similarly, the larger and more complex the sculptural program, the more elaborate becomes the architectural setting. No single standard plan exists even though through the years artists have agreed—unconsciously—that the one already discussed (fig. 9) is usually the most suitable. Even that type has varied roof shapes; a common earlier form, made with palm mat shingles, is a conical roof raised on a tall central post (pl. 26).[5] Some individuals, however, favor other plans. Akalazu frequently uses a cross plan (figs. 10g and h) for medium-sized houses while Ugwuanya has employed a modified "T" plan on several occasions (fig. 10f). All mbari of these types—and hence probably the invention of these two plans, are attributed, respectively, to these artists. When building larger mbari, other artists have increased the number of stepped buttresses on occasion (figs. 10i, j, and k), and if a cloister is present, some new departures usually mark the designs of these outbuildings.

Although columns too have a prevailing squared profile and section, figure 11 clearly illustrates that innovative solutions of many types are welcome. I found no evidence of any special meanings being attributed to variants of either plans or column designs, which instead testify to the inventiveness and independence of artists who observe the existing convention to some extent when solving visual problems, but who nevertheless more or less constantly add to and reinterpret forms. Innovative artists are allowed plenty of creative latitude.

The architectural space of a medium-large unadorned mbari is analogous to that of outdoor monuments, for one walks only around the structure and not inside it (figs. 10m, 10n, and 12; pls. 10, 11, 22, and 75). These clay structures create a public and open series of spaces as if conceived more for crowds than for intimate groups of visitors. The visible spatial organization is an orderly, predictable succession of masses and voids; yet one knows there is something behind the heavy wall, inside the block, and is somewhat puzzled about it since the area cannot be seen. This is especially true when there are windows and sealed doors leading inward, but no real means of access. If a cloister or gallery rings the mbari on three or four sides, the experience of space is altered to become somewhat like walking through the street of a miniature village in which the houses have no façades (color plates 5 and 6, pl. 75, figs. 10m and n). An mbari house may be relatively small, but when empty of its clay inhabitants, it lacks a sense of scale and the illusion is of a large and spacious environment.

Although the hidden interior puzzles the visitor, the part he does see is honest, simple, and severe. Without sculpture, the heavy columns and buttresses enclose neutral voids (pl. 18). Lacking paint, an mbari is barren, an unrelieved mass of clay. The plates and "slivers of iron" inserted in the mud, however, tend to modify blank surfaces somewhat by diminishing the impression of unyielding solidity (pl. 20). The plates and slivers appear to have been pushed in, as if this actually difficult task were simply and quickly done,[6] and the modified mud surfaces then become visually ambiguous; they appear less impenetrable at this stage, but they remain stark and heavy.

Sculpture

The empty stage set of an mbari needs actors to enliven it, to bring it into perspective and scale, to give it meaning. Modeled clay figures and animals do this admirably by transforming bleak architecture into an exciting, entertaining environment (color plate 11). Indeed, we have already seen that an "ordinary building" *becomes* mbari only with the insertion of plates, the activity that signals the onset of "yam collection" and figure modeling. Sculptures then do not only "adorn" mbari; they actually create it.

Although confronted by a bewildering variety of sculptured images, I tried to discover what figures were essential. Several artists[7] listed the figures which they felt should "be included in a proper mbari." Not surprisingly, their lists varied somewhat, particularly when they exceeded ten or twelve figures. A conflation of five lists follows:

The owner of the house
Ijeremgbe (two or four)
Amadioha
Mamy Wata
Leopard
Python
"Hippopotamus," or elephant
Okpangu
"Displayed" woman
Woman in childbirth
White man (*beke*)
Policeman, soldier, or court messenger
Ada (1st daughter of the *agbara*)
Pretty girl or pregnant woman

Most artists extended the list, however, with such statements as: "The artist has to put in all those essential things, and out of his mind can put in some new things. You know the world is always changing, so we try to represent the changes."[8] Variations and surprises must therefore be included in the sculptural program of mbari art along with the more formalistic, inherited, and expected figures that normally take precedence over them.

Unvoiced rules dictate both the organization of sculpture within the entire mbari and the placement of individual figures within each side. To ease the identification of the various mbari sides in this section I will number them from one to four (fig. 6). The four sides of an mbari are usually balanced both internally and with respect to one another, creating a visible order of sides and of parts within each side. The side belonging to the "owner of the house," for example, is never in doubt. The artist establishes her absolute preeminence both by choosing as her side the one most open to access paths and by hierarchical arrangements on that side (pl. 27, color plate 1, fig. 10). His formal devices include: placing her well back in space; seating her higher than other figures, with her feet raised on a bent iron bar; hedging her about with as many as eight or ten subsidiary figures of varying smaller sizes ranked in front, behind, and to the sides; and rendering her in a style different from that of other figures. The owner's pose and those of her nearby subordinates are frozen in rigid frontality. In many mbari houses, moreover, all the figures on side one are frontal and more or less formally posed, thereby extending the hierarchical impulse outward from the central niche (color plate 1). Side three often contains another central and formal deity or group to balance that of side one (pl. 28). Side three usually ranks second to side one in formality, side two comes next, and side four last. This hierarchy may be seen in a schematic diagram of the relative formality of figures in the mbari at Umugote Orishaeze (fig. 13).

In the architectural plan, the breadth and depth of the central niche on every side is calculated to accommodate a specific figure or group; the space of these niches plays a part, therefore, in the hierarchical arrangement that descends rhythmically to the corners. The schematic elevation of side one at Umugote Orishaeze (fig. 13) for example, reveals the following rather involved rhythm (*A* = clay column or wall, *B* = figure): *A b a bbb B bbb a bb A*. That at Umuahiagu is: *A bbb a bb Bb bb a bbb A*. All sides have well-defined central niches and firmly anchored corners. Symmetry is often modified with figures in varying numbers, sizes, shapes, and positions, so there is sometimes considerable irregularity. And on some sides and corners, there may be considerable informality, more especially if, as at Lagwo and Umuowa (fig. 10f, pl. 29) two sides have modified plans, without central niches.

If side one contains the most formal arrangement and poses, often with all figures frontal, seated, and stiff, this rule seldom applies to side four and never to the cloister, where groupings are rather arbitrary or random, and individual poses far less formal than in the mbari proper (color plates 1, 5, and 6; fig. 12). It also follows that an mbari with a cloister is more formal on all four sides than one without, since the cloister can house oddly constituted groups and those less calculated to sustain grandeur and dignity. A hierarchical principle similar to that found in medieval manuscript illumination may be observed here: aberrant poses or activities, fabulous semi-human creatures, and figures showing the closest observation of naturalistic form usually appear in the least prominent places. In mbari these may be at corners, up under the roof, in the cloister, or at the very least in subordinate positions away from the most visible and central parts of the house.

Figural Styles

The compositions and figural styles of individual sculptures and groups are analogous to the interplay of materials and structural elements of mbari architecture. Again we have a light framework overlaid and weighted with clay. But in mbari architecture the massive additions transform and almost entirely obscure the framework, whereas in sculpture the skeletal armature determines the final shape of the figure. As in figural placement, we find a balancing of hierarchical, formal traits with those of more random, irregular, and informal character.

Like most figural traditions in African art, mbari style can best be explained by a continuum, each point on which represents a different admixture of polar traits: hierarchical and informal, schematized and naturalistic, static and lively, monumental and familiar. Before attempting to isolate the common denominators of all mbari sculpture, four divisions in this stylistic continuum may be examined. Of these four modes, two are major, two subsidiary. The main formal divison, here called Iconic, includes most deity groups and is in fact limited to them. It is balanced on the *informal* side by the Popular mode. The minor modes include Schematic, falling within the Iconic, and Idealized, a transitional mode between the Iconic and the Popular. This continuum and the modes on it may be visualized on the diagram below:

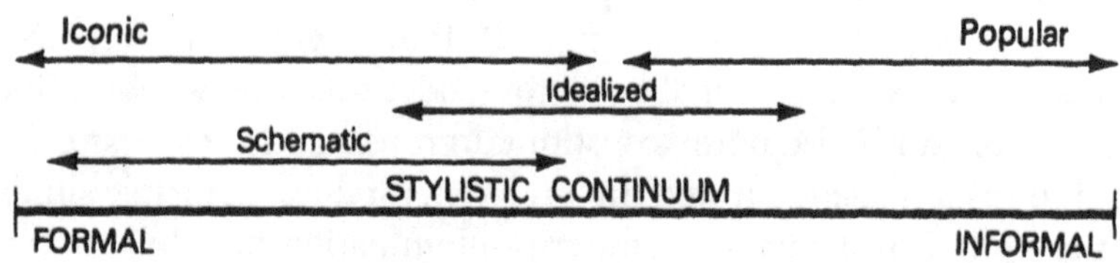

In discussing these modes I will begin with the work of a single "mainstream" mbari sculptor, Nnaji, and supplement his work with other examples.

The Iconic Mode: Sculptures in the iconic mode are central and dominant within mbari sides, and are often supported by descending ranks of architectural and sculptural forms (pl. 27, color plate 1). The word "Iconic" is chosen to indicate the essential link between morphology and iconography by suggesting a narrow segment in a formal and metaphysical hierarchy largely composed of supporting, more "popular" sculpture. Although most *agbara* figures fall into this style category, its apotheosis is seen in the owners of fairly large mbari houses, such as the Ala group at Ndiama Obube (color plate 4). The stylistic and compositional traits manifest here crystallize the character of the Iconic mode: an hieratic setting, symmetry, frontality, monumentality, and in general a distinct formalism. This hierarchical group is an essential element in the sculptural conception and thus has an effect on the style and impact of Ala herself. The backdrop behind her helps to define the structural space, closed on three sides, in which the group is placed.

Ala is stiffly posed within a pyramid of space in which she forms the dominant organizing element. The pyramid's weighted base is the lower pedestal seat and the python (originally longer but now broken); the apex is just over Ala's head. The entire group is rigidly frontal, with a strict symmetry broken only, significantly, by Ala's knife. The pyramid subdivides both vertically and horizontally. A strong vertical axis is modified by spatial interplay between diagonal and horizontal elements, and finally checked by the white face and the "T" form of Ala's hairdress. This triangle, formed by headdress mirrors, is repeated several times in the balanced, rather complex composition.

The style and posture of the goddess herself echo the hieratic nature of the group. The rigidly erect and elongated torso column contrasts with lesser tubular shapes, the children and all the limbs, which are supporting elements. In this mode, too, artists use massive volumes and precise detailing to complement one another. Sculptural refinements and surface detailing are insignificant at a distance, but emerge at closer range to elaborate and particularize an image (color plate 4, pl. 27). Human proportions are also contrived to augment the impact of monumentality; the scale established in the attenuated torso of Nnaji's Ala becomes greater still in her heavy neck and in the face and headdress unit. In contrast, the arms and legs are reduced in size. An illusion of greater monumentality stems from the placement of this idealized figure among smaller and more naturalistically proportioned figures, including Ala's children, on the same side.

Despite excessive distortions, however, Ala's figure reveals the conventionalized but fairly organic naturalism, based on the observation and simplification of human forms, that is a general hallmark of mbari figural sculpture. Surfaces are smooth and flowing, especially in the torso, where the navel rupture and breasts swell organically to simulate flesh. Arms and legs project and articulate realistically. Although flesh-like surfaces are simplified, muscles are sometimes indicated, as in the calves which expand in a natural manner under the simulated brass leg bands.

Naturalistic details in the head, on the other hand, are expressively subordinate to bold patterns and large-scale masses. In this and most other female *agbara* figures (color plates 4 and 7, pls. 27 and 28), four units make up the cross-shaped head ensemble: a thick, attenuated neck, considered an ideal of beauty by Owerri Igbos; three flanges (sometimes five, see color plate 10) of dressed hair, which balance the neck and combine with it to form the arms of the cross; and the central facial area. Despite the emphasis on striking shapes and color contrasts, however, detailed accents in the face contribute to and refine the general expressive statement. Most female *agbara* have shallow concave facial profiles resulting from the bulky size of the hairdress. But because they are generally seen frontally, faces of such deities required no greater depth.

The face of one goddess (pl. 30), a masterpiece of mbari sculpture, is modeled in rounded, subtly merging planes. The forehead is long, about one-third the height of the face, a ratio common to most figures in the Iconic mode (color plates 4 and 7). Realistically observed eyebrows in low relief funnel this plane downward into a fleshy nose with flared nostrils; the plane also flows into shallow eye depressions and out again in the mouth area to create a mild prognathism. Such naturalistic surfaces surround and integrate the more conventionalized eyes, mouth, and ears. Eyes and lips are simple cowry-shell shapes applied onto the facial surface, just as semi-naturalistic ears are pressed on beside the lateral hair wings. These elements combine to express a passive, aloof aura in this and similar figures. Some artists, however, prefer the more lifelike and alert expressions achieved by inserting white plate fragments in the eye sockets (color plate 10).

However, not all sculpture in the Iconic mode conforms with these two monuments, for all the figures, like the mode itself, are part of the formal continuum of mbari style. Thus in a single mbari all other deities differ somewhat from the owner of the house in composition and style, just as the owner (i.e., principal figure) of one mbari differs from the owner of the next. Such variations within the mode appear arbitrary at first glance; they are in fact arbitrary to the extent that each new mbari is more or less different from all previous solutions, that each artist combines traditional artistic components for each local situation while giving his own fresh interpretation to the tradition.

Formalism in the Iconic mode is so strong, however, that two general rules can be observed: Other deity figures in an mbari are subordinate to its owner, and the number of hierarchical elements present in any *agbara* group varies with the size of the house. Medium-sized mbari therefore bring fewer hieratic conventions to bear on the structure of the owner and in the house as a whole than are seen in large mbari. The main deity of a lesser house (pl. 22) is more like the larger mbari's side three *agbara* (pl. 28) (who will of course be subordinate to its owner [pl. 27]).

In these cases the reductions affect both composition and stylistic emphasis: fewer or less rigidly posed children and thus a smaller, less formal composition; less weighty pedestal seat; reduced size and scale of torso and head units, contributing to more naturalistic proportions;

decreased complexity and interpenetration of surrounding space; less strict frontality; greater asymmetry; and of course reductions in the extent and nature of external hierarchical support, whether figural, spatial, or architectural. Despite these variables, however, some conventions of the Iconic mode do remain constant. Expressive emphasis of the neck and head remains unchanged, as does the frontality and essential symmetry of the deity, though the children may become very informal. The figure is always seated and central, with symmetrical legs raised on an iron bar. The same components of naturalism in faces and body surfaces obtain in these subordinate god figures, and because of the more realistic proportions a closer reflection of life forms may be observed.

Among the subsidiary deities that manifest less rigid principles of hieratic structure are Amadioha (color plate 9), Mamy Wata (pls. 10 and 31), and the goddess with many children (pl. 8), often identified as Ekwunoche, who, when present, usually occupies a subsidiary side in larger houses owned by Ala or another deity.[9] The Amadioha at Orishaeze (color plate 9), who is balanced by his wife and is attired less formally than most female *agbara*, conveys an informal impression consistent with his subordinate placement.

Mamy Wata and Ekwunoche may lack the backdrop of a central niche, being placed in one of the corner spaces that are open to the rear (pl. 8). Their poses and elongated proportions, however, keep them in or on the margin of the Iconic mode. Mamy Wata usually sits with her legs crossed[10] (pls. 10, 13, and 31) and with her arms raised in a position identified as a favorable one for women to assume. Her neck is elongated and often ringed, qualities also equated with dignity and beauty. Other proportions, however, like her only slightly elongated headdress, may keep her style more in line with that of other female figures than with grandiose *agbara.*

The goddess with two children posed actively but symmetrically on each side (pl. 8) shows the extent to which the medium of modeled mud can be taken within the Iconic mode, for the smaller forms of the children's torsos and limbs are a cagelike structure woven around the sides and front of the central torso. This web of interconnecting forms, impossible in wood on this scale and seldom matched even in small wooden figures, dramatizes the expressive potentialities of the clay medium in spatial activation and interpenetration. Although the contrasts between formal *agbara* and less formal ones such as the Ekwunoche, Mamy Wata and Amadioha figures are great, their common structural characteristics nevertheless clearly set them apart from figures in the Popular mode discussed below.

The Schematic Mode: Before turning to informal style traits, it is important to discuss a class of figures that forms a minor mode, the Schematic, clearly related to the hieratic Iconic mode. See color plate 4 and pls. 17, 22, and 27. Standing figures in relief, *ijeremgbe,* constitute this separate category because of the degree to which they are conventionalized, even in comparison with the more formal deity groups. A pair of these figures usually appears in every mbari that contains more than ten or twelve figures. As elongated, spare, standing images, *ijeremgbe* are proportioned according to their pose and their expressive possibilities which, in turn, depend on the unvarying placement of the figures in a tall, narrow space, either behind the *agbara* (to the sides of the small door) or on column surfaces. *Ijeremgbe* are always attenuated in legs, torso, and neck, and they generally have bold lateral patterns of dressed hair. The variable treatment of arms and hairdress signals a recurrent feature of mbari sculpture as a whole, for throughout the genre these two elements receive the most arbitrary sculptural handling. With the exception of the arms, which occasionally project out from the wall on armatures, all *ijeremgbe* body parts are integral to the wall surface, though in very high relief. Arms may be proportionate to torsos, but more often they are either reduced or further elongated, depending upon the expressive pattern the artist desires.

Thus, in spite of high relief, artists conceive of *ijeremgbe* more as two-dimensional geometric designs than as palpable human beings. This is their greatest difference from the other figures, which without exception and despite frequently rigid poses, exist as corporeal entities in circulating space. From afar *ijeremgbe* appear to be part of the surface decoration of the wall or column, for they are often pinioned midway between top and bottom, with their feet several inches above the ground. Variations in their poses can be conveyed nearly as well in stick-figure sketches as in photographs (fig. 14).

Such unnatural attenuation and schematic pattern-making does not, of course, allow the same degree of naturalistic treatment seen in the Iconic mode. In fact *ijeremgbe* are inorganic and unnatural, with emaciated parts drawn out and stiffly articulated, conforming more to abstract design than to life. Almost all larger body parts are simple pipelike shapes of varying size. Yet at close range one sees about the same degrees of conventionalism and naturalism as characterize figures in the Iconic mode. Surfaces and details—beads, bandoliers (*ohihe*), necklaces, anklets, and staffs—are carefully rendered, as details are on all mbari figures (pl. 17). The faces of *ijeremgbe* are also subtly modeled, with the same overlay of schematic features as in Iconic figures. Never, however, does such detailing intrude upon the distant impression of *ijeremgbe* as minor actors filling a prescribed, supporting role in the structure. In meaning, too, their role is supportive; they represent *ndimgbe* themselves, who are only means to an end and not the end itself.

The Popular Mode: This brings us to the less formal side of the stylistic continuum. As the word Popular implies, this style is preeminent in respect of sheer numbers of modeled figures. No such figure may outclass an iconic deity. Such informal stylistic tendencies are quite rare in African figure sculpture, which is generally formal, frontal, symmetrical, and rigid. In this sense the informal mode is more like African masquerades (as distinct from the masks themselves), which are often popular rather than hieratic arts, and in which motion, asymmetry, and naturalistic expression are inherent if only because the positions and actions of the masker must necessarily begin with the human dancer inside the costume. It should not surprise us, then, to see a masquerader (color plate 3) in mbari rendered as informal, natural, and poised for action in an informal space.

The Popular mode includes all figures in which the sculptor has attempted to freeze motion, to render an activity with some realism, graphic on occasion, through emphasizing in sculptured form those aspects of position and pose which recall people in actual situations (pl. 32). Not that the Popular mode is lacking in conventions, for many are still present even if they are less evident than in more formal figures, where they seem to support the rigidity of the style. This mode manifests a relative lack of formalism partly because sculptors often evoke a realistic or plausible human scene, while in other modes they use symbols, hierarchies, juxtapositions of scale and proportion, and the architectural space itself to express an abstract concept of supernatural power and dignity.

A good indicator of this mode is a figure's location within the mbari—off center, without a solid backdrop, in a corner, up under the roof, or off in the "kitchen," as the cloister is often called. The activities of these figures, too, signal their style. Many are genre subjects, people engaged in common, easily recognizable pursuits like divination, blacksmithing (pl. 32), or dancing (pl. 33). Such ordinary human activity, set in unstructured space, leads to informal poses and naturalistic proportions.

Smooth fleshlike surfaces can integrate parts into a whole that has a relatively unambitious expressive role in the mbari structure. Once again form and content dovetail, for "popular" figures, limited as they are in meaning, appear simpler and less forbidding than *agbara* figures, which have a visual complexity corresponding to their multifaceted roles at the philosophical apex of the Owerri hierarchy.

The Popular mode is well represented by a female figure seated on a low mbari wall (pl. 34). If she were to be placed near an Ala of the type discussed above, the deity would dwarf and intimidate her. She has a relaxed and unceremonious manner yet is by no means the most informal figure found in mbari art. Her body position is in fact very similar to that of the Ala discussed above, which makes her contrasting expressive message all the more remarkable. Despite the frontal pose, however, she faces to the side, perpendicular to the mbari front, has no formal backdrop behind her, and therefore automatically becomes a subordinate figure in the structural program. The artist has relaxed her and given her an unassuming informality. Arms once poised in mid-air now drop to comfortable positions. In contrast with the Ala figure, the body is less stiff and the facial expression less proud and aloof. Except for an enlarged head on a slightly attenuated neck, this woman has normal proportions, and they give her a familiar human scale contrasting with Ala's superhuman monumentality. There is dignity here but no grandiosity. Organically integrated body parts and smooth surfaces combine with the more natural proportions to reflect a closely observed naturalism. Her torso is a fluid surface from which the organic navel rupture and breasts erupt with realistic vitality. The artist has not only indicated fingers, he has also articulated wrists, giving the hands relaxed positions. Rather than suggesting much bony structure or indicating muscles, the sculptor achieves his naturalism by making smooth flowing surfaces that suggest skin and by lifelike posing that shows a sensitivity to real body positions.

Despite the lifelike nature of this mode, there are no portraits and little facial expression. Rather than give a face expressive lines and wrinkles, deep eye sockets or hard angles, artists smooth over facial planes into an idealized form that suggests neither age nor idiosyncrasy. The occasionally particularized blemishes of diseased mbari figures noted by Kenneth Murray in the 1930s would seem to be records of oddities rather than efforts to individualize.[11] Children are not given infantile features or baby fat; they are simply small editions of the prevailing agelessness so characteristic of most African figural styles.[12] Emotional expressions—of anger, laughter, sadness, and so forth—are equally absent in mbari unless one counts rather impassive faces projecting a certain aloofness and dignity, which would seem to derive more from modes of conventionalization than the conscious desire to capture mood. Attenuated necks, high foreheads, and blank stylized eyes contribute to this convention, and all such traits are more common in the Iconic than in the Popular mode.

The gigantic triangular hairdresses that contribute so much to the formality of female *agbara* are absent in the Popular mode. Without that bold, heavy shape the sculptor can concentrate on the roundness and plasticity of the head and the hairstyle. Ears may be positioned farther back on the head, and the face itself may project forward in a more rounded, three-dimensional manner. Since many of the figures in the Popular mode are seen from different vantage points, they must have fully round heads. Women's hairstyles of the "everyday" type have radial projections (plaits), rounded knots or pigtails, curved lateral bands (pl. 4) or shaved curvilinear patterns (pl. 33), all of which contribute roundness to the head mass. The hairstyles of this mode are those in use when the particular mbari was made; thus the hairstyles seen in the Whitehouse mbari of 1904 (pl. 6) are quite different from those observed in recent years (pl. 34). Female *agbara,* in contrast, are still graced with the old-fashioned ceremonial *ishiojongo* (color plate 7, pl. 30), which Igbo women no longer affect.

The overall effect of most figures in the Popular mode is alertness but reserve, informality with a slight sense of tension. There is no reaching out or up, no insistent proclamation of dogma or superiority. Instead, human scale and proportions, along with relative organic naturalism and quite realistic body positions, accord with the roles of these make-believe villagers as somewhat idealized but essentially normal members of the temporal community.

Despite the naturalism of pose, proportions, and surface modeling of genre figures, however, the nature and variety of body positions are limited and remain rather conventionalized. Figures seldom bend at the waist or turn their heads. Rarely do they twist in space. In both respects the female figure shown grinding camwood is rather unusual (pl. 35). The vast majority of figures stand, or sit, on a raised seat, with feet planted firmly and usually symmetrically on the ground, though occasionally legs dangle in space or are twisted around the seated torso. But the arm positions, particularly, give the impression that the body is not at rest or even natural, and the pose thus imparts a sense of quiet tension and, sometimes, of a slight stiffness. The arms convey these impressions because sculptors tend to avoid the most restful arms-at-side position. They prefer to take advantage of projecting armatures, keeping upper arms out from the body and elbows bent, forearms thrusting upward or forward, hovering in space. Such positions may be seen as expressive on dancers (pl. 33), but the convention is clearly recognized as such when this arm position is noted on virtually all figures.

This conventionalization is least noticeable, however, in the Popular mode and particularly in figures occupied with a definite activity or, occasionally, in some active, seated figures whose arms are supported by something other than a projecting armature. Whether the figure holds a demijohn of wine or a bottle (figs. 15 and 16), a flashlight, a gun, or a guitar (pl. 10), attention is drawn away from conventionalizations and the viewer feels himself in the presence of remarkably anecdotal figures or scenes. Poses that avoid strict frontality and torso stiffness, as in scenes of wrestling (fig. 17) or childbearing (pl. 4, color plate 5), tend to be the most graphic. In these and other genre activities such as writing at a desk (pl. 22), riding a bicycle, playing drums, or dancing, the sculptors take advantage of both the armature and the presence of open, unstructured space, often in the gallery or cloister rather than in the main house.

Popular figures involving odd poses and interesting genre activities, particularly when contrasted with formal sculptures, give the mbari-viewing experience its movement and dynamism. A few feet along from the god's niche in one mbari, for example, we encounter the figures of two rainmakers blithely perched on an openwork fence (pl. 36). There is no greater contrast to the weighty solemnity of an *agbara* than this jaunty interpenetration and projection of forms in informal space. Or again, we note the oblique pose and asymmetry of the hunter who stands between a figure of Mamy Wata and another of an august, deified hero (pl. 10).

The Idealized Mode: The fourth stylistic grouping is the transition between the Iconic and Popular modes; it embraces those figures in which naturalism and conventionalization are most nearly balanced. Like Iconic figures they are frontal and symmetrical, with parts geometrically disposed and carefully aligned in space (pl. 37). Like popular figures, they are of human scale and proportion, yet they seldom appear in central niches with a formalized backdrop wall. The best exemplars of this mode are seated females who are stiffly erect with their arms raised as horizontal extensions of the shoulders, elbows at right angles, and forearms projecting upward (pl. 37); or standing men, usually uniformed, whose firmly planted feet and akimbo arms convey a sense of serene power (pl. 29), or people who are seated, with arms symmetrical and hands on hips (pl. 38). Common to all these is their lack of activity, their aloof poise, their sense of permanence, impressions that are produced by bilateral symmetry, erect posture, and in the case of the females, the unnatural but confident (and often repeated) arm position.

The mode has been called Idealized because of the figures' dignified inactivity and because body proportions, particularly in the neck and head, distort reality into something that is more than human, although by comparison with *agbara* and *ijeremgbe,* still less than supernatural. Unlike those of *agbara,* heads are fully round and may be seen from the side. The convention of a heavy, elongated torso does not prevail here and legs are naturalistically proportioned and organically articulated. Unlike *agbara* or *ijeremgbe,* these figures remain on the edge of the human realm and are not distorted expressions of belief. Standing males are tall and bulky, but their relatively natural proportions save them from being overbearing or severe. In sum, while the Idealized mode is less often used and is less important than either the Iconic or the Popular modes, its identification enables us to visualize a real continuum rather than a simple and misleading polarity. Most large mbari, too, contain several figures of this kind. If the edges of this and other modes are blurred, as they certainly are, the overlapping at least varies in kind from one figure to the next, thereby reinforcing the complexity of mbari's expressive program.

Animal styles vary from relatively stiff and formal sculptures often centrally located on a side or end, to dynamically posed beasts placed in odd or transitional positions or climbing around in the mbari structure (color plates 6 and 11, pls. 11 and 21). Indeed, the placement of an animal figure—whether on a formal side of the main house or "off in the kitchen"—determines its stylistic rendering more than does the type of animal or even its association with a local deity. Like many mbari images, however, a number of animals have been repeated often enough to yield a fairly stabilized and conventional pose. The leopard, *agu,* is frequently seen either descending the steps of a buttress or eating a goat (pl. 23), while the python, *eke,* is almost invariably found coiled on a wall or column surface (color plates 1 and 11, pls. 10 and 13). These are certainly the most common animals. Simplifying conventions govern these and other animal images, and some, apparently through replication in the absence of natural models, have departed quite markedly from their prototypes. This is particularly the case with the hippopotamus, *enyimiri*, sometimes called an elephant, *enyi*, even by different informants at the same mbari (pls. 39 and 40). These have become rather whimsical, fanciful creatures that lack both realism and ferocity, as if tamed for inclusion in the mbari scene. Whatever inventiveness is sacrificed in the modeling of these beasts is more than made up for in the painting of them. Many animals, on the other hand, betray a variety of poses and attitudes which bespeak playful license on the part of the artist. Monkeys climb posts (pl. 11) or ride on the backs of horses, birds are perched atop walls (pl. 10), dogs sit back on their haunches or stand idly on a wall (fig. 3), and Okpangu appears alone (pl. 15) or ensnared by a policeman (pl. 41), or copulating with one of the foolish girls he has lured off into the bush. Considerable variation also characterizes python images, as if artists became tired of the prevalent coiled form (pl. 42). The treatment of animals, then, is varied in spite of recurring conventions and therefore reflects the amount of individual choice open to an artist, a matter discussed at greater length in the next chapter.

General Style Tendencies

The many apparently disparate stylistic strands in figural art may now be drawn together in a statement that applies to all mbari sculpture regardless of mode. The most important traits relate to and partially derive from the two components of the mbari medium, clay applied over a light wooden framework. Heavy, solid clay transforms a figure's armature, yet the figure's final shape depends on the linearity of that armature. At a distance, the bold mass of mud dominates, but as one moves closer, the spatial penetration of smaller supporting forms, as well as the play of details and painted surfaces, becomes increasingly apparent.

Like the mbari building itself, most sculptures have a solid unbroken mass oriented centrally in space and aligned vertically. Partially surrounding this core and connected with it is a subsidiary web of interconnected diagonals that support the central column while reducing its severe weightiness. Thus, while the final impact of mbari sculpture generally stems from bold and simple shapes, these are refined, supported, and enlivened by smaller detailed forms and subtle surface treatment.

Compositions and poses tend to be simple, frontal, and symmetrically balanced, but they vary according to location in the mbari; they follow hierarchical and geometric principles when central and focal, veering toward asymmetry, informality, and spatial liveliness when in subsidiary positions, especially in galleries. A similar balance may be seen between conventionalization and organic naturalism. Central figures and their supporters show the greatest distortion of human proportions, resulting in extremely elongated torsos and necks, and oversized heads, with a complementary reduction in the size and scale of appendages. The proportions of other figures may be extremely naturalistic, as if to support a correspondingly realistic pose or activity.

All figures, however, have certain standard and recurrent conventionalizations: an oversized neck and head; arms that hover, never flush with the torso; neglected or simplified musculature; smooth, unbroken, unlined flesh surfaces; relatively naturalistic faces of shallow but subtle intersecting planes overlaid by schematic details that remain on the surface. In contrast, however, limbs are articulated organically and one senses the underlying armature skeleton. But there are no attempts at imitative realism; sculptors are more interested in expressive evocations based on nature than the strict imitation of life forms. Hence even the most naturalistic figures have a stiff, slightly unnatural tenseness and a distant, impassive facial expression.

Painting

Painting completes an mbari house. If the addition of figure and animal sculpture populated and complicated the mbari stage, painting animates and enlivens sculptured forms and partitions their backgrounds. Color transforms the mbari from the familiar red-brown ever-present in the real world to an airy, cheerful place apart, vibrant and inviting (color plate 12). The only real formal analogues in the Owerri world to a resplendent mbari are bustling markets and large meetings or festivals, where bright-colored fabrics appear in busy, contrasting profusion.

Mbari artists use color in different ways depending on the section of the mbari being decorated and according to the effect desired. Painting may reinforce form, in the case of sculpture (color plates 4 and 9); subdivide and fragment form, as on steps, columns, and lower walls (color plate 11); or, as on the large planes of upper walls, introduce illusionistic designs unrelated to the background surface (color plate 12).

Figural Painting: The simplest of painting techniques and effects embellish three-dimensional sculptures and reliefs. In all such cases the painted patterns correspond to and clarify the shapes and contours of human or animal figures. Painting sometimes even complicates surfaces with an effect of intensifying the expressive impact of the form, particularly for close-range observations (color plate 7). Most often, however, painting is simple and descriptive (as on the Amadioha figure in color plate 9), differentiating flesh from clothing or identifying details and facial features. An artist begins by blocking out major sections in solid, often contrasting colors: white for the helmet, shirt, and knee socks; black for shorts and shoes; pink for head, hands, and knees. Shallow details are then highlighted, or sometimes painted in (the collar and necktie), again in contrasting tones. The effect of the contrasts is to make major forms intelligible at some distance, and then for the close-up view, to render subjects more realistically complex and credible by emphasizing small, sometimes arbitrary but descriptive details.

The support that painting gives to both distant and close views is apparent in female figures, particularly *agbara*, in which carefully detailed embellishments parallel other types of hieratic elaboration. In the Ala group discussed previously, for example, the distant view is of white heads, hands, and legs, contrasting with apparently solid-colored torsos (color plate 1). Only when the observer is close does he perceive meticulous body painting, a rich overall pattern of contrasting parallel curvilinear lines (color plate 4). Thus painting reinforces the dichotomy observed in sculptured form between large blocks of contrasting colors that identify major body forms clearly at a distance, and details of dress, surface, and facial features designed for close scrutiny. For the most part figure sculptures are clothed in realistic or descriptive colors and painted patterns. Elaborate female body painting, for example, comes directly (although it has been somewhat idealized) from a usage once common for Owerri women on ceremonial occasions (color plates 4 and 7). Two exceptions to realistic painting may be noted, however, as further links between artistic form and meaning. The first is that mbari artists make no effort to render skin color in the various shades of brown flesh seen among these peoples. Instead, a variety of light tones—pinks, whites, and even yellows—are used, a tradition that relates to a system of color symbolism to be discussed in chapter 6. Suffice it to say now that light tones are used for both aesthetic and philosophical reasons, and that they do not necessarily identify mbari figures as white men. Another tradition is the adding of real clothing and jewelry to completed figures. Cloths (wrappers) and earrings may be rendered in clay and/or paint, but the real objects add prestige to the figure and to the mbari as a whole (pl. 8).

The painting of certain animals, on the other hand, may be described as arbitrary, a prime example being the fanciful "hippopotamus," or "elephant," whose sculptural form is also a conventionalization. The usual handling of these animals is an overall, tightly-spaced pattern of detailed, repetitive geometric designs that derive ultimately from women's body painting, *uri* (pls. 39 and 40). Rather than a solid color, as in life, the painting here is far richer, and provides diverse visual effects at various distances.

If this painting is most idiosyncratic when applied to animals, however, other kinds of paintings are still far from imitations of nature. Leopards, pythons, goats, birds, and other creatures are rendered in patterns that may evoke nature, yet they remain essentially imaginative solutions, many of which achieve a kind of standardized currency through repeated usage (color plate 6, pls. 10 and 42). In most cases one or more small units (dots, triangles, lines, etc.) overlay a single base color. In painting a bird, for example, dots of different colors and sizes are used to differentiate the parts: white ones for the wings, large black dots for the underbody, and smaller black ones for the rest of the body. Considerable virtuosity is seen in the application of these simple patterns, especially in the painting of pythons, which are nearly ubiquitous in mbari houses.

Architectural Decoration: Painting on stepped walls, niches, and columns is a more complicated matter that reflects great variety in the aesthetic basis of painting and in resulting solutions. Three fundamental principles, however, do govern this type of decoration: the use of geometric patterns and combinations of rectilinear and curvilinear elements; subdivision of basic architectural shapes into smaller units; and contrast in the coloring of pattern sections. Wall designs are always applied with considerable care and control. It is also clear that these patterns, which are found in the lower section of mbari and so are visible from some distance away, act to lighten the solidity and severity of the walls and columns. The plates and "slivers of iron" (or wood) imbedded in the walls (before the onset of painting activity) help considerably to determine the final geometric designs. Of these, the plates are the more decisive, for the "slivers" are inserted later, if at all, and in consideration of plate positions. Of the mbari houses extant in 1966-67, moreover, only one contained these "slivers of iron," *mkpeshi igwe* (pl. 20). Thus the geometric subdivision of wall surfaces has two apparent sources: rounded or curvilinear patterns reflecting or magnifying the circular plate aperture, complemented and further complicated by rectilinear forms introduced by slivers, if they are used. More fundamentally, however, painting reflects and upholds the basic geometry of the building, its straight lines and angles. Blended in a single program, various patterned designs transform the weighty planar surfaces of solid structural clay into something apparently transient and insubstantial, like painted canvas on a theatrical flat (pls. 21, 29, and 43). As in the execution of stage flats, there is no emphasis here on mathematical precision. Whether the pattern is round or square, the designer needs no compass or T-square. Most frequently we see unruled straight lines, even though straight sticks are sometimes used to sketch out the pattern at the beginning. These preliminary lines are simply guides (pl 24).

In designing geometric wall patterns an artist considers primarily the relatively small surface before him, whether this is the column side, step series, or the wall of a niche; each is a semi-independent surface to be broken up into smaller patterns. Each small unit contrasts with its neighbor, or, as one Owerri man put it, the "designs kill one another." The various patterns may compete with one another, but the artist considers it important that they are all more or less homogeneous, with no one patterned area drawing particular attention to itself. Artists are traditionally limited to three colors, occasionally four, including red-brown or black, the usual outline or guide colors. The most interesting designs are not simple subdivisions and never, not even among the dullest patterns seen, do artists reduce them to simple checkerboards. Instead, patterns generally occur meaningfully within other patterns; a bold design will first be marked out that reflects somewhat the shape of the space or that divides it into several large sections: a large triangle (pl. 43), a dominant "X" (pl. 28), or a series of rectangles. These are again subdivided systematically, yet with small, sometimes whimsical details and variations. Rectangles or triangles break down into curvilinear elements (pl. 43) or smaller geometric units of assorted shapes and sizes (pl. 31).

Though these painted "building blocks" are simple enough, they combine with amazing variation in a single mbari, always observing the principle of contrast, each color unit playing against those around it. And although colors are often used in the same way, that is, brown or black for outlines, white and tan or yellow for infilling, sometimes, as if to surprise the viewer, brown or yellow will outline (color plate 9, pls. 27 and 44). Occasionally for variety, colors are used in solid blocks without outlining (pls. 22 and 35). This seems to have been a more common practice in the twenties and thirties. Or again, a black outline will swell into a pattern of its own, setting up an ambiguous relationship between figure and ground, outline and outlined (pls. 17, 29, and 30). In better geometric painting the artists give considerable attention not only to variety, the keynote, but to what strikes us as whimsy and good fun, as if to announce the playful element in mbari, in contrast to its drudgery (pl. 44).

The designs of course vary greatly from one mbari to the next, from one artist's hand to another's. One artist may delight particularly in framing or embellishing the plate opening (pls. 27 and 43), while a second punches a wall full of small holes, then weaves his design around them (pl. 39). Others may prefer bold color blocks, interspersing them now and again with simple figural motifs, perhaps a fish, a fowl, or a floral abstraction. Or the organizing decorative program may be different, as in the examples (pl. 45) in which curvilinear abstractions again appear to be variations on themes developed for women's body painting, which was once itself an abstract art of great versatility in Igboland. An example of recent wall painting breaks away from the control of more traditional designs, substituting an expressionism atypical of this genre (pl. 46). These paintings, executed by a man without a craftman's apprenticeship or long mbari experience, have freedom and considerable strength, but they compete with the sculpture more than is usual (and generally acceptable) and tend to lack unity. They do, however, show the possibilities of innovation and change in this aspect of mbari art.

Whatever the type of decorative pattern, the viewer is struck with their frequent subtlety and the endless variety achieved with such simple means. The background decoration in a single mbari generally shows the unifying hand of its directing artist, but never boring sameness. The pattern on one column surface differs in conception from that of its neighbor, and the background of one niche is varied from the design of the next. Within these variations—both in a single house and from one to another—there is constant stress on contrast of light and dark, curvilinear and rectilinear elements, figure and ground. We also note considerable emphasis on openings and edges; attention is constantly drawn to plate holes by encircling them, enlarging upon them, by contrast with other design principles. Similarly, the edges of steps, columns, and walls are dramatized, repeated, and clarified by repeated framing and edging and by the frequent use of straight lines in the patterns.

Illusionistic Painting: The varying figural or illusionistic paintings on upper mbari walls (color plate 12, pl. 47) contrast with the abstract geometric patterns on columns, buttresses, and lower walls. The latter serve as nonsymbolic decorative backgrounds to the sculptural program while the former, applied to large spaces relatively free of competition from sculpture, are fields for independent paintings that add dimensions to the form and content of mbari. Significantly, the upper surfaces on which these appear are not visible from a distance; the viewer must be well within the ambience of mbari, and he will have seen much of it before his eyes are lured up under the roof. Different in concept and style from the rest, these paintings are at once a refreshing contrast to, and an extension of, the mood of mbari. Similar paintings are sometimes also seen on the walls of the cloisters.

Two important kinds of painting on these upper walls may be considered, for the sake of discussion, prototypical of all such illusionistic decoration: representations of rectangular cloths, which by their nature are neatly framed within their own borders (pl. 47), and a series of celestial and other motifs which generally float, unframed, on the large flat surfaces (color plate 12). Nearly all mbari with more than six or eight figures display at least one cloth and at least one sky symbol. Almost invariably, a cloth is painted on the front side wall above and behind the owner of the house, and in larger mbari houses this may be one of seven or eight cloths decorating the four upper walls. These symmetrically placed rectangles have the effect of reiterating the basic geometry of the house and its subdivision into patterns of small contrasting units (pls. 22 and 47). Some painted cloths are "copies" of real ones such as the "elephant" or "George" cloth imported from India (pl. 48), while others are freer variations on figured prints of the type imported from Holland or made in modern Nigerian factories (pl. 47). The majority of cloth patterns, however, spring from the imaginations of artists, and a good many are of sufficient visual interest to be considered independent paintings within the larger work of art. Variation is great, from meticulous geometric divisions and subdivisions to seemingly "modern" abstractions consisting of a few bold shapes inside an embellished border. Artists give themselves great freedom within the rectangular frame.

The few framed paintings seen in mbari that are not cloths may in all likelihood have originated from the idea of cloth. One example (pl. 49) groups a number of zoomorphic motifs and objects of common usage together in a random composition. The objects chosen by the artist have no apparent relationship to one another and their distribution within the frame is rather arbitrary and haphazard. More often, however, such heterogeneous objects as knives, fish, lamps, combs, and umbrellas are simply painted on the large wall surface, whose only frame is the edge of the wall mass (color plate 12, figs. 18 and 19). These are the "floating objects," among which are found the sun and the moon, sometimes stars and almost invariably the rainbow, *egurugru*, represented as a double-headed python. Of all these motifs, only the rainbow is used as a device for composition. It is an arching shape that often spans the other motifs on that wall (pl. 50, fig. 19), though in one instance (pl. 47), it is a band running around the entire central block, dividing the upper walls into two zones on all sides. Sometimes celestial motifs are grouped together on the same wall, or they may be scattered.

A catalogue of the widely disparate motifs found painted in mbari houses—real objects (fig. 22), figures (figs. 19-21), and animals or plants (fig. 24); semi-human or monstrous forms (fig. 4), abstractions of several types (fig. 23)—would include a great many parts of the Owerri world, real and imaginary. The upper walls of one typical large mbari (at Ulakwo Obube), for example, display the following:

Side One: Two large cloths (the Indian "George" cloth of the type illustrated in fig. 48), two machetes, and two folded umbrellas.

Side Two: Walking stick, two sheathed knives, small arching rainbow eating a fish with one of its mouths, cow with rope around neck, man holding an abstract shape resembling a palm tree, an open umbrella.

Side Three: Two large cloths, several small units of abstract body painting designs, two machetes, top view of open umbrella, two combs, two small fish.

Side Four: (fig. 50) Two small fish, one headless "stockfish,"[13] top view of open umbrella, small checkered cloth, large arching rainbow, moon inside circle, sun inside circle, several small insects and birds.

Wall paintings that include more abstract or fantastic motifs, as well as human figures (pl. 49, fig. 18) are difficult to catalogue because several items or activities are ambiguous or not clearly recognizable, even to local people. No real purpose would be served by listing here all the motifs seen on upper walls, although many will be found in Appendix B and in figs. 19-25. The list above and the illustrations, however, do show the extraordinary range of painted objects: from tiny insects to bicycles and trains, and a boat containing three trees and five women (pl. 51).

No explicit rule governs either the types or numbers of objects which are painted on the walls of any given mbari, although, as we have seen, cloths and celestial motifs are nearly always present. Both the nature and the amount of painting depend instead on the size of the mbari and the predilections of its artist(s). There may be a few rather widely spaced motifs, as in several houses of medium size (30-40 figures), or these and larger houses may have a great profusion of paintings executed out of what approaches a *horror vacui* (pl. 47, figs. 18-21). The compulsion to embellish all mbari walls more or less densely tends to prevail; only rarely are any large unadorned white spaces found. In contrast to the orderly geometry of lower decorations, upper walls are free, sometimes chaotic, in both composition and subject matter, as if the artist had burst the bonds that restrained him when painting the lower parts. Here he is quite free to let his imagination run and he often responds with great inventiveness. The upper walls of mbari houses almost never resemble one another, even in a series executed by a single man. Clearly these surfaces encourage an unrestrained virtuosity that many artists enjoy greatly.

Occasionally artists break the "rules" confining abstract and largely geometric paintings to lower walls and illusionistic ones to upper walls; and paint actual objects, figures, and (rarely) scenes on lower surfaces. Yet these subjects are seldom if ever visible in the main house from the approaches to an mbari, and so the rule remains effectively intact. The permissible areas are the sides (occasionally backs) of niches on sides 2, 3, or 4, or in the gallery—areas never visible when the viewer first perceives an mbari.

Concepts of scale, perspective, and shading are outside the mbari-painting canon. Instead we see motifs sized at random and spaced irregularly, often in curious and apparently arbitrary combinations. Rather than use devices that would produce an illusion of plasticity, artists usually outline each individual motif with a fine black line, then fill in with solid, flat colors, as many as can be found or mixed, and not the limited few used on walls below. The background and prevailing color in these upper (and occasional lower) spaces, as throughout the mbari, however, is white, which seems to recede spatially under the contrasting motifs and with the help of sculptures spotted at intervals around its lower margins.

Beside these lively surfaces, populated as they are with all manner of creatures and objects, the geometric decorations below seem tame and conservative. From this artistic dichotomy one gets the impression that a whole new order of things is being catalogued on the upper walls. Many of the designs and motifs—like cloths and the sun or moon—would in fact be extremely difficult to execute in modeled clay.

Form: A Summation

As an aesthetic unity, an mbari house is surely greater than the sum of its parts. This is clearly demonstrated by a brief analysis of the scale and illusory size of mbari which results from the combination of architecture, sculpture, and painting. By the standards of Owerri building, mbari houses are extremely large. In physical dimensions they have no peer; few traditional buildings are even one-fourth the size of larger mbari. But mbari houses are made to seem much larger even than they are. The architectural setting is made up of a series of minutely graded steps that recede and rise in space until they meet the solid, apparently terminal wall, the outside of the closed box; this magnifies real distances and sizes (color plate 4, fig. 9, pls. 39 and 52). And when windows are punched in the walls, the impression of depth and scale is greater still (pl. 50). Painting modifies the architecture by atomizing it into hundreds of small geometric components that further augment the real measurements of steps and regressive courses. Sculpture completes the illusion of monumentality. Usually a few *agbara* figures exceed life-size, but the majority of subjects are sized in proportion to their distance from the outer edge of the side, so that those figures perched on top of the "ground floor" of the house may only measure three feet from top to bottom (color plate 4, pl. 39).[14] Some subsidiary adult figures are about one-third the size of the *agbara,* and several grades fall in between. All components of mbari combine to produce an illusion of great size, of monumental scale overall.

Thus the impact of an mbari house rests on the integration of all its elements, great and small, even if its fundamental character may be reduced to the various kinds of relationships between clay and the frameworks that lie beneath it. The tectonic foundation is solid, orderly, enduring. It divides space into spatially open compartments that are hieratic because of the solid backdrop in the central niche. If the building is primarily massive mud, then the sculptures disposed within it are preeminently armature. Sculpture enlivens through the capacity of its projecting armatures to interrupt and activate space. Painting subdivides and describes; it reinforces the plastic, volumetric character of figural sculpture but it lightens architectural massing, rendering it apparently insubstantial. Some paintings and figure sculptures, furthermore, lead independent, free, and informal lives of their own, as if to defy their architectural confinement. More than anything, however, color provides a kaleidoscopic effect, a mosaic of flashing contrasts, which lends a spectacular note, especially in contrast to the prevailing environment of the village.

Expressed differently, mbari is the meeting place of light armature and heavy mud, of orderly rectilinear space and liberated, irregular space, of relaxed informality within a framework of hierarchical control. It is the nexus of formalism and freedom, convention and virtuosity, straight line and circle, light and dark, familiar and monumental. Mbari is subdivision, repetition, contrast, variety, a consciously staged illusory world. Many aspects are expected, regular, and predictable, but odd juxtapositions and whimsical surprises always lurk in the wings.

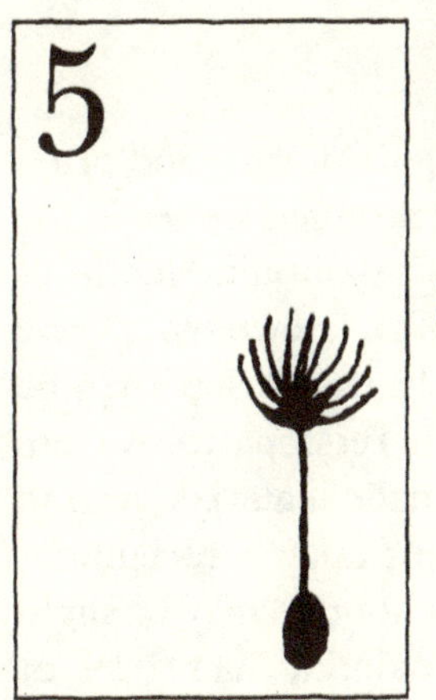

5 Inspiration, Individuality, and Aesthetics

The enormous variety of subjects represented in mbari calls for some examination of artists as both transmitters of culture and innovators. At the same time, the observable variety of personal styles requires explanation, especially in view of the alleged "communality" of the enterprise. We have seen that an artist works simultaneously in four sculptural and two or three painting styles, but how much does the hand of one artist differ from that of the next? We may ask, too, about the extent to which individuality, both in the invention of forms and in the modes of their execution, is sanctioned, recognized, or required of artists by their patrons. We may explore the reactions of these patrons to specific subjects or motifs in mbari, to an mbari as a whole, and to its formal configurations. To what extent does aesthetic criticism exist and how is it articulated? In this chapter, then, we will discuss the artist's inspiration, his individuality, and responses to his work by the community at large.

INSPIRATION

No matter how much artists follow established patterns of image making, each large mbari contains a new selection of figures, perhaps one or two wholly new images, variations on earlier themes, and a fresh mixture of subjects in its program of sculpture and painting. What, then, are the sources of mbari subjects and to what extent does an artist work to invent new forms?

A comparison of dozens of mbari, each distinct from the next, clearly reveals the extent to which artists draw upon the work of the past. The traditional corpus of sculptural types is the artist's source, his "copybook." As an academician, he is given little license either to disregard or to question the assumptions (and artistic products) of his teachers, who have been similarly trained. In this respect mbari craftsmen are no different from most African sculptors. Original forms (and often their meanings) may be lost in history, and the products we see in the twentieth century are often replicas of replicas. About nine-tenths of the subjects listed in Appendix C, a catalogue of all known types, have been used more than once to my knowledge. In the period 1945-66 comparatively few new forms were introduced. Yet departures from past models and the introduction of new thematic material, even in this period of apparent decline, were incumbent upon conscientious and ambitious artists. Variations from available sources may be slight or incremental, as in changes of clothing, body painting, hair styles, or in new juxtapositions of existing subjects, but change has nevertheless been continual, at least since Whitehouse (1904, pl. 6), and undoubtedly, before. An important part of the inherited mbari tradition is the license, indeed the mandate, to update, change, and innovate. Both copying and inventing are sanctioned by the institution and the society in which artists operate. Nearly all artists acknowledge this, as Ezem's commentary indicates.

> When you are doing your own [mbari] you go to another to see if there is anything you would like to copy. You look at the man's work and select those you like but have not tried. You add them to the ones you have in your mind. Then you keep your mind working and you can produce some out of your own imagination. Of these, the people who come to look will judge which are better. . . . Each person has his own way of working.

Another artist, Ugo, when asked "if there is anything [subjects] we have not seen in mbari," replied:

> You have not seen anything. When our children grow up they will not do the same as we have done. They will have to make their own figures, and they will put in their own new things, but quite unconsciously, without knowing it, things we have done will pour out. . . . There are many things our predecessors used to put in, and we don't have any of them now: people who have guns, warriors, people who are taking care of fowls, and people who have bags [*ogwu*] on them for war. But now we have clothes and every figure we make has some clothing on it. And now we put on shoes. The old people used to show the toes and the toenails very clearly.

Indeed, we need only compare the mbari houses photographed in 1904 or in the 1930s to those I recorded in 1966-67 to see many of these changes, both incremental and boldly innovative. Despite the greater numbers of images in the very large mbari of the thirties, since that time several new subjects[1] have been introduced, and many older images have been updated or changed somewhat. We shall later see the extent to which this dualistic, complementary approach to mbari imagery—adherence to tradition and the need to innovate—reflects the world view of the Owerri area.

When asked to name their sources for specific figures or groups, artists commonly answer either "I saw it in another mbari" or "It came from my imagination"—sometimes both. Neither of these statements reveals the ultimate inspiration or motivation for the panoramic range of subjects illustrated here. We need to go beyond such answers to find the remote sources for both previously existing imagery and imaginative additions to the corpus. Several kinds of inspiration may be identified: mythology, stories, proverbs, historical occurrences, and the observable life of the contemporary world. The psychology and mode of transformation from a "model" to a finished clay sculpture remain mysterious, but no more so, perhaps, than the mental and manual processes employed by an artist in any culture to transpose one kind of reality—tangible, verbal, or imaginary—into another. Fidelity to the model may be seen, but the new image also reflects the conventions of the artist's own culturally determined bias, along with his personal vision. Although mbari artists often rely on the stock of extant imagery, someone, of course, had to invent all the clay forms. Since we cannot recapture those original artists' intuitions and creative processes, we must be content to identify some of their sources and prototypes. At the same time it is useful to pinpoint the religious, social, political, or economic relevance of various subjects, as a preview of mbari content, which will be discussed in more detail in the following chapter.

From mythology or folklore come the images of Okpangu, already discussed, the rainbow (always painted), and the orphan. Myths say that the rainbow (color plate 12, pl. 50) originated as a python which fed for years in a river until it had reached sufficient length to arc over the entire sky. Diviners read the presence of the rainbow as an important omen, for good or evil, but more significant still is the "falling of a rainbow" when, people believe, an important man will die. The place the rainbow "falls" is said to be suffused with a light or haze of miraculous color, and presently a "big man" dies in or near that area. The rainbow is consistently painted on the upper walls of medium-sized and large mbari, with heads at either end of its arching form. One or both of the heads may be shown engorging a human (pl. 53) or another animal which is about to strike a human (fig. 19). A messenger of *agbara*, often of Amadioha, the rainbow will strike those who have offended the gods but will protect those who are innocent. Thus the various myths about the marvelous life and deeds of the zoomorphic rainbow are predominantly spiritual in orientation.[2]

Orphan mythology and folk stories, on the other hand, are primarily social and economic: The orphan, always deprived and ill-treated as a youth, surmounts his deprivations and with dedicated hard work, becomes more successful and more wealthy ultimately than his peers. The orphan image illustrates one of the more recurrent and touching parts of this varied mythology; the child cracks *odara* nuts, which are his only food since other children have taken and eaten the tree's nutritious fruit. His foster mother gives him only hard nuts which he must work strenuously to crack. In one version, however, he plants a seed and, miraculously, an *odara* tree richly laden with fruit grows up almost overnight. The tree is *his*, and he is of course justified in refusing its fruit to the eager members of his compound. The moral and economic lessons in such stories are nearly endless, and the mbari orphan image surely recalls several more pages in the encyclopedia of Owerri life.

Many of the morals of orphan, Okpangu, and monkey stories are crystallized in proverbs so these images may refer equally to these didactic maxims. One man said: "Okpangu is a proverb about all the humans who have been hurt by spirits." Another sculptured group, three superimposed levels of three women each, surmounted by a jug of palm wine that had fallen from its original upright position (pl. 54), is titled by the proverb "wives whose husband loves them very much" or "the favorite wives of the husband" (*nwanyegbavuruololo*). This proverb and group refers among other things to the prosperity of a man with nine wives, the ideal of solidarity among co-wives, and the services (such as bringing palm wine) that a man can expect from his women. The significance of the groups is thus social and economic, and it may of course be interpreted from any of several points of view. Notably the proverb says nothing about the number of wives, which varies in mbari interpretations, or about their distinctive superposed positions, which are constant. For these we can refer only to the inventiveness of the initiating artist and the whim of the copier.

Both Basden and Meek have indicated stories or pictures as sources for modeled mbari figures. Meek cites a traditional folk story about a baboon riding on an elephant,[3] whereas Basden (a missionary) feels that "ideas of obscenity" originate not in traditional belief but as "crude tangible replicas of indecent photographs, or modeled reproductions of seaport and smokeroom stories as gleaned by steward boys and others."[4] Both reporters may be right although I believe Basden underestimated traditional sources of sexual imagery. These figures clearly buttress a variety of moral injunctions that seem to have been in force long before "seaport stories" could have made an impact. One traditional sexual group, for example, has the name "man is goat," *madu bu ewu* (pl. 55), a proverb that refers to foolish behavior.[5]

The most significant mbari image owing its existence to a picture is that of Mamy Wata, whose cult, as we have seen (pp. 00-00), may stem largely from external visual sources. Igbo people have assimilated Mamy Wata to such a degree that details of one common print, such as the necklace and waist sequins (indicating riches), are interpreted by aspects of the cult or vice versa, although such details are seldom reproduced in mbari images of her. This lithographic image (pl. 14)—a woman with luxuriant hair, richly sequined blouse, and mysteriously docile snakes draped about her—appeals to Igbo people; abundant hair and fancy clothing are signs of beauty and prosperity, while the ability to tame and control pythons and dangerous snakes, many of them sacred in Owerri, is clearly a supernatural gift echoing images of Cretan snake goddesses,[6] and the crownlike headdress on several Mamy Wata sculptures (pl. 10 and 13), may well have stemmed from still other photographic sources. Interesting too are the sculptural variations in handling Mamy Wata's legs, which are not shown in the most common print (pl. 14). The most literal interpretation seen (pl. 56) omits the legs altogether. When legs are rendered, they are usually crossed (pls. 10, 13, and 31) in a manner atypical of Igbo posture, and sometimes the waist is marked by severe constrictions and inorganic ridges (apparently belts, see pl. 13). Both these features are clever structural expressions of Mamy Wata's "foreignness" and allude to her alleged mermaid characteristics, indeed, her classification as a deity. In some paintings of Mamy Wata, in fact, the mermaid conception is fully realized (pl. 57).

Despite the prominence of Mamy Wata, however, mbari sculptures or paintings that directly betray European or any other non-indigenous influence are quite rare. One of the few other clearly derivative images, in addition to paintings of cloths, is a winged angel (fig. 25), probably inspired by illustrated mission literature or a Christmas card. Another figure, more important for the silent comment it makes on modern Owerri psychology, however, is the mud image of Christ crucified (pl. 58). Properly speaking, "crucified" is the wrong word, for the cross has been omitted. The figure has been harmoniously positioned on the flat column face, however, and even the nails and crown of thorns have been included. The artist admitted he had seen the large concrete crucifix in the mission hospital compound at Emekuku, but because that figure's ankles are not crossed, as the mbari Christ's are, he must also have seen pictures that depicted the cross-legged convention, perhaps in a Bible belonging to a younger member of his family. This artist also said that he had attended a few worship services at the Emekuku mission. Such visits by him (and by earlier artists) may have inspired the occasional inclusion in mbari houses of a priest at an altar and kneeling catechists.

One may ask why a crucifix is modeled in a manifestly non-Christian monument. Its presence is a candid recognition of the existence of Christianity as a socio-religious force. Pragmatic and sensitive to the changes occurring around them, mbari artists even depict the child of a traditional deity with a cross around his neck (pl. 28).[7] Although some older people lament the Christianity of their children, they recognize the many benefits the new religion has provided either directly or indirectly: education, hospitals, permanent dwellings, wells, clothing, bicycles and cars, radios, and bottled beer. It is not unlikely that conversion-hungry missionaries have overemphasized the correlation between the Christian faith and a higher standard of living. Ironically, mbari have become billboards advertising modern life, the very life that is hastening the demise of mbari as a traditional art form.

But it is the job of mbari to advertise life, and from life itself comes the majority of mbari imagery. Thus the natural habit of the python to coil itself is exploited by artists, who often find new decorative effects and positions for this versatile form (pl. 42). Variations on the theme of the python exemplify the extent to which artists experiment with the form of even those subjects they appear to have "copied" from life. Whether he models a diviner seated on the ground, a woman with a bottle or jug of wine (figs. 15 and 16) or a sewing machine (pl. 59), a hunter (pl. 10), or a masquerader (color plate 3), the artist usually has alternative ways of depicting his subjects. He may decide upon a figure or group he has seen elsewhere, but he seldom copies it slavishly. In the first place the "model" is not available at the site of the new house. As far as I could determine, furthermore, a sculptor never uses an actual model while molding clay figures. He works instead from memory and on impulse, letting the form itself show him the way, as Ugo testifies:

> At times when you work you fail to put in what is in your mind. You only succeed in making something else. The next day you will be wondering to yourself, "How did I make this type of figure?" However, you will be satisfied with what you did. . . . Usually you have no control over what you are doing. The way it goes you follow.

Still, artists need only look around them to find many common mbari subjects: dancers and musicians (pl. 33), women preparing camwood or cracking palm kernels (pl. 35), a wine tapper ascending a palm tree, hunters, or blacksmiths (pl. 32). The prevailing mode for representing genre themes, the Popular, seeks as much realism as possible except for the conventions noted above.

The sources of numerous other mbari figures are obscure; they might have originated in stories, in life, in the artist's imagination, or from some combination of these. Rainmakers, for example, are indeed present in the culture, and appear, as in mbari, with vials of medicine, grass switches, and blackened bodies (pl. 36). But nothing in life accounts for the openwork fence on which they are perched, so we must conclude that this, like the akimbo arms and legs, is a creative exploitation of the mud-on-armature medium rather than a reflection of life or meaningful content. But rainmakers, at least, have a place in Igbo culture, which can hardly be said for the figure of a "boy on an ostrich" (fig. 26), seen in mbari houses at least since the 1930s.[8] Informants say this image came from stories about "what happens in the North." Beyond its value as a curiosity to amuse visitors, reason enough for its repeated inclusion, I could discover no significance for the group.

If the "boy on ostrich" originated in a story (or picture), the somewhat analogous image (pl. 60) of a three-headed woman riding on a horse (or perhaps it's a goat) stems only from the imagination of the artist, who disclaimed both a name and a significance for the curious group. Called either *mmuo* or "only 'fancy' " by informants, the image stands as a tribute to the artist's power to invent.[9] It is just this kind of virtuosity that artists often cite as their way "to beat other artists." Another especially charming virtuoso work is the "general" (pl. 61), a figure appearing in an mbari second-story window. The image is a clever visual pun, for the general's decorated blouse is simply painted on the wall; the window frame is thus half real, half *trompe l'oeil.* Though surely originating in a picture, quite possibly a colored magazine illustration, this delightful general has been transformed by the humorous imagination of the artist.

Thus there are two strings to the inventive bow of mbari artists: the practice of transforming existing imagery from stories, myths, proverbs, and life forms into tangible clay models; and, more infrequent, the invention of totally new images. In addition to the examples already cited, the transforming process may be exemplified by the following. Nwa Alakandu was a dwarf who lived in Ulakwo as the "caretaker" of an mbari until his death, ca. 1950. Nwa Alakandu was an odd and popular local character, and an artist decided to memorialize him in an mbari he was making. The resulting caricature (pl. 62), a legless figure with vestigial, winglike arms, has since been repeated by the originating artist and others and is now an established, although not widely copied, mbari image. Although Nwa Alakandu was a "normal" dwarf, his distorted figure in mbari, and thus the man himself, is sometimes now called *mmuo,* because all grotesque images are so named. The progressive transformations here are interesting: the creative interpretations the artist gave to a life form in turn have given rise to an mbari meaning—*mmuo*—quite different from the original.

The same artist who was first to memorialize Nwa Alakandu, Ezem, is well represented also on the creative side of image-making—he has made a figure of a long-legged ostrichlike bird giving birth to a human head. With the possible exception of the ostrich-with-rider, I know of no source for this unusual figure. The most distinctive aspect of the image, the representation of parturition, can be accounted for only in the psychology of the artist who made it. Ezem revealed on several occasions a somewhat atypical preoccupation with females and sexual matters.[10]

Several artists spoke of dreams as sources of inspiration. Onuegbu, for example, said: "In a dream at night the deity will show me the shape of the figure and in the morning I will not forget it, and it will have the shape the god likes." Ezem was still more specific about dreams:

> Last night while I was dreaming I built a certain figure and I called my wife. I have been having terrible dreams. I dreamed I was building a frightful figure. I shuddered with fear when I woke up. Any [mbari] work I get next I will first do this one I dreamed of, before doing any other figure. That this is utterly new and frightful. It is terrible in my

> eyes and nobody has ever built it, that one I built last night. . . . I have never seen any mbari where it was present; and nobody knows its name.

The spirit of competition between artists also helps to account for new imagery. Ezem, when queried about an unusual figure he had made, said "it is the kind of thing I compete with, which shows people how clever I am." In the same vein is Ugo's remark that "anyone who can do anything [original] to beat another artist will do it." Recent experiences, moods, family relationships, and activities within the mbari enclosure may stimulate innovation as well. Nothing is too common, too sacred, too bizarre, for inclusion, and indeed there is every reason to believe that strange and exotic subjects, like lurid ones, are strong magnets for drawing the appreciation and laughter of patrons and other visitors: "When they see ugly or funny things they say, 'Hey, look at this woman displaying herself! Is this really the way women are?' When they meet [mbari images of] people copulating, they say, 'Ewe! ewe! They are copulating—come and see them! Then all the people around will go to that place and laugh and shout.' "

The portrayal of time can also be superimposed on the assortment of imagery to reveal further the wealth of mbari sources. In a large mbari the visitor sees representations of historical occurrences, scenes dealing with the present, and the references to the future. The relationships between these overlapping periods also elucidate concepts of image-retention and change in mbari art. The introduciton of new, usually topical, imagery in past years has made extant mbari houses sources of historical data. Some innovations are never repeated a second time and hence are lost when the mbari disintegrates. Others are preserved for generations through replication. Both personalities and events have been recorded. About 1910, for example, a huge Igbo policeman from the northern Igbo town of Ogidi (and known by that name) was assigned to the Owerri area where he made a profound impression on the local people; they quickly appropriated him to mbari, where he became still larger even than in life (fig. 27). After his introduction as the "giant policeman," a topical character who may have also represented newly imposed law and order, Ogidi became a legend. Even today one frequently encounters his huge caricatured form.

In the 1920s and 30s a common mbari scene was the confrontation of German soldiers and British Maxim gunners (pl. 2), which presumably reached Owerri in stories or pictures, perhaps from Nigerians who fought on the British side in the Cameroons Campaign of 1913-14. But this scene, often made up of a boat and eight or ten figures and sometimes including a whimsical Gatling gun (fig. 29), was dropped sometime in the late 1930s and is no longer seen. Though that war is no longer relevant, it would not surprise me at all to see allusions to the Nigeria-Biafra conflict of 1967-69 in mbari houses made recently.

The figures of white men, Ogidi, and Nwa Alakandu, the dwarf, reveal certain flexible principles of image introduction and retention. It seems that a form may be initiated and tenaciously repeated under the following conditions:

1. If initially its subject is sufficiently strange or of widespread local interest.
2. If the image is odd or out-of-the-ordinary, with continuing "human interest" appeal.
3. If the image or stories about it continue to be relevant, funny, or memorable.
4. If the figure is suitable for mbari, both in relative ease of modeling and the possibility for harmonious inclusion within the sculptural program.

By these standards the 1913 war was no longer topical, and was, as well, sculpturally complex, space-consuming, and therefore difficult to repeat; hence such images were dropped. A complex scene of a white man being borne in a litter, photographed around the turn of the century by Whitehouse (pl. 62), was also dropped, perhaps as the custom of litter-bearing was discontinued, or because of its complexity. Simpler scenes of white men, Ogidi, and Nwa Alakandu, however, meet the retention criteria. The white man is ever present and always relevant; he is thus recorded in an overlapping series of changing images. Nwa Alakandu became a spirit and Ogidi a legend. As a single figure each of these can be included easily in any empty spot, or can even be placed in curious juxtaposition with other images, as when Ogidi "captures" Okpangu (pl. 41) or when Nwa Alakandu sits, placidly, under the belly of a "hippo" (pl. 62).

Merging with and frequently ousting historical imagery are those many figures and groups that document the present. Historical documentation is in fact both less frequent and less conscious than is the prevailing penchant for showing things as they are today or as they might be. In some instances the "here and now" only overlays traditional forms, as when Ala is clothed in a brassiere or Mamy Wata is decorated with the Christian cross (pl. 31), but in others, when bankers, cars, bicycles, and sewing machines are modeled, modern life appears in full force. To say that European clothes on mbari figures only represent the superficial adoption of Western culture, however, is to miss the point. For many an Owerri man today, pressed trousers, a shirt and shined shoes symbolize full involvement, at least to the extent now economically feasible (since a car, the ultimate symbol, is so expensive), in modern, evolved, European-style Nigerian life. It cannot be denied that there are strong vestiges of traditional Igbo life among even the most modern, as expressed for instance, in the action of university graduates who are known to use *ogwu* to pass examinations, but calling attention to such residues seldom dissuades younger people from their belief that they have superseded, and thereby cancelled, ancestral ways. What is remarkable is that mbari, ostensibly a traditional religious art form, so candidly and explicitly mirrors current anti-traditional views.

Mbari houses clearly manifest the desire to be "up-to-date." We see mirrors, clocks, western clothes, gin bottles, umbrellas, trains, and imported cloth. Machines, modern occupations, and even the plates themselves (mbari) directly reflect the consciousness of status and prestige associated with modernity. More revealing still is the imagery of that grey area in which the world as it is now merges with what is hoped for. Herein lies the apotheosis of mbari as a social and psychological document, as proof of the Igbo thirst for innovation and change.

Fundamental to this expression of hope is the very form of the mbari itself, a two-story house with a zinc roof. When this modern form evolved, in the 1920s or early 1930s, some few British colonial offices and residences were the only other buildings so constructed in Igboland. Indeed, a district officer's two-storied house still stands in the township of Owerri. Once the deity is housed in the most prestigious of buildings it can only be a matter of time, the people today hope, before she will filter similar benefits back down to them, particularly if they continue to honor her with such presents as mbari. One scene in particular symbolizes the merging of present realities with benefits a town hopes for in the near future. This view of a modern maternity clinic shows a mother giving birth, attended by midwife and two uniformed nurses (color plate 5). How sharp is the contrast between this and the traditional scene of parturition (pl. 4). The town where this mbari is located recently built a maternity center, and this group may thus be taken as a form of mere reporting, a quite direct translation of observable data (nurses with uniforms) adapted to an often-repeated type (scenes of women giving birth). However, the same mbari also documents as-yet-unrealized hopes for modernization, as it is linked up with a telephone system, although the town, Agwa, is actually twenty miles from Owerri and the nearest operating telephone. Telephone poles stand at each corner of the main house (fig. 12, pl. 75); on the walls of the clinic (color plate 5) and "office building" (pl. 3) there are mud telephone receivers constructed of used flashlight batteries. At the end of the cloister an animated operator relays silent messages (pl. 76). In another part of the same mbari stands a small airplane, built high on stilts, which because of its small size and summary handling looks quite unreal and amusing, somewhat in keeping perhaps with its current distance from realization in the village (fig. 12). In these three scenes we see three stages of the future: a maternity clinic, hoped for and now a reality; a telephone system, attainable, but only after some years; and the airplane, something "heard about" and seen in the air, but not really within the local scheme of things in the near future. In a similar sense the man shown in a white shirt and necktie, in this case a representation of Amadioha (color plate 9), may be taken in other situations to represent the local schoolteacher, one of the few citizens who might wear a tie (in use since early in the colonial era); or the townsman who has "gone abroad" to Onitsha or Lagos, Europe or America, and whose high status and "advanced" way of life are symbolized by his attire; or it may look forward to the time when such apparel (and the high standard of living it reflects) will be common in Owerri towns and villages. Therefore the costumes, occupations, and other modern references in mbari, like the honorific arm-raised pose of female figures, may represent projected ideals of form and behavior even more than they reflect the reality of the here and now. This sort of ambivalence will be discussed in the next chapter.

Mbari artists are very much integrated into community life. Their choices reflect, to a large extent, the shared world view, and in this sense they are transmitters of culture. Occasionally, as in the case of Ezem, personality may affect the subject and content of imagery; in these and other new forms, artists, as innovators, may be considered prophets, even creators, of culture. Usually it is difficult to classify individual mbari artists' work according to content. As the next section indicates, however, it is certainly possible to identify their work on stylistic grounds.

INDIVIDUALITY

Mbari artists, like African sculptors in all media, possess individual, sometimes idiosyncratic personal styles, just as some will be more inventive and original than others. This fact is acknowledged, if not stressed, by many Owerri people: "Skilled workers always do what comes out of their minds; they each do their own work and their handwork is varied. Their work cannot be the same"; or, "Artists work differently"; or, "The way an artist learns his work he will *always* work. The hand work of two men will always differ." The craftsman himself is of course most aware of his artistic origins and the fact of his individuality. Moreover, artists are especially conscious of their physical skills, their *hand*work, as if their aesthetic interests were as much manual and tactile as they are visual. Ugo said: "Mbari is in the hand," suggesting that the visual results of creative processes were somehow taken for granted. "Each person has his own way of working (i.e., style). . . . You are free to work the way you like. If necessary you can invite a fellow artist to lend you a hand, and you can see the two hands in the mbari." "Everybody works differently according to the dictates of his own mind. Some artists give all their figures similar faces, others vary them. All this depends on how you learned your work and what is in your mind."[11]

Against such acknowledged individuality, however, must be balanced the more general and pervasive comments of the viewing public and especially the people who have built an mbari. Here ideology obscures personality; an mbari is made by and for a specific community, and this, rather than the handwork of Nnaji or Ezem, is the sociological reality. The obviousness of this statement is not always recognized by those who stress the personal styles of African artists (see Cole 1969c). We have seen how spirit workers ritually deny their "hand" in the building effort, and how they avoid speaking about "their" mbari on subsequent occasions. No such stricture inhibits the professional artist although he is not acutely conscious, as western artists and scholars are, of which sculptures he modeled or even which types of figures he originated. On two occasions an artist mistook the work of another man for his own. As someone trained to recognize stylistic idiosyncrasies, I was more aware—in an mbari in which five men had modeled figures—than the mbari priest and his family were, of which figure was constructed by which man.

Furthermore, there are no regional styles in mbari sculpture. Rather, mbari work manifests a regional Igbo style that is internally quite homogeneous, and distinct from other, primarily woodcarving, modes elsewhere and even nearby in Igboland.[12] Although there is some concentration of a man's work in a radius extending outward from his own community, this cannot be counted as true regionalism; mbari artists were accustomed to travelling twenty-five miles or more from their homes to accept commissions. Hence, there are several personal styles visible in any small area, and not enough clustering of related personal styles to constitute a "school" or regional mode.

It is possible, on the other hand, to identify the personal styles of some artists with that of their masters or teachers. Data are available only for Nnaji and Ezem, contemporaries who worked together from time to time (color plate 9, pl. 28), both of whom were apprenticed to Uwama (pl. 28), perhaps the finest mbari sculptor of the twentieth century. Nnaji's style of modeling and Ezem's are closely related, both to each other and to the style of their teacher, as Ezem openly acknowledged: "My own handwork is better [than Nnaji's], but in fact our work is similar; both of us are on the same level. . . . I do not mind if people confuse our work; after all, a common mother (teacher/master) holds us together." The differences between Ezem's work (color plate 9, right) and Nnaji's (color plate 9, left) are small; Ezem's noses are shorter and his jaw lines tend to be more distinct. Nnaji spaces his eyes wider and tends to carry the fleshy nose bridge up into the forehead. The flare in Ezem's nostrils is more emphatic, and he sometimes models eyebrows (pls. 30 and 38), while Nnaji seldom does. Such subtle diagnostics are found only on heads; bodies modeled by the two artists are indistinguishable. Their painting styles, however, are quite different. Ezem's palette, especially in recent years, has been rather more colorful and flamboyant than that of Nnaji, who is also more conservative in his geometric designs on columns and lower walls. Ezem also seems more adventurous and inventive than his colleague in the "free" paintings applied to upper walls as well as in modeling unusual figures or groups.

All in all, Ezem's work shows more variety, a bit more creative flair both in subject matter and style. Nnaji, on the other hand, has remained the "classic" mbari craftsman, highly accomplished, precise, and clear, and his work shows little change over the years. Ezem's work is more uneven; sometimes it reaches greatness (pl. 30), while recently, perhaps as a consequence of his failing strength in advanced years, it has occasionally been somewhat sloppy and inconsistent from figure to figure.

I had a long discussion with Ezem about the relative merits of various artists. In general his opinions coincide with my own, a fact that suggests, if it by no means proves, that qualitative standards have cross-cultural consistency. When I asked Ezem to compare the work of Nnaji to that of Ugwuanya, he snapped back: "How can you compare an elephant to a beetle? Of course Nnaji's work is far better." Other parts of this conversation are worth recording:

> *Questioner*: Can you tell me about the work of some of the living artists?
> *Ezem*: There are these: myself, Nnaji, Akalazu, Ugwuanya and Akakporo. This is how Akalazu's figures usually are! (facial expression of derision)
> *Questioner*: His work is good?
> *Ezem*: No, it is poor.
> *Questioner* Akakporo and Akalazu, which is better?
> *Ezem*: Akakporo's work is better.
> *Questioner*: Do you know Ugo?
> *Ezem*: Ugo of Ihitte? Yes, the heads of his figures are always the size of my hand.
> *Questioner*: Ugo and Akakporo, who is better?
> *Ezem*: Ugo does better work than Akakporo.
> *Questioner*: Akalazu and Akakporo?
> *Ezem*: Akalazu's work is like turds!

In the following section on aesthetics we will find independent—and rather more circumspect—corroboration for Ezem's opinion of Akalazu.

Ezem also singled out one of the significant personal traits in Ugo's work, his small heads, which are at the same time more naturalistic than the elongated ones of Ezem and Nnaji. Ugo also has a penchant for small-unit details and sometimes shows a *horror vacui.* Precision detailing, approaching a kind of rococo filigree, is especially evident in his female deity sculptures (color plate 10). His emphasis on crowding and filling available space may be seen in his paintings (figs. 18-22). Ugo's work overall, when compared with that of Nnaji, tends to emphasize fussiness and small subdivisions, while he (Ugo) is quite adventurous in two-dimensional painting.

Akalazu's figural style, as opposed to Ugo's, is in the monumental tradition of Ezem and Nnaji. Yet Akalazu lacks the crisp precision of the other three; his faces often have an amorphous quality sometimes approaching lumpiness (pl. 37). Igbo critics of his work (see next section) find it uneven or unbalanced, lacking in smoothness, clarity, and precision, at times sloppy. They find his noses too large and his mouths too small, his bodies sometimes off-balance, lacking desirable straightness. People identified the "rough bumps" in some of Akalazu's work with the representation of old age, which they implied is not appropriate to the idealized nature of mbari statuary.

Ezem did not especially favor Akakporo's work. Notably, however, both Akalazu and Akakporo had plenty of commissions in the 1960s, so we must assume that their public reception was more favorable than Ezem's perhaps elitist judgement. In fact, mbari patrons appear to find the work of all available professionals acceptable although, as we shall see, they are not loath to make qualitative differentiations when asked to do so. As far as I know, however, no completed mbari has ever been rejected, although some have been severely criticized. The artist Nnaji told me of two instances in which the deities for whom mbari were made refused to accept them, the verdict presumably handed down through divination. In each case the townspeople, who despite the allegedly inferior quality of the houses had spent much time and energy constructing them, implored the gods to accept. In one case they claimed that the mbari expenses had already crippled them and they could not afford to start again. In each case the god relented and the mbari was opened. Since divination determines (theoretically) if an mbari is acceptable aesthetically, the diviner is (again theoretically) perhaps the ultimate critic. Yet this man had long been involved with the mbari and was most likely present when the elders came inside the enclosure to formally criticize the house, so his opinion probably represented a consensus.

Akakporo's personal diagnostics (pls. 22 and 42) include especially long necks, shaped as truncated cones, and small, high noses with sharply pinched nostrils, the latter sometimes giving his figures a squinting effect. Akakporo told me of an interesting fact, which I have no reason to doubt, that bears on the consciousness of individuality among artists; as an apprentice he soon learned how to model heads, and after that his "master" would construct only the bodies, turning the figure over to Akakporo, who modeled all the heads and faces.

Space does not allow a discussion of all the artists' personal styles. Suffice it to say that there is indeed a notable range of formal solutions to the problems of figural modeling in clay and painting wall surfaces. The illustrations dramatize the point more clearly than words can. One artist from Etche extends the nose bone into the forehead; another achieves individuality not so much by sculpture as in decorative face-painting; still another models small, narrow noses.

Personal styles must then be seen as facts despite the minimal emphasis given named individuals, as such, by most of the public involved with mbari. Artists may be aware of idiosyncrasies but even they, visually the most highly trained people in the Owerri world, place no great emphasis on acute individualism. Formal distinctions seem much more the result of subconscious manual tendencies, like those accounting for most differences in handwriting, than of style consciousness *per se* or deliberate efforts to develop personal or individual modes.

AESTHETIC RESPONSE

In the past several years[13] Africanists have been increasingly interested in the aesthetic responses of Africans to their own works of art. Under the stimulus of these efforts to gain insight into native categories and principles, I went to the field hoping to discover what the Igbo might contribute to this discussion.[14] Unfortunately my interviews geared specifically to aesthetics came at the end of fieldwork and were terminated, perhaps one-third complete, by my departure from the area at the onset of the Nigerian Civil War. Still, enough data are available for a preliminary report on Owerri attitudes in this realm.

During other discussions about mbari, and before specific interviews on aesthetics took place, several factors bearing on the subject emerged. Neither artists nor the general public volunteer aesthetic analysis; reactions to works of art are not readily separated from functional and cultural considerations; men and women *can* be good critics, but the Owerri value system seems to place little emphasis on this activity. In short, analytic response to works of art is not an "isolate" in Owerri thought,[15] as storytelling, sacrificing, or dancing might be. Each of these points was corroborated repeatedly during my work on aesthetics.

After several months of intensive questioning of all kinds, often at or near mbari houses, I heard only two or three voluntary comments concerning their relative quality or the design principles that governed their creation and decoration. I did on several occasions elicit such information, but nearly always I came away frustrated by what I considered "unsatisfactory" answers which skirted that issue, however informative they may have been in other respects. I became repeatedly aware that all mbari were beautiful and good, and more important, that excellence in form is for most Igbo synonymous with excellence in concept, purpose, and result. Gratuitous corroboration for such emphasis on the wholeness and significance of "art" works came from other situations, for example when a man was asked to describe an "ideal" woman in terms of the way she was formed. His initial response was to refer to the *whole* woman: "I wouldn't know anything about her inside, only her flesh." On a different occasion, when a man was asked to choose between two female mbari figures, he inferred that the question was unfair: "I might like the way she walks." Still another response to the same question: "No woman is any more beautiful than another one—unless the second is barren." This merging of cultural and aesthetic responses is well-stated by one of Robert F. Thompson's informants in the Banyang area of Cameroun: "We say people are not judged by physical beauty but by the quality of their heart and soul" (Thompson 1973: 42). The Owerri man first sees the total significance of a "work of art" and concludes that its forms express well what is intended: "The person who has done it has done it well; after all, he is not Chineke. Of course I can't come out and tell you something here [in the mbari] is bad; they are all fine and beautiful." Or: "This belongs to the god who owns us; I cannot tell you that this figure here is beautiful and that another is ugly. All the figures here are good and beautiful. It is our tradition." Asked if people talked about the *form* of mbari, another man said: "They praised it and [at its opening] they killed a goat and a fowl with which to talk about the beautiful figures." Almost invariably the "owner of the house," the deity for whom the mbari was made, was considered the finest figure, although occasionally the female relief figures, *ijeremgbe,* were preferred. I realized that no cultural provision exists for the separation of purely formal considerations from those of a general ideological or functional nature. An mbari is supposed to be fine, it is meant to be beautiful, and therefore it is. Such attitudes are of course patently logical. After all, an mbari is rare for any single community, one of the unique climax events in an otherwise relatively drab succession of common daily activities; in this sense there is no cultural provision for it to be either artistically inferior or spiritually ineffective. I began to see that "unsatisfactory" responses to aesthetically oriented questions were in fact telling me a great deal about the place of "art" in Owerri life, and not a little about my own preconceptions.

The ambiguity in Igbo thought between "artistic" and "practical" beauty may be seen in the Igbo language, for example in the word *nma.* This adjective can signify goodness (moral), usefulness (functional), beauty (artistic or physical), enjoyment (as of a performance), suitability (as of an occasion or time), or fit (a garment "fits" well). The intended nuance often, but not always, may be inferred from the context in which the remark is made. The word *njo* or *ojo* (bad, ugly, unsuitable, etc.) has the same multiple valence. Notably, speakers often do not *intend* to qualify these words, for all nuances may be implied. Thus to say "mbari is *nma*" is to make a powerful, multi-faceted statement embracing moral, aesthetic, and social values.

Aware of these general attitudes, I nevertheless established a semblance of laboratory control[16] to further plumb people's responses to mbari. I chose two houses, each of which contained figures by two prominent, well-established artists, Ezem and Akalazu, whose styles are markedly different. Fifteen people were interviewed, hardly an adequate sample for conclusive results, yet trends and tentative finds seem to be consistent and therefore valuable enough to set down. Each informant was asked approximately the same questions; all were cult devotees (priests, spirit-workers, and *amala*) who had some greater-than-passing interest in the mbari used for testing. Each person interviewed was told in advance that he would be given a standard five shillings for taking the time to answer our questions. I was well-known in the two communities and hence encountered little general suspicion although several people found the nature of the questions (asked by an interpreter trusted by the people) decidedly odd; for example, when a man was asked *why* he felt the work of Ezem (pl. 63) was superior to that of Akalazu (pl. 64), which he readily admitted, he said "that is not what we are judging. We do not ask a lot of questions." To the same query another replied, "All I can say is I like this better. There is no more I can tell you." All but one critic preferred Ezem's figures to those of Akalazu.

In view of the prevailing reluctance to find fault with an entire mbari, it is significant that most informants were willing to discuss the relative quality of individual figures or parts of the whole structure, and that they were more adept still at picking out parts and details of such figures for praise or, more rarely, criticism. This tendency accords exactly with Vogel's experience with Baule critics (1973: 15-16). Few informants, however, felt quite comfortable in saying *why* one figure was superior to another, although with repeated questions, some of a probing nature, five individuals gave answers that I would consider analytic rather than simply descriptive. When comparisons were elicited the most common replies were like the following: "This one sits upright, but this other one is bent," or "Her form is good, her neck is beautiful because it is long and not too thin; the hair is fine because of the way it was dressed." Or "I like this figure [pl. 63] because of the way it was made; it is filled out just right. And look at the wristwatch; that makes him look nice. Look at his legs; see how they stand erect. His head is straight and upright, and the cap fits well." Such essentially descriptive commentary could be multiplied twentyfold from these interviews.

A theoretical question arises, however, about the extent to which such descriptive comments—either appreciating or depreciating—may be considered aesthetic *criticism*. A good many of Thompson's eighteen Yoruba aesthetic criteria, which he refers to as "named abstractions," seem to be descriptive points of reference primarily.[17] Most of Thompson's criteria were preferences remarked also by Susan Vogel among the Baule, and most came up in my interviews as well. Neither Vogel nor I found our informants enumerating aesthetic criteria *per se*, and the same appears to be true of Thompson. Speaking of an mbari female figure, for example, one informant said: "Everything about her is so complete, her face, her hair, her neck, her breasts." Asked about her disproportionately long neck (that is, in relation to that of a real human being), the same man said: "Look, we have two kinds of necks, short ones [gesture of derision] and then we have long necks for tall beautiful women [gesture of approval]. This one is long and upright." "Completeness" and "uprightness" (or straightness) can be extracted from these responses; this, I take it, is how both Thompson and Vogel arrive at their aesthetic criteria. Description certainly comprises an aspect of the concept and syntax of criticism, yet I see articulated analysis, which is based to some extent on comparative judgment, to be the essence of this activity. A prerequisite for true voluntary analysis in this sense would seem to be a range of possibilities within a type and thus the existence of contrasts and comparisons. There must then be a local valuation of the verbalization of comparative judgments over enough time to create a tradition of critical analysis. This kind of artistic criticism I found lacking among those interviewed. I believe it is equally true, moreover, that few Americans or Europeans approached on the street at random would qualify as true critics in this sense if asked about modern art or architecture.

Analytic commentary was rare then, but did occur occasionally. A few such responses may be cited. One man explained why he preferred the body painting of one figure to that of another: "Skill differs; it's like haircutting. A barber can give you a brilliant haircut that suits your body and you will be very pleased; but the same haircut on another man might be bad." In comparing two geometric column paintings another man stood back to say: "You have got to make many patterns; this one with several different patches—it is good. If you make just one design/form (*odi*) it is not good. It would not be good having them all resemble each other. If you have a light pattern here, put a dark one next to it. If first a tall person, then a short one. If ten people are on the road, are they all equal in height? There must be variation." Here the informant began with a description, only to abstract from his observation, by comparison, the analytic concepts of contrast and variation. Other comments of this nature touched upon ideas of composition, unity, and idealized human form.

Composition: In response to a question on how mbari walls should be painted to make them beautiful, a woman said: "You have to divide the wall up into pieces and put them in the right position. You have to combine them very cleverly, put one against another so they kill one another [i.e., contrast]; when one kills the other you will use another color to separate them." Another person observed of a female figure: "Look at her body and head; everything seems balanced and proportionate. Everything is complete and in the right position."

On unity: Answering our question about *why* he preferred an Ezem male figure to one by Akalazu, a man said: "The way the painting is outlined; it has unity." Another: "The face here is unified and well-balanced." Still another: "The work on these two figures is not the same; here the body, legs, and face are all unified. . . . This is better."

Mbari informants were mostly aware of the real difference between living people and those portrayed in mbari, and they commented on each according to traditional ideals. At the same time they clearly recognized and appreciated the skill of the artists. "The person who did this [figure] made it in the *form* of a human being; he succeeded" (emphasis mine). Asked if he liked a figure, a man said : "Yes, the artist did it well." Why do you like it? "You know the work of an artist is just a trick. What they do is make figures that make people laugh and others that are so beautiful." Asked to choose between two female figures, another man said: "Both of them are fine, well-made, and they resemble the way Chineke made human beings, but an Igbo man made them by hand, modeling mud. If they were alive they wouldn't be sitting here day after day." The priest in charge of one mbari overcame his reluctance to criticize any figure and chose Ezem's seated female over that of Akalazu, principally because of her long neck: "People have long rainbow necks. I've never seen a woman with a neck this long even though I've seen long-necked women. But this has been worked by a skilled hand; the person did what came out of his mind. This is what he did with his hand, and he does it so people will praise him. 'Do you see this neck?' people will ask, and no one will say this neck is bad for being too short.' " We can put these few analytic responses together with data from the many descriptive comments to infer some abstract principles of a provisional nature. Manifestly, however, the abstracting process for most of this material is the author's, not the Igbos'. The principles may be no less valid for that, but caution should be introduced lest we impute this translation to the traditional Igbo and include it as a normal part of his system of valuation and articulation.

We cannot doubt, however, that Igbo people analyze form intuitively; the consistency of their judgment, the clarity and tenacity of their opinions, as well as the very quality (in our terms) of the art work itself assure us that this is true. Before attempting to outline inferred principles governing form and quality in mbari, then, it is well to indicate what verbal and other mechanisms Igbo people employ to make these judgments.

Thirteen of the fifteen people interviewed were able to separate reactions to form from functional or ideological considerations after sometimes-repeated explanations about the nature of our experiment. Most were clearly more comfortable, however, expressing themselves in terms of "good-better-best" rather than "good or poor." Two absolutely refused to make any comparison between specific figures, insisting that "the artist did well" or asking "have you ever seen a person do a deliberate bad thing?" Several, as we have seen, entered into the spirit of the interview even though most seemed puzzled by the questions—the kinds of questions another Igbo would never dream to ask. Queried repeatedly on *why* he preferred one figure over another, for example, one man became annoyed: "Why do you keep on bothering me? If you see a good thing don't you know it?" Still, levels and types of responses can be quite easily discerned.

Nearly all people approached were able and willing, eventually, to say which figure in a pair (one similar figure each by Ezem and Akalazu) they preferred (pls. 29, 63, and 64). The responses were in fact remarkably consistent, for out of 35 chances, 34 reactions were the same.[18] This near-unanimity may have stemmed from what I believe to be markedly disparate levels of skill and accomplishment in the two artists, but the fact that both had frequent commissions, and considering the rather bizarre nature of any sort of articulated qualitative ranking, those interviewed showed themselves to be sharp observers. The question remains: Can they be called critics? I prefer to call most of them able "appreciators," for they remained on a *reaction* level, avoiding articulated *analysis* unless pressed. We may assume that intuitive analysis precedes the judgment. Relatively uncomplicated statements of appreciation were in fact very frequent during the interviews, as we have seen: "It is well made," "Everything about the figure is complete," "Her features are even [proportionate]," "This figure is off-balance," "The mouth isn't good at all; it is like this [puckering gesture] and it is small, resembling *nkapi* [a type of rat], the body is not smooth and the face is ugly."

Gestures of approval or derision, as well as laughter and handclapping, were clearly part of the "vocabulary" of appreciation. These gestures were made with hand, body, or face and sometimes with all three at the same time. Indeed, my impression was that physical responses were both more frequent and more expressive in dramatizing feeling levels in Igboland than in our own culture.[19]

An aspect of articulated response that particularly drew my attention was the coinage of words, modified or made up on the spot, which were well understood in context but not necessarily intelligible alone or easily transferable to other situations. Five or six respondents coined words in this manner. The words themselves are both alliterative and onomatopoetic in Igbo: *kwagarakwagara* for "haphazard" or "sloppy," *ngringri* for "vibrates," *yigiyigi* for "rough" or "shabby," *gbagaragbara* for "dignified." Often, the newly modified or coined word was combined with an appropriate gesture to clarify and emphasize its meaning.

Notably, the Igbo language also contains a great many commonly understood words appropriate to a discussion of formal qualities. The following is a brief sample: Oneness, or unity, *otu, nzuko;* balance, *kwa-*

bim; off-balance, *ndahere;* complete, *ozurezu;* position, *onodi;* shape or form, *odidi;* design or form, *odi.* And although the context of the statement naturally contributes a great deal, many fine distinctions or near-synonyms allow nuance to be clearly expressed. The following, for example, are variations of intensity and focus on the idea of straightness or uprightness, a clearly preferred trait, all of which were used in the interviews:

straight or erect	*guzo*
very straight	*guzuruegus o*
straight, upright	*kwaroto*
upright	*ebegere*
standing proudly upright	*kwekere*

We have seen that several people were aware that mbari figures did not look like real humans, but showing instead proportions associated with ideal form. The most commonly noted ideal feature is the long, ringed neck—a widespread convention among African people: "Long necks are always beautiful; you will admit that yourself." "I like the way he made the neck because it is sufficiently long and erect, and it has these coils around it. It is the *ihe egurugru na olu,* 'coiled rainbow on the neck.' " Susan Vogel emphasizes the point that Baule critics prefer sculpture to adhere to traditional *sculptural* ideals rather than to observable nature, and she indicated what is nearly a universal trait, that "art imitates art far more closely than it imitates nature" (Vogel 1979: 318). Baule and Igbo informants agree on this point, preferring sculptural figures that "look like a person" (i.e., the sculptural ideal) and criticizing those sculptures that fall short. Such figures, called ugly, were compared to old people, foreigners (especially Hausa, the active enemy in 1967), deformed or diseased persons—obviously those outside the preferred norm. Exceptions to the ban on indicating age are Ala and other important female deities, for reasons that will be discussed in the next chapter. Also appreciated were straight, upright postures and a youthful (young adult) appearance and carriage. This quality of youthfulness is noted as important to Baule critics, reported by Vogel, and is among Thompson's criteria. Proportions skewed to emphasize the torso and especially the neck and head of a figure were praised. Informants preferred figures with straight thin noses, long faces, and light-colored skin.[20] Nor did the short legs often seen on seated figures disturb people: "If she stands up she will be something to laugh at—her legs would be too short and would not suit her body; but as she is seated here, it is good for her."

Few of these ideals are expressed both in mbari statuary and in approving reactions to it are physically present in the community itself, at least in such extremes. In this respect people clearly differentiated art from life, illusion from reality. The artist Ugo, for example, said: "Nobody will try to make an mbari figure (*ewuwu*) resemble a human being. If an artist deliberately makes one look like a human being it will turn out very ugly." They take the mbari for what it is: "These things are modeled in clay. They are things done by man's hand." Several people acknowledged artists' skill in modeling intentionally "ugly" figures such as Okpangu: "When we see the ugly ones, we say so; but these usually cause laughter and people shout with glee. Even these ugly ones are well made. . . . The artist who made it did it purposely, to cause laughter."

In this regard we may note how concerned most observers were with artists' technique. Comments on skill or facility—or the lack of them—must be recognized as a dimension of critical response; indeed, sloppy workmanship tended to catch a person's eye and concern him considerably more than did other aspects of form. One man said, after comparing the work of the two artists, "There are people whose work becomes very powerful and pleasing to the eye. The work of others is rough and shabby." The frame of reference for fine, "powerful" work (an abstract idea) is that of poor technical competence. Commenting on two examples of body painting, another person said: "This one is just splotchy; it vibrates in a bad way. But see how this other one was drawn; it was marked out precisely and carefully." Another: "Ezem's faces are usually smooth and good, but when Akalazu models his figures, either they jut out their mouths or they bend to one side." Such comments on technique, like the descriptive reactions which they closely resemble, certainly contain the seeds of analytic criticism. On the other hand, the same commentators usually remain silent on abstract formal properties and relationships between parts.

Technical dexterity would certainly number among Owerri Igbo formal principles. A number of others can be inferred from the interviews although, as noted, few of these ideas were stated as abstractions. A single composite statement (compiled from several interviews) might run like this: "Individual figures should be based on a prototype of idealized naturalism, with smooth surfaces, clearly rendered parts, and precisely finished detailing. Surface painting should mark parts off from one another so they are clearly visible. Technical competence means that figures will be complete and without blemishes, for blemishes suggest human abnormality or old age. Faces and poses should reflect youthful vigor; flesh, for example, should appear firm and compact, while postures should be proudly erect. Women's breasts will be high and full. Distortions of human anatomy are condoned only when they conform to recognized ideals (i.e., the long neck) or for specific, purposely "ugly" subjects such as Okpangu, the mythical ape-man. The whole mbari program should show variety but in a unified way. Individual parts should contrast with one another—in size, shape, color, and emphasis—with order and balance; and undue attention should not be drawn to any part except, perhaps, the owner of the house. Work that appears sloppy, haphazard, or rough is not tolerated. All parts, as well as the whole, must be complete and carefully finished."

Precision, balance, straightness, and order were among the words most commonly used in these interviews, and while they were used in response to specific figures or mbari parts, they, like the other words in the paragraph above, may be taken as abstract design principles that do in fact govern the aesthetic basis of mbari.

In conclusion we may observe that the Owerri "critic" knows clearly, if intuitively, what he likes and has both the vocabulary and expressive nuance to back up his reaction; yet he is not often constrained to explain his position in detail or in analytic terms:

> *Questioner*: Do mbari visitors ever discuss these figures?
> *Informant*: Yes, people come to look at the figures.
> *Questioner*: Do they *talk* about them?
> *Informant*: They will move around and say this is good/beautiful, this too, this one more beautiful, and they leave money at the one they like best.
> *Questioner*: But they don't give reasons?
> *Informant*: They don't. They just say the artist has done well here and here; he has made a mistake here.

Another situation:

> *Questioner*: You recognize a beautiful thing, but do people talking about it say why it is beautiful?
> *Informant*: No, they do not say why. They say "This is beautiful," clap their hands and go on to another and say "This is ugly. It [Okpangu] was done purposely."

6 Meaning

Attempts to unravel the complexities, contradictions, nuances, and deeper meanings of mbari are at best difficult. To give a truly full explanation would be tantamount to defining what Owerri people feel is the meaning of life itself. And they, of course, are loath to analyze either life or mbari. The institution, in both process and form, has an ineffable quality analogous to the artistic and ritual culture of the Abelam people as discussed by Anthony Forge (1965, 1974). For the Abelam, as for the Igbo, art and ritual constitute a system of communication independent of words, expressing things for which there are no real verbal equivalents. It is possible to discuss such concepts as the motivation, function, meaning, and content of mbari, as the following analysis indicates, but these interpretations go well beyond those of any single Igbo informant.

Several attempts have been made to define the meaning of the word *mbari*. Talbot,[1] echoed later by Leith-Ross,[2] translates it as "fine" or "decorated." "Beautiful," said Whitehouse;[3] Spörndli called it "celebration."[4] Owerri people, when asked the meaning of the word, respond by defining the whole phenomenon, the concept of mbari, the reason for mbari, or what mbari does for them or other people. This variety of answers arises out of the role of the informant, whether priest, artist, mbari worker, or villager, and must be interpreted in the light of his or her vested interests. In the broad sense all these "synonyms" are correct; and the fact that none of them is an inclusive definition of the word should not cloud our realization that mbari, as a complex and long-term festival, means many different things.

Etymology, however, reveals the probable origin and thus something of the real meaning of the word itself. *Mba* means "town" or "village,"[5] *eri* is the infinitive of the verb "to eat." When these words are combined and elided, a common practice in making Igbo words, the result is mbari, "the town eats."[6] Thus mbari is a time and a place where the whole town (or village) eats, or more precisely, where representatives of the town's various segments converge for a prolonged major celebration. Like many African peoples, the Igbo invest considerable social and symbolic value in the sharing out of food and its consumption. Nowhere are these valuations more clearly demonstrated than in a festival setting, like mbari, when men and the gods share the same sacrificial foods in a carefully choreographed act of communion.

Although a fundamental motivation for mbari is the fear engendered in the hearts and minds of the people by a major catastrophe or a series of minor ones, other factors are involved. Mbari is thanks as well, and a tangible prayer for further benefits. One explanation for the delay in construction—as much as five or ten years after divination reveals the need for mbari—is that these motivations take time to crystallize. By the time of "walking the iron," various interest groups, spearheaded and mobilized by the priest and the host village, have spread word of potential dangers to other people in the village group to bring about a community of conscious and subconscious fears, desires, and expectations. Motivations have ramified in myriad, sometimes conflicting, directions. Only by analyzing the activities, interest groups, and forms of mbari can we begin to understand the many meanings of the entire phenomenon.

The etymological definition of mbari reveals a basic distinction between the processes of erecting an mbari and the resulting forms. The meaning of the word and the responses of Owerri people to questions about the meaning of mbari stress process as much as form. Because the motivations for mbari and the socio-religious significance of the process are not necessarily the same as the meaning of the completed building, its sculpture and painting, *process* and *form* can, at least for analysis, be differentiated for separate discussion.

THE MEANING OF THE MBARI PROCESS

"Mbari is our god."
"Mbari is a sacrifice to the god who owns us."[7]

These quotations underscore the fundamentally religious character of the mbari process. Because of its great size and infrequent occurrence, mbari is the most elaborate and time-consuming sacrifice offered in Owerri culture. In what ways is mbari a spiritual expression, and how does it constitute a sacrifice? Not only individual sacrifices within mbari but the whole process is an elaborate mystery play shrouded in secrecy, where only initiates and a few closely involved professionals are admitted into the sacred enclosure. Symbolic sacred objects are employed, countless prayers invoked, and various rites and sacrifices carried out to assure mbari workers a beneficial relationship with the gods and therefore a long and productive life for the whole community. In addition, the entire mbari process satisfies Hubert and Mauss's concept of sacrifice" ". . . a religious act which, through the consecration of a victim, modifies the condition of the moral person who accomplishes it or that of certain objects with which he is concerned" (1964:13).

The great sacrifice involved in the activity of building an mbari containing, say, seventy-five figures and dedicated to the dominant god of a given town starts with a modest and conventional ritual, the offering of a single fowl or goat. Over the next ten or twelve years, however, those animal sacrifices multiply a hundredfold and are supplemented with countless other goods and the efforts of hundreds of people. The development of an mbari may in fact be visualized as a constant unfolding, each subsequent step being revealed through the various forms of sacrifice (and thank offering) involved.

The first effective ritual activity surrounds "tying the head on iron" and the following tour of "iron people" with this symbolic object, initiating the ceremonial festival of "eating yams." The "head of iron," *ishigwe,* represents the deity for whom the house is to be made. Short of mbari itself, the iron bar, *igwe,* represents the most important form of sacrifice, for each bar was presented to the god with a human slave, *osu.* The symbol is carried through the town by old women (*ndishigwe*), who are neutral and unable to contaminate the god-symbol or be greatly contaminated by it. The tour of these women, with their dangerously powerful object, is analogous to a tour by the goddess herself. It is as if the assembled priests and diviners had called the god into their midst to witness their ritual promise to erect mbari, then sent her out through the town, in symbolic form, to rally and intimidate the entire community. During this tour the goddess comes close to all her people, indeed too close; goats and fowl are offered in turn by every village to urge the *agbara* to withdraw, which she does, figuratively, each time the old ladies move to the next village. In effect, the dozens of sacrifices over the next few years are repeated supplications, asking the goddess to return to that neutral distance from which men and women may continue their lives in peace and prosperity.

The festival of "eating yams" is an uneasy proclamation of joy by the community that has agreed to build a "house" for its god. Because the god is thought to rejoice at the prospect, the people, too, must rejoice. Informants said that the god expressed her joy with wanton "friendships" among her fellow deities; so must the people capitalize on the brief period of spiritually sanctioned sexual freedom. Perhaps too this period of abandon and chaos is necessary before the longer period of denial and discipline that follows when the structure begins. All frivolity, then, must cease before the real work begins, for the people must enter this undertaking with reverence and solemnity. The god has come to visit, has established new and stricter laws, and has turned the whole community to the coming monumental task.

The actual building cannot begin until the mbari workers have undergone elaborate preparations for their sacred work. Their initiation is conceived of as a symbolic death followed by their rebirth as spirits, and it is divided into several phases: preparation, including a vigil and ordeal with attendants; walking the iron to cries of "Goodbye, go well"; being cut with a knife while lying on banana leaves (which are used for corpses in actual burials); seclusion in a special hut; sexual restrictions; new cloths and attributes (*ofo igwe* and *agalegbe*); new names and spouses; ritual feeding when they emerge; repeated purifications and acts of strengthening. The complexity of the initiation, moreover, suggests that *ndimgbe* are repeated sacrifices:[8] human sacrifices when they "walk the iron," the symbolic bridge which conveys them to their death, or limbo, of three weeks in *eke nwaori;* and "spirit-sacrifices" when their spirit identities are ceremonially cast away and burned at the end of the process, before they are reborn to the outside world as ordinary mortals.

Some informants recognize that *ndimgbe,* after their initiation, become spirits. Ezem said that:

> If someone should see *ndimgbe* while they are working collecting yam, they will go to his house and take goats and fowls. The man will not see them, or see that these things have been done. The *ndimgbe* are not *amala* inside. They are doing the work of the deity. . . . They are regarded as spirits (*ndimmuo*) because everything ordinary people do, they do not do. They won't plant cassava with us, cut bush with us, or keep the roads in good order. When yams are planted, they don't plant, and wine tappers will not tap. They are spirits. When they finish they undergo a ceremony, and then they can go back to do what the *amala* are doing.

Another informant clearly revealed that each member of the spirit-worker group is a sacrificial offering: "He is used to free all his people from the wrath of the god. He represents them all. He is used in sacrifice."

The four-day-workers, on the other hand, remain *amala* or ordinary villagers (or slaves). They rub protective medicine on their bodies and are purified at the opening, but they do not undergo symbolic death. They live as members of the normal community during most of the building period and must fulfill their "civilian" responsibilities. This dichotomy between *ndimgbe* and four-day-workers explains the ambiguous relationship between the groups. Human beings (four-day-workers) work the hardest, but the spirits (*ndimgbe*) must be careful not to offend them lest the humans leave them and turn to other gods.

The difference between spirit-workers and four-day-workers parallels the distinction between anthill clay and ordinary clay or mud. The core of the "ordinary house" is made with mud which is, significantly, dug and prepared by four-day-workers. Spirit-workers may not enter these mud pits. But anthill clay (yam), used to mold the mbari figures, must be dug by *ndimgbe*. Anthill clay itself, and the collecting of it, is dangerous for spirit-workers; anthills are resting places for deities, spirits, and human souls. Common mud may be dug in the daytime, but "yam" must be collected at night, the time of spirits, with many restrictions. While only the mud is being modeled, the emerging building is not yet considered mbari, but after the turning point of plate and iron insertion, when the work with "yam" begins, the atmosphere becomes spiritually charged, and the building is first identified as mbari. Because figures are modeled in "yam" only, this symbolic clay may be seen also as a food offering to the god. Modeled mbari figures are spirits, *umummuo*, in three senses: they are the children of the god for whom the mbari is built; they are made from spirit clay; they are made *by* spirits, the *ndimgbe*. The plates and irons imbedded in the mbari walls are also important sacrificial materials. Plates are brought by *ndimgbe*, individual compounds, and families, carrying the concept of sacrifice into all segments of the community. The fact that these plates are not actually used for eating, and that the huge number of them represents a great financial outlay by the community, suggest that they also function as an important part of the sacrificial complex.

Irons, too, are sacrifices. One man described the use of many previously-sacrificed irons, *igwe*, in the walls and columns as "showing off"; indeed, these irons are reminders of the wealth and power of the god (pl. 21). The repeated and varying uses for iron act in mbari as a reprise of all the major (human) sacrifices in the twenty-five to forty years since the last house was built. Re-sacrificing these symbolic objects in a new, still more important context demonstrates emphatically the ramifying nature of sacrifice in the mbari process, and at the same time points up its display of wealth.

The final ceremonies, as mbari is unveiled, further extend the concepts of sacrifice. The small, incomplete first-figure is uprooted to be thrown away as a scapegoat carrying with it any lurking difficulties that might disturb the success of the project. The curses spirit-workers raise upon themselves before their expulsion, stating that they are "lost . . . burnt, and dead," suggest that their former spirit identities are killed, also as scapegoats, in the fires lit to consume the first-figure and the fence debris. After the workers are purified and "release their heads" from the god, they run out into the free world, reborn again as human beings.

All aspects of mbari are sacred. The sanctity of the entire building period is ritually established at the "tying of head on iron," when special laws governing behavior are enacted. Through the symbolic role of *ndimgbe,* who represent all lineages, the entire community is embraced in and contributes to the activity, to enter the "face of the god" (*ihu agbara*) by proxy, thereafter to establish and enthrone the god in an elaborate and holy house. The process also instigates a rebuilding of spiritual life in the community. The *agbara* is present and particularly forceful at this time, reminding people of their continuing obligation to her and punishing severely any transgressor.

At the completion of an mbari, people wait for their desires and expectations to materialize.[9] In their piety they have paid heavily in a complex of sacrifices, and the god must compensate them in return.

"Mbari is to tell the god not to kill us."
"Mbari is for giving life and giving children."

These are statements of spirit-workers in 1966 while still inside the mbari enclosure, under obligation to their god. Their first preoccupations are with children and with preserving themselves and their families. In the narrow sense, to workers, mbari means protection from imminent death. Asked why she liked being an mbari worker, one woman replied, "It is work for our mother who will kill anyone refusing." Another said, "I like it because I am alive. If you work as *onyemgbe*, you will live longer." Since each worker represents a family or lineage, by extension that group will benefit from its member's service to the god. "I went to mbari for peace and our lives. It is to save my family, and they will have great praise names for me for doing this."[10]

In a broader sense, mbari enriches the lives of these spirit participants by virtue of their extraordinary activity. Mbari is a respite from the cares of family and world, and at the same time an entertaining dramatic performance, a festival, and a "school." Some verses of a song sung by the *ndimgbe* on the paths to the "yam farm" (anthill) emphasize this learning experience:

> When you come back from *mgbe* you know many things;
> He who returned from *mgbe* knowing nothing, that is his own fault.

A worker would have to be very insensitive not to gain from the unique experience. Those I spoke with enjoyed their life even though they complained about it.

As a result of mbari, all participants expect more and healthier children, one of the primary preoccupations of agrarian peoples, who have long been plagued by a high rate of infant mortality. "Because of this mbari, the deity will give the town many children." Or again, "Mbari will make our yams large and our wives bring forth children." Mbari means increase in all species, human, animal, and vegetable. Although actual results are difficult to measure, increase probably does occur in the more favorable domestic climate that mbari fosters. Men are at home, undistracted by local disputes or larger wars; they can devote more attention to their wives and their farms. Energy once dissipated in destructive projects can now be directed to productive ends.

"Mbari is a time when a god and its priest gather wealth."

The priest in particular gains measurably while the house is being constructed and on its completion. "Public subscriptions are raised to provide the priest with a new wife, pay any debts he may have, and add to his comfort generally."[11] It would not do for the directing priest, now in the community spotlight, to have any outstanding obligations; his family should be a model of prosperity and well-being. The people must look to him for spiritual and moral leadership, and as we have seen, leadership of all sorts depends upon financial solvency. Before a major mbari is begun, the deity and her priest must already be relatively wealthy. "The *agbara* we regard as grown up is the one with wealth. If a god has no money, she cannot have mbari." Furthermore, a god's (and her priest's) income is increased during the building period, because normal laws are more strictly enforced and carry higher penalties. A usual payment of a cock or a goat will be much increased, as in this instance:

> If in the course of making an mbari two people fought and drew blood, the penalty would be to produce an *osu*. This is better understood when you know that mbari is a time when a god and its priest gather wealth.

Apart from increased income from sacrifices made for normal infractions, a great deal of wealth is "killed" in connection with the mbari effort. Countless fowls and goats come under the knife of the male leader of spirit-workers named the "goat killer," *ogbokiri*. Shares of all such sacrifices go to the priest and his family. The plates, iron, and "yam" of mbari, on the other hand, are on a level of symbolic consumption and display, with the apotheosis of this symbolism, of course, the splendid new house itself. A finished mbari both advertises wealth and acts as a magnet to attract still more, in the form of many gifts for the newly housed deity.

> *"Mbari is building a house for the god to make her feel happy."*
> *"Mbari will let our god speak among other gods—will make her come of age."*

Wealth is tantamount to social status. For a deity and her priest the new house both shows off and validates positions of prestige, leadership, and status. Mbari, in the building process, acts out symbolically the buildup of a god's wealth and status, for each addition to the house adds to the pride of the god. As a worker said while an mbari was under construction. "Ala comes here always. She is happy and proud. She will be very harsh to those gods who have no mbari. She will kill other small deities because they are now junior to her." Another said, "Of course she knows this mbari is being danced. She asked for it. She knows and is happy. When we open the fence, she will invite other gods to see it, and if they have no house, they will worry their priests to build one." In this sense, of course, mbari is a gift of thanks, a dance of praise. For the priest, as for most townspeople, the building period and especially the unveiling are times of unrestrained pride. He probably will build but a single mbari during his tenure, and the activity projects him to center stage. If he can capitalize on the sharply focused adulation of his own and nearby communities, the priest who oversees the building of a large mbari can make substantial gains in the constant battle for position. A priest seems to rely heavily on the increased prosperity brought by mbari, and though he may complain of debts, his long-term gains, measured not only in wealth but, perhaps more important, in terms of status and leadership opportunities, usually seem to outweigh his short-term losses.

"Mbari guides people."
"Mbari is for the peace of our town."

As a "guide for the people," mbari encourages solidarity, equilibrium, and socio-political control on all levels, family, lineage, village, and town. These integrating factors also dramatize the difficulty of separating social, political, and economic benefits, even for analysis, for by chain reaction mbari affects the secular man and his relationships, just as it affects the moral, spiritual, and psychological sides of human life.

Mbari becomes the focus of the community in many ways, even long before it is opened. Its god, and hence its priest and the diviners, become powerful regulators of human conduct. Strengthened moral and legal sanctions are directly attributable to the spiritual mystery that is unfolding within the mbari enclosure, to the sacred, peaceful period that prevails in the community at large. At the same time the building of an mbari helps to define a community, to set it off from its neighbors, to point to other groups neither wealthy nor generous enough to erect such a splendid house for their own god(s).

The salutary effects of mbari on a single worker exemplify the interweaving of several facets of spiritual and secular discipline. Some rebels or rogues are chosen purposely as spirit-workers, presumably with the hope that the rigors of mbari will bring them into line:

> The people who own a rascal will caution him before he goes away to mbari. They will say "You are going to do this type of work—be careful. If you are going to do the kind of thing that will kill us all, go ahead." When he goes out then he has to cool down. He will have to stop all those things he used to do.[12]

A worker must submit to these disciplines and indignities, because should he fail, he not only destroys himself but may also wreak havoc in the lineage he represents.

Within the enclosure, especially, there is no room for dispute or asocial behavior. The controls and sanctions there, in the hands of diviners, artists, and priest, seem to be enough to ensure a smooth-running team of buildings. *Ndimgbe* are struck by the friendly, democratic atmosphere and the virtual absence of conflict inside the fence: "I like the peace of mbari, how people are very happy here." The lack of both quarrelling and differentiation between the sexes underscores the uniqueness of mbari activity.

The accord within the enclosure is echoed in the whole community, now subject to strongly enforced laws against all fighting and other dispute. Hence the mbari process confers overt socio-political benefits on town and village levels. The semi-autonomous and sometimes openly conflicting segments of a village group are forced to pull together for the common good; it is as if a people put aside their intramural squabbles to unite against a common enemy. This integrating function of mbari is analogous to the current efforts in Igboland to "get a town up," in which internal differences are forgotten while a community works by self-help for the improvement of its prestige and economic position in competition with other towns. A large mbari, when complete, stands as a monument to a town's ability to mobilize disparate factions in the face of disaster, to transform common danger into common benefit. If no lasting unity results, at least the moratorium on intervillage wars and other squabbling provides a climate of cooperation and peaceful coexistence, and for a time creates a greater sense of community.

While gathering human and material resources for mbari, a community re-establishes and strengthens its lines of communication. Authority and responsibility continually subdivide and filter down so that most nuclear families are affected, each being asked to make contributions at one time or another. Each spirit-worker comes to his initiation with three attendants and a basket full of goods. He must be sent food periodically, and a child messanger is chosen to carry it. Each worker is greeted with food and gifts at least once and often several times during construction and generously feted when he "emerges from suffering." By sending one or more worker, each lineage goes to mbari collectively, if vicariously; it is important for the lineage leader, the senior *ofo* holder, to communicate this involvement by distributing responsibilities. Nearly all families must provide construction materials,[13] food, and plates for incorporation in the structure. The family, farm, debts, and other commitments of the absent spirit-worker must be provided for. All these obligations, passed down through successive layers of authority, help to solidify and validate the kinship system in a way that may surpass even the changing of village sites.[14]

When a village shifts to a new site, lands and responsibilities are redistributed to account for new lineage divisions and the current relative strength, numerically and otherwise, of lineage segments. People seem to know, perhaps unconsciously, that only a single mbari will be built while they occupy a particular tract of land. By reflecting and reiterating the rites and activities of these infrequent site changes, mbari tests and presumably strengthens the alignments that have been in force since the physical move to the new village. At the same time, in drawing attention to the natural productivity of farms and human beings in a healthful new environment, mbari is an instrument and a symbol of security, continuity, and growth.

"Mbari is a dance for our god."
"Mbari is a thing of good heart; it is joy and happiness."

As a major festival only held at long intervals, mbari is capital entertainment for Owerri people. The process is high drama: perhaps ten years of crescendo, a hundred costumed actors, a mysterious setting, an unfolding, developing spectacle. It is a unified theatrical presentation created for three audiences: the gods, the people inside the fence, the community at large.

Nearly all ritual activity in Igboland, as in West Africa, has inherently aesthetic components. A diviner's performance interweaves poetry and song with the sounds of rattles and gongs in a theatrical setting. Rituals invoke music and the dance, chant and gesture, often in patterned calls and responses. Other artistic elements in ritual are symbolism and metaphor, stylization and embellishment for dramatic effect. Moods are set, activities have rhythmic pace, crescendos, and resolution. With this realization we may understand what Owerri people mean when they speak of "dancing mbari." Throughout the whole process varied aesthetic elements are introduced as counterpoint to the heavier and more tedious rhythms of actual mbari construction. In mbari, as elsewhere in Igbo life, it would be unthinkable for any single artistic activity, whether sculpture, drumming, singing, dance, or prayer, to exist or be performed by itself. A multidimensional, polyrhythmic aesthetic experience is the rule, particularly in festivals.

Owerri people realize that mbari contains a great deal of *abaraka* or *uroro,* words in which pride, bluff, fun, showing off, and playfulness all are implied:[15] Mbari is a deadly serious joke, a pretentious game played according to strict but arbitrary rules. As one man said, "This [phrase] 'dancing mbari' serves to cover every small detail of work and life inside the fence, so that nobody will know what materials were used in making mbari." Much mbari symbolism is both *abaraka* and simultaneously spiritually significant. Anthill clay is yam; ants are thorns. This "yam," however, is consecrated, the stuff of spirits living in anthills, which are spirit houses; thus an ant-bite may be seen as a spirit-wound. It may be laughed at, but it is terrifying nonetheless. Sticks are considered the bones of modeled figures. The body of a sacrificial goat is called chaff—but is later eaten. The mbari columns are called "eyes on the road," *anyanama;* the cloister is called the "long kitchen." Spirit-workers may not enter the mud pits. They curse one another and later pretend to have had nothing to do with their mbari, although they parade proudly through the market a few days after the completion of the building. One perspicacious informant was able to see through the ceremonial rules and secrecy of mbari to point out the playfulness of some of the basic symbolism. With tongue in cheek Ugo said, "Do you see that thing for which they entered *mgbe*? Everyone should buy a *plate* [his emphasis], *efere*. That is what is going on; that is mbari." Then he laughed.

Spirit-workers manifest the idea of playful *abaraka* in many ways, creating fun while they work. One man said,

> We dance mbari. We sing mbari. In the morning we make ourselves beautiful. We keep washing and rubbing camwood on our bodies. We kill wealth. . . . We have drums too. We beat drums and dance. . . . Mbari is a thing of good heart.[16]

Physical beautification is ostentation, *abaraka;* workers dress up for themselves as well as for the goddess who comes to visit her mbari. People joke with and about their "husbands" and "wives." When they rename each other they may give an old man the name of a young boy or vice versa. They steal goats. They sing, and many of their songs recount the glorious past of their town and their own bravery as "great women" and warriors. The theme-song of several *ndimgbe* groups runs like this:[17]

> Are we suffering? There is no time we shall suffer.
>
> Woman, run away from your husband and come to *eke nwaori.*
> Nothing bothers us; is there any way it can bother us?

When our townsmen take their knives to work
We take our knife to kill a goat.

The talk of *ndimgbe:* changing, changing.
Things we say in the morning are not things we say at night.

When the dove sings, we sing a different song.
When the cock crows, we speak a different thing.

Things we say at night are not things we say in the morning.
When bush fowl cry we jump about, when doves hoot we jump around.

This song expresses the sense of play, pretense, and even foolishness that grips life inside the fence. Other songs are made up, or inherited from previous mbari, for different phases of the activity: walking the iron, marching to the "yam farm," digging "yam," pounding it, rubbing bodies with camwood, and so forth. The "song of the yam" is a good example of the playfulness and ambiguity that obtain:

You people have legs like those of the yam people;
The legs of the yam people are like dry sticks of wood;
The arms of yam people are like the powerful dance of Okonkwo;
You people have legs like those of yam people.

These "yam people," the workers, refuse to allow themselves to suffer. They create a drama for their own enjoyment; they themselves are both actors and audience.

Artists and diviners, as the leaders of mbari, also indulge in playful diversions, enacted at the expense of the workers, and sometimes, the priest. As the walls near completion, "We will tell the people of the town that we are going to give the *ndimgbe* great greetings, and they will cook us a lot of food. We diviners and artists always rejoice when such things come up. At the end of it, we will greet them, yes, but we will carry away the meat and fish," said one artist, smiling. Speaking of the ceremonies during the three weeks' seclusion of the *ndimgbe* in *eke nwaori,* another man said, "We diviners are looking for money. We might invent some other ceremony and let the workers go through it." This "dance for the god," therefore, is choreographed by the diviners and artists, who delight in "spicing the soup" with a series of minor festivals inside the fence.

Despite the closed and apparently secret life of *ndimgbe,* townspeople are aware of the progress of mbari and its current stage of development, although no one tells them in so many words. Villagers can hear the singing and drumming inside the fence that proclaim each new phase. For the town as a whole, the mbari activity is, paradoxically, a thinly veiled mystery. Yet the people support these guileless deceptions with elaborate formality, much as Americans preserve Santa Claus for small children.[18] Such deceptions, after all, are part of the town's entertainment, and although people do not actually see the mbari take shape, they are very much caught up in the crescendo of its development. Mbari is one of the few great festivals in a lifetime, so people take advantage of it and subscribe willingly and with mounting anticipation to the mystery of its unfolding. Display and illusion, ritual and art, play and seriousness merge to create the dramatic nexus of mbari.

"Mbari is Life"

Like life itself, the mbari process may be seen as an interplay between the united but separable concepts of continuity and change. The history of all mbari, as well as the development of a single one, can be visualized as a dialogue between a conservative adherence to tradition and a series of breaks with that tradition. Ultimately, mbari means security—the preservation and cyclical repetition of known and expected secular and ritual acts aimed at maintaining human life against the threats or ravages or war, disease, drought, and death. More than that, however, mbari means security in the more active sense of continuity, involving forward motion, the developing sense of human existence, including procreation and the incorporation of new ideas and forms within older patterns. Igbo culture may be called a borrowing culture, for the Igbo people adapt, delete, and innovate, and have been doing so since well before prolonged European contact. "The Igbo—traditionally accustomed to thinking, acting, and making decisions in terms of a range of alternatives—are more at home in the culture contact situation than members of societies with other orientations."[19]

Receptivity to change affects mbari directly, and only by examining change in the mbari process can we understand its survival. The mbari houses constructed between about 1960 and 1967 remained culturally and aesthetically viable only because a liberal attitude toward change is fundamental to Owerri (and other Igbo) psychology. Progress and change, side by side with stability and repetition, are rules of the mbari process. There have been profound changes in ritual activity, for example, over the last forty years. No longer do *ndimgbe* work every day or live in *eke nwaori*. No longer is their life funnelled into an arbitrary, detail-filled routine. *Ndimgbe* do not rub camwood, wear fancy hairdresses, or wear the uniform of *ohihe*. Hired hands, paid wages in currency, help dig mud and "yam," and carpenters nail the machine-sawn structural timbers together and nail down the zinc roof, lately shipped by truck from a modern factory in Port Harcourt. But mbari survives. The *ndishigwe* still tour with their symbolic iron, the priest prepares and installs the god's *chi,* and the cow still parades through the market. *Ogwu* is still used and countless sacrifices performed, though for libations, London Dry Gin is now preferred over palm wine.[20]

Hisorically, mbari has always embraced change. Two basic symbols, the plate and the iron, are European products, and it may be possible someday to attribute the very existence of mbari houses, now so firmly rooted in Owerri culture, to European influence or at least some form of stimulus from outside the Owerri area.

A probable reason for the incorporation and importance of progress and change in the mbari process is that mbari is as much a social institution as a religious one, which is another way of saying, again, that Owerri religion is basically pragmatic. As an outlet for current aspirations and a source of answers to contemporary problems, traditional Igbo religion is as viable as Christianity (or more so); however, the era of Christianity has provided school education, a capitalistic economy, and modern status, now coveted.

Change is also embraced because mbari, the most profound religious offering known in the society, contains, somewhat paradoxically, much that is not spiritual. Perhaps this is because mbari is also a gift of praise, a dance, a celebration. It is an aesthetic drama (and monument) overseen by a professional craftsman who is chosen partially for his ability to innovate, to respond to things that are socially and economically relevant. Then, too, the construction process is *abaraka,* an ostentatious game for the entertainment of all concerned. It provides also for the reiteration of fundamental laws which, despite the spiritual sanctions underlying them, are primarily social and political. Even while an mbari is being built people know that it will never be as sacred as the central tree on the *ihu agbara,* the wooden Agwushi figures, or the forest of the god.

Mbari is most profoundly social, however, in the stress given secular forms in the sculptural program. In the iconography, as in the process, the dialogue between stability and change continues, mirroring in miniature the conflict between traditional and modern life that has preoccupied Owerri people since mbari houses were first recorded. With its preponderance of popular and secular forms, the artistic program reiterates the fundamental social and practical orientation of Igbo thought.

THE MEANING OF FORM

Although no Owerri villager would suggest that mbari houses are erected without reason or simply to beautify the town, a good many people, when asked why various figures have been included and what they mean, answer simply, "for 'fancy' " (i.e., decoration). Others say that "all these figures are the children of the god and are included only to make her house beautiful." An artist said: "Mbari is only 'art work' (*ihenkarinkari*). You cannot go to it and swear on the god." These statements dramatize the difference between the spiritual adventure of an mbari in progress—the unfolding of sacrifice—and the finished mbari as an assemblage of tangible, largely secular forms. When an mbari is opened, it is no longer highly charged with spiritual power: it is now a public monument. The sacrifice has been presented and accepted; since this fundamental purpose has been served, the mbari is never repaired. In the old days it was permissible to replace worn-out roofing mats, but never could crumbling, rain-washed figures be repaired or repainted. Yet the life and function of mbari in the community are far from finished. Despite the quotations above, it exists as more than simply art work; mbari remains a significant religious and social document although its relevance changes from being essentially spiritual to being predominantly secular.

The scenes in mbari come from real life, dreams and imagination, from spiritual belief, mythology, law, and custom, from the modern world as well as from the times of the ancestors. The range and variety of forms and scenes in a large mbari are so great one is tempted to think there is no system of inclusion beyond the ten or twelve figures considered essential to each new house. An approach to the systematization of the bewildering content of mbari houses, however, is the brief but incisive analysis provided by one observant old man:

> You will come to understand that they put four things into mbari: very fearful things; things that are forbidden; things that are very good (and/or) beautiful; and things that make people laugh.[21]

The lists he provided for each of these categories are as follows:

Fearful	*Forbidden*
Okpangu	Twins
Leopard	Hunchback
Python and other snakes	Other deformities
	Mgbekenwaokpere
Ekwensu	Ekpekele

Good/Beautiful	*Laughter*
Pregnant woman	*"Madu bu ewu"*
People with money	People wrestling
People with children	*"Beke ime ala"*

Although the informant did not explain his choices, he did say: "Some things, like the leopard, are both beautiful and fearful; a deity like Ala kills people but also gives children." Thus he offered not only a valuable inclusive categorization of mbari imagery, but observed as well the frequent Igbo practice of assigning more than one meaning to a single thing. Another man's comments, basically supporting the statement above, also add an interesting point: "You put in some good things and some bad ones; you can't have only good things. . . . When you come to mbari you see things with meaning and meaningless things." Nor is the distinction between the meaningful and the meaningless always very clearcut. Non-content-bearing forms such as imaginative figures and much of the painting, especially that on the lower walls, serve to point up the inherently decorative and artistic character of mbari.

Closely analyzed, the four-part classification above reveals a great deal about both the content of mbari houses and the world view of Owerri people.

Fearful Subjects

Both the natural world and the realms of imagination and bad dreams are inhabited by dreadful, potentially harmful creatures, recorded in mbari. Many of these strike swiftly and without warning. Among them are pythons (pls. 10 and 42), and in the old days leopards (pl. 23, color plate 6), elephants, and even hippopotamuses (pls. 39

and 40). Such bush or swamp animals are known especially to hunters who, depending upon local taboos, either stalk them or avoid them for fear of offending the deity who "owns" them. In either case all hunters (pl. 36) wear elaborate preparations of protective *ogwu*, for even animals that are protected as sacred and are considered friendly sometimes attack. When leopards or pythons leave their natural homes to enter villages, either they or signs of their visits, such as dead goats (pl. 23), are discovered by villagers, who seek an explanation through divination. Diviners usually read the presence of these (as well as other animals and even insects) as supernatural signs of impending tragedy or even death, and sacrifices to avert the evil are required. If misfortune strikes anyway, as it frequently does in Igboland, where accident and mortality rates are high, the sacrifice already offered is adjudged insufficient for the angry god who sent the creature. It is in such circumstances that an *agbara* may call for mbari. The inclusion of these sculptures in the mbari program is an appropriate memorial to animals owned by the gods and sent by them on evil errands.

Tales about animals and other creatures represented in mbari are the constant fare when old men gather with palm wine to tell stories by an evening fire. The turtle, *nabe*, is a favored "wise man" in folktales; curiously, however, few turtle images are to be found in mbari. A ram-headed male figure, called "*madu* (man) Amadioha," recalls the story of a foolish person who offended Amadioha and was ordered by him to carry a basket containing all the silly or useless things found on the road for the rest of his life. Especially welcome to the inevitable youthful audiences at such sessions, however, are stories about Okpangu (pls. 15, 32, and 41). Though a mythical creature, Okpangu is very real to the children of Owerri. He is a symbol of everything bad that can happen to foolish or lazy people—those who refuse to help on the farm or who forget to carry a knife (as a weapon) when travelling through dense bush, or even mothers who go on errands leaving unprotected young children behind. Okpangu likes to wrestle men and rape women. He pelts lonely night travellers with the rocklike seeds of the *ngu* tree that he carries at all times. If you chase Okpangu, you suddenly hear his voice behind you. If you throw something at him he catches it and heaves it back at you, accurately. Okpangu is thought to wear his feet backwards so as to confuse anyone who attempts to follow him.[22] Intelligent people can extricate themselves from Okpangu's snare, but the cleverest are those who find ways to avoid him entirely.

Okpangu stories are a rich catalogue of native custom. When mbari visitors encounter ugly black Okpangu, with his huge spiky penis, they are inevitably reminded of one story or another, amusing but instructive, that they heard from the old men.

Ekwensu is the evil side of all *mmuo,* especially of *agbara.* It is the Igbo word Bible translators adopted for the word "Devil" and in mbari the iconography, a pink or red beast with a tail (fig. 4), should probably be traced to Christian imagery. For traditional Igbo people, however, the color is equally meaningful since anything red is dreaded. Ekwensu may also represent any deity, however, for all are known as evil-doers.[23] Thus when an informant uses the word "Ekwensu" he may be referring to Ala, Opurogo, Uramurukwa—virtually any god in the pantheon, to Okpangu or especially to those otherwise unnamed spirits that plague men in countless ways.

The wicked side of Ala's character, and the iconography of images of all female mbari owners, is revealed in these praise (or curse) names: "Ala, queen among women who cuts/kills with a knife," and "Ala, she who eats and shuts her mouth"—this referring to Ala as the personification of the earth, who kills a person and swallows him unconcernedly. Another man said: "Ala is the god of peace. When she demands peace and someone breaks it, the knife is a symbol for us people of the world. If anyone breaks the peace, or causes it to be broken, Ala will kill him with the knife." Asked why Ala is always seated in mbari, with her feet on an iron rod (color plate 4), an informant said: "Don't you know that Ala is bad? If she stands people die. . . . If I were a great person, I would not want my feet on the ground but would have them raised to show off my title."[24] The god's seated position also may reflect people's desire to control her by rendering her relatively immobile. When mbari visitors see frightful creatures or signs of wrath, power, or tragedy, their minds may wander in any of several directions, to a local misfortune, to a moral lesson, or more indirectly, to the necessity of periodic conciliatory rites.

Forbidden Subjects

A number of natural occurrences or human activities, forbidden in native law generally because they defile the earth and thus offend Ala, are represented in mbari. Twins (pl. 65) were outlawed, and formerly killed at birth, because (among other reasons) "only animals gave birth to litters. Are we animals?" People with physical deformities were sometimes also forbidden life, perhaps because their handicaps would place them in the lowest competitive position and at the same time would drag their families down. In a society governed by "survival of the fittest," those who were plainly unfit were given no chance, and according to Igbo beliefs such homicides would be considered humane since the dead child's *chi* would soon be born again in a complete and healthy body; souls that stay on earth only briefly also reincarnate quickly.[25]

Mgbekenwaokpere, a woman named "Mgbeke," "child of open legs," *nwaokpere,* appears in several forms in mbari (pls. 29 and 66, figs. 20 and 30). She is legendary, a woman sometimes considered insane, who lived in a nearby town and simply liked men too much. She displayed her sex, even in the marketplace, and taunted men, luring them off into the bush with her. Occasionally she is considered a prostitute, but more often she represents a woman without restraint or common sense. Her presence in mbari houses is a clear injunction to people of both sexes to mind their sexual manners. Images of her, and stories about her, are greeted with raucous jeers. Characteristically, she always seems to belong to "other people" (those from other villages, that is, foreigners), never to those questioned about her. Another image of a shameless woman called Mgbekenwaokpere, bent over at the waist, has a hunchback copulating with her (pl. 66). This relationship between physical deformity (the hunchback) and abnormal or illicit sexuality is recurrent in mbari imagery, although the precise reason for it remains speculative. Most erotic images illustrate sexual activity outside the moral order, which apparently was believed to result in physical or mental aberrations of different sorts. Despite the lack of direct corroboration for this analysis, it is consistent with Owerri thought. Okpangu, for example, was transformed from man to ape-man, with a huge, grotesque penis, because he failed, as a young man, to live up to expected standards of social behavior: he refused to plant and tend yams on the farm.

All mbari sexual imagery lies well outside the accepted social code. Even scenes of natural intercourse, which may be seen from time to time, are immoral for the simple reason that, leaving aside the *display* of sexual organs, the very mention of sexual matters in public is a breach of etiquette. Igbo attitudes toward sex and the mention or exposure of genitalia are strictly modest and often seem somewhat prudish.[26]

Ekpekele[27] is an anomalous hermaphroditic creature of the bush whose character and physical appearance are not firmly fixed in people's minds. It is a dreaded monster, occasionally called *mmuo,* whom some men nevertheless claim to have shot and killed. Though its flesh may be eaten by men, it is forbidden to women. Even to men, however, Ekpekele is strange and evil, possibly symbolizing some abhorred transgression of hunter's laws, although there is no substantiation for this view. Informants said the artist gave it human form "for no particular reason"; nor had they any explanation for the winglike arms or the four small hands.[28] In the absence of any real explanation, the statement of one artist about this creature seems most plausible. "Most of these things made in mbari we have not seen at all: we have just heard stories about them. When you hear of such things, you try to picture them in your mind and put them into mbari to beat the other artists."

Another perhaps fearful but probably more amusing erotic group is that of a dog shown copulating with a woman (pl. 67). This scene probably has its source in a once common epithet hurled at dreaded and hated neighboring villagers: "They give their virgins to dogs."[29]

Good/Beautiful Imagery

Mbari figures considered *nma,* good and/or beautiful, constitute the largest single grouping in the sculptural program. Many of them, such as seated men (pl. 38), women (pls. 29, 34, and 37), and couples (color plate 1), in fact may appear to convey little because they are often unnamed and do not elicit lengthy stories or explanations. Such figures may have been left unnamed purposely, so they may be taken for any member of the community. These are illustrative figures which, in addition to "decorating and filling up the house," are models of propriety and status, often idealized in pose, body decoration, and dress for expressive emphasis. Other figures in this category, however, are immediately identifiable as good because of some positive distinguishing feature, including representations of pregnancy (pl. 68), childbirth (color plate 5, pl. 4), and suckling. Such images are very common in mbari and appear to refer directly to concepts of fertility and increase. More indirectly, they represent harmonious and productive family and village life by showing useful, happy people of all ages. They can, of course, raise more than one association.

Far more visually prominent than these figures, on the other hand, are the "owner of the house" and her servants, *ijeremgbe*. And of all mbari figures, these simultaneously good and beautiful ones can be changed least by artists. Notably they are the representatives of the Iconic and Schematic styles. It appears that the central deity (color plate 4) is not changed because she represents the entire spiritual motivation for the house, the stable, underlying essence of it, and the dimensions of the multifaceted Igbo word "*nma.*" *Ijeremgbe* (pls. 17, 22, and 27) are probably not changed because, in representing spirit workers (*ndimgbe*), they symbolize at once the people and processes of mbari, the tradition-based ritual activity that is re-enacted, with some variation, each time this great sacrifice or "dance" is performed. How far back in time the iconography of these two figures was established cannot be known, probably, until the origin of mbari is known. Their iconography can be accounted for and elucidated, however, by contemporary information and analysis.

Ala's pose (or that of any female god), identified as one of dignity, grandeur, and power, is clearly honorific (color plate 4). Her erect, elongated body is an idealization much revered, particularly on aesthetic grounds, and her proportionately short legs are dismissed as "things which people should not put their eyes into." As quoted above (pp. 180–81), she would be laughable if she stood up, but as a seated figure she is fine. Her breasts droop because she is now a great woman, past child-bearing, older, a man among women." She and other powerful female deities are the only exceptions to the idealized rendering of female mbari subjects with full, upstanding breasts, women in the bloom of youth. Ala's feet are raised on an iron bar because "a king [or queen] never puts his feet on the ground." The unnamed children beside her are those whom she controls, those for whom she peels yam. Surely they represent the community at large, and her rather impersonal relationship with them also bears this out. Never is she shown suckling.

The few parts of Ala's image that vary according to each artist's predilection are the patterns of body painting and the shape of the hairdress, details that would naturally vary in different contexts when affected by Igbo women themselves. The elaborate hairstyle, whose generic name is *ishiojongo* (color plates 4, 7, and 10), incorporates ideas of pride, grandeur, great size, and stateliness. In short, the correspondence between form and meaning is detailed and full. It seems probable that this close bond is to a large extent responsible for the immutability of these deity images. Though gods are changeable in their dual capacity for good and evil, they are nevertheless stable. One could say that Igbo people expect them to act unexpectedly.

Outfitted with beads, *ohihe,* body painting, *agalegbe,* bracelets, anklets, and fancy hairdressing, *ijeremgbe* images clearly represent spirit-workers, *ndimgbe.* Yet the native interpretations of these figures are rich and varied. "*Ijeremgbe* are beautiful women but not human beings. They are something said by the mouth"—that is, symbolic. In these figures are concentrated all the roles and ideals connected with mbari workers: as daughters of deity they are her guardians, stationed beside the door to the inner chamber containing her *chi;* as her messengers and followers, "they are very strong"; as manifestations of ideal beauty and goodness, they are modeled with long torsos, ringed necks, and their U-shaped arm pose. Curiously, this is always described as the proper position for *ijeremgbe* arms despite the fact that many are actually rendered with arms in other poses (fig. 14). Odd, also, is the common statement that *ijeremgbe* should be the most beautiful and morally the most superior figures in mbari, surpassing even its main deity. Most curious, however, is that *ijeremgbe,* alone among anthropomorphic figures, are in relief. This rendering cannot be explained, as distortion and elongation can, by reference to any ideal of beauty. Instead, the semi-human relief precisely reinforces the interpretation of *ndimgbe* as spirits, partly human and partly supernatural, whose feet need not, and in the sculptural rendering of *ijeremgbe,* often do not, touch the ground.

In representing spirit-workers, *ijeremgbe* seem to apotheosize man's ideal relationship with the gods. Men should guard and follow their gods, and should, like *ndimgbe,* lead lives of submission, purity, and sacrifice. *Ijeremgbe* serve as stately models of useful, beautiful, moral human existence. That they remain relatively immutable in mbari, as well as essential to it, is another way of expressing the stability of the human ideal of constant and virtuous service despite man's fallibility. The word *ijeremgbe,* meaning "you have gone to *mgbe* (mbari)" is a constant reminder of the mbari process itself, that the people of the town, symbolically, have gone to mbari and therefore have rendered the ultimate sacrifice to their god. *Ijeremgbe* figures stand in the house to represent this commitment.

A good many other mbari subjects may also be considered good/beautiful. Most of the countless genre activities, for example, fall into this group. For that matter, all imagery may be included—even the "ugly" figures—because all are well-made, all contribute to the beneficial magnetic display which any "good" mbari must be.

Imagery Causing Laughter

Like good or beautiful things, those that provoke laughter draw attention to the entertainment value of a completed mbari house. If the construction process is an ongoing drama for the spiritual refreshment of its participants, the finished product is a unified exhibition of art for the enjoyment of spectators, a museum containing a series of dioramas. Artists assert unanimously that an mbari that does not stimulate laughter is a failure. The traditional group called "*Madu bu ewu*" (pl. 55), "man is goat," is humorous and edifying at the same time. Goats are considered the most foolish creatures in the Owerri world, and among the most lewd, with a reputation of wanton sexuality and procreation akin to that of rabbits in popular American thought. The scene depicted is an act of sodomy between two creatures, each of which is partly goat. This human-animal combination bears out the occasional designation of this group as *mmuo,* and reinforces the interpretation expressed previously that deviant sexuality and physical abnormality are linked. Partially because of the antiquity of the image, however, it has no single interpretation. "*Madu bu ewu*" is meant to cause laughter and to warn against all kinds of foolishness, especially sexual frivolity. It may enjoin as well against sodomy, which would certainly defile the land, although there is little evidence beyond this and the "dog-woman" group (pl. 67) that sodomy has ever been practiced in the area.[30]

The inclusion of people wrestling (fig. 17) in the informant's list reveals particularly the spectator value of mbari imagery. Many such "pictures within a picture" refer to ordinary human activity. Among them are other sport scenes such as boxers (pl. 69), footballers, and village scenes of men climbing palm trees and women cracking palm kernels or pounding yam (pl. 35). Like most mbari figures, these amuse people because they are simultaneously real and unreal; they show human action in tangible, lifelike poses, and yet, as miniatures half life-size, rendered in positions that are often recognizably stilted, they cannot be taken as other than clay; it never occurs to people to criticize conventionalized poses or schematized faces.

"*Beke ime ala,*" "white man in the ground" (pl. 70), recalls the myth of the white man's origin; he simply emerged from a hole in the ground or in another version, from the depths of the sea. In this, as in most of the varied renditions of white men, there is an element of caricature. The nose is long and thin, and almost invariably supports a pair of eyeglasses. The hair may be shown with two or three parts, or the head may be covered with a pith helmet, originally associated only with whites but taken over by Igbo men, as early as the 1920s, as a status symbol. Another legendary image of the white man shows him Janus-faced with another face on his chest, and in some versions, yet another on his back (pl. 71). The multiple-headed versions, according to one informant, refer to the reputation white men had, in the early days of contact, for omniscience and omnipotence, as well as to the deviousness of the slave traders. They also suggest that white men are not quite human. *Beke* has always been held in awe and still is, in many quarters, because of his appearance, forcefulness, and wealth. It is possible that the virtually mandatory inclusion of his image also reflects a desire for the psychological control, even the capture, of his awesome power. When it first appeared, the imagery may also have related to an analogous desire hypothesized earlier, namely, to rid the Owerri world of a formidable enemy by modeling his "portrait," and thus expecting the angry god to kill him. Today such figures are no more than caricatures or historical and legendary recording, but there is no incompatibility between these meanings and the hope for control or even annihilation.

The several other images of the white man that have appeared over the years include the following: a white man in a litter; the first two colonial district commissioners in Owerri, Douglas and Connell, looking out of second-story windows (pl. 50); Beke on horseback (pl. 72), seated in a chair (color plate 2), or as a radio announcer (pl. 73). These varied interpretations of the Beke motif reflect the view of one informant who said, "The ways of the white man are different. We try to show these differences in mbari." Whether he was laughing at the white man or simply trying to record what he had heard or seen, the artist probably first incorporated the myth, before Owerri became an administrative center and before many white men were seen by Owerri people, then changed that interpretation from his own observation, showing the European visitor in a litter. Later Beke was placed in different and particularly elevated parts of the "house." When the people came to know two-story buildings through contact with white men, they immediately appropriated such houses for the gods, and Beke quite naturally appeared in the windows of what was, after all, a tall house of his invention (pl. 50). The mbari images of white men, like those of Igbo people, change with time and incorporate the latest developments in clothing, house types, and technology. Laughed at and sometimes despised, white men are nevertheless respected as powerful harbingers of progress.

It is equally true to say that the entire mbari (excepting deities) is designed to provoke laughter. Good and beautiful things may please the crowds, but frightful and forbidden images, as comic relief from the daily round, attract them first. As one man said of sexual imagery, "When we want to play tricks, we put figures in poses that excite laughter. Wherever the bad things are in mbari, that is where the people flock. They even call them the most beautiful." Light-hearted entertainment is therefore one of the decisive motivations for the creation and variation of all mbari imagery, an embodiment of, and a tangible parallel to, the playfulness characteristic of the construction process. Still, the motivation for including any single figure or series of figures may be only tangentially related to any of the reasons why mbari are built.

Ambiguity

No analysis of mbari meanings would be satisfactory without discussion of the ambiguities built into the sculptural program. We have seen how varied the interpretations may be of a single word such as "*nma.*" Images too have multiple meanings, both intentional and ascribed, as well as those which vary in the eyes of different beholders. Then too, determining how mbari messages are assimilated and interpreted by Owerri people is not easy; Igbo culture relies more heavily on unexplained, sometimes inexplicable, intuitive responses than on verbalized analysis. The four-part classification of mbari imagery above is thus extraordinary, and in approaching the range and diversity of mbari subjects the analytic westerner must be very wary of imposing neat categories on material that remains largely unclassified and unquestioned in Owerri thought. Most fitting, perhaps is an analogy with the iconography on the tympanums and capitals of medieval churches and cathedrals; not always comprehended even by the stonecarvers or priests, much of the symbolism was unintelligible to the public, who simply believed. As in medieval churches, the origins and meanings of some mbari iconography have been obscured by replication, tempered by drifts and reinterpretations over decades or even centuries. Certain common motifs, on the other hand, are quickly understood even by children. These may safely be called icons or iconic symbols because of the immediate response triggered in the local viewer, a response which, like that to the Madonna and Child in Christian cultures, goes quickly beyond an identification of subject matter (i.e., a stately seated woman holding a child and a knife, an attenuated relief figure with crossed bandoliers on her chest, or a black ape with prominent sex) to an intuitive understanding or knowledge of meanings that are not in fact visually expressed. Shared, consensual cultural values render any articulated "explanation" of these meanings among Owerri people unnecessary, even redundant. Everyone knows what *agbara, ijeremgbe,* and Okpangu "mean," although the precise associations called forth in any individual will vary according to his or her age, experience, sex, psychology, and so forth. At the other end of the spectrum are those non-recurring, non-traditional images, often invented by sculptors (pls. 60, 61, and 73), which call forth no automatic associations and which do not in fact *mean* anything at all specific to most or even all observers. These they may find puzzling, amusing, frightful, clever, or fancy; there is no stock response. Five people queried about the "name" or "meaning" of one such figure (pl. 60), for example, had five distinct replies: 1) only decoration, 2) *mmuo,* 3) something from the artist's imagination, 4) a thing to draw people to this mbari, 5) a deformed human being. We would err in choosing one as "correct," for no two of these "meanings" are mutually exclusive. A beautiful thing may at the same time be frightful. The artist in this case may well not have had anything special in mind when he modeled the figure: ". . . the way it goes, you follow."

In other specific instances when I asked artists to identify their newly completed sculptures, they reacted in various ways: they named the figure, viz., "It is Ada Agbara" (the god's first daughter); one man said that "the people who paint the figure will name it"; and another replied, "when people come to visit this mbari they will decide whom this figure represents." In the latter two cases the artist fostered ambiguity deliberately (it would seem) by leaving the identification open for interpretation by participants or other observers. As in these examples, the bulk of mbari iconography lies somewhere between the extremes: the Iconic, prompting a conditioned understanding, and the "newly invented," which elicits varied, non-specific, and often vague responses. This middle range is made up of recognizable, more or less conventional imagery—conventional not so much in that it is repeated (although it often is), but because a plausible and obvious natural situation is represented. Dancers, diviners, various animals, seated or standing people, paintings of cloths, umbrellas, or cows, and a host of other genre scenes and familiar objects are found. Once again, however, native response may often ramify well beyond the "title" or obvious subject matter, depending on the receptivity, imagination, mood, occupation, or status of the observer. One mbari, for example, depicts a traditional birth scene, and nearby stands a man whose gun points at the mother. One observer disclaimed any relation between the two tableaux, while Ezem, who modeled the figures, said that the gunman, who was the woman's husband, planned to kill her if she failed to produce a (culturally preferred) male child. I do not believe, however, that Ezem meant to have his meaning the *exclusive* one for this group, to be associated with it dogmatically until the figures fell apart and were forgotten. A birth scene, perhaps unlike a hunter or blacksmith, calls forth unpredictable and widely varied responses, despite the fact that the imagery in both cases is quite fixed and easy to "name." It may be didactic to a wide-eyed ten-year-old, for example, sentimental to an aged grandmother, and to a promiscuous unmarried youth, nerve-racking. A person sees in it what he chooses to find; just as experiences vary so will these "meanings." If responses are not ambiguous here, they are certainly varied.

Regardless of category, on the other hand, some imagery is culturally ambiguous. An Ala figure, traditionally wielding a knife in her right hand, is a case in point; it may denote malice or beneficence, or a person's response might be neutral. "It is her kitchen knife; with it she peels yam and prepares food for her children. This comes from the proverb, 'Ala, woman, save some yams', which is her praise name."[31] "No," said another man present at this interview. "The knife signifies that before a person can get something to eat he must work hard with a knife. We go to farm with knives." Both men, of course, are right, as are others who said, "It is the knife with which she brings up her children," and "She uses it to control (herd) her crowds"; each statement may denote her beneficence or malevolence, depending on the situation. Meek, writing of the Owerri area, speaks of a knife as a "symbol of defense against evil spirits."[32] Again interpreted neutrally, Ala (with her knife) may more or less unconsciously remind a viewer that the deity is strong, commanding, or imperious. Many symbols of importance in this culture have faceted meanings, some of which may seem to contradict one another but which, instead, reveal a richness of thought and a virtual absence of the belief that any one thing is either totally right or wrong, good or evil.[33]

In still other cases, as we have seen (Nwa Alakandu, pl. 62), meanings may change in time. Undoubtedly many such "fluid" topics escaped my notice, but a few can nevertheless be cited. When a miniature two-story building was (I believe) first erected as part of a cloister in the 1950s (at Obinze, fig. 31) it was specifically labelled "Zik's House," referring to the prestigious home owned by the Nigerian Nationalist leader, Dr. Nnamdi Azikiwe (an Igbo), pride of many Igbo people. The next time such a structure appeared (pl. 3), however, it was simply called an "office building." Football players, wrestlers (fig. 17), or boxers (pl. 69) may originate as specifically named individuals, such as the internationally known Dick Tiger, for example, but in time they tend to lose their individuality, to become generalized. I also noted this in the case of Ogidi, who in some places was known only as a "giant policeman" and not as a specific historical personage. Some white men, such as Douglas and Connell (pl. 50), also once named, have lost their individuality. It may also happen that a generalized figure will, some months after an mbari is opened, be linked with a topical personality; this happened after the opening of the mbari I participated in at Nnorie, when a generalized light-skinned man seated at a table was given my name after someone placed a few of my discarded yellow Kodak film boxes on the table.

Components of ambiguity in the building process may also be reiterated. Word games (i.e., clay = yam), ritual play, and in fact the leitmotif of *abaraka* (playful deceit, bluff, etc.) that underlies the entire construction program should be seen as equivocal, as should the uncertain positions of spirit-workers, who are at once spirits and men, "sufferers" who nevertheless do not really work very hard and get only the finest of foods.

Ambiguity, whether in process or form, serves to reinforce the human dimension of mbari. Men, Igbo people will admit, are not always logical any more than they are totally good or wholly evil. Contradictions and complexities mark the real world, so they are equally present in mbari.

Colors

The symbolism of color in the Owerri area, both in and beyond mbari contexts, is characterized also by ambivalence, multiple reference, and a certain ambiguity. It would be erroneous, for example, to ascribe symbolic valuation to all colors in mbari. Colored pigments are mostly descriptive and are used primarily for artistic reasons. This is true even if the same colors also have symbolic charges in certain ritual contexts. The four most important colors in mbari ritual (indeed in all ritual) and art are white, black, yellow, and red (or red-brown). More fundamental, however, is the opposition between light and dark or white and black. In moral, utilitarian, and aesthetic senses, light things are generally good while dark things are bad,[34] an opposition that may be clarified by a brief tabulation of the four predominant mbari colors and some of their associations.

White (light)[35]	*Black (dark)*
Goodness, purity, cleanness	Evil, impurity, dirtiness
Daytime	Nighttime
Life, wealth, children	Death, sickness, barrenness
Beauty, handsomeness	Ugliness, disfigurement
Clarity, truth, visibility	Obscurity, falsehood, shadiness
Childbirth (semen, milk)	Sterility, illicit sex
Ancestors (beneficial)	*Mmuo* or Ekwensu
Weakness, delicacy	Hard work, strength
Amadioha	Ala
Yellow (light)	*Red (dark)*
Peace, coolness, pride, showiness, brightness, prestige	Fighting, terror, death, danger, power, heat, blood, sacrifice, defilement, Ekwensu

Red is the most ambiguous color, and I was only moderately successful in uncovering its various meanings. Red (*Oche obara,* literally: "the color of blood") is considered dark, and yet sacrificial blood may be associated with beneficial desires. Turner (1966:60) found red ambivalent among the Ndembu, who believe red things can act for good and ill, and so it seems to be in Owerri. Its relative absence among mbari pigments was explained by one informant as stemming from the difficulty of procuring it, but because red camwood (*uhie* brought in from Hausa country in the North) is in common usage for decorative body painting, this reason seems inadequate. Another man suggested that all the blood spilt in mbari sacrifices was sufficient use of the color red, which he said, "enrages and reminds [people] of death." In general red is not considered a pretty, good, or beautiful color, and its infrequent use stems from this fact in combination with its powerful ritual associations.

To be good (and beautiful) mbari houses must be light, bright, clean, and cool, hence the predominance of white and yellow in the decorative program. In many ways mbari reflects the aesthetic, moral, emotional, and psychological dimensions of the concept of "cool" surveyed by Robert Thompson.[36] It is built to "cool the land" and its light-colored program accords with Igbo valuations of light-colored things and their positive, "cool," associated meanings. One house whose geometric patterns use blue and black in above-average quantities was labeled "dark and dirty" by a mainstream artist, and it is not surprising that the neophyte craftsman who made that mbari was largely self-taught. Black is essential in some *mmuo* figures, like Okpangu, whose color accords perfectly with his black heart and dark deeds, while other statues, just as clearly and unambiguously evil *mmuo,* were painted with light colors. Hence, the "rules," often broken, seem to be quite arbitrary.

But why are the skins of the Igbo people, and particularly of "dark Ala," always rendered in light colors? Primarily because mbari and their inhabitants are idealized expressions of physical beauty and moral rectitude, as well as emotional coolness, and must therefore be portrayed in colors that connote these traits. Even if people do not always adhere to high moral standards, it would be unthinkable to portray them, and their gods, as they actually are. To do so would approach portraiture, which is shunned, and would in general run counter to a basic motivation for mbari, which is to glorify the deity and thereby seek its blessings—children, prosperity, purity, health—all of which are "light" things.

White is thus the color of beauty, purity, and "things of good heart." Yellow is for peace and coolness. Both colors are decidedly good and are sometimes used interchangeably. In rituals (both those connected with mbari and those that are not) a yellow powder (*odo*) is usually sprinkled on fresh sacrificial blood, as if to counteract its danger and power, to cool its heat. The yellow pigment (*uvovo*) used in mbari is a different substance, but since it was repeatedly called the "head, leader, and most important of all mbari colors," we may assume that its artistic use parallels ritual uses of *odo*. Furthermore, *uvovo* is difficult to obtain, involving a trip of great length, alleged danger, and some expense. If mbari builders did not think it was ritually as well as aesthetically important as a declaration of community coolness, pride, and peace, they doubtless would not trouble to obtain it, personally, from the banks of the Imo River at Ife.[37]

The significance of other mbari colors is minimal, with the possible exception of the red-brown of the earth itself. After an mbari is painted none of the building core or the original mud-colored sculpture surface shows, although the same red-brown color is often used later in geometric patterns. If the uncorroborated information I have is correct, modeled figures were once painted black after the walls and columns were whitewashed; these antithetical colors must have been applied to neutralize the red-brown color (of blood and perhaps of the defiled earth) for symbolic reasons which now can only be surmised. It is possible that the red-brown figures, considered spirits (*umummuo* or *umuagbara*), were blackened to identify them ritually as sacrificial scapegoats, analogous to the incomplete first-figure. The whitened architectural setting would then be their "home," an environment of wholesome purity and goodness. The eventual painting out of these symbolic colors is important and necessary both ritually and aesthetically, for the completed monument must reflect ideals of moral harmony and physical beauty. Support for this notion comes from the color symbolism of traditional funerals, in which these polar colors are also used, black apparently to acknowledge earthly death and the potential malevolence of a wandering spirit, white in the hope that the spirit will hurry "home" to clean and productive land of beneficent ancestors before returning to earth through reincarnation. Even if this interpretation, based on scant evidence, is not correct, the fact remains that color symbolism is of some importance in mbari art and content despite the primary use of colors for artistic purposes.

The Cultural Telegraph

Mbari houses are communicating devices of great complexity and sophistication. They telegraph Owerri Igbo culture in its breadth and depth, in both processes and forms. Some messages are clear and direct, others cryptic, as if in a secret or private code; some are light and optimistic while others, dark, report or foretell disaster or evil; meanings are singular or ambiguous, and some have disappeared. Nor is every activity or figure or painting laden with significance, either direct or symbolic. It would be a mistake to search all figures and all wall paintings for hidden content: "When you come to mbari you don't expect only good things; you see things with meaning and meaningless things," as the wise older artist, Ugo, remarked to me.

As communication, mbari touches every aspect of Igbo existence. The mbari process is living ritual, an ever-unfolding complex of sacrifices that, though it may spring from a spiritual commitment, touches all life. In it are re-enacted religious mysteries and social facts, political competitions and agricultural processes, the life-cycle in symbolic form and the playful entertainment that enables people to endure a hard life. In the completed form many references are again made to these facets of human existence, but usually from different points of view. In process, mbari is more openly didactic, and in form, more passive and reflective. Life is spread out before the viewer in the completed house, the harsh reality of life as it now is and the ideal of life as it might be. Similarly, mbari is a celebration of yam, which as the major prestige crop in a subsistence economy, is often the focal point in Owerri life. Yam and other symbols of Owerri culture are tangibly crystallized in sometimes confusing or ambiguous relationships between spiritual and secular life and between the stability necessary for the continuation of life and the change essential to its healthy development. These interwoven dialogues are dramatized in the images of mbari, modeled not as static replicas of traditional behavior, but like yam itself, as living organisms reaching out for the future with confidence and hope.

7 Conclusions

We may visualize mbari first as a dramatic synthesis of arts, in which all the creative resources of the Owerri community are marshalled to the greater glory of man and god alike. The transient arts—body painting, drumming, dancing, singing, chanting—are orchestrated for the building process. More tangible and permanent forms—architecture, sculpture, and painting—combine in the completed monument. All these arts are unified in the festival "dance of mbari," a phrase that applies equally to artistic activities and completed structures. This entire multifaceted scenario is surely one of West Africa's great artistic achievements.

We may also visualize mbari as a dramatic reenactment of creation, as mythology made tangible. Only through such an interpretation[1] can we grasp the ramifying symbolism of mbari, and only with this realization can its complexities and ambiguities be resolved into simple, not to say self-evident, terms. Mbari is a reiteration of cosmic beginnings, a contemporary image of renewal and regeneration that links the real world with creation, tying man to his supernatural forebears, revitalizing the community by reactualizing sacred history.

An mbari is begun because nature and the gods who personify its forces threaten to disrupt or annihilate the world of men. More accurately, perhaps, profane man has brought this wrath down upon himself, for he has defiled the earth, "caused good lands to become bad." Man's eternal need for spiritual renewal recalls to him cosmic beginnings, when man, as spirit, inhabited a sacred world. Perilous crises precipitate the Owerri man's promise to relive creation and thereby to rededicate society as a whole. The pledge, "tying the iron leader," is followed directly by a dissolution of the old, defiled, and profane condition—in the free sexuality of "eating yam." This brief orgy is a ritually necessary return to primordial chaos, a wiping clean of the cosmic slate before renewal.

The process of cosmic disintegration is completed by the classic[2] initiation of *ndimgbe,* which represents the death of society itself. Already the stage is set for world renewal, for the whole community must obey "new" laws, which in fact signal a return to sacred time. Both sacred time and sacred space are of course intensified within the mbari enclosure where spirit-workers live a life apart, as sacred actors in the cosmic drama. Oblivious of the "real" world outside their enclosure, *ndimgbe* live in a twenty-four-day limbo, perhaps as if in Ala's very womb.[3] *Ndimgbe* are reborn as supernaturals that they may repeat the cosmogony. More than that, they undergo rebirth, growth, marriage, and death, after which they emerge again into the "civilian" world outside, into a society that by their very sacrifice has been purified and renewed. The telescoped life of these spirit-workers recalls in brief the life cycle of every individual, which has as its model the primordial process of death and regeneration.

Renewal is also symbolized on other levels. The cycles of the farming year, the lunar year, and changing village sites are all recalled in mbari rites. There are many obvious parallels to the rituals of the agricultural calendar, including clearing the ground, burning debris, planting, harvesting yam, and finally, a reprise of the New Yam festival itself at the mbari opening when the priest offers his god a "porridge of yam." The fires that consume construction evidence—and mbari fences—are analogous to fires that "consume" the old lunar year (in New Year rituals) to cleanse the world, making way for the new. Mbari rites also recall ceremonies of the major cyclical renewal of real village life, also brought on by crisis, when people abandon one village and rebuild their community in another place. Notably, too, the twenty-five to forty-year mbari cycle is parallel to site shifting; each new community can theoretically[4] accommodate only one mbari for any single god during those years.

The correlations between mbari and recorded creation mythology, on the other hand, are more oblique. Perhaps this is because verbally articulated creation stories were rather fragmentary, at least as I was able to collect them.[5] In submitting to the demand for mbari, man undertakes once again to reorder and recompose nature—the land—in an ideal form. At this time, as at creation (see p. 4), spirits (*ndimgbe*) outnumber men (four-day-workers) and a house is made with four rooms (the central niches on all four mbari sides). Some few mbari have four doors, one real and three false, leading to the interior sanctum; these recall the four doors (or eyes) of anthills, which like mbari are spirit houses. Some creation stories also speak of Chineke modeling the four original men from lumps of clay.[6] There are also hazy references, now largely lost in mbari lore, to the creation of the four days and markets and cardinal directions, each being assigned to different gods who take up positions on the four mbari sides. Mbari processes of fence, path, gate, and habitation construction recall the subdivision of nature that took place at creation; untamed nature is thereby ordered, prepared for civilization. And the four essentials that Chineke provided then—cloth, the basket, the knife, and yam—all figure prominently in mbari activity and form. A cloth is painted behind the owner of the house, and real cloths are given to the deity as gifts during unveiling festivities; baskets used by workers to collect "yam" often are preserved in the gallery (color plate 6); we have seen the wealth of knife and yam symbolism. Spirit-workers, like the first men, have plenty to eat. On another level the progressive ordering of nature in mbari parallels the ideological control of nature which is a constant preoccupation; the pains taken and sacrifices offered to increase the productivity of nature—especially of the yam crop—and to reduce the hardship brought on by extremes of heat and wetness are all focused in mbari.

The materials and workers in mbari reflect the three cosmic divisions: the real world, the underworld, and the sky world, which are also present tangibly in the completed edifice. By erecting a house of ordinary mud or clay, men (four-day-workers) create the real world, which is then transformed by spirits (*ndimgbe*) with the addition of powerfully charged clay from the underworld. If men reincarnate from anthills, moreover, their clay is the most appropriate medium for the re-presentation of idealized, original man in mbari. When the artist paints in the celestial motifs, sun, moon, rainbow, the tripartite cosmos is complete. The central poles used in some older mbari (possibly once very common) may then be seen as a world axis that allows communication between the three world layers.

An artist is neither *onyemgbe* (spirit) nor four-day-worker (man) but intead, someone apart from and superior to all workers as their leader, the master builder. When the artist Ezem half-facetiously said, "I consider myself the Chineke of every figure," he did not in fact misrepresent his role. The artist is responsible for the overworld in particular and the creation of an entire new world in general; myths have Chineke building the first house, with four sides, four rooms, and so forth. Furthermore, painting counteracts the dark lower worlds of the unpainted structure in a symbolic process of cosmic ideation: the faces of the people and their gods, as well as the walls of their home, are lightened and purified, and in being purified, they are rendered simultaneously beautiful, good, and cool.

As a cosmic symbol, however, mbari is not all light, ideal, and good, for many references document as well the harsh dark realities of everyday existence: terrifying animals, dread deformities, defiling sexuality, feared spirits, and not least, a potentially homicidal god. Yet all the real or latent evils are composed artfully within an ordered, compartmentalized, open environment in which they may be apprehended and thus, perhaps, controlled. The completed house is then a microcosm in which the order, complexity, and contradiction of the real world are articulated. The extent to which mbari seeks to embrace the totality of real and imagined life is well crystallized in the words of Ezem: "... you can never finish all that should be done in mbari before you pull down the fences. If you tried to finish all that must be done, you might spend ten years building one house." His statement is tacit admission that even fine, large mbari are inherently imperfect, as any structure that attempts to summarize the world must be. In its iconographic program, mbari also reflects what may be considered the proper relationship between men and their gods. Larger than life, supernatural beings must dominate and control. Men, though more numerous, must occupy subordinate positions of submission and obedience.

Mbari may also represent the juxtaposition, merging, and ultimate union of several kinds of cosmic polarity observable in the Owerri world. These can be reduced to two primary oppositions: male versus female and light versus dark. Recalling the union of *chi* and *eke* in the creator, Chineke, men and women in mbari marry and procreate, if only symbolically, to populate the new world. As a community, the clay souls found in a completed mbari are both the children of the artist and *ndimgbe,* who made them, and of Ala, who demanded their creation. Such metaphors of primordial procreation are reiterated vividly in clay scenes of actual copulation and birth. Yet the opposition and differentiation of the sexes are actually obscured and underplayed in mbari activity, almost as if the *ndimgbe* are meant to be neutral, androgynous spirits beyond petty human distinctions in their role as primordial creators. With *ndimgbe,* too, are identified iron (male) and plates (female), which are respectively dark and light, strong and weak. Since real people, like gods, are combinations of good and evil (light and dark), men must also provide plates and women carry iron (*agalegbe*).

Straight dark irons and round white plates, notably, are together responsible in large measure for the decorative program in mbari, which is a unity made up of contrasting opposites in color, texture, shape, and symbolic charge. The introduction of these apparent (but unarticulated) symbols of sexuality also transforms the building process, quite literally, by infusing it with new life, with new sacrificial "blood," as a "house" becomes mbari.

The symbolism of light and dark is further articulated by the necessity of day and night work and by the juxtaposition of modeled figures from the light, ideal world with creatures of the dark underworld. Darkness is inherent in initiatory death, in the cosmic night inside the mbari fence, in the house before it is painted, and at the underworld "yam" farm. While inside mbari, *ndimgbe* experience the "suffering" of cosmic death, yet they live with the expectation of their own rebirth, the dawn of creation. Once painted, mbari is primarily light, the color of birth and life itself. The unveiling, first to the light of cosmic fires that blaze in one final act of purification, and then to the stronger daylight of a world renewed, symbolizes the triumph of light over dark, of life over death.

The same opposition is of course found when the light sky world of Amadioha fuses with the dark earth world of Ala, the great mother: "The land and the sky are the same." This union, seen also as rain fertilizing the earth toward greater productivity, is one of mbari's most crucial results. Yet the earth, Ala, is the great and dreadful constant of Owerri life. "There has always been land. The land existed before we met it." When men build mbari they reshape this dark earth with a light, idealistic vision of a new world in which natural forces are, for a time, controlled.

But in the cyclical nature of things, the natural environment reasserts itself, the bush invades, and the mbari ultimately melts and disintegrates; it fuses again with the very earth of which it was made and which, personified as Ala, called it into being (pl. 74). This is the ultimate sacrifice of mbari; having revitalized the world by a return to beginnings and new growth, the idealized world falls.

But, thirty years later, in the cyclical nature of things, man will pledge once more, a new world will take shape. For as the Owerri people affirm, mbari is life.

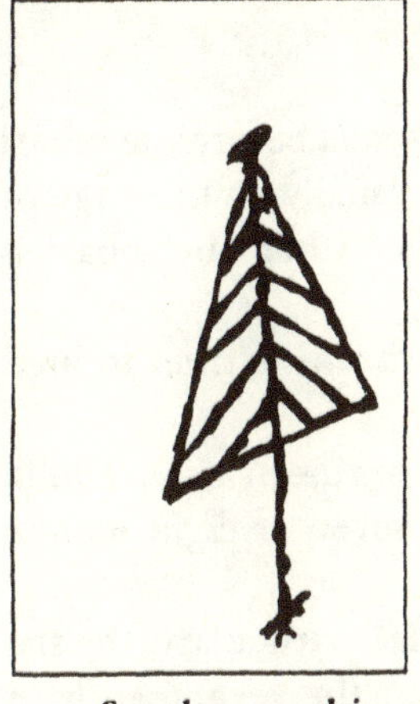

Glossary

Áfọ̀: One of the four days, that day reserved for the worship of Amadioha. Also means year.

Ábāràkā: Playfulness, bluff, joking.

Ágbàrā: God or gods, such as those of the land, thunder, the sun, yam, rivers, etc.

Āgēlégbè: The iron staff given female *ndimgbe*. Looks like, and takes its name from, the ramrod for a Dane gun or musket.

Ālà: Goddess of earth and the deity for whom most mbari are made.

Āmādīōhà: God of thunder and lightning.

Āmálà: "Owners of the land." All adult freeborn men who live on the land of their ancestors.

Bēké: The generic name for white man or men.

Chí: A person's soul or guardian spirit, which is usually incorporated into a small shrine. Has a male association.

Chínèkē: The high god or creator.

Díbìà: Diviner and native doctor, who consults Agwu or Agwushi, directs sacrifices to *agbara* and makes *ogwu.*

Chúkwū (Chiukwu): "Great chi" (spirit); the high god.

Édeàlā: Intricate body painting made with a vegetable substance that irritates and therefore swells the skin, so that a pattern remains on the body after the paint is washed off.

Éfērē: Plate or saucer. Has female assocations.

Ékè: The female counterpart of *chi,* but without the connotation of independence and spiritlike quality associated with *chi.* The word is also the verb "to create" and can signify creation. As *Ēké,* is also one of the four days, that set aside for honoring Agwushi; it is therefore the day sacred to diviners. As *Ékē,* also means python.

Ēkēlé N̄dìmgbē: "Greeting the mbari workers." A ceremony that is performed at least once during the building of an mbari, during which townspeople assemble at the mbari site to honor, feast, and give presents to the *ndimgbe.*

Ēké Nwàorī: The house built for *ndimgbe* by the *amala* before the mbari is begun. Is adjacent to the mbari site and usually on the edge of the priest's compound, for he takes it over when the mbari is completed.

Ēkwēlèm: "I have agreed." One of the *umuagbara* shrine trees located on an *ihu agbara.*

Ēzúmēzù: "Completeness." Part of the *chi* and *eke* shrine in a household.

Īgbò: The language, of the Kwa family, of the seven or eight million Igbo, or Ibo, people.

Ígwè: The sky. Also the word for iron (and bicycle), particularly the six- to seven-foot-long iron bars introduced in the seventeenth or eighteenth century as a trade currency. Used in the Owerri area as a sacrifice that must accompany the presentation of an *osu.* Iron has multiple ritual uses inside and outside the mbari process, and has male associations.

Īhú ágbàrā: "The face of the god." The plot of ground on which a god's principal community shrine is located, which contains many subsidiary shrines as well.

Ījērèmgbē or *nẃāījērèmgbē:* The female relief figures found in mbari on columns and particularly beside the door to the interior chamber. Literally means "you have gone to *mgbe*" or, with a different pronunciation, "have you gone to *mgbe* (mbari)?"

Íkē īshì: "Tying the head." A ceremony that *ndimgbe* undergo shortly after "walking the iron."

Íkē īshígwè: "Tying the head (or leader) of iron" or "tying the head to iron." The first major mbari ceremony.

Íkō: Concubine. The name given to one of the villagers who assists an *agbara* priest at rituals.

Ịkụ̀ īgwè: "Hitting iron." The process of embedding the slivers of iron or wood in the mbari walls and columns.

Ịkwáchị̄chị: "Clearing the stumps and debris." A ceremony enacted annually during the farming cycle, as well as in mbari.

Ịrùọ̄kà: "Planting the skill (art)." The ceremony of sinking the "backbone" armature in the *agbara*'s pedestal seat. This rite initiates all modeling.

Ízọ̀ígwè: "Walking the iron." The ceremony in which *ndimgbe* are initiated into their mbari work.

M̄bárī: Probably a contraction of "the town eats," *m̄bá ērí.* The structure that is the subject of this study. Also the name given to the plates inserted in the walls and columns of mbari houses.

Ḿgbè: Another word for mbari (used especially in Etche), usually used in the Igbo language as a suffix, and probably meaning "seclusion" or "retreat," a time and place set apart from the everyday world.

M̄gbọ́tọ̄: Women who have left the town of their fathers and gone elsewhere to live with their husbands.

M̄kpátākù: "The coming in of wealth." A shrine, personal or for an *agbara,* located in a man's meetinghouse or on an *ihu agbara.*

M̄kpéshì ígwè: "Slivers of iron." Refers to the iron strips, or their wooden surrogates, that are embedded in the walls and columns of an mbari house.

Mmárụ̀: "End." The ceremony of bringing *ndimgbe* out of *eke nwaori* after their three-week (24 days) period of seclusion.

N̄díchìè: Ancestor or ancestors.

N̄dímgbè: Those people chosen (by divination) by an *agbara* to work on its mbari house.

N̄dīshígwè: "People at the head of iron." A group of women, usually past the age of child-bearing, who announce the promise to build an mbari by carrying the iron bar prepared at the *ikeishigwe* ceremony to all villages of the town.

N̄dīọ́hà: "People of peace." Lineage elders among the *amala* and, in the old days, the group most important in making decisions affecting a community.

N̄díọka: "People of skill (art)," or artists. In this study, specifically those artists who take charge of and largely build an mbari house.

N̄dīọ́nụ̀ábàlīanọ́: "Four-day-workers." The "civilians" chosen to help with mbari work. Given this name because they are required to work only one day out of four. In early times some or all may have been *osu.*

N̄kwọ́: One of the four days, that set aside for the worship of Ala.

N̄wáọ̀kwàójọ̄: "Child of bad mortar." The name given to the first crude and incomplete figure modeled at the mbari site.

Óbì ágbàrā: "Heart of the god," a symbol found in gods' shrines.

Ōbīámā: "House on the road." The meetinghouse of a compound.

Ōbīámā ágbàrā: Heart and/or meetingplace of *agbara.*

Ọ̄fọ́: The ritually important short, stafflike symbol of authority. Held by priests, *okpara,* and diviners.

Ọ̄fọ́ígwè: The iron-based short staff carried by male *ndimgbe,* resembling the ancestrial *ofo* (see above).

Ógènē: Iron gong. A musical instrument.

Ọ́gwụ̀: Medicine or magical substance prepared by diviners.

Ōhíhē: Strings rubbed with *ogwu* which were once worn, crossed over the chest bandolier-fashion, by all *ndimgbe.*

Ọ̄kwā: "Bowl." Also the name given to those (selected by divination) who help a priest on ritual occasions.

Ọ̄kọ́hià: "Big forest." Many prominent *agbara* have an *okohia* reserved for them, in which their most important symbol is located.

Ọ́kpārā or *ọ́pārā:* "First son."

Ọ̄mụ́: Young palm leaves, usually tied together, which are used to mark off sacred places.

Ónyēīsīāgbàrà: The priest of an *agbara;* literally, "person at the head of the deity."

Ōnyémgbē: A single person among the *ndimgbe.*

Ōnyēọ̄jọ̀: "Bad person." The name given to the first crude figure made in the mbari process. See also *Nwaokwaojo.*

Ōnyēọ̀kā: An artist.

Órìè: One of the four days, that set aside for honoring the ancestors.

Ōsú: A living human slave, dedicated to a particular cult.

Ọ̄vụ́vụ̄: A yellow earth color used extensively in mbari painting.

Ōdò: A fibrous yellow pigment used in rituals.

Úlọ̀ ágbàrā: House of the god. Usually a small house, and always located on the *ihu agbara* in which the priest receives sacrifices for his god.

Úmùágbàrā: "Child of the god." Refers both to the figures made in *m̄bárí* and to the shrine trees located on an *ihu agbara.*

Úmūnnà: "Children of a father." A patrilineage.

Ụ́wà: World or destiny.

Appendix A
Tree Altars

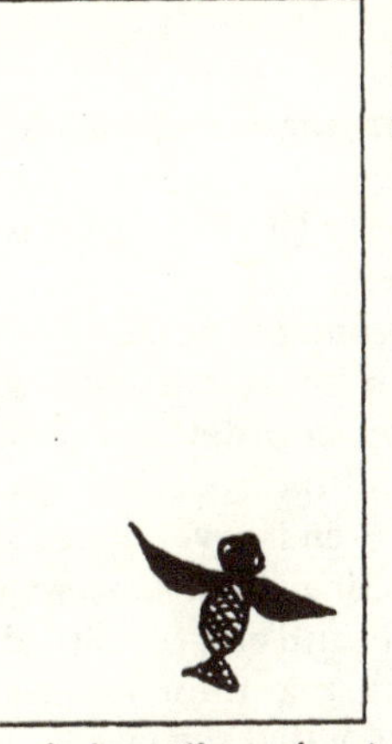

Ritually planted trees figure prominently on all sacred sites (*ihu agbara*). Each tree is regarded as a subordinate shrine or altar, a "child," *umuagbara,* attached to the "parent" *agbara.* This limited anthropomorphism sometimes includes gender, in which cases the sex of the shrine tree is indicated. Divination determines where a given sacrifice should be made, whether at the main tree or at one of the "children." The following list of commonly encountered *umuagbara* altars gives the general character of each; some of the occasions when sacrifices are made are included in parentheses.

These are not given in any significant order, and the positions of most trees on *ihu agbara* seem to vary.

Iwu: "law" (to mark the ratification or breach of laws).

Ozuzu: "completeness" or "may we remain complete" (during sickness or pregnancy, or dissension in village affairs).

Ogazi: an abbreviation of *ogazielam,* "may my path be smooth" (before any important undertaking).

Ekwelem: "I have agreed" (after agreeing to do something for a person or *agbara*).

Ndiukwu: literally "people of the waist," signifying the unity of a family or lineage (at family rites, such as the death of an important member, or when a rift is healed.).

Afo: "year" (female; at the year's end and/or beginning).

Oku: "property," signifying the completeness of property (if something has been stolen, or if goats or palm trees are sick).

Onoka: (for long life, placed by older men).

Opara: "first son" (in thanks for the first male child).

Anyawu: "sun" (male; for success in an undertaking).

Ihuoma: "the face of goodness" (in praying for children, or when something goes well).

Ekwensu: signifies the evil side of *agbara* or *mmuo* generally (on death, natural or unnatural).

Mkpataku: "the coming in of wealth" (on going to farm, to or from market or a trading trip).

Ejialo: "go and return unharmed" (before taking a long trip or going to war).

Oraura: purification after defiling (after a major infraction, such as defiling the earth).

Chukwu: reference to the high god, literally the "great chi," which is another name for Chineke (in requesting children).

Ajiokuji: yam goddess (at various stages in the farming cycle).

The names of the trees suggest that they really represent impersonal principles or concepts that relate directly to the social order and to other practical aspects of everyday life. These "children of the gods" are not visualized in anthropomorphic or zoomorphic terms even if several are called male or female. They are in fact abstractions reflecting ritual concern with interpersonal relationships, economic success, the health and fertility of the family, safety, prosperity, and so forth. It is notable that these shrines are visibly ordered within the sacred precinct, suggesting that the Owerri man began at some point to consciously organize the tangible world so as to make the intangible more intelligible and hence, perhaps, more controllable.

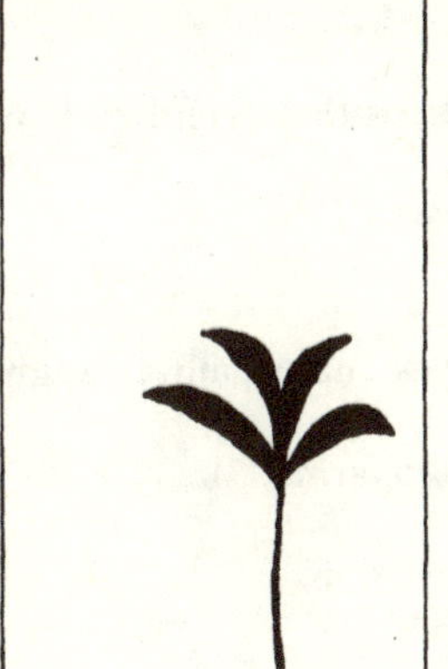

Appendix B
Ndimgbe Names

Igbo names, characteristically, are meaningful, but most of those below are not used as "real" names for Owerri people. Several names here refer to jobs or characteristics of specific people, e.g., "goat killer," for the male leader of the mbari workers, who is in fact the one who prepares sacrificial animals after the rite. *Ogaram,* "messenger," is a messenger, and so on. Still other names are traditionally given to those who exhibit traits contrary to those implied by the names—i.e., the shortest man in the group may be named *Agube,* "tall man," while *Abọzi,* meaning "strong man," may be given to a relative weakling.

Abọzi, m.: "Branch of *iroko*" (the tree); a large, strong man.

Agalauzoubi, f.: "Don't walk on the road to farm."

Agube, m.: "A tall man."

Ajaranma, f.: "Beautiful clay," a name given to one praised for her beauty.

Anyaegbu, m.: "Eyes cannot kill" (a proverb); given to a stubborn person.

Mị-ọku, f.: "Hot wine" (illicit gin).

Mkpeshi uri igwe, f.: "Piece of black iron."

Njaozi, m.: "Most handsome."

Nwaeluekwe, m. or *f.:* "Child atop the drum."

Nwaeriogu, f.: "Person who does not like ogu" (a vegetable used for soup).

Nwaezi, f.: "Child of a pig."

Nwaijeremgbe, f.: "Child who went to *mgbe* (mbari)."

Nwambari, f.: "Child of mbari" (or "child of plate"). This name is also given to a child born to an *onyemgbe* during the mbari process.

Nwamgbe, f.: "Child of *mgbe.*"

Nwanyawu, m.: "Son of the sun."

Nwaụlarị, f.: "Child of the head tie"; i.e., a beautiful woman.

Nwauodo, m. or *f.:* "A deaf person."

Ogaramonyemgbe, m. or *f.:* "Messenger"; this name is usually given to any *osu* who are among the *ndimgbe.*

Ogborkiri, m.: "Goat killer"; the male leader of *ndimgbe* and usually the son of the priest.

Ogozi, m. or *f.:* "Messenger"; also used for *osu,* but not exclusively so.

Oguncha, f.: "Cake of soap."

Ojiemba, m.: "Traveller."

Okazi, f.: The name of a vegetable used for making soup.

Ọkwamma, m.: "Knife sharpener"; in some areas he is the second male in command.
Ọkwauhie, f.: "Uhie bowl"; given to a preparer of *uhie.*
Ọlụkpọ, f.: "The caller."
Ọmuhie, f.: "*Uhie* [camwood] rubber."
Ọrieanụ, f.: "Meat eater"; the female leader of *ndimgbe* and usually a daughter of the priest.
Ọsọnụejeubi, f.: "She who dreads work but still goes to farm."
Otiri, m.: The name of a tree.
Udelu, f.: "Pomade"; given to a person with very dark skin.

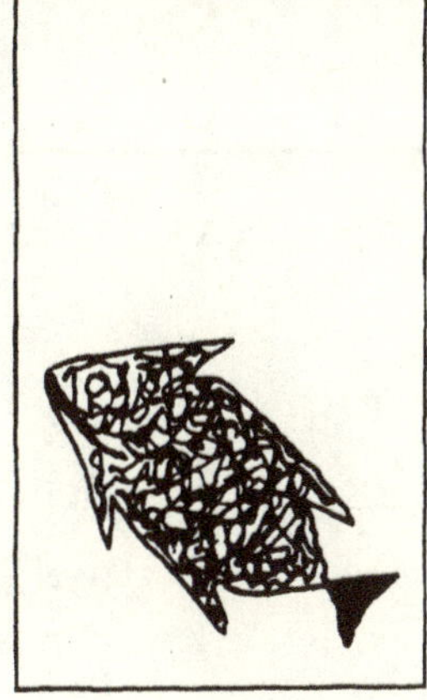

Appendix C
Master List of Mbari Subjects in Sculpture

Key to sources

W = articles by A. A. Whitehouse, 1904
T27 = Talbot, 1927
J37 = Jones, 1937
M37 = Meek, 1937
C69 = Cole, 1969
(C) = Unpublished Cole photo (or notes)
(J) = Unpublished Jones photo
(M) = Unpublished Murray notes

Key to symbols of frequency
C = found in virtually every mbari that has 25 figures or more
R+ = a very recurrent inclusion
R− = repeated, but not noted frequently
A = arbitrary inclusion; noted only once

1 = Number of figures
2 = Date of first documented appearance
3 = Source of illustration
4 = Source of verbal description
5 = Frequency of inclusion
6 = Illustration # in this book

DEITIES	1	2	3	4	5	6
Female with knife (& children)		15	T27		C	c1
Female with mirror (& children)		15	T27		R	
Male & female	2	15	T27		R	
Male with title insignia		15	T27		C	c9
Male with gun		36			R	p7
Ekwunoche (deity with many children)	5, 7	15	T27		C	p8
Mamy Wata	1, 2	36	(J)	J37	C	p13

DEITIES	1	2	3	4	5	6
Ijeremgbe		15	T27		C	p17
Motorcyclist, w/wife in sidecar		36	(J)	J37	A	
GROUPS (Number of figures included follows)						
Madu bu ewu ("man is goat")	2	36	(C)	(M)	C	p55
Twins	2	62			A	p65
Diviner and client	2	15		T27	R	
Blacksmith and apprentice	2	36			R	p32
Boxers	2	63			A	p69
Rainmakers	2	63			A	p36
Seated couple	2	36	(J)		R	c1
Woman with schoolboy	2	59	C69		R−	
Woman and dog copulating	2	36			R	p67
Hunchback and woman copulating	2	63			R	p66
Court scene	8	36		(M)	A	
Priest with catechists (Christian)	4?	36		J37	A	
Woman giving birth (traditional)	3, 2	15		T27	C	p4
Woman giving birth (modern)	4	36		(M)	R	c5
Woman suckling child	2	15		T27	R	
Woman holding child	2	04	W		R+	
Woman with child on head	2	36			R−	
Boy on ostrich	2	36		J37	R+	f26
Musicians (ensemble)	3, 4	15		T27	R+	
Drummers	2, 3	15	(C)	T27	R+	
Xylophone players	2	36	(C)		R−	
Superposed figures	2, 3	15	T27		R−	
Radio announcer/politician	2	63			A	p73
Nwanyegbavuruololo	9	50			R−	p54
Burial scene	3	15	T27		R−	
Soldiers in boat	4?	36		J37	R−	p2
Dressmakers	3	36		(M)	A	
Europeans at club table	4	36		(M)	A	
Ndimgbe (mbari workers)	4	36	(J)		R	
District officers at windows	2	36	J37	J37	R+	p50
Children playing mancala	2	36			A	
Teacher and students	7	36		(M)	A	
Traders at market	3	36		(M)	R−	
Man and woman copulating	2	15		T27	R	
Bandmaster with band	5?	37		M37	A	
Children carrying firewood	3?	37		M37	A	
Truck with driver	2	36		(M)		

GROUPS	1	2	3	4	5	6
White man in litter	3	04	W		A	
Three-headed woman on horse (?)	2	48			A	p60
Wrestlers	2	15	T27		R−	f17
Man with machete threatening woman	3	62	(C)		A	
Woman scarifying child	2	04	W		A	
Men with feather decorations	2	62	(C)		A	
Woman painting body patterns	2	36		J37	A	
Woman dressing girl's hair	2	04	W		R−	
Equestrian	2	04	W		R+	p72
Ogidi holding Okpangu captive	2	62			A	p41
Dancers (traditional)	3, 4, 5	36	J37	J37	R	p27
Dancers (Highlife — modern)	3	63	C69		R−	
Men in office	2	54			R−	f31
Man copulating w/sheep or antelope	2	15		T27	A	
SINGLE FIGURES						
Okpangu		15		T27	C	p5
Court messenger		15		T27	C	p63
Giant policeman, Ogidi		35			R+	f27
Police		15		T27	C	p63
Hunter		15	J37	T27	R+	
Orphan		36		(M)	R	
Wine tapper		45		(C)	R−	
Football (soccer) player		58		(C)	A	
Office worker		54			R−	p3
'Displayed' woman		04	W		R+	
Man with goat's head		36	(C)	(M)	R	
Hunter with goat's horns		36		J37	A	
Ekpekele		34			R−	
Hunchback		63			R−	p66
Hausa man		36	(C)	J37	R−	
Cooper		36		(M)	A	
Man rolling barrel		36		(M)	A	
Prostitute		36		(M)	A	
Beggar woman		36		(M)	A	
Woman pounding yam		36		J37	R−	p35
Woman with jug		36			R	f15
Woman grinding camwood		15		T27	R−	p35
Woman with handbag		45	(C)		R+	

SINGLE FIGURES	1	2	3	4	5	6
Woman holding plate		36		(M)	R	
Woman holding mirror		15	T27		R+	
Woman drinking and holding bottle		36			A	f16
Pregnant woman		04	W		R	p68
Masker (Okorosia)		15	T27		R−	c3
Seated woman		04	W		C	p34
Chief		15		T27	R	p10
Seated man		15		T27	R+	p40
Priest (Christian)		36		(M)	A	
Diviner		15	(C)	T27	R	
Airplane pilot		65	(C)		A	
Woman seated, with arms raised		36	J37		R+	p37
Woman making cassava flour		36		(M)	A	
Man with one leg		36	J37		A	
Man with decayed nose		36		(M)	A	
Man with swollen testicles		36		(M)	A	
Girl with cut arm		36		(M)	A	
General (white man)		55			A	p61
White man emerging from hole		36	J37	J37	R+	p70
White man in easy chair		59			R−	C2
Hermaphrodite		60	(C)		A	
Man with guitar		63			A	p10
Market woman		36		J37	R−	
Telephone operator		63			A	p76
Woman pounding palm fruit		35			A	
Priest (native)		36		(M)	A	
Figure with heads on hands, knees, feet		36		(M)	A	
Banker at vault		62		(C)	A	
White man at desk		15		T27	R	p22
Bird giving birth to human		60	(C)		A	
Woman at sewing machine		36			R	p59
Janus-headed man		36			A	p71
Child blowing trumpet		36			R−	p7
Angel		36	C	J37	A	F25B
Naked man with head between legs		36		(M)	A	
Moon-faced child		15	T27		A	
Fisherman		15		T27	A	
Soldier		04	W		R+	
Drummer		04	W		R+	
Slit-gong player		63	(C)		R	
Nurse		15		T27	R−	

SINGLE FIGURES	1	2	3	4	5	6
Midwife		36			R+	p4
Man on bicycle		63			R−	p1
Mmuo with pointed head		65			A	p11
Man (*mmuo?*) with buck teeth		65	(C)		A	
Crucifix		36		(M)	R	p58
Dancer (male & female)		36		(M)	R+	
Goat with human head		36	J37		R−	
Nwa Alakandu		56			R−	p62
Blacksmith		15	T27		R	
Osu		04	W		A	
District officer on ladder		15		T27	R−	
Clerk		15	C69	T27	R+	
Woman fixing hair		15		T27	R+	
Photographer		36		J37	A	
Man at sewing machine		36		J37	R−	
Prisoner		36		(M)		
ANIMALS						
Ọkpangụ		15		T27	C	c6
Leopard		15		T27	C	c6
Leopard eating goat		15		T27	R+	p23
Goat		15			R+	p23
Cow		36	(J)		R−	
Elephant or hippopotamus		15		T27	R+	p39
Python		15		T27	C	
Python eating goat		55	(C)		A	
Dog		04		T27	R−	f3
Lizard		55	(C)		R−	
Turtle or tortoise		63	(C)		R−	
Monkey		04	W,(C)		R	
Bird (guinea fowl, parrot)		15	(C)	T27	R−	
Lion		62			R−	c6
Crocodile		60	(C)		A	
Fish		35	(J)		R	
Monkey riding elephant		37	(C)	(M37)	A	
Ostrich		36	J37		A	
"Hippo" eating child		04			R	p40
Chimpanzee		58		(C)	A	
Sheep		15		T27	A	

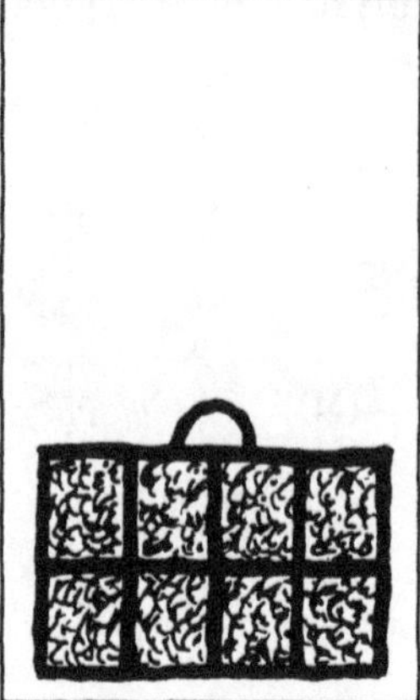

Appendix D Mbari House at Obaku, Oratta clan, Owerri

The late Kenneth C. Murray, former Director of Antiquities for Nigeria, recorded the following information in 1946 at what must have been one of the largest mbari complexes ever built. It seems best to reproduce his text in full to indicate the size, content, and figural variety. In this house, notably, there are many scenes or groups of related figures, more of these than were observed in the 1960s. The figures counted in the left margin are approximate. See note at the end.

The descriptions that follow are exactly as written by Mr. Murray.

The plan is roughly a rectangle round three sides of which a low shed is built, and in the central area there are five houses.

Number of figures

22 A. *Amadiọha* on a motor cycle, with *Lọlọ* his wife, with other figures around representing his children, including *Ada*, his eldest daughter, at the back of the building. The shed contains about 22 figures including a cow.

8 B. Native court: prisoner, witness, 2 clerks, 3 court members, court messenger.

15 C. *Eze Nwaye*, the Queen, with four other figures on front side, including a woman carrying a child on her head.

On side: an animal with a woman's head; a clerk, policeman and prisoner; a leopard eating a goat.

Back: a Janus figure, a large animal. The other figure had been destroyed.

Side: Mammy Water and *Ada 'la*, the eldest daughter of the land — *Ala*.

16 D. *Iyafọ* and his wife who nurses a child, two other girls.

Side: Woman nursing child; a chief; a woman and a lunatic (?) child, the daughter of *Iyafọ*.

Back: A leopard descending from the back wall eating a goat. Two women.

Side: Two men seated.

E. *Eze Ala* and his wife holding two children, accompanied by two girls and a man at sides, a girl and boy seated in front, and two girls in relief at sides of door behind the group. Two girls and a man at side.

Annex: Court scene with 7 figures.

14 Native doctor and two girls with another girl in relief on back wall.

Pregnant woman and a girl, with girl in relief on back wall (court scene).

24 At side of main building. Beggar woman and child breaking kernels.

The woman with many children (4)

Man on horseback.

Back: Midwife delivering a child.

A group of devils painted white. Male and female (faces on knees). Two double figures (one figure on another).

Woman grinding cam wood. Man seated (naked).

Side: An elephant? and a black coloured hunter with medicines fixed to his body. Two seated men.

4 (On top of his house is a kind of rectangular umbrella of corrugated iron, on top of which is a small figure of a dog and a dove, with beneath, wooden figures of man and woman.

Side sheds. Left:

11 *Ndi Ala* (the people of Ala): *Ala Lawa* and wine jars. 6 people, a monkey, a man riding an ostrich, and an ape (Okpango).

Side gallery (front) in order:

24 Cooper, man rolling barrel, 3 men in canoe; crucifixion with two angels; 3 soldiers; a warden and 3 prisoners; 2 wrestlers; a girl with mirror (a dancer), a Hausa man; a Lagos man, a figure now destroyed, a woman. Along the front of this gallery is a snake for "Mammy Water." Mammy Water figures (2).

26 Back: Masked *Okorosia* figure; teacher and six scholars; 3 women making garri (cassava) flour in basins over fires; 3 women dressmakers; 3 women selling garri; 2 traders at market; 2 youths making "Yanga" at market; a man seated who wished to have connection with a woman, himself in act, (destroyed) the woman in bent position; a girl with mirror (dancer).

8 Back: Two figures of Mammy Water.

Hospital scene (destroyed).

8 Dog having connection with woman.

3 cows along back wall.

43 Two women, 8 dancers and musicians (*Odi Nma*): lorry with European driver and two pedestrians; 4 Europeans seated round table at Club; gorilla (black, with fruits under arms and on shoulders, very large penis); seated woman; woman lying naked on bed, hand held over face in shame having connection with dog (dog destroyed); white-ant hill; 5 dancers, *Ute* dance; *Beke amala* — white man from underground (emerging from sewer?); girl, Hausaman; native doctor; 2 cows at back; Hausa

man; *Maduewu* — a naked man with a head emerging between his legs, in front a figure with head, arms and tail (fairy); clerk; two girls; "House of Goblins" with 4 goblins (fantastic distorted figures).

24 Side: Crucifixion (cross legs, screws instead of nails); 6 exam. candidates; two rich Africans seated and drinking, with the wife of one handing drinks at side; a woman bending over for copulation with a parrot looking at her vagina; canoe fight; 3 soldiers and a dog, and a woman at side; the machine gun; 4 soldiers in canoe; a woman; a chief (with his naked son on horseback); 2 ladies.

261*

---

* Mr. Murray calculated 230 figures, but when I added his marginal numbers up, the total came to 238. He seems, moreover, to have omitted two counts in the margin altogether, for in cross-checking the numbers with the descriptions, I counted a total of at least 261 figures, and I have taken the liberty of emending the numbers to reflect this calculation.

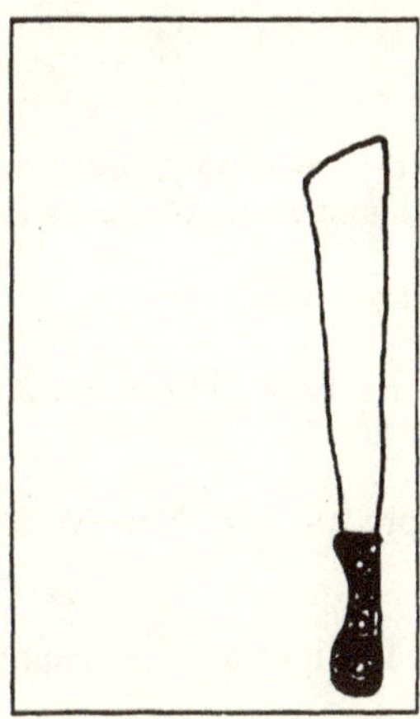

Bibliography

Achebe, Chinua. See Morrell 1975.

Anene, J.C.
1966 Southern Nigeria in Transition, 1885-1906. Cambridge: Cambridge University Press.

Ardener, Edwin W.
1954 "Some Ibo Attitudes to Skin Pigmentation." Man 54(101):71-73.

Arinze, Francis A.
1970 Sacrifice in Ibo Religion. Ibadan, Nigeria: Ibadan University Press.

Basden, George T.
1938 Niger Ibos. London: Seeley, Service and Co. Ltd.

Beier, Ulli
1960 Art in Nigeria 1960. Cambridge: Cambridge University Press.
1963 African Mud Sculpture. London: Cambridge University Press.

Ben-Amos, Paula
1973 "Symbolism in Olokun Mud Art." African Arts 6(4):28-31, 95.

Bohannan, Paul
1961 "Artist and Critic in an African Society." *In* The Artist in Tribal Society, proceedings of a symposium held at the Royal Anthropological Institute. Marian W. Smith, ed. Pp. 85-94. London: Routledge and Kegan Paul.

Boston, John Shipway
1960 "Some Northern Ibo Masquerades." Journal of the Royal Anthropological Institute 90:54-65.
1977 Ikenga Figures among the North-West Igbo and the Igala. London: Ethnographica in association with the Federal Department of Antiquities. Nigeria.

Carpenter, Edmund
1968 "We Wed Ourselves to the Mystery." Explorations 22.

Chadwick, E.R.
1937 "Wall Decoration on Ibo Houses." Nigerian Field 1(3):134-35.

Child, Irvin L. and Leon Siroto
1965 "Bakwele and American Esthetic Evaluations Compared." Ethnology 4(4):349-60.

Cole, Herbert M.
1969a "*Mbari* is Life." African Arts /Arts d'Afrique 2(3):8-17, 87.
1969b "*Mbari* is a Dance." African Arts/Arts d'Afrique 2(4):42-51, 79.
1969c "Art as a Verb in Iboland," African Arts/Arts d'Afrique 3(1):34-41, 88.
1975 "The History of Ibo *Mbari* Houses: Facts and Theories." *In* Af-

rican Images: Essays in African Iconology. Boston University Papers on Africa. Vol. 6. Daniel F. McCall and Edna G. Bay, eds. Pp. 104-32.

1981 (In press). "Mbari Sexual Imagery." African Arts 15(1).

Cole, Herbert M. et al.

1970 African Arts of Transformation. Santa Barbara: The Art Galleries of the University of California.

Coomaraswamy, Ananda K.

1956 [1943] Christian and Oriental Philosophy of Art. New York: Dover.

Correia, J. Alves

1921-1922 "L'animisme Ibo et les divinities de la Nigeria." Anthropos 16-17:360-66.

1923-1924 "Le Sens moral chez les Ibos de la Nigeria." Anthropos 18-19:880-89.

Crowley, Daniel

1966 "An African Aesthetic." Journal of Aesthetics and Art Criticism 24:519-24.

d'Azevedo, Warren

1958 "A Structural Approach to Aesthetics: Toward a Definition of Art in Anthropology." American Anthropologist 60:702-14.

Dike, K. Onwuka

1956 Trade and Politics in the Niger Delta, 1830-1885. Oxford: Clarendon Press.

Drewal, Henry

1976 "The Iconography and Distribution of Mami Wata Imagery." Paper read at the 4th Triennial Symposium of African Art, Washington, D.C.

1979 "The Impact of Printed Media on Mami Wata Art and Ritual in West Africa." Paper read at the meetings of the African Studies Association, Los Angeles, California.

Ejiogu, N.O.

1935 "The Owerri *Mbari* Houses." Nigerian Teacher 1(4):9-11.

Eliade, Mircea

1958 Rites and Symbols of Initiation: The Mysteries of Birth and Rebirth. New York: Harper and Row.

1961 The Sacred and the Profane. New York: Harper and Row.

1963 Myth and Reality. New York: Harper and Row.

Fagg, William B.

1965 Tribes and Forms in African Art. New York: Tudor.

Fernandez, James W.

1966 "Principles of Opposition and Vitality in Fang Aesthetics." Journal of Aesthetics and Art Criticism 35(1):53-64.

Floyd, Barry

1969 Eastern Nigeria, A Geographical Review. London.

Forde, Daryll and G. I. Jones

1950 The Ibo and Ibibio-speaking Peoples of South Eastern Nigeria. London: International African Institute.

Forge, Anthony

1965 "Art and Environment in the Sepik." Proceedings of the Royal Anthropological Institute, pp. 23-30.

1974 "The Problem of Meaning and the Art of New Guinea." Paper 28, Art of Oceania Symposium, Hamilton, Ontario.

Fraser, Douglas and Herbert M. Cole (eds.)
1971 African Art and Leadership. Madison: University of Wisconsin Press.

Gennep, Arnold van
1960 [1909] The Rites of Passage. Chicago: University of Chicago Press.

Green, Margaret M.
1941 Land Tenure in an Ibo Village. London School of Economics. Monographs on Social Anthropology, No.6. London: Percy, Lund, Humphries.
1947 Ibo Village Affairs. London: Sidgwick and Jackson.

Hall, Edward T.
1959 The Silent Language. Garden City, New York: Doubleday and Co.

Henderson, Richard N.
1972 The King in Every Man. New Haven and London: Yale University Press.

Horton, Robin
1962 "The Kalabari World-View: An Outline and Interpretation." Africa 32(3):198-219.
1963 "The Kalabari *Ekine* Society: A Borderland of Religion and Art." Africa 33(2):94-114.
1964 "Ritual Man in Africa." Africa 34(2):85-106.
1965a & b "African Traditional Thought and Western Science." Africa 35(2):50-71; (3):154-87.

Hubert, Henri and Marcel Mauss
1964 [1897-98] Sacrifice: Its Nature and Function. Chicago: University of Chicago Press.

Huizinga, Johan
1955 [1950] Homo Ludens: A Study of the Play-Element in Culture. Boston: Beacon Press.

Ilogu, Edmund
1974 Christianity and Ibo Culture. Leiden: E.J. Brill.

Isichei, Elizabeth
1973 The Ibo People and the Europeans. London: Faber and Faber.

Jeffries, M.D.W.
1956 "The Origin of the Names of the Ibo Week." Folk-Lore 67:162-67.

Jensen, Adolf E.
1963 Myth and Cult among Primitive Peoples. Chicago and London: University of Chicago Press.

Jones, G.I.
1937 "Mbari Houses." Nigerian Field 6(2):77-79.
1938 "The Distribution of Negro Sculpture in Southern Nigeria." Nigerian Field 7(3):102-8.
1956 The "Jones Report": Report of the Position, Status, and Influence of Chiefs and Natural Rulers in the Eastern Region of Nigeria. Enugu: Government Printer.

1963 The Trading States of the Oil Rivers. London: Oxford University Press.

1973 "Sculpture of the Umuahia Area of Nigeria." African Arts 6(4):58-63, 96.

Leith-Ross, Sylvia

1937 "Notes on the Osu System among the Ibo of Owerri Province, Nigeria." Africa 10:206-20.

1939 African Women. A study of the Ibo of Nigeria. London: Faber and Faber.

Leonard, A.G.

1906 The Lower Niger and its Tribes. London: Macmillan.

Meek, Charles K.

1937 Law and Authority in a Nigerian Tribe. London: Oxford University Press.

1943 "The Religions of Nigeria." Africa 14(3):106-17.

Moore, G. and U. Beier

1956 "Mbari Houses." Nigeria Magazine 49:184-98.

Morell, Karen L. (ed.)

1975 In Person: Achebe, Awoonor, and Soyinka at the University of Washington, Seattle. Seattle: Institute for Comparative and Foreign Area Studies, University of Washington.

Murray, Kenneth C.

1935 "Body Painting from Umuahia." Nigerian Teacher 1(4):3-4.

n.d. "Notes on *mbari* Houses." Unpublished typescript.

Njaka, Elechukwu N.

1974 Igbo Political Culture. Evanston: Northwestern University Press.

Noon, John A.

1944 "A Preliminary examination of the Death Concepts of the Ibo." American Anthropologist 44(4), part 1:638-54.

Nsugbe, Philip O.

1974 Ohaffia: A Matrilineal Ibo People. Oxford: Clarendon Press.

Odita, E.O.

1970a Igbo Masking Tradition: Its Types, Functions, and Interpretations. Ph.D. Dissertation, Indiana University.

1970b Contemporary Art in Africa, by Ulli Beier, (book review) in African Report 15:39-40.

Ogbalu, F.C. and E.N. Emenanjo (eds.)

1975 Igbo Language and Culture. Ibadan: Oxford University Press.

Okparocha, John

1976 Mbari: Art as Sacrifice. Ibadan: Daystar Press.

Ottenberg, Simon

1959 "Ibo Receptivity to Change." *In* Continuity and Change in African Cultures. William Bascom and Melville J. Herskovits, (eds.) Pp. 130-43. Chicago: University of Chicago Press.

1968a Double Descent in an African Society: The Afikpo Village Group. Seattle: University of Washington Press.

1968b "Statement and Reality: The Renewal of an Igbo Protective Shrine." International Archives of Ethnography 51:143-62.

1971a "Humorous Masks and Serious Politics among the Afikpo Ibo."*In* African Art and Leadership. D. Fraser and H.M. Cole, eds. Madison: University of Wisonsin Press.

1971b Leadership and Authority in an African Society: The Afikpo Village Group. Seattle: University of Washington Press.

1971c Anthropology and African Aesthetics. Typescript of a paper presented at the Institute of African Studies, Legon, Ghana.

1973 "Afikpo Masquerades: Audience and Performers." African Arts 6(4):32-35, 94.

1975 Masked Rituals of the Afikpo. Seattle: University of Washington Press.

Peek, Philip M.

1976 "Isoko Mud Sculpture." African Arts 9(4):34-39.

Prussin, Labelle

1976 "Fulani-Hausa Architecture." African Arts 10(1):8-19, 97-98.

Rattray, R.S.

1927 Religion and Art in Ashanti. London: Oxford University Press.

Rubin, Arnold

1968 "Uta and Utumu: Kutep Mud Sculpture." African Arts 1(3):18-20, 93.

Salmons, Jill

1977 "Mammy Wata." African Arts 10(3):8-15.

Scheinberg, Alfred

1975 Ibo, Ibibio, Ogoni: Art in Wood from three South-Eastern Nigerian Tribes. New York: Endicott-Guthaim Gallery.

Shaw, C. Thurstan

1970 Igbo-Ukwu: An Account of Archaeological Discoveries in Eastern Nigeria. 2 vols. Evanston: Northwestern University Press.

Shelton, Austin J.

1971 The Igbo-Igala Borderland: Religion and Social Control in Indigenous African Colonialism. Albany: State University of New York Press.

Sieber, Roy

1961 Sculpture of Northern Nigeria. New York: The Museum of Primitive Art.

Smith, Marian W. (ed.)

1961 The Artist in Tribal Society. Proceedings of a symposium held at the Royal Anthropological Insititute. London: Routledge and Kegan Paul.

Spörndli, J.I.

1942-1945 "The *Mbari* Question." Anthropos 37-40 (4/6):891-93.

Starkweather, Frank

1968 Traditional Igbo Art. (Exhibition catalogue). Ann Arbor, Michigan: Museum of Art, University of Michigan.

Talbot, P. Amaury

1926 Peoples of Southern Nigeria. 4 vols. London: Oxford University Press.

1927 Some Nigerian Fertility Cults. London: Oxford University Press.

1932 Tribes of the Niger Delta. London: The Sheldon Press.

Thomas, Northcote W.

1913-1914 Anthropological Report on the Ibo-speaking Peoples. 6 volumes. London: Harrison and Sons.

Thompson, Robert Farris

1968 "Esthetics in Traditional Africa." Art News 66(9):44-45, 63-66.

1969 "Abatan: A Master Potter of the Egbado Yoruba." *In* Tradition and Creativity in Tribal Art. D. Biebuyck, ed. Berkeley and Los Angeles: University of California Press.

1972 "Yoruba Artistic Criticism." *In* The Artist in Traditional African Societies. W. d'Azevedo, ed. Bloomington: Indiana University Press.

1973 "An Aesthetic of the Cool." African Arts 7(1):40-43, 64-67, 89.

1974 African Art in Motion. Berkeley and Los Angeles: University of California Press.

Turner, Victor W.

1961 Ndembu Divination, Its Symbolism and Techniques. Manchester: Manchester University Press.

1964 The Ritual Process. Chicago: Aldine.

1966 "Color Classification in Ndembu Ritual." *In* Anthropological Approaches to the Study of Religion. Michael Banton, ed. Pp. 47-84. London: Tavistock Publications.

Uchendu, Victor C.

1965 The Igbo of Southwest Nigeria. New York: Holt, Rinehart and Winston.

Udo, Reuben K.

1970 Geographical Regions of Nigeria. Berkeley and Los Angeles: University of California Press.

Vogel, Susan M.

1974 Gods of Fortune: The Cult of the Hand in Nigeria. New York: Museum of Primitive Art.

1979 "Baule and Yoruba Art Criticism: A Comparison." *In* The Visual Arts, Justine M. Cordwell, ed. The Hague: Mouton.

Welmers, Beatrice F. and William E. Welmers

1968 Igbo: A Learners Dictionary. Berkeley and Los Angeles: University of California Press.

Whitehouse, A. A.

1904a "An Ibo Festival." Journal African Society 4(13):134-35.

1904b "Note on the 'Mbari' Festival of the Natives of Ibo Country, Southern Nigeria." Man 4(106):162-63.

Wieschoff, Heinrich A.

1941 "Social Significance of Names among the Ibo of Nigeria." American Anthropologist 43:212-22.

1943 "Concepts of Abnormality among the Ibo of Nigeria." Journal American Oriental Society 63:262-72.

Willett, Frank

1967 Ife in the History of West African Sculpture. London: Thames and Hudson.

Wittmer, Marcilene K. and William Arnett

1978 Three Rivers of Nigeria. Atlanta: The High Museum of Art.

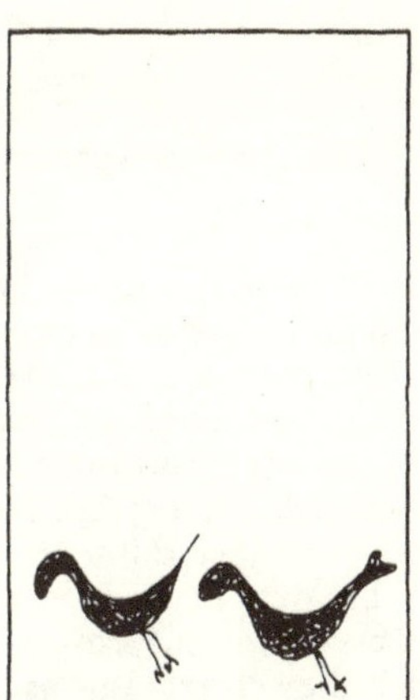

Notes

Preface

1. Mud or clay sculpture has become better known since the publication of Ulli Beier's pioneering but general book on Nigerian and Dahomean traditions, *African Mud Sculpture,* 1963. More recent publications include Ben-Amos 1973 and Peek 1976.
2. Igbo people speak a language of the Kwa group. The name of the people may be spelled with or without the "g".
3. See Starkweather (1968) for a reasonably complete bibliography of Igbo art. The most complete survey of Igbo art (especially masks) yet to appear is a doctoral dissertation by E.O. Odita (1970a).
4. Forde and Jones 1950:9: "Before the advent of Europeans the Igbo had no common name and village groups were generally referred to by the name of their putative founder." See this work and Uchendu 1965 for general ethnographic accounts. A full-scale Igbo ethnography has not yet been published for the Owerri area, although important recent books are available on other Igbo areas; See Ottenberg (1971 and 1975) for Afikpo, Shelton (1971) for Nsukka, Nsugbe (1974) for Ohaffia, and Henderson (1972) for Onitsha. The most detailed works for the Owerri area remain Meek 1937 and Green 1947.
5. See Boston (1960) for a good example of the wealth and variety of masks in a single small area of Igboland, or Cole 1970, Scheinberg 1975, Wittmer and Arnett 1978 for selections of Igbo masks from several areas.
6. Demographic data are imprecise at best. These figures have been interpolated from Meek (1937), Forde and Jones (1950), and Floyd (1969). See Floyd (1969) for a treatment of eastern Nigerian geography. Today there are approximately nine million Igbo people.
7. In the field each *mbari* I saw I recorded on a mimeographed sheet, with the following data tabulated: location, deity honored, approximate size, number of modeled figures, approximate year built, name of principal artist, and any unusual features. Regrettably, this valuable file was not available for this study because it, along with other personal effects prepared for shipment at the beginning of the Nigeria-Biafra conflict in 1967, was lost.

1. Introduction

1. Floyd 1969:39.
2. The mbari area came under British control shortly after 1900, the year all Igboland passed from the hands of the Royal Niger Company to the British Crown. Owerri then became an administrative center under Douglas

in 1901, and a government school was opened in 1906, the time that the missionaries arrived.

3. Dike 1956:41.

4. Many authors (Meek 1937:24, 44-47; Basden 1938: 91-92) discuss the once-powerful oracle at Umunoha, a village group about twelve miles from Owerri, on the northern fringe of the mbari area. Like Ibinokpabe at Arochukwu, this oracle, called Igwekala, was consulted by individuals and groups from many parts of Igboland. Despite its proximity, however, the oracle seems to have been outside the mbari world and to have been a different sort of spiritual enterprise, which appears not to have influenced mbari procedures in any way remembered by mbari builders in 1966-67.

5. A few older men, among the most knowledgeable of my informants, actually preferred to speak of this earlier era, which they clearly saw as a kind of "golden age" of mbari: "Those were the *real* mbari," as opposed to "the small patches of tin" made in the 1960s. Most people were well aware of the kinds of shortcuts employed recently in both ritual and structural processes.

6. A composite of two stories told by Ugo during two different interviews.

7. Uratta refers both to a "tribe" (or clan) and a village group within it. See Forde and Jones 1950:41-41. Talbot (1927:23) implies that "Orata" people were the first mbari builders, on information obtained in Etche, a distinct people south of the Uratta, some village groups of which also build them. My informants in Etche corroborated this history, as did those in Inyeogugu (Isu people), Mberichi, and Agwa, the latter two on the western and southwestern edges of the area, respectively.

Several Uratta and some people outside those groups claimed Ulakwo, a village group of the southeast Uratta, as the actual point of origin, while a few people attributed origin to Egbu. Either, but especially Ulakwo (favored by informants), would account for the adoption of mbari by close Ngor neighbors (in Emerienwe, Obike, and Umuhu) to the southeast, and by some southern Isu village groups to the north. Some of the southernmost mbari builders in Etche trace migrations to Ngor areas, which probably accounts for the southern extension of the institution.

8. Interpolated from Forde and Jones 1950:39-42.

9. Ibid., p. 38.

10. My data are somewhat inconclusive on both the frequency of village resettlement and the spread of this practice, which seems to have stopped in the 1930s and 1940s. The erection of more permanent buildings such as administrative offices and schools, and more recently, private homes, concrete market stalls, and other community improvements, naturally reduced the impetus to move.

11. Although men may eat yam—the main prestige food crop—for most of the year, women and children must often be content with cassava, which is cheaper and lower in nutritional value.

12. Precise data on trade goods and their distribution to interior areas are hard to establish for specific dates, and variations occur depending on the proximity of a village to Owerri town or to other major markets or roads. The modest village in which Green lived (1934-37) claimed no bicycles, one sewing machine, some carpentered chairs, a few enamel basins, and metal spoons. " . . . imported goods had only begun to scratch the surface of people's lives though there were few households from which they were

entirely absent . . ." (1947:32-33). Today, in the same village, one might expect to find universal ownership of several items of western clothing, many bicycles, radios, sewing machines, perhaps several concrete houses with metal roofs and a few cars—the latter two items often owned by people who live elsewhere and return "home" once a year or less frequently. Villages nearer major roads, and of course Owerri town, have still more visible modern wealth.

13. Uchendu 1965:15.

14. Ibid., 19.

15. See both Ottenberg (1959) and Uchendu (1965) for analyses of the historical roots of "Igbo receptivity to change," the title of Ottenberg's important paper.

16. Again, this pattern does not hold for all of Igboland. Onitsha, under the influence of Benin, has a king; and the priest-kings (*ezenri*) of Nri, a clan in Awka Division who are ritual specialists especially linked with the Ozo title system, may have exercised some form of widespread ritual authority (probably not extending to temporal affairs) perhaps since the 9th or 10th centuries A.D., the dates of the well-known bronze artifacts from archaeological sites in Igbo-Ukwu. See Shaw (1970).

17. See Uchendu 1965:15; Meek 1937:114; and Green 1947:67-77.

18. For details on this important symbol, see Green 1947:58-60, 67-72; and Meek 1937:63-65 and passim.

19. Forde and Jones 1950:15-16.

20. Green 1947:17.

21. Lineages were constantly breaking off from each other; some were expelled, others sought new political liaisons, some split so the two halves could intermarry, or divided because one half feared the power and domination of the other. For a detailed discussion of kinship in the precise area in question, see Meek 1937:88-115. The subject is treated only briefly here because the convolutions of kinship do not seem to elucidate mbari houses, for they can be made by any social unit that embraces a cult, from a single extended family to a group of villages. The larger, more important mbari, however, are made by villages or village groups.

22. See Meek 1937:93 and Green 1947:16-17, 22.

23. Meek 1937:242-43, and Green 1947:255.

24. G. I. Jones, personal communication, 1972.

25. Meek (1937:174) did not find the Ozo society in Owerri itself, although some Uratta peoples, and especially the Isu, have long had it. Ozo or similar title regalia have long been a part of mbari imagery.

2. The Gods and the People

1. For improvements on this chapter I am indebted to G. I. Jones, to Simon and Nora Ottenberg for many helpful suggestions, to several works by Robin Horton (1962, 1963, 1964) and to Austin J. Shelton's work on Northern Igbo religion (1971).

2. Parts of creation stories related by the cult priest of Afo at Umuoye Etche.

3. In many parts of Igboland, as in Owerri, the high god is also called Chukwu, an elision of *chi* and *ukwu* ("great"), but in Owerri Chineke is the more common usage.

4. Meek (1937:55*n*) translates *chi* as "a genius or spiritual double" and (p. 57) *eke* as "creation."
5. It is, however, universally accepted that Chineke is male. See Shelton 1971:87.
6. Some informants felt they also had an *eke*, but were unable to define it. People speak frequently about their *chi*, but seldom if ever about their *eke*.
7. See Uchendu 1965:16.
8. A person's destiny, *uwa*, is symbolically incorporated with his *chi* and *eke* in the personal shrine. A man with a family sacrifices to this shrine in a yearly renewal ceremony and at times of distress or misfortune. He may chide his *chi* for its laxity and ask it to help him with a debt or dispute. These shrines also are concerned with the fertility, health, and completeness of a family unit, for they receive sacrifices when women are in labor and are reconsecrated on the birth of the child.

These shrines are small pottery bowls containing clay mixed with other symbolic or magical ingredients, out of which project three or four small sticks. The sticks represent *chi*, *eke*, and *uwa:* a fourth, *ezumezu*, or "completeness," may be added when a man becomes a grandfather. See Meek 1937:57*n*, and 58-59.
9. All supernaturals, except Chineke, can be called *mmuo*, the most precise translation of which is "spirit." Because of imprecise usage, however, the word *mmuo* can be confusing. See Arinze 1970:12-13. I will use it to refer to the class of "Other Spirits" which are neither ancestors (*ndichie*) nor tutelary deities (*agbara*).
10. This group may be a territorial unit living within a single compound; more commonly, as we have seen, several compounds make up a single lineage that traces its descent to one man represented by the oldest male, the *ofo*-holder.
11. Shelton 1971:35.
12. Statement by Ugo. The inclusive word for such deities varies regionally; for example: *agbara* are called *alusi* in parts of Igboland farther north.
13. An amalgamation of two very similar testimonies, one by Ugo, the other by Christopher Onuigwe. Meek's (1937:24-32) account of Ala is still the fullest in literature. He discusses Amadioha briefly (p. 24), while Talbot (1927) provides a more lengthy, if less scholarly, treatment of the male god. Both authors mention Igwe, the sky, as an object of religious rites, yet they agree that Igwe is subordinate to Amadioha as a god of the upper or sky world. Arinze, the most recent analyst of Igbo religion (1970:16), sees Amadioha and Igwe as synonymous, the names being local variants. In view of the fact that the mbari area contains few if any shrines for Igwe, Arinze's explanation seems the most plausible. It is further buttressed by the fact that Owerri people consider sacrificial iron rods, *igwe*, symbols of Amadioha.
14. Meek 1937:25.
15. Arinze 1970:16.
16. Though not a god, the rainbow is, like thunder, a most auspicious phenomenon, whose exploits in zoomorphic form are recounted in mythology. Sometimes the rainbow is considered a messenger of gods, especially of Amadioha. See Okparocha 1976 for useful information on rainbows and their relationship to pythons. Albino and red-skinned Igbos are called Amadioha's children. In the past these "children" were often taken by their families to the senior Amadioha shrine at Ozuzu. See Talbot 1927:56. Talbot

went to the senior Amadioha priest in Ozuzu and gives a vivid account of his visit (1927:52-58).

17. Many of the gods "wealthy" or important enough to have had mbari built for them are noted in the lists of illustrations.

18. Whenever the word "town" is used, "village group" would be a more precise term because there were no real towns in the mbari area before the coming of the whites.

19. Although Talbot's (1927:12) observation that only town chiefs may aspire to the priesthood of dominant cults was not corroborated by my fieldwork, it is indicative of the socio-political importance of the priest.

20. Priests are said to be "married" to their gods. A freeborn man is *diala*, "husband of the earth." A "small" Ala in the town of Obube will be the mother of those people living in her village, as well as the daughter of Ala Umuajaka, the oldest Ala. Ala Umuajaka is the mother of all Alas in Obube. . . . "It is like sending your daughters out to be married." It is notable that while each village group or town has its senior Ala, there is no "parent" Ala for the entire area, unlike the Amadioha of Ozuzu. Yet while Amadioha Ozuzu is the father of all others, there may be no senior Amadioha in a given town (Meek 1937:24).

Most *agbara* have husbands, parents, children, and even concubines or paramours among *agbara* of neighboring towns, though the relationships are not deep and frequently seem arbitrary. So, while cults clearly have the same tendency to fission that villages and towns have, the spirits are not always genealogically parallel. In the cited case of Obube, for example, some of the "small" Alas might claim parentage from Uramurukwa or Ngwoma, two other powerful female *agbara* in the town, though in theory all Alas should be the daughters of Ala Umuajaka. Or, in Umuowa, a "small" Amadioha is said to be the son of the locally powerful (male) Ogirishi, rather than Amadioha Ozuzu, theoretically the head and father of all Amadiohas. What should be the case theoretically is often altered by local conditions or "power politics" in the spiritual sphere.

21. The other main area, reserved for only the most prominent of *agbara*, is a sacred forest, *okohia*, visited infrequently and then only by the priest and a few important diviners who penetrate its depths to the most sacred representation of the god, a huge tree. For most occasions and most people, the *ihu agbara* is the essential spiritual sanctuary.

22. Many towns that share the same sacred animals claim no historical relationship with one another, and the origin and ultimate meaning of these "quasi-totems" remain obscure. Animal associations no longer necessarily distinguish exogamous groups, for example, although they may once have done so.

23. As Shelton (1971:58) has observed for the Nsukka area, a real distinction between public and private cults is difficult to draw in every case. This will become particularly clear below when divination is discussed, for while most diviners' clients are private individuals, often their most important clients are a few men acting on behalf of an entire village or village group.

24. "Agwu" is the deity's proper name, but he is commonly called "Agwushi," so I will generally use that form. Some informants call Agwushi an *agbara;* see preceding note.

25. Even though Agwushi is consulted at frequent intervals by everyone, both individuals and groups, his only real worshippers seem to be diviners, who maintain Agwushi shrines as part of their divination apparatus.

26. This is a somewhat abbreviated version of Ugo's testimony.
27. Agwushi seems to combine the roles and personalities of the Yoruba deities Eshu, the trickster, and Ifa, god of divination and order. Igbo stories and myths about Agwushi, however, are far less detailed and explicit than those of the Yoruba.
28. The newness of Mamy Wata, spelled here phonetically because the English words have been assimilated into Igbo, is clearly recognized by the people, who say they borrowed the cult from the Niger Delta area. The cult has existed in Owerri at least since 1937, when Mamy Wata's distinctive image was modeled in an mbari at Obokwe Obike and photographed by G. I. Jones and K. C. Murray. See Salmons (1977) for Ibibio interpretations of Mamy Wata. Henry Drewal has surveyed manifestations of the same cult among the Yoruba, Ewe, and still further west along the coast of Africa.
29. Arinze (1970:81) differentiates between oblations, or offerings of inanimate objects, and "sacrifice in the strict sense," of living victims, from minor crops to human beings. For our purposes, however, any ritual offering can be considered a sacrifice.
30. Both compounds and large communities mark periodic agricultural and yearly cycles with sacrifices. Like the offerings given at such life crises as birth, marriage, and death, at the installment of priests and diviners, and at minor expiatory rites, these are usually small and predictable. More unexpected, irregular rituals and sacrifices mark heinous individual breaches of the social code, such as murder, or major community disasters like drought, war, or famine.
31. *Osu* and other forms of Igbo slavery have been officially outlawed for many years, although in Owerri *osu* sacrifices are still offered; today, however, cows take the place of humans, and thus the present tense is maintained. This unusual form of cult slavery is discussed at some length in Meek (1937:203-4 and passim), Green (1947:23-24 and passim) and Arinze (1970:90-92).
32. A freeborn person becomes an *osu* if he or she marries one; neither may he have sexual intercourse with an *osu* nor buy seed yams from one for fear of contamination. Once dedicated to a god, a male or female *osu* partakes of that god and is therefore dangerous, taboo (*nso*), as well as sacred, and thus enjoys immunity from bodily harm or even retribution after theft (Talbot 1927:59). An *osu* offering, beyond the not inconsiderable price of a human being, includes several necessary subsidiary items: yards of cloth, jars of palm wine, a turtle, an egg, palm oil, vegetables, yams, fowl, and an *igwe*, a long flat bar of iron, which is important.
33. It is unclear whether, in the old days, all *agbara* had *osu*. Possibly they did, yet the hierarchy of *agbara* cults, ranging from those very wealthy and powerful to minor ones with little apparent sway, suggests that they probably did not.
34. See Shelton 1971:62. *Ogwu* can be used for either beneficial or harmful ends in a manner analogous to the white and black magic of popular legend. It is used to protect people against, or control, dangerous and unruly *mmuo*, to fortify people in the presence of *agbara*, or, therapeutically, to heal malaria or a broken leg. Or it may be used to strengthen a hunter or warrior, to weaken a foe. The parallel use of *ogwu* and sacrifice in several rites suggests that they are intended to serve a similar end—the activating or influencing of supernatural powers. In one mbari ceremony, for example, an iron bar, *igwe*, is rubbed with an *ogwu* intended to protect the person car-

rying the iron from the same *agbara* to which it was earlier offered in sacrifice. At other times both *ogwu* and sacrificial blood are employed to increase the effectiveness of an object, such as *ofo*.

35. See Horton, 1965a:65-68. Except for the lack of figural representation of ancestors, this hierarchy seems to fit Horton's observations: "When theory is founded on analogy between puzzling observations and familiar phenomena, it is generally only a limited aspect of such phenomena that is incorporated into the resulting model" (p. 65). Thus, the "other spirits"—those most removed from the human model—are thought of in the least anthropomorphic terms.

3. The People and Processes of Mbari

1. The reasons cited for shifting village sites are analogous, and often identical, to those given for building an mbari, i.e., some kind of current or impending crisis. Some informants indicated that mbari were sometimes built to thank or honor a god, or to show her relative wealth in comparison with other gods, all of which count in the composite motivations and values represented, but generally there seems to have been a crisis as catalyst. See Meek (1937:49) and Basden (1938:100).

2. Account by Ugo, an artist who first participated in mbari activities about 1920.

3. Or the diviner may simply identify major lineages, each of which is expected to provide one old woman, who would then be selected locally, probably again by divination. I witnessed none of the selection processes.

4. As the illustration shows, I observed one *ikeishigwe* ceremony (in Umuokpaa Obube), but I did not witness the tour of *ndishigwe* or the "yam festival" that followed it. In 1966 I was told these were much modified versions of what used to occur.

5. What is not clear from the data is the composition of the *mgboto* group that follows *ndishigwe*. Informants have implied that all *mgboto* follow them, but logic suggests that only *mgboto* from a particular village would await the arrival of the men. I was unable to determine the village affiliation of the men. In fact, data on this "yam festival" are varied and ambiguous, probably reflecting a good deal of temporal and regional variation.

6. See Meek 1937:49.

7. If the mbari is a large one built for the strongest god in the town, as in this hypothetical case, several diviners may be involved.

8. Most of these schemes, which all have ritual content, are part of the "play" element in mbari, which is discussed in chapter 4.

9. Mbari artists as a group are clear-thinking and sensitive men. And as the quotations throughout this volume indicate, I found them the most knowledgeable and objective informants, both because of their varied experiences with mbari and because of their lack of vested interest in a single building effort (conversely an mbari priest often aggrandizes his own mbari in terms of its cost, importance, and artistic quality).

10. *Mgbe* is another word for mbari; in Etche it is used for the house itself, and elsewhere it is used with other words as a modifier. See glossary. The etymology of *mgbe* is not clear, but it may derive from *mgbede*, the word for the "fatting or fattening house" where in the old days unmarried adolescent girls were secluded for several months to prepare for marriage. This interpretation is corroborated by G. I. Jones, who suggested that *mgbe* means the

seclusion of a person from the profane world, analogous to what Christians call a "retreat" (personal communication 1971). See also Okparocha 1976:15-16.

11. Talbot (1927:16), Meek (1927:49), and Basden (1938:102) have conflicting reports on the numbers, sexes, and ages of *ndimgbe* as well as on the method of selection. These differences are in all likelihood regional and perhaps temporal variations and also depend on the size of the mbari constructed. As Basden indicates (p. 102), males and females were equal in number. Meek (p. 49) says that grey-haired people are not chosen, and while a few of such age were *ndimgbe* in the principal mbari I observed being built, their presence may perhaps be attributed to recent changes in the building process. Okparocha (1976:15) confirms my impression that *ndimgbe* were usually of child-bearing age.

12. One trusted informant (Ugo) made it clear that in the old days diviners, who are also makers of native medicine, were empowered to enforce rules made in the names of gods, even to the extent of poisoning and therefore killing an offender, although undoubtedly this was done extremely rarely.

13. The statement was made by a spirit worker, on the job inside the mbari enclosure at Umuedi Nnorie, in 1966.

14. Any except Orie, the day given to worshipping ancestors.

15. Although the basket contents are variable, in one instance the following items were reported by informants: camwood for beautifying the body, a cloth, some money (cowry shells and manillas in the old days, pennies and shillings in recent years), an antelope skin, a stool, a fowl, and other food (fish or meat). *Ndimgbe* almost always had special stools; either each person brought his own, or they were made for the entire group by the artist and presented to the workers on still another ritual occasion. The baskets and sometimes the stools are occasionally preserved in the completed mbari, as at Umuofeke Agwa, where baskets are visible under the roof in color plate 6.

16. Where an *osu* is among the workers, he may be the first to walk the iron; if there are two *osu*, the other will be the last.

17. Information from Ezem. I did not observe this rite, but it or variants of it were reported by many informants. My reconstruction drawing (fig. 6) is based on these accounts and was checked by informants for accuracy.

18. See Basden 1938:102, Okparocha 1976:15–16.

19. See Basden 1938:103, who says that a single long washstand was erected at which all workers, men and women, washed at the same time. His report is corroborated by Okparocha 1976:16. The practice of housing *ndimgbe* in the priest's compound seems to have been abandoned in the 1950s.

20. Okparocha 1975:18.

21. One artist stated that in one mbari he worked on one day out of four was set aside, with no work accomplished, so *ndimgbe* could indulge in sex the night before.

Yet it is doubtful that mbari was the continual, ritualized orgy suggested by some authors (Basden 1938:103), at least during the building period. As noted, however, general license prevailed before the construction period and may have again in the festival atmosphere of its opening, as Meek asserts (1937:51). Again there was doubtless much temporal and regional variation.

22. Most of its ingredients, however, are different. The ancestral *ofo*, for example, is modeled over a branch of a special tree (*Detarium Senegalense*) rather than iron. *Ofo mbari* also contains special protective medicines, and

in some instances, manillas (traditional currency), which the ancestral *ofo* does not have.

23. In some areas they may not eat coconut or palm nuts (Talbot 1927:18).

24. No *eke nwaori* have been built in recent years. Basden (1938:103) says that after the month's seclusion workers moved to huts within the mbari enclosure. This is perhaps another regional or temporal variation. See also Talbot 1927:17-18 and Okparocha 1976:17-19.

25. One informant remarked this usage of palm leaves as yet another instance of *omu*, the tender young palm leaves which signify the presence of the *agbara*. This may be true even though the leaves are not necessarily young in this case.

26. This quotation suggests that four-day-workers may have originated as a group of *osu*, but I have no proof for the hypothesis.

27. "*Mgbe*" in this instance referred to the period of seclusion, as in a fatting house; see note 10 above.

28. Statement by Ugo. Commercial European plates were trade goods in the nineteenth century and perhaps before. Informants were by no means clear about what preceded them; some said shells, others white chalk.

29. Statement by Nnaji.

30. Of the 150 or so mbari I saw in 1966-67, only one, completed about 1935, contained *mkpeshi igwe*, and these were the wooden surrogates in the illustration. Apparently, however, real iron was once used in some places, for informants spoke of blacksmiths being specially hired for the job. One man insisted that only wood served as *mkpeshi igwe*, however, suggesting again the likelihood of regional variations. A few men claimed these "slivers" quite necessary as guides for painting geometric patterns. Since all but one mbari I saw were painted without them, however, the reason for their use—or claims of their necessity—is probably to be sought elsewhere than in technical requirements. The problem is addressed again in Chapter VII.

31. "*Ewuwu*" is a word that seems to have been created especially for mbari, for it is used in no other context that I could determine. Its etymology is not clear, but it may derive from the common word for goat, "*ewu*". If this interpretation is correct, mbari figures are, metaphorically, "yams and goats."

32. Obviously, preliminary holes or pedestal seats will vary for different figures and groups: four large holes for the legs of an elephant; a small pedestal for a seated figure; perhaps a combination of holes and pedestals for a person seated at a desk.

33. These are said to break if a person who has recently had sexual intercourse comes near them.

34. The lack of quarreling may possibly be explained by the fact that *ndimgbe* worked only every few days rather than more or less constantly as they did fifty years ago. Basden corroborates this finding, however, by saying that a man who quarrels with his (mbari) wife "must forfeit a fowl as penalty" (1938:104).

35. Basden 1938:104, Okparocha 1975:19.

36. One man insisted that the "real" mbari of the old days, as opposed to the "small patches of tin" made today, contained four relief figures. Although the number four is consistent with much mbari (and other Igbo) symbolism, I only know of two houses with four *ijeremgbe*, one of which is illustrated in Beier 1960:16-17.

37. Or if the owner is Amadioha, a white ram.

38. Only women ground colors in the mbari I witnessed, and I neglected to ask if this was always the case.
39. I did not witness this visit.
40. Leonard (1906:409) noted this in his brief passage on mbari: "A curious, and in a sense significant feature in connection with these figures of human beings is the fact that they are made to represent images of certain prominent or dangerous enemies whose death is religiously desired as an advantage to the community." Despite repeated inquiries about this matter in the field, only one man said that enemies might have been "disposed of" in this manner, and G. I. Jones (personal communication) feels this sort of magical control over enemies is inconsistent with other mbari procedures. It remains a moot point, although the prohibition against portraiture, upheld by several informants, was probably enforced.
41. I witnessed this and the following rites at Umuedi Nnorie.
42. See Talbot 1927:20.
43. In the mbari I saw (Nnorie), the blood was dripped on Amadioha, Nguma (Ala's mother), Ada (Ala's first daughter), Mamy Wata, the two *ijeremgbe*, and the leopard.
44. Talbot (1927) records two instances of this interior room's actually being used. A person accused of an infringement against a god could be locked up in the room at night; if innocent, he would be alive in the morning, but if guilty he would be found dead (pp. 20 and 44). I found no corroboration of such ordeals, but Talbot was in the area circa 1915, and they may well have been abandoned soon after that.
45. After the ceremony I saw, the workers simply went home. In earlier years, however, the flight of *ndimgbe* to a neighboring town seems to have been universal—it was reported by many informants.
46. See Talbot (1927:18-19).
47. This spectacle did occur in 1966; it is also reported in Talbot (1927:20).
48. In the old days women painted their bodies with the same elaborate kinds of designs still retained for mbari figures of female *agbara*. They also wore similar, though probably less elaborate, hairdos, along with beads, anklets, and other jewelry. Men wore new "wrappers," dressed their hair with feathers, and may also have rubbed their bodies with camwood.
49. See Meek 1937:51.

4. Form

1. Sebastian Onuegbu of Umueke Umuayo Eziobo.
2. I am not aware that the Owerri man himself consciously differentiates between these two types.
3. The mud-casing of wooden structural members does at least partially prevent termite damage. However, timbers that are structurally important but aesthetically unnecessary are not enlarged with mud. See color plate 1, pl. 10.
4. Probably 50 to 60 percent of mbari with more than 20 figures adhere to this basic plan.
5. Ugo, an artist, said plans with a central column were the "correct" ones although few such mbari were seen in 1966-67.
6. Curiously, the Igbo verbs used to describe the activity of inserting plates and slivers are "push in" and "hit in"; so the final visual impression accords well with the metaphoric language of mbari construction.
7. Ugo, Ezem, Nnaji, Akakporo, and Ugwuanya.

8. Akakporo.
9. Amadioha and other male *agbara* (Opurogo, Otamiri Ogirishi, and others) rate medium-sized or large mbari houses less frequently than female *agbara* do, but when they are so honored the full catalogue of hierarchic traits is enlisted in their behalf. Amadioha often has a small house next to the main mbari, as at Umuowa and Agwa (fig. 12, pl. 75).
10. The cross-legged pose is very uncommonly assumed by Igbo people, and is considered especially poor taste in women, so its use in mbari is of some interest. See chapter 5, p. 161.
11. Observations recorded in unpublished field notes kindly supplied to the author by Mr. Murray.
12. Three important exceptions to the overwhelmingly predominant "ageless" or "idealized young adult" demeanor may be noted: in ancient Ife (see Willett 1969:pl. V and p. 72), among the Yoruba (see Thompson 1968:64-65), and among the Fang (see Fernandez 1966:56). The two former examples deal with old age, the latter, with infantile sculptural expression. "Monsterized" or grotesque violations of human facial anatomy are another matter, for they are reasonably common, especially on masks. See Cole 1970:48.
13. Folk stories link the stockfish—salted, dried fish imported usually from Scandinavian countries, used in stews and soups—with Mamy Wata. The dried fish, as imported, comes without a head; Mamy Wata is popularly linked with the mermaid, so her torso connects with a tail rather than legs. To the white man, mysterious and often deviously clever, is attributed the severing of Mamy Wata's tail to create the stockfish. Mamy Wata is then thrown back into the sea to grow a new tail so the process may be repeated, and the white man gets richer!
14. Measurements taken at the mbari to Uramurukwa at Ngwoma Ulakwo Obube are: 103 inches from the tip of the seated *agbara*'s hairdress to the soles of her feet; as opposed to 45 inches measured the same way on an upper seated figure whose back is about four to five feet behind that of the *agbara*. The distance from top of hairdress to base of neck are, respectively, 34 and 13 inches. It is worth noting that *agbara* figures are among the largest figural sculptures in West Africa; this may be accounted for by the relative flexibility of the additive clay-on-armature medium as compared with the prevailing subtractive technique of woodcarving.

5. Inspiration, Individuality, and Aesthetics

1. For example: the "ostrich" giving birth, a radio announcer (pl. 73), boxers (pl. 69), airplanes and telephones (pl. 75), an office building (pl. 3), and a "general" (pl. 61).
2. See Okparocha (1976:44-57) for several stories and myths about the python and the rainbow.
3. 1937:51.
4. 1938:106.
5. See p. 202 for further comments on sexual imagery.
6. G. I. Jones, in pointing out the parallel between Cretan snake goddesses and Mamy Wata (personal communication 1971) correctly warns against the attribution of this image to a single source. Since my research was conducted, two other scholars have been exploring the distribution and nature of the Mamy Wata cult; see Salmons 1977 and Drewal 1976, 1979.

7. Crosses may in fact be seen around the necks of numerous other figures (pl. 31).
8. Meek observed a similar group (1937:52), probably the same one that G. I. Jones photographed circa 1936.
9. Okparocha (1976:29-30) reports a figure with four faces, *agbara ihu ano*, also recorded by Jones and Murray, and says that such an image "might be a way to show that whatever people do cannot be hidden from the gods."
10. This preoccupation perhaps stemmed from his childlessness, a condition that embarrassed and chagrined him; it seemed to me that he attempted to cover up or minimize his embarrassment by bringing up sexual matters and speaking of his exploits. I believe his overt sexual imagery, of which this is but one example, can be explained the same way.
11. Both statements by Ugo, on two different occasions.
12. Two distinct woodcarving styles, for example, can be found in and near the mbari-producing area; one is for Okorosia masks, the other for wooden deity figures (Mbiere-Mbaise). See Cole 1969c and 1975a.
13. The onset of this focus can be quite precisely dated to 1957, when Paul Bohannan reoriented attention from the artist to the critic in his paper at "The Artist in Tribal Society" symposium (see Smith 1961). His paper, "Artist and Critic in an African Society," set the stage for subsequent research and analysis, most notably the work of R. F. Thompson 1968, 1972, 1973. See also W. d'Azevedo 1958; I. L. Child and L. Siroto 1965; D. J. Crowley 1966; J. Fernandez 1966; E. Carpenter 1968; H. M. Cole 1969, 1970; S. Ottenberg 1971; and *The Traditional Artist in African Societies*, W. d'Azevedo (ed.) 1973. Vogel 1979 compares Thompson's Yoruba material with hers from the Baule.
14. Robert F. Thompson's pioneering work among the Yoruba was the real catalyst (1968, 1972, 1973).
15. Hall 1959, p. 106ff.
16. Several pairs of similar figures or other mbari parts (column or wall paintings, animal figures), one each by Ezem and Akalazu, were chosen for comparison at each site. Each interview was recorded and later transcribed with the aid of my interpreter, Herbert Opara, and another person, Charles Nwaebo, both adept at distinguishing linguistic nuances.
17. See Thompson 1972. I suspect the major differences between Thompson's report and mine (beyond the fact that he interviewed eighty-eight people to my fifteen) are in the interpretation of the data. On the other hand, perhaps the Yoruba, whose culture is in general considerably more aristocratic than that of the Igbo, have evolved more analytically articulate responses.
18. Most of the 15 informants were queried about more than one paired comparison, so there were 35 separate "tests."
19. A dimension of nonverbal response that is linked to ideological values is the practice of giving coins (formerly, cowrie shells) to one or more of the mbari figures: "Usually what we do is offer money to the owner of the house and say it is given to praise the beauty of all these figures." See also Thompson 1973:20-21.
20. It would be tempting to attribute ideals of light skin and thin noses to European influence within the past hundred years. Yet this would, I feel, be a disservice to Igbo values and their persistence. Possibly European influence in the last five hundred years may account for these "un-African" features, but in crediting primarily the British presence of the last seventy years with these values we either have to admit that the Igbo is capricious

and open to an immediate and wholesale assimilation of new ideals of physical perfection, or we have to explain away a number of masks (really "spirit heads") and figures of deities with thin features and light-colored faces. While I have no explanation for the genesis of the ideal, I do believe it to be of considerable antiquity and not the result of the recent—or even the ancient—presence of white men. See note 16, chapter 2.

6. Meaning

1. 1927:10.
2. 1939:146.
3. 1904b:162.
4. 1942-45:891.
5. See Meek 1937:89.
6. E. O. Odita, 1970:40, mentions this meaning for the word, and another, complementary one: "M-bari means to break apart. This is derived from the image of the yam, which breaks open the earth as its vine climbs upward to the fresh air and sunlight."
7. Despite the importance of these two quotations and others which introduce sections in this chapter, I have decided not to cite each individual informant, because to do so would interrupt the text unnecessarily. The authors of the statements, and all others quoted directly in this book, are recorded in my field notebooks.
8. Hubert and Mauss (1964) document analogous rites of death and rebirth in their section on "Entry in the Sacrifice," pp. 20-25. It is notable that *ndimgbe* seem to fulfill multiple, overlapping roles in the mbari sacrifice scheme, as sacrificers, sanctifiers, priests, and the sacrificial victim itself.
9. As in so many of the stated purposes and results of mbari, these are all but impossible to prove or document. My field techniques were in some cases too insensitive, and in other, more long-range instances like these, there was no opportunity to observe actual results even if it had been somehow possible to measure them.
10. Several of these responses seemed automatic, as if from an "authorized version" of mbari behavior, which of course does not actually exist. In mbari, as elsewhere, when people are confident of a result, it will often occur despite the lack of a "scientific" explanation.
11. Meek 1937:49.
12. Statement by Ugo. Although a son and a daughter of the officiating priest are automatically chosen for mbari and become leaders of the *ndimgbe* group, it is not altogether clear how and why other members of the group are chosen or to what extent the disciplining and educating of people is a factor.
13. Meek (1937:50) reports: "The materials for the building are provided by the townspeople, each contributing a bamboo pole, a piece or matting, and some twine." Many of these contributions could probably have been purchased in markets (as construction materials often are today), if money had been collected instead. The actual practice, however, seems to have involved the community with the mbari and its socializing effects.
14. In theory, at least. There was no real opportunity to observe this, as there was none to test most "functions," either direct or latent.
15. The elements of play in mbari coincide remarkably with J. Huizinga's (1955) analysis of the "play-element in culture." See especially pp. 1-27.
16. Statement by Nkwocha Ibe of Nnorie.

17. Slight variations in this song were heard in several villages, so the basic song is widely used for mbari and is of some antiquity.
18. See Huizinga 1955:22-23.
19. Ottenberg 1958:139.
20. All of these survived during my period of fieldwork.
21. Statement by Uchehara Meziobi of Nekede.
22. All *mmuo* are said to have this characteristic, and when *ndimgbe* turn around to enter the enclosure backwards, we have a ritual echo of this trait associated with spirits, which the workers have become after "walking the iron."
23. Notably, the Ekwensu symbolism of removal, that is, a *red painted* form as opposed to a sculptured figure of a more acceptable color, like other mbari figures, is paralleled in *ihu agbara,* in which trees labelled "Ekwensu Agbara" are always planted apart and never in line with other *umuagbara* trees.
24. Statement by Ezem. Important people all over the world proclaim and buttress positions of socio-political and moral leadership with physical elevation so that they may look down upon their people both actually and figuratively (See Fraser and Cole, 1971).
25. See Arinze 1970:17.
26. Talbot (1927) devotes several pages (32-36) to a discussion of sexual codes and "breaches" of them observed in mbari. See also Okparocha 1976:34-5.
27. Also called Ana Obibi by people living near the town of Obibi.
28. In the field it is sometimes difficult to tell whether a paucity of information stems from ignorance or evasion, although with questions about Ekpekele I suspect the latter.
29. Basden 1938:108.
30. Talbot's (1927:32-36) discussion of sexual matters refers to sodomy in marginal Igbo areas (Ekpahia) and among neighboring peoples.
31. A closely analogous proverb is cited by Arinze (1970:115) for Chukwu (Chineke), the high god: "God has both knife and yam, to whom he slices off a part, that person eats."
32. 1937:311.
33. Probably they also vary according to who asks the question. I suspect that the "Ekpekele," for example, would have elicited a fuller, more meaningful response had the interviewer been a local Igbo. See note 28 above.
34. These data on color symbolism, especially regarding black (dark) and white (light), are closely analogous to those reported by Ardener (1954) who worked among the Mbaise Igbo, about twelve to fifteen miles northeast of our area.
35. The associations noted can be explained in each case by behavioral examples, such as the rubbing of white chalk on newborn babies (to make them smooth and healthy, and because babies are a blessing) and on the eyes of diviners (to make them see clearly and speak the truth), but they are omitted here because this study is primarily art historical rather than anthropological.
36. Thompson 1973.
37. This Ife, located about fifteen miles from the eastern edge of mbari country, is of course not the famous Yoruba city, which is some 300 miles farther west.

7. Conclusions

1. No Owerri person called mbari a cosmic symbol in so many words, so this judgment, like many of the other conclusions drawn here, is interpretation based on observable facts. What is remarkable is the extent to which mbari dovetails with worldwide patterns of sacred thought and activity. See work cited by Mircea Eliade for comparable material.
2. See Eliade 1958. Many aspects of mbari cleave very closely to widely diffused patterns of behavior in initiations of many kinds.
3. See Eliade 1958:51. *Ndimgbe* enter *eke nwaori,* the distinctive long house built for them, for their twenty-four-day seclusion. Although informants could not interpret the etymology of the name of that house, it may mean "python" (*eke*) "child of Orie" (*nwa ori*[*e*]). Its length, uncharacteristic of other Owerri structures, makes it somewhat like a python, which in this case could then be the initiatory beast who "kills" and later disgorges initiates. In Africa, Oceania, and elsewhere a common theme in initiations is a legendary beast who swallows novices and spits up young adults, now socialized in the school of the initiation process.
4. "One mbari per village site" is true in theory but not always so in actuality. The fact of a second mbari being built on the same site as an earlier one may, however, be explained by the increasingly widespread practice of erecting concrete houses, market stalls, etc., which more or less forces a village to remain at its current site.
5. The suggestion may also be advanced that mbari *is* mythology, that is, that the very existence of the mbari institution, analogous as it is to more usual forms of verbalized mythology, renders the latter less necessary here than elsewhere.
6. See file in the Religious Studies department of the University of Nigeria, Nsukka, for stories collected among Igbo who were not localized. This is, moreover, a widespread West African story type.

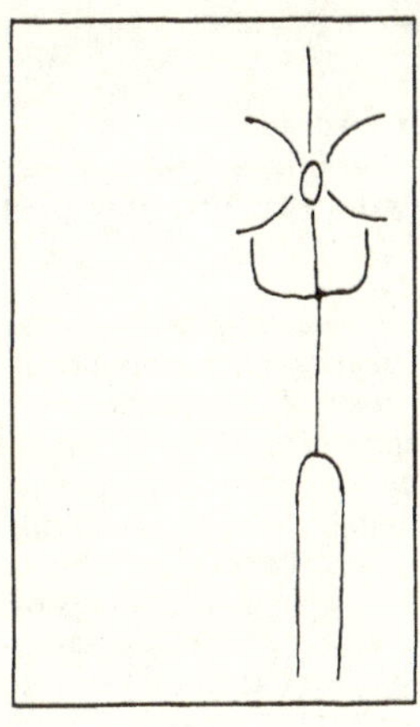

Index